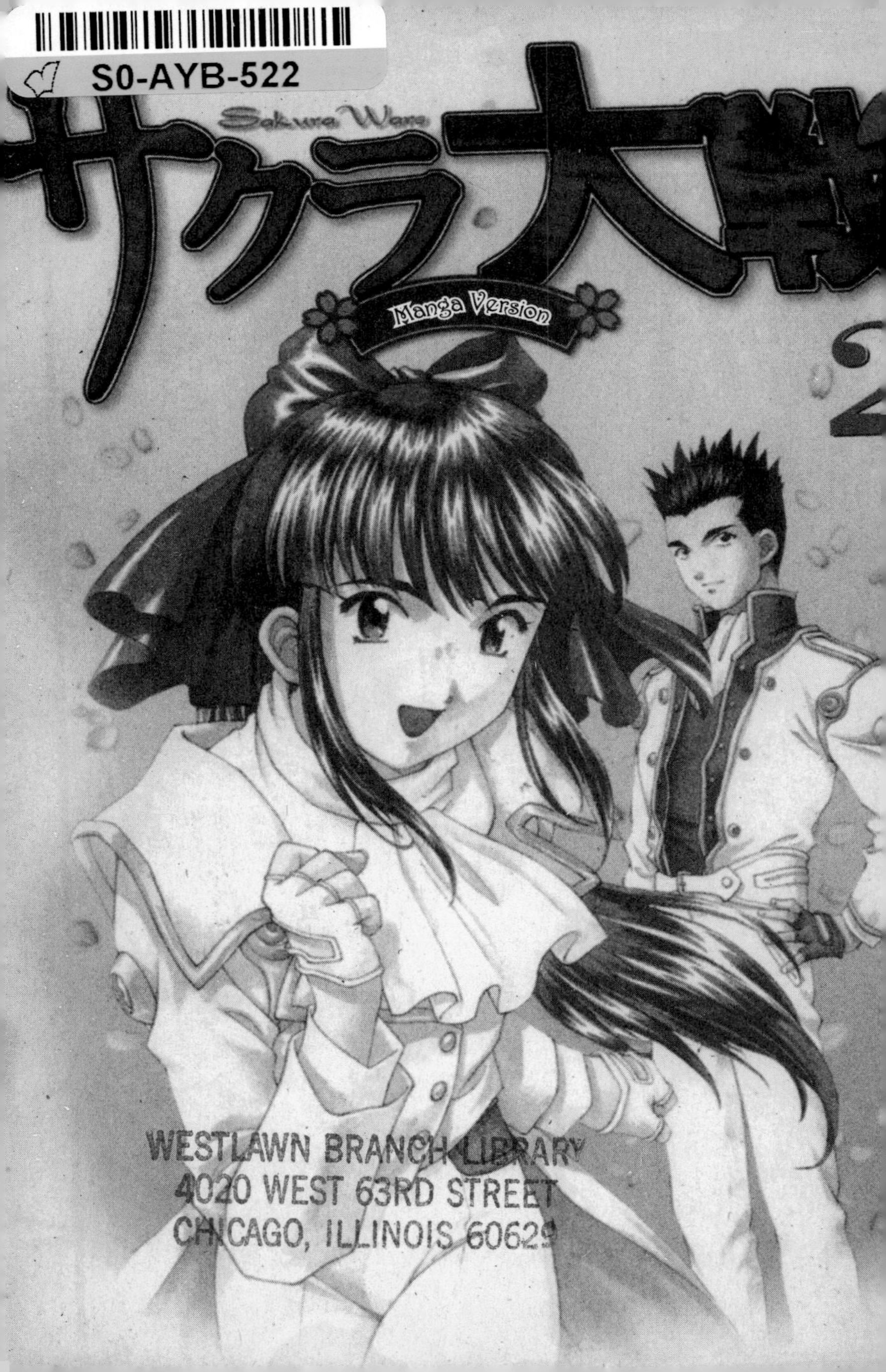
サクラ大戦
Sakura Wars
Manga Version
2

Sakura Taisen Manga Version Volume Two
Table of Contents

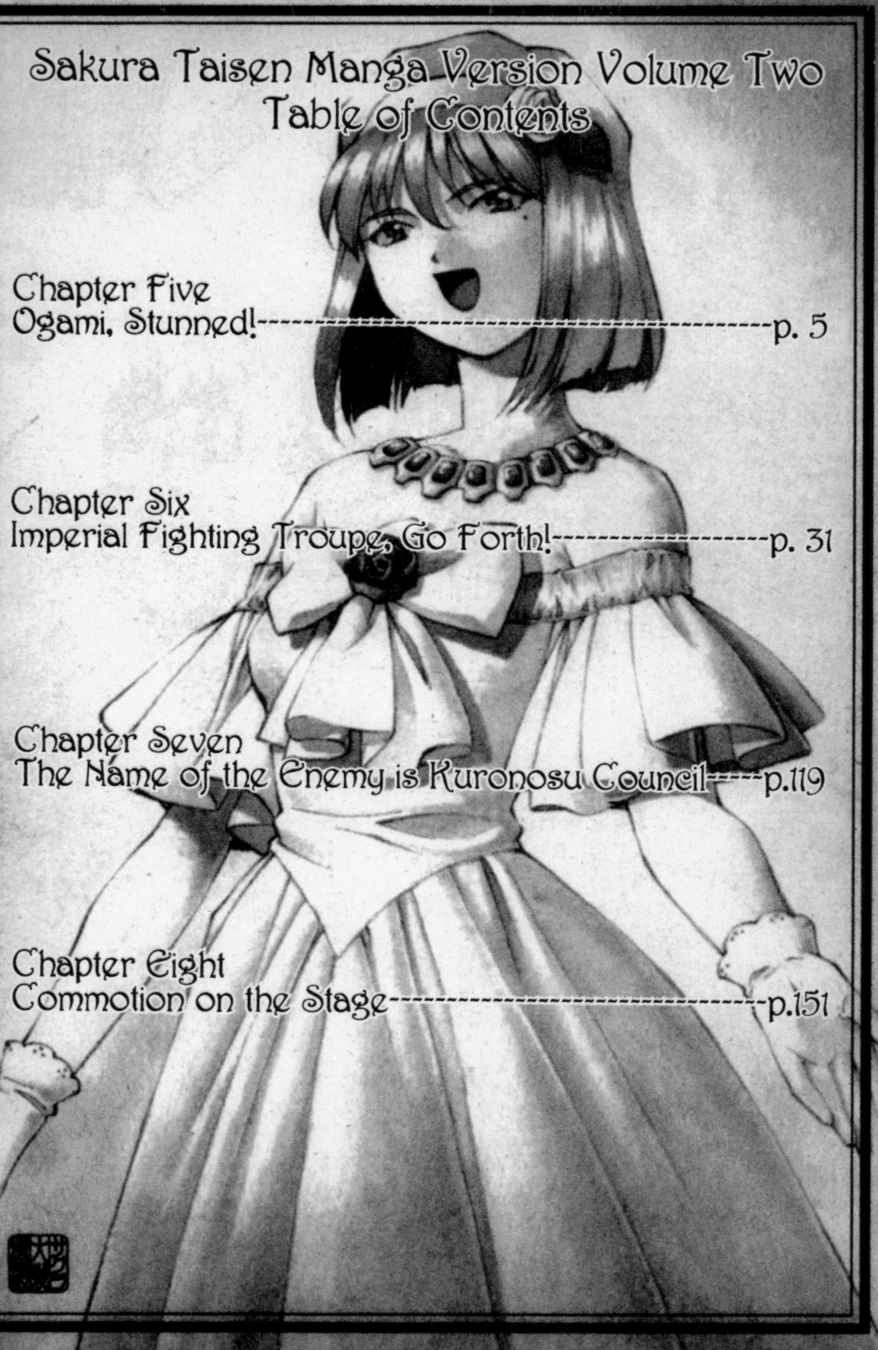

Vol. 2

Story By
Ohji Hiroi

Art by
Ikku Masa

Characters by
Kosuke Fujishima

HAMBURG // LONDON // LOS ANGELES // TOKYO

Sakura Taisen Vol. 2
Story by Ohji Hiroi
Art by Ikku Masa
Characters by Kosuke Fujishima

Translation - Yuko Fukami
Retouch and Lettering - Mike Graniel
Production Artist - Bowen Park and Jose Macasocol, Jr.
Cover Design - Jorge Negrete

Editor - Lillian Diaz-Przybyl
Digital Imaging Manager - Chris Buford
Pre-Press Supervisor - James Dashiell
Production Managers - Jennifer Miller and Mutsumi Miyazaki
Managing Editor - Lindsey Johnston
VP of Production - Ron Klamert
Publisher and E.I.C. - Mike Kiley
President and C.O.O. - John Parker
C.E.O. - Stuart Levy

A  Manga

TOKYOPOP Inc.
5900 Wilshire Blvd. Suite 2000
Los Angeles, CA 90036

E-mail: info@TOKYOPOP.com
Come visit us online at www.TOKYOPOP.com

ISBN: 1-59532-943-9

First TOKYOPOP printing: December 2005
10 9 8 7 6 5 4 3 2 1
Printed in the USA

Ueno

Toeizan
Kaneiji
Temple

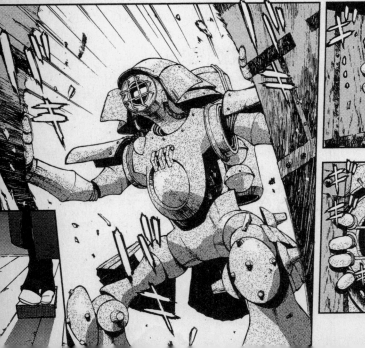

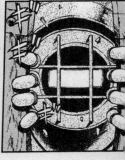

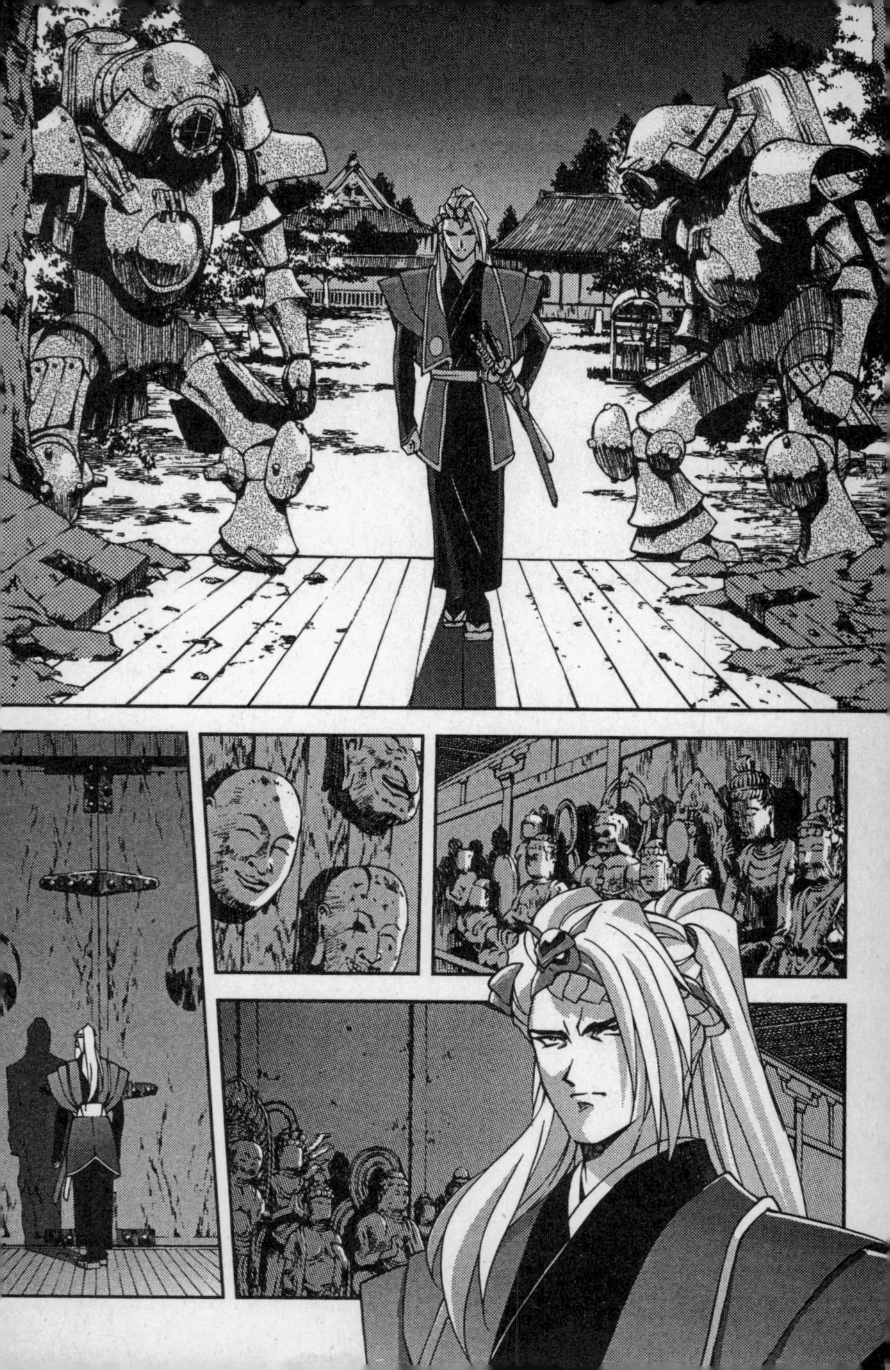

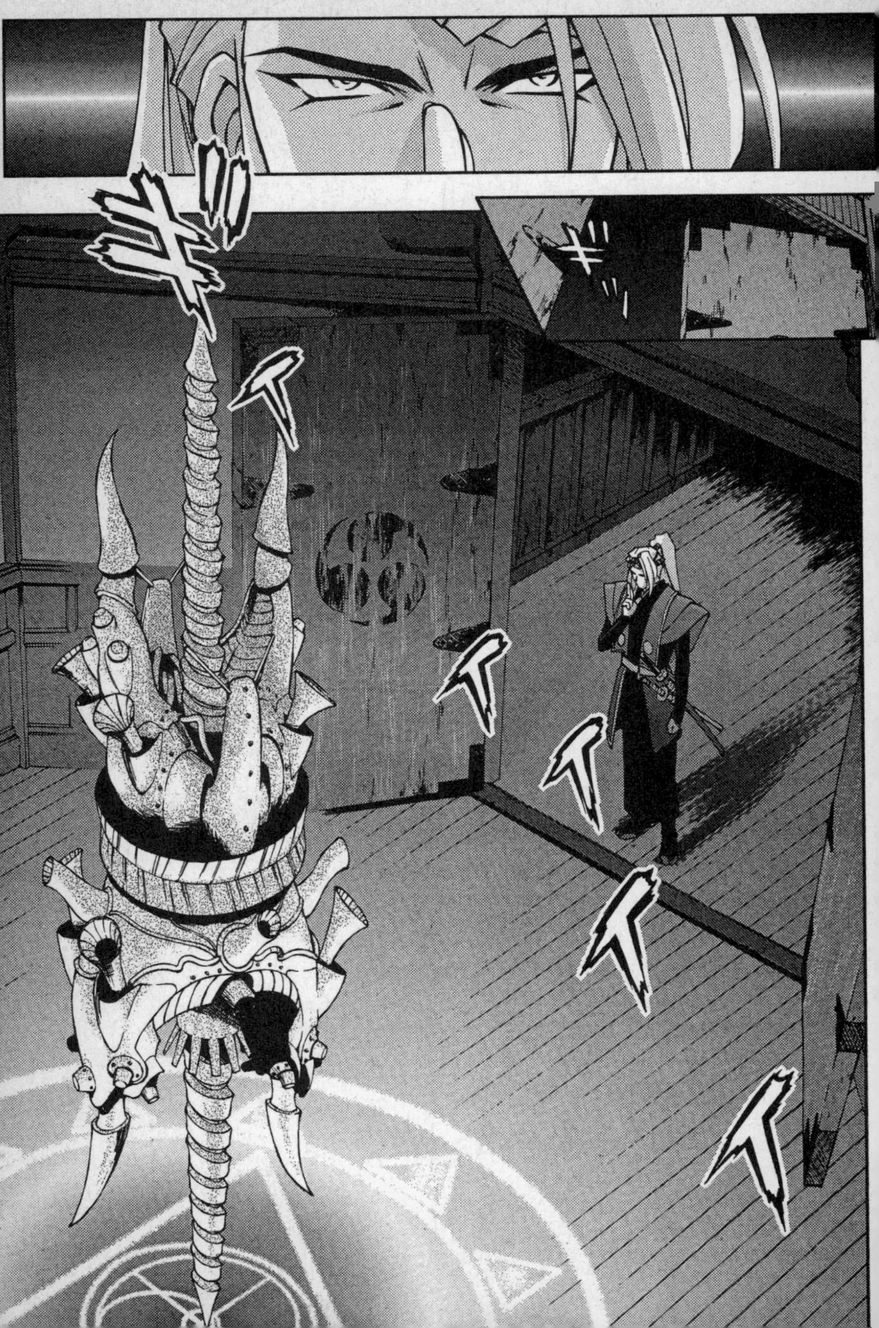
ズ
ズ
イ
イ
イ
イ
イ

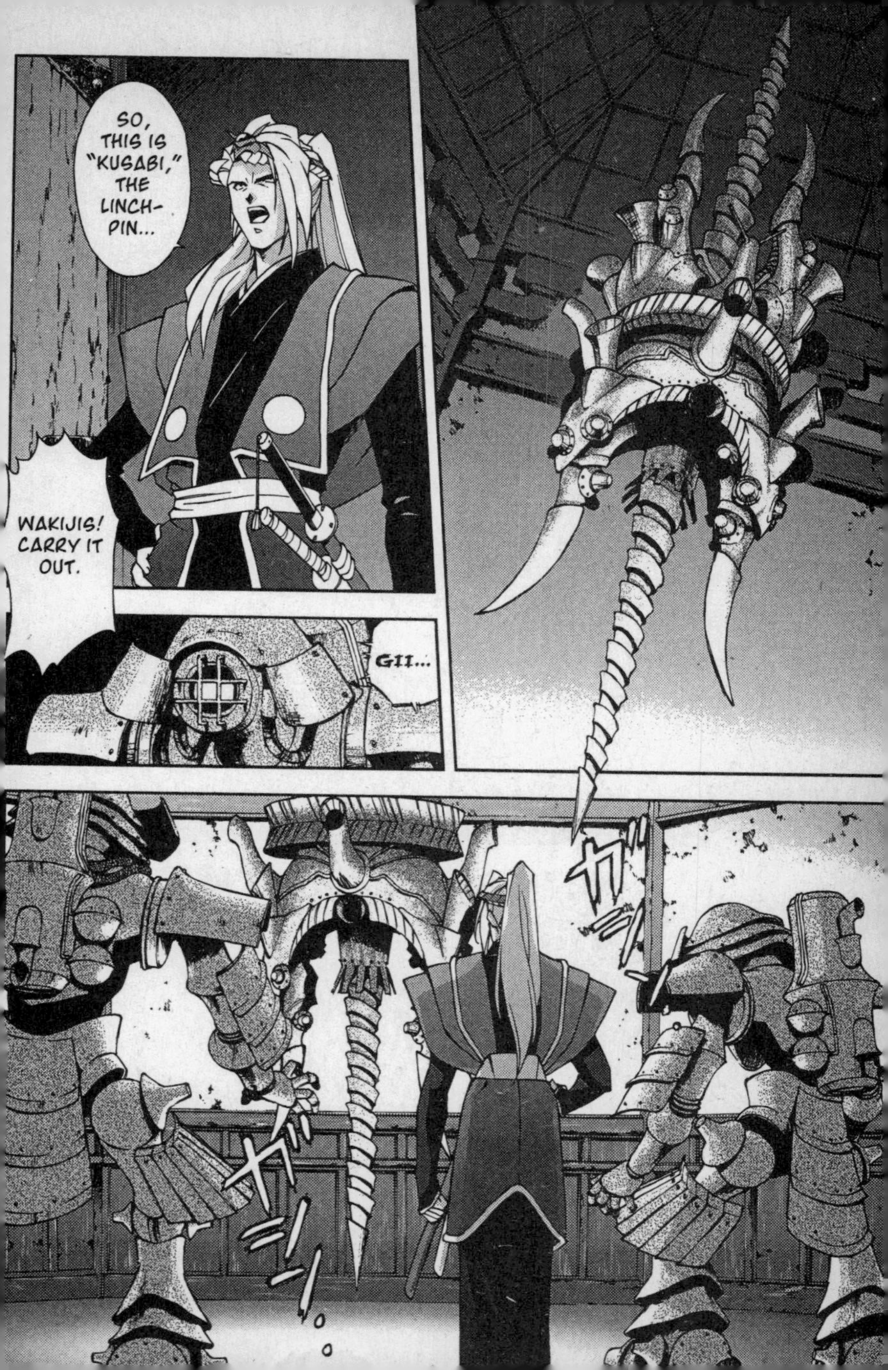
SO, THIS IS "KUSABI," THE LINCH-PIN...
WAKIJIS! CARRY IT OUT.
GII...

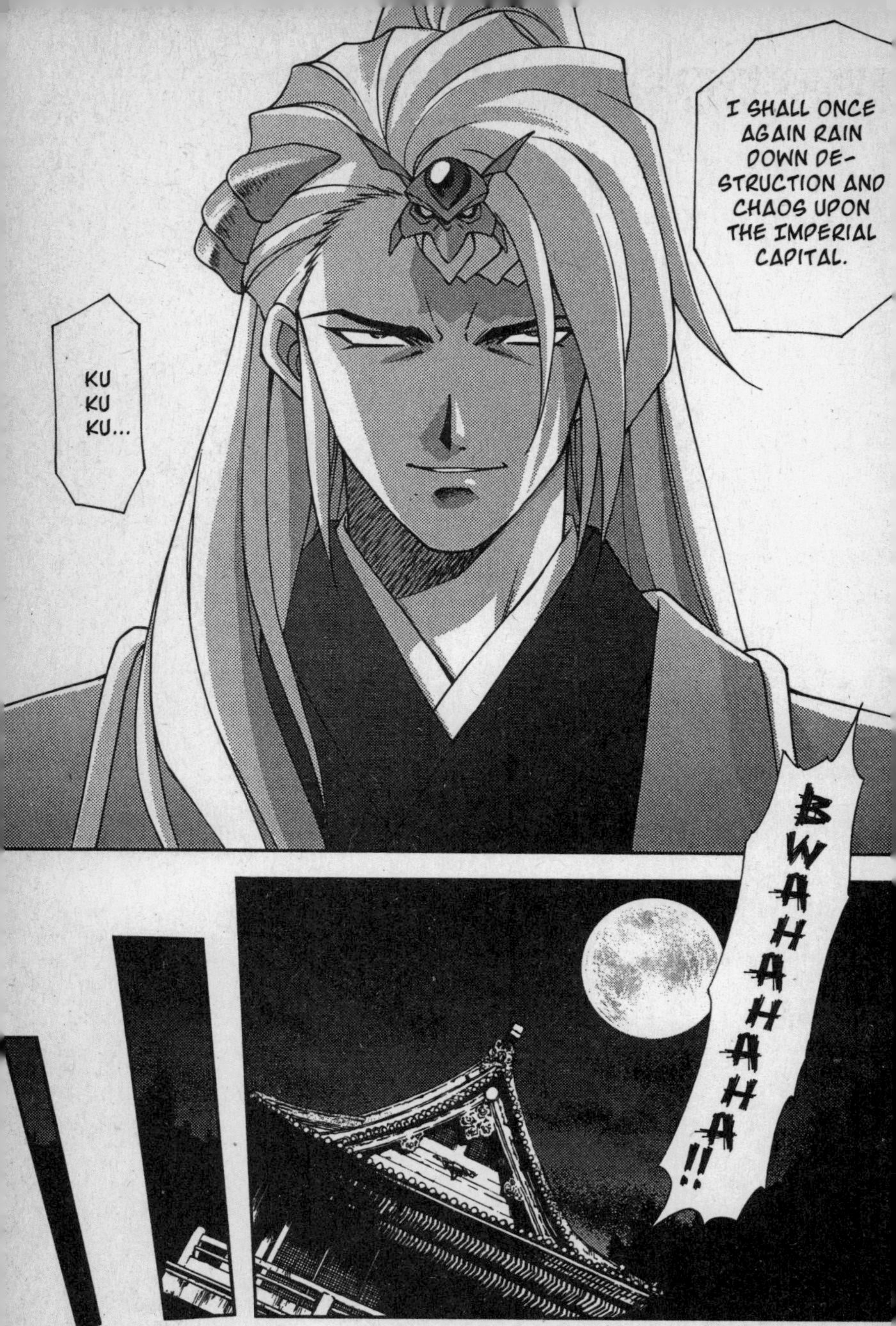
I SHALL ONCE AGAIN RAIN DOWN DE-STRUCTION AND CHAOS UPON THE IMPERIAL CAPITAL.
KU KU KU...
BWAHAHAHAHAHA!!

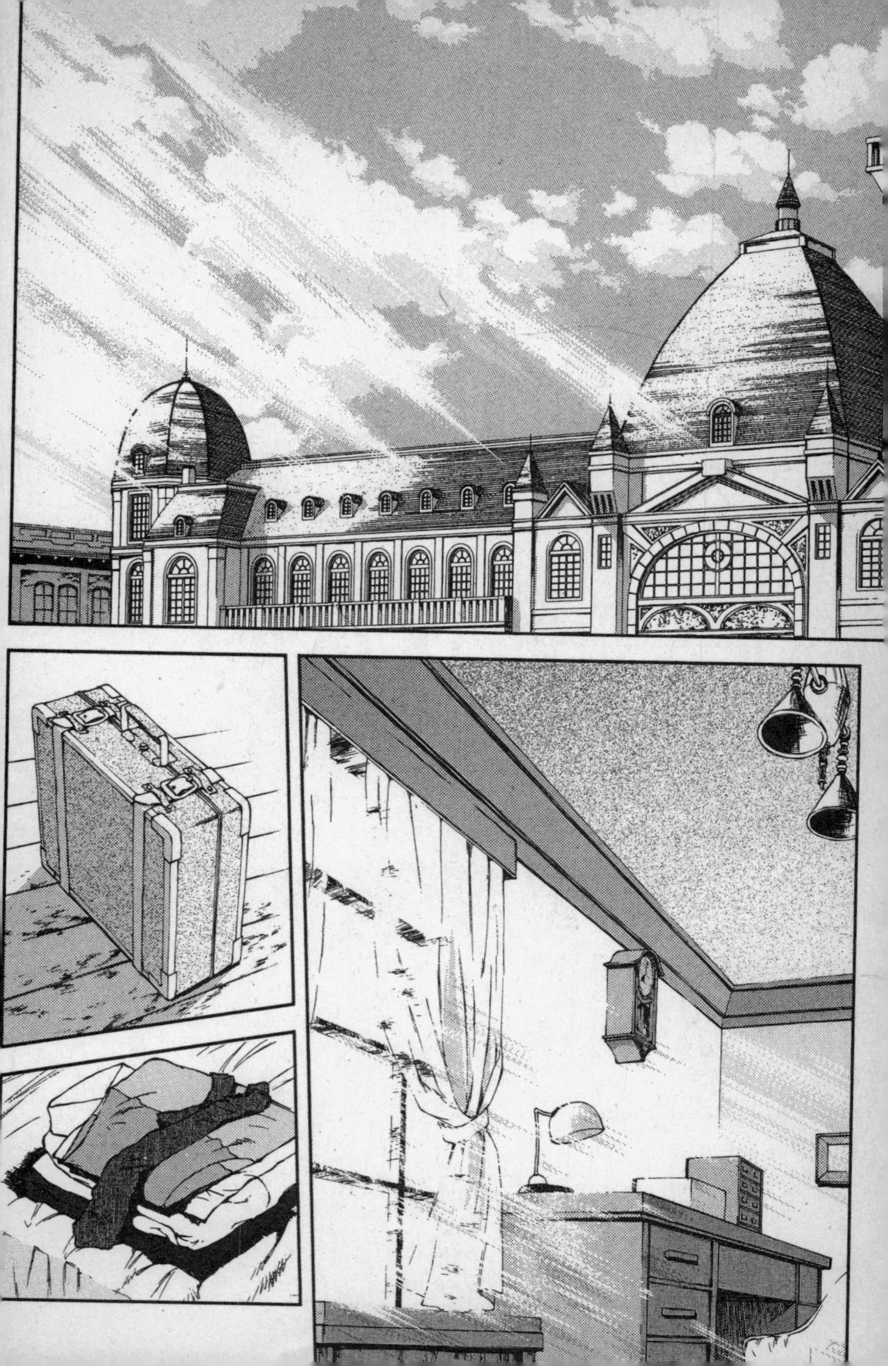

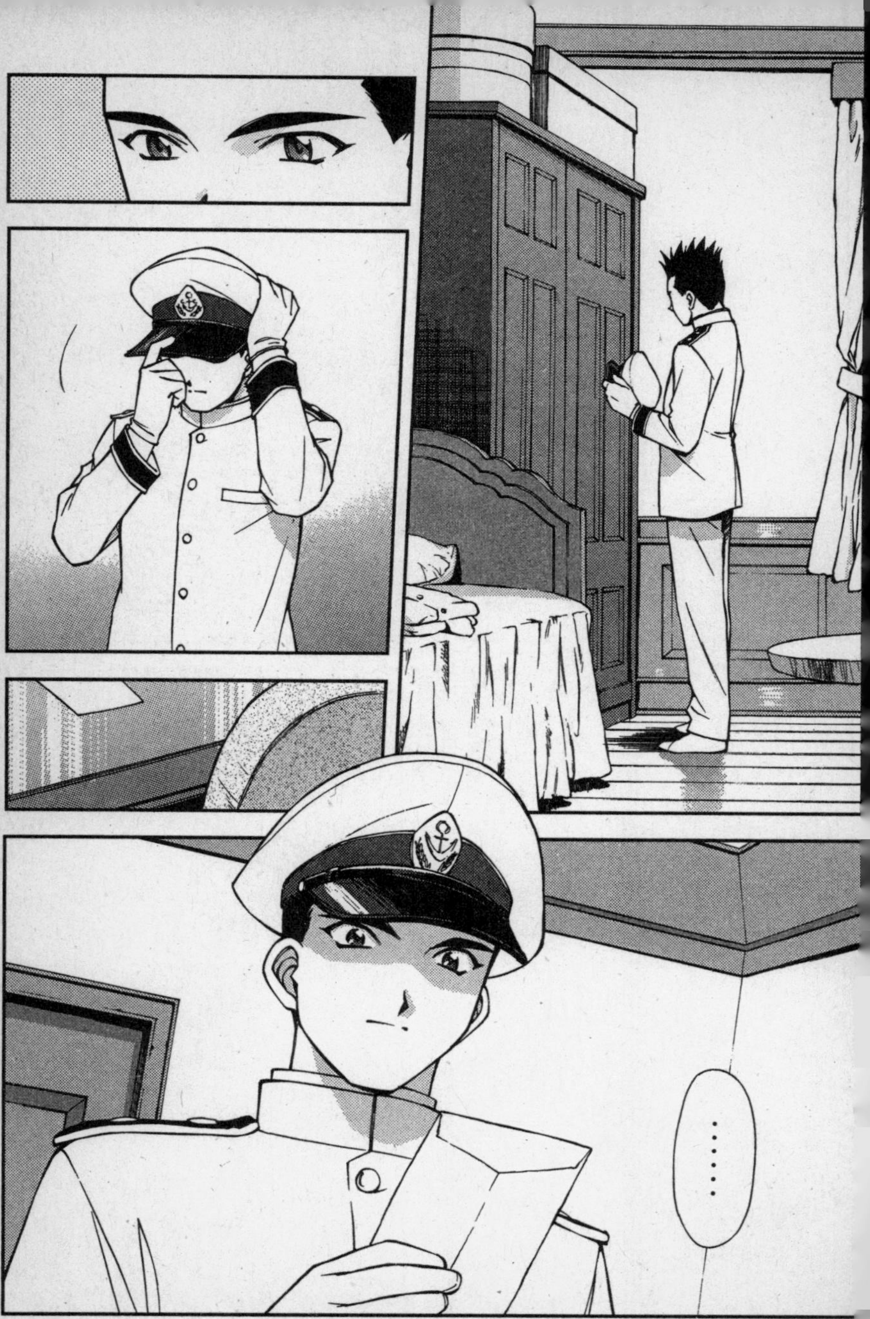
......

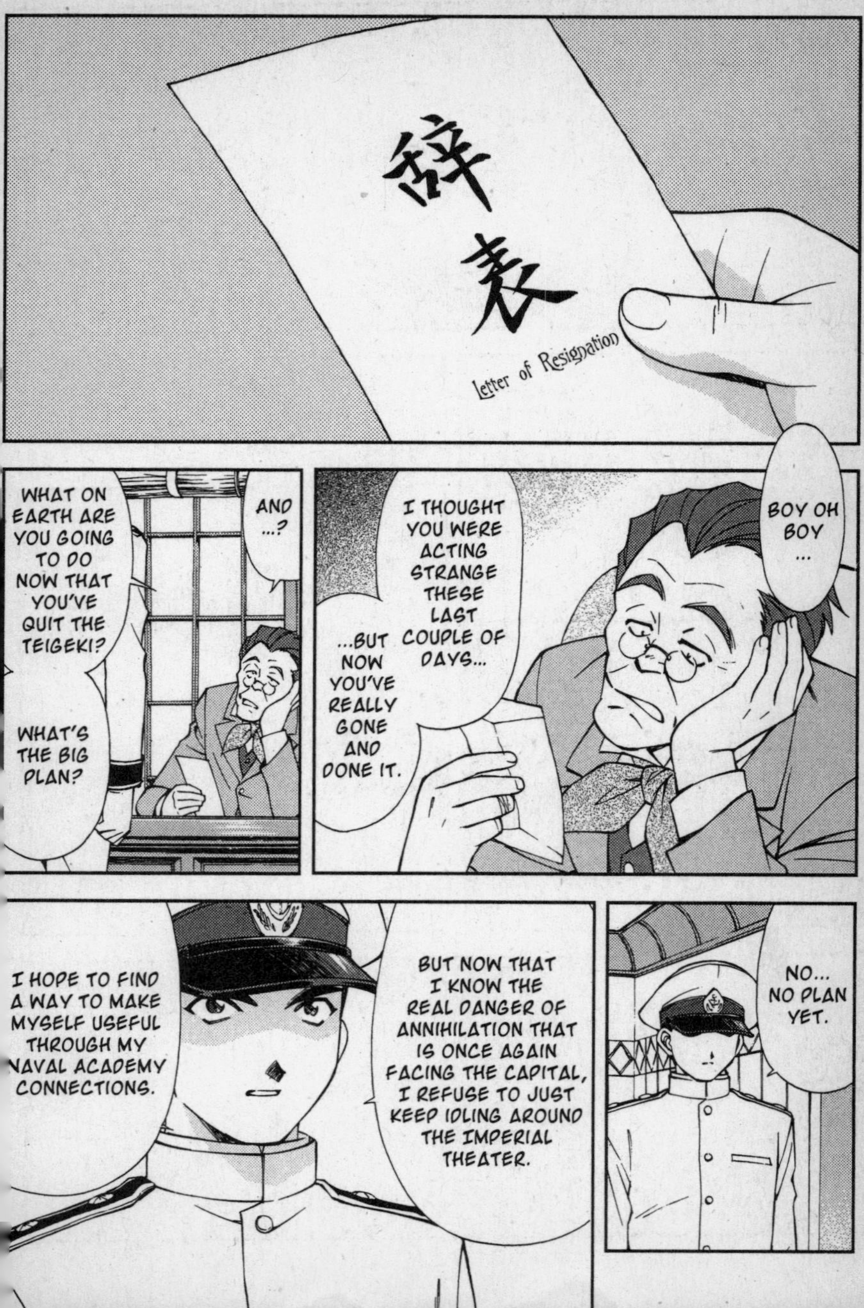
辞表
Letter of Resignation
BOY OH BOY ...
I THOUGHT YOU WERE ACTING STRANGE THESE LAST COUPLE OF DAYS...
...BUT NOW YOU'VE REALLY GONE AND DONE IT.
AND ...?
WHAT ON EARTH ARE YOU GOING TO DO NOW THAT YOU'VE QUIT THE TEIGEKI?
WHAT'S THE BIG PLAN?
NO... NO PLAN YET.
BUT NOW THAT I KNOW THE REAL DANGER OF ANNIHILATION THAT IS ONCE AGAIN FACING THE CAPITAL, I REFUSE TO JUST KEEP IDLING AROUND THE IMPERIAL THEATER.
I HOPE TO FIND A WAY TO MAKE MYSELF USEFUL THROUGH MY NAVAL ACADEMY CONNECTIONS.

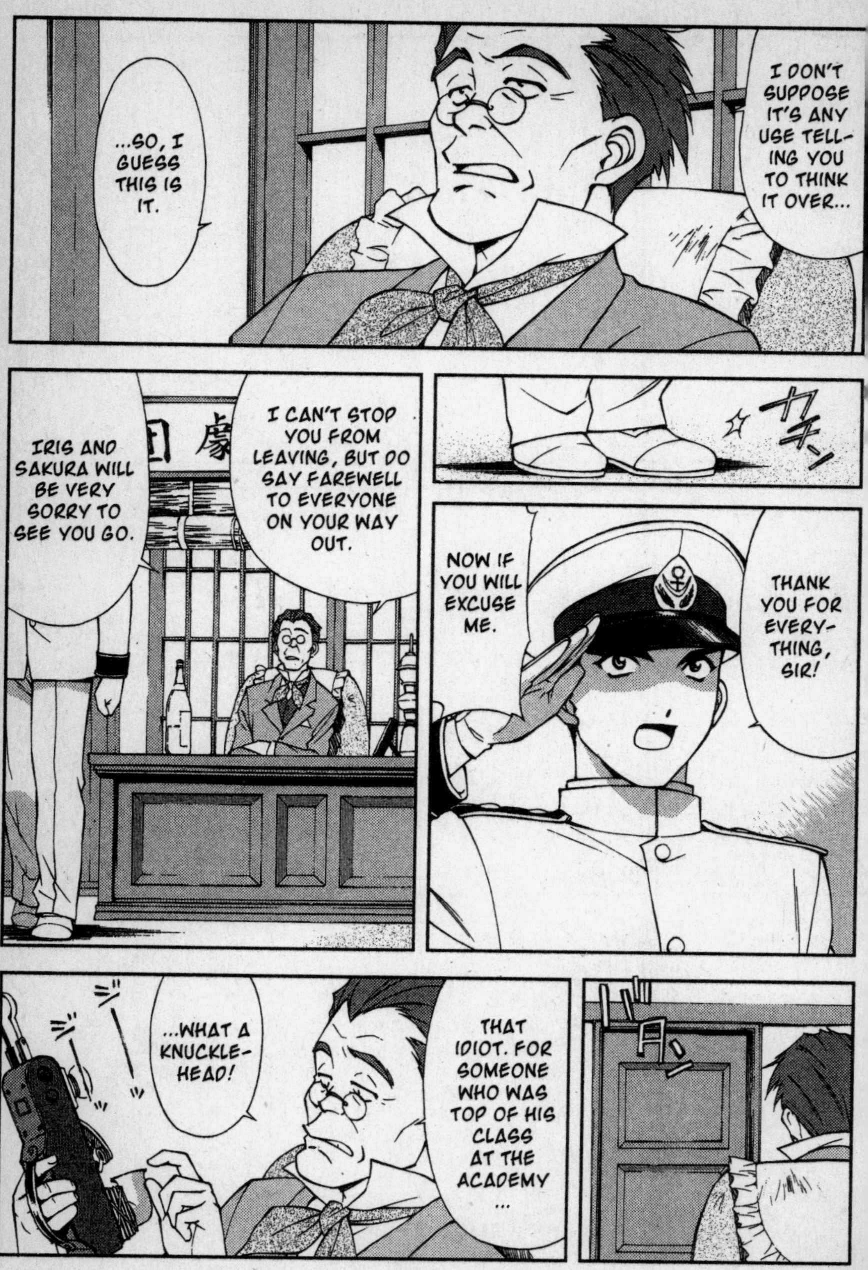
I DON'T SUPPOSE IT'S ANY USE TELLING YOU TO THINK IT OVER...
...SO, I GUESS THIS IS IT.
THANK YOU FOR EVERYTHING, SIR!
NOW IF YOU WILL EXCUSE ME.
I CAN'T STOP YOU FROM LEAVING, BUT DO SAY FAREWELL TO EVERYONE ON YOUR WAY OUT.
IRIS AND SAKURA WILL BE VERY SORRY TO SEE YOU GO.
THAT IDIOT. FOR SOMEONE WHO WAS TOP OF HIS CLASS AT THE ACADEMY ...
...WHAT A KNUCKLE-HEAD!

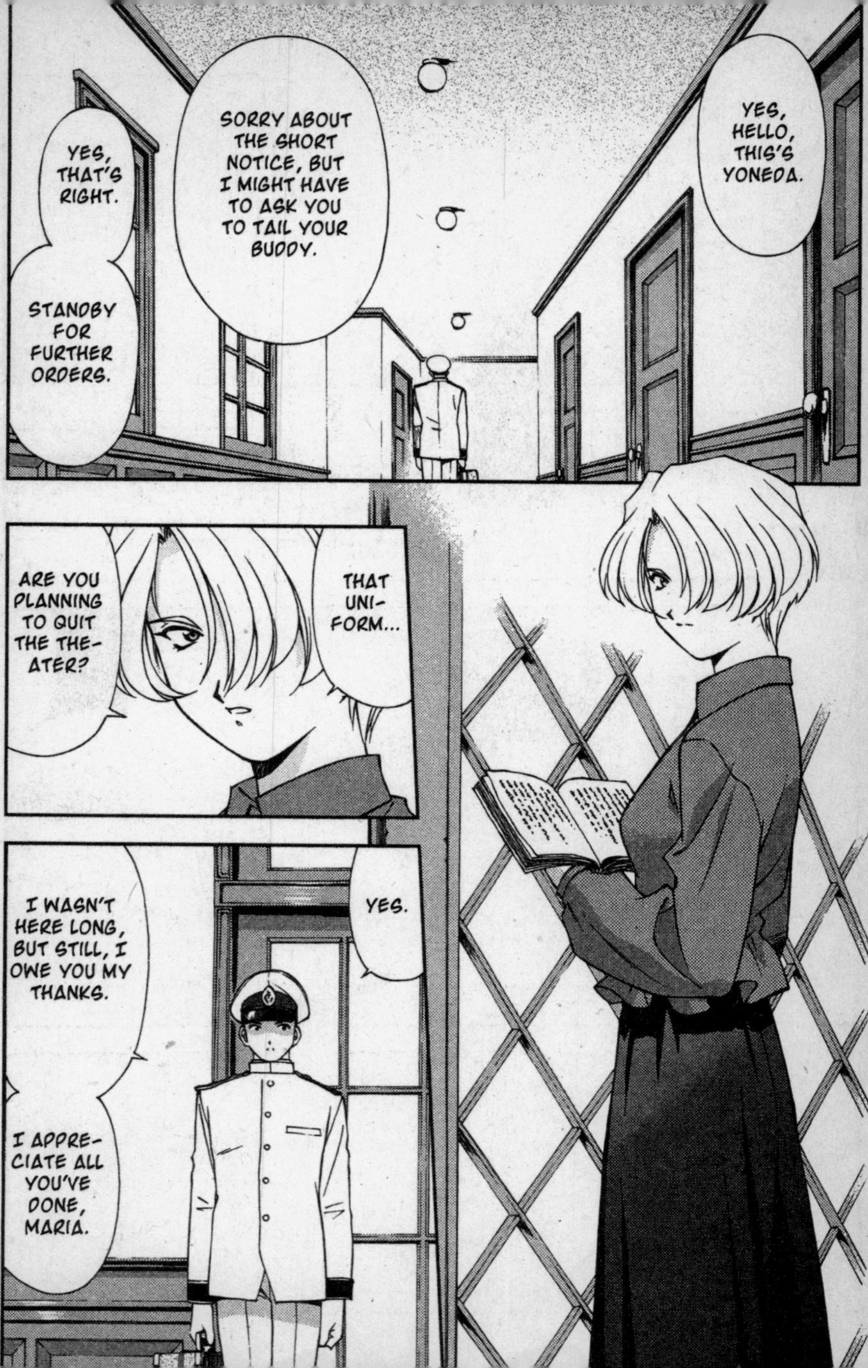
YES, HELLO, THIS'S YONEDA.
SORRY ABOUT THE SHORT NOTICE, BUT I MIGHT HAVE TO ASK YOU TO TAIL YOUR BUDDY.
YES, THAT'S RIGHT.
STANDBY FOR FURTHER ORDERS.
THAT UNI-FORM...
ARE YOU PLANNING TO QUIT THE THE-ATER?
YES.
I WASN'T HERE LONG, BUT STILL, I OWE YOU MY THANKS.
I APPRE-CIATE ALL YOU'VE DONE, MARIA.

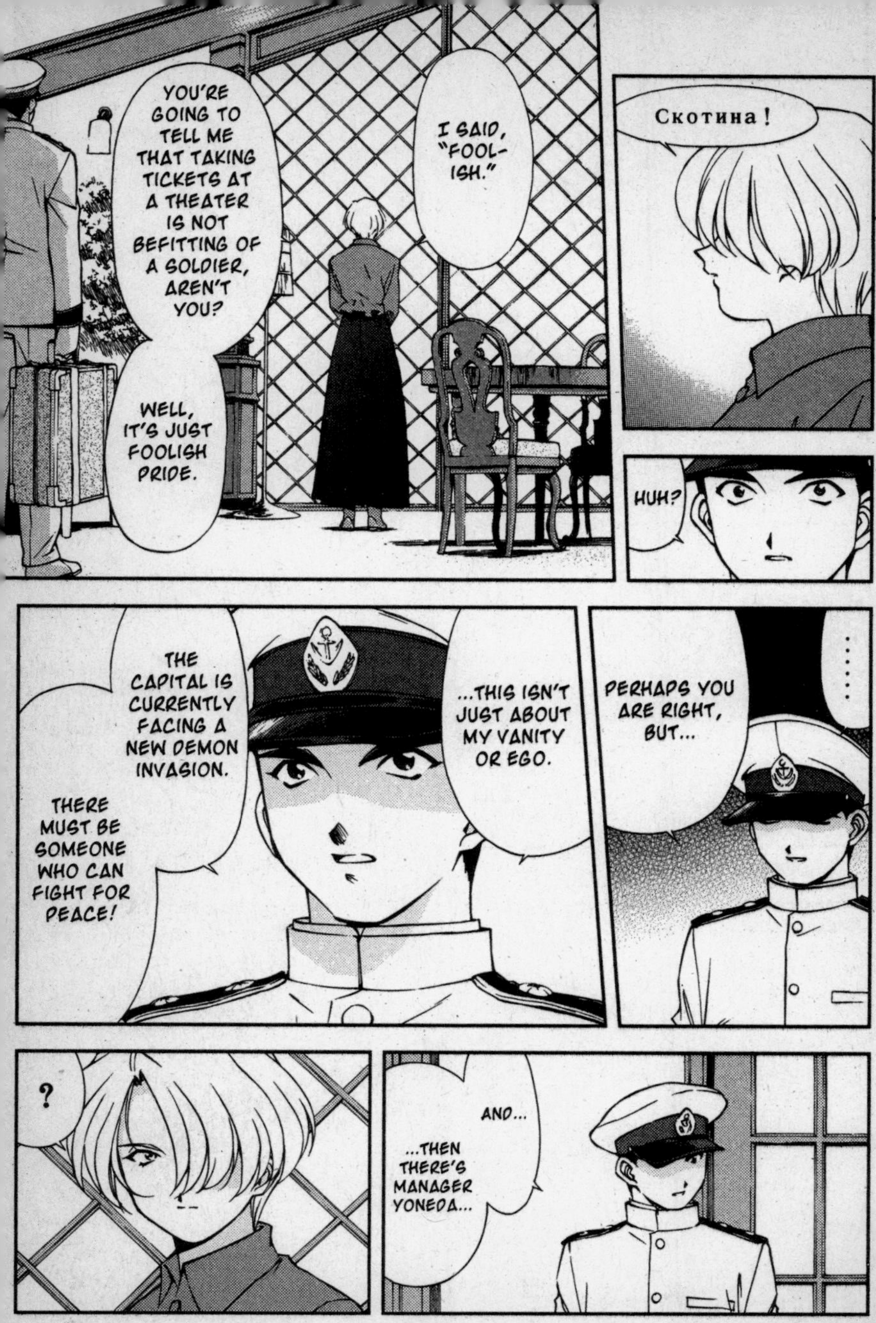
Скотина!
HUH?
I SAID, "FOOL-ISH."
YOU'RE GOING TO TELL ME THAT TAKING TICKETS AT A THEATER IS NOT BEFITTING OF A SOLDIER, AREN'T YOU?
WELL, IT'S JUST FOOLISH PRIDE.
......
PERHAPS YOU ARE RIGHT, BUT...
...THIS ISN'T JUST ABOUT MY VANITY OR EGO.
THE CAPITAL IS CURRENTLY FACING A NEW DEMON INVASION.
THERE MUST BE SOMEONE WHO CAN FIGHT FOR PEACE!
AND...
...THEN THERE'S MANAGER YONEDA...
?

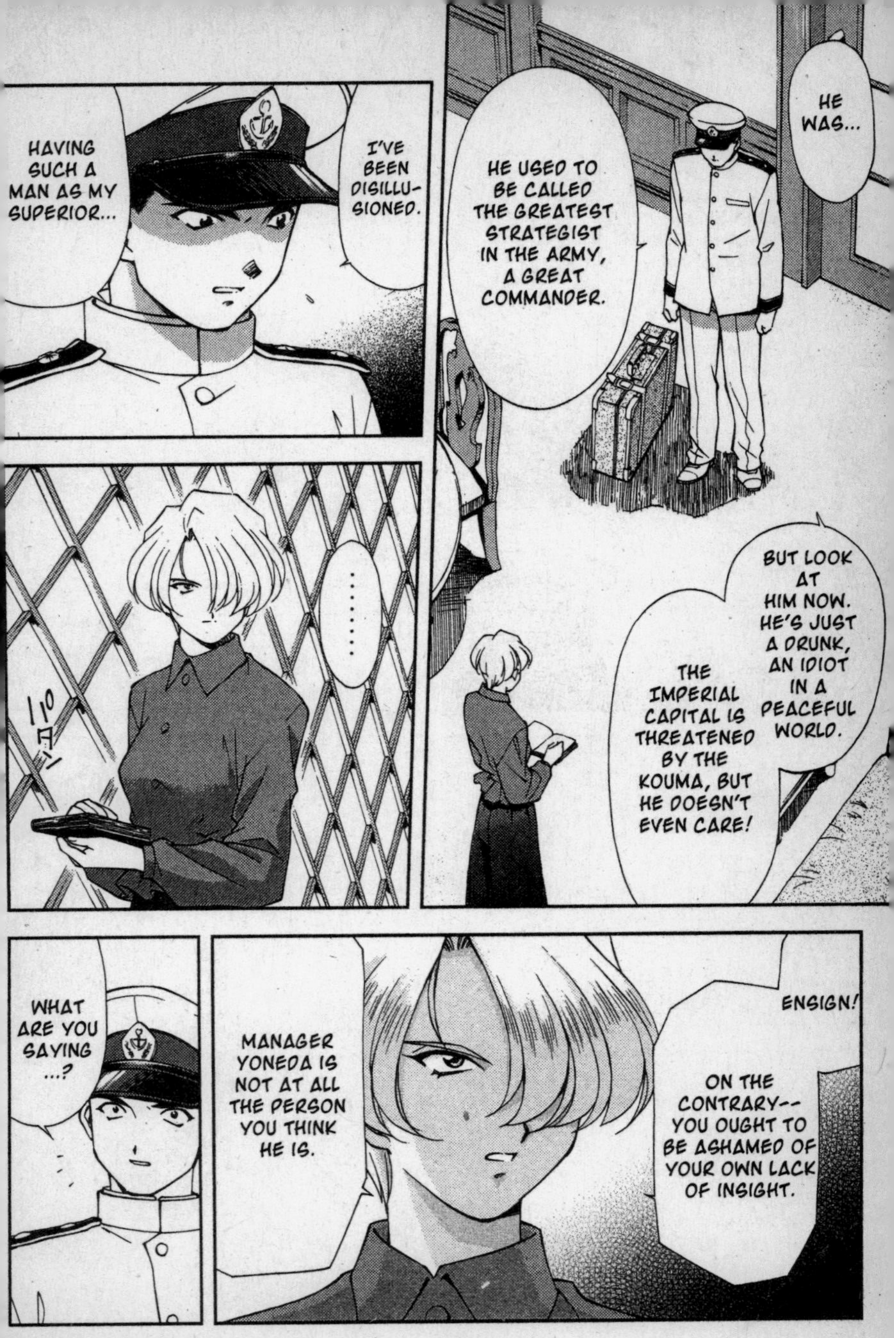

HE WAS...
HE USED TO BE CALLED THE GREATEST STRATEGIST IN THE ARMY, A GREAT COMMANDER.
BUT LOOK AT HIM NOW. HE'S JUST A DRUNK, AN IDIOT IN A PEACEFUL WORLD.
THE IMPERIAL CAPITAL IS THREATENED BY THE KOUMA, BUT HE DOESN'T EVEN CARE!
I'VE BEEN DISILLUSIONED.
HAVING SUCH A MAN AS MY SUPERIOR...
......
ENSIGN!
ON THE CONTRARY-- YOU OUGHT TO BE ASHAMED OF YOUR OWN LACK OF INSIGHT.
MANAGER YONEDA IS NOT AT ALL THE PERSON YOU THINK HE IS.
WHAT ARE YOU SAYING ...?

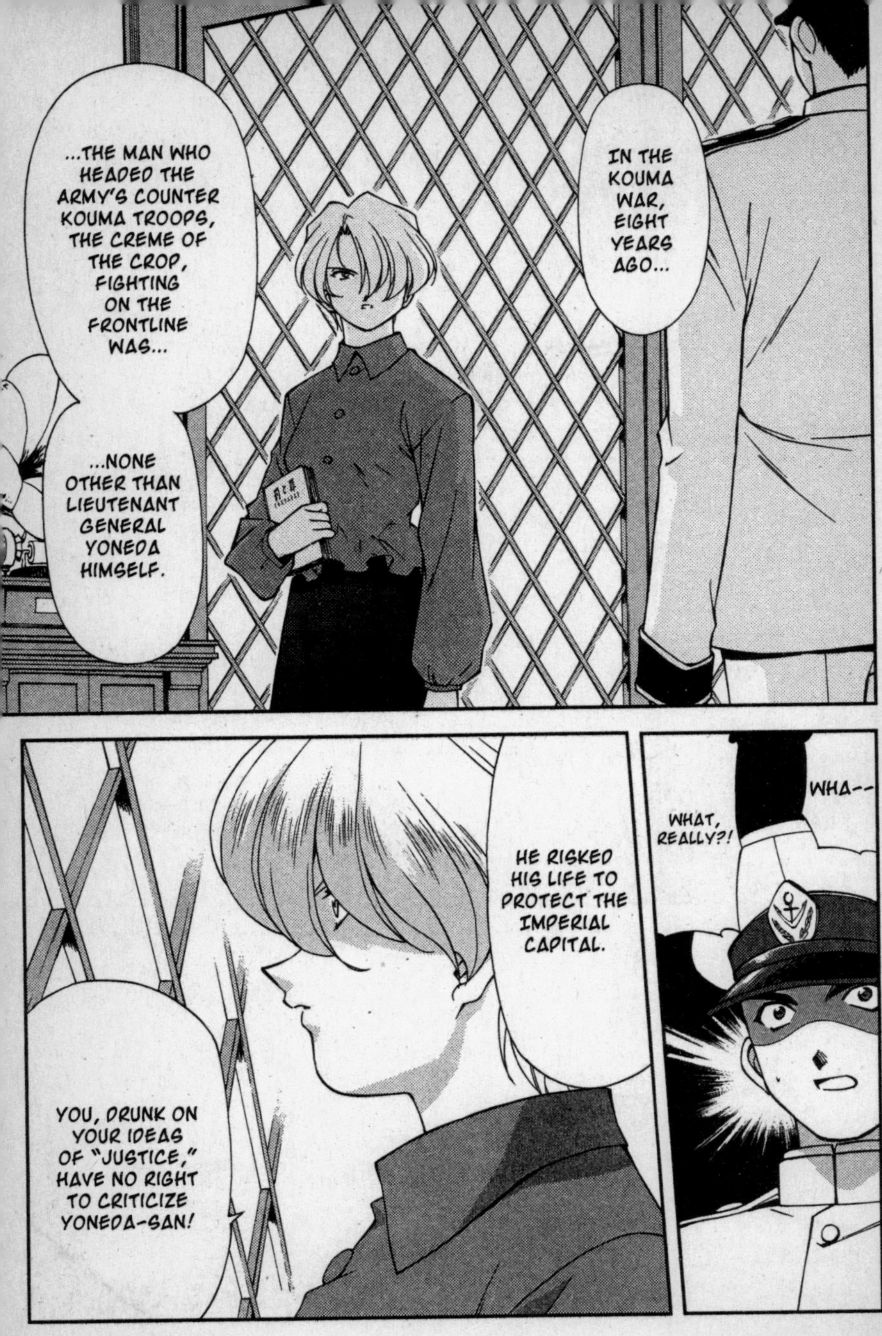
IN THE KOUMA WAR, EIGHT YEARS AGO...
...THE MAN WHO HEADED THE ARMY'S COUNTER KOUMA TROOPS, THE CREME OF THE CROP, FIGHTING ON THE FRONTLINE WAS...
...NONE OTHER THAN LIEUTENANT GENERAL YONEDA HIMSELF.
WHA--
WHAT, REALLY?!
HE RISKED HIS LIFE TO PROTECT THE IMPERIAL CAPITAL.
YOU, DRUNK ON YOUR IDEAS OF "JUSTICE," HAVE NO RIGHT TO CRITICIZE YONEDA-SAN!

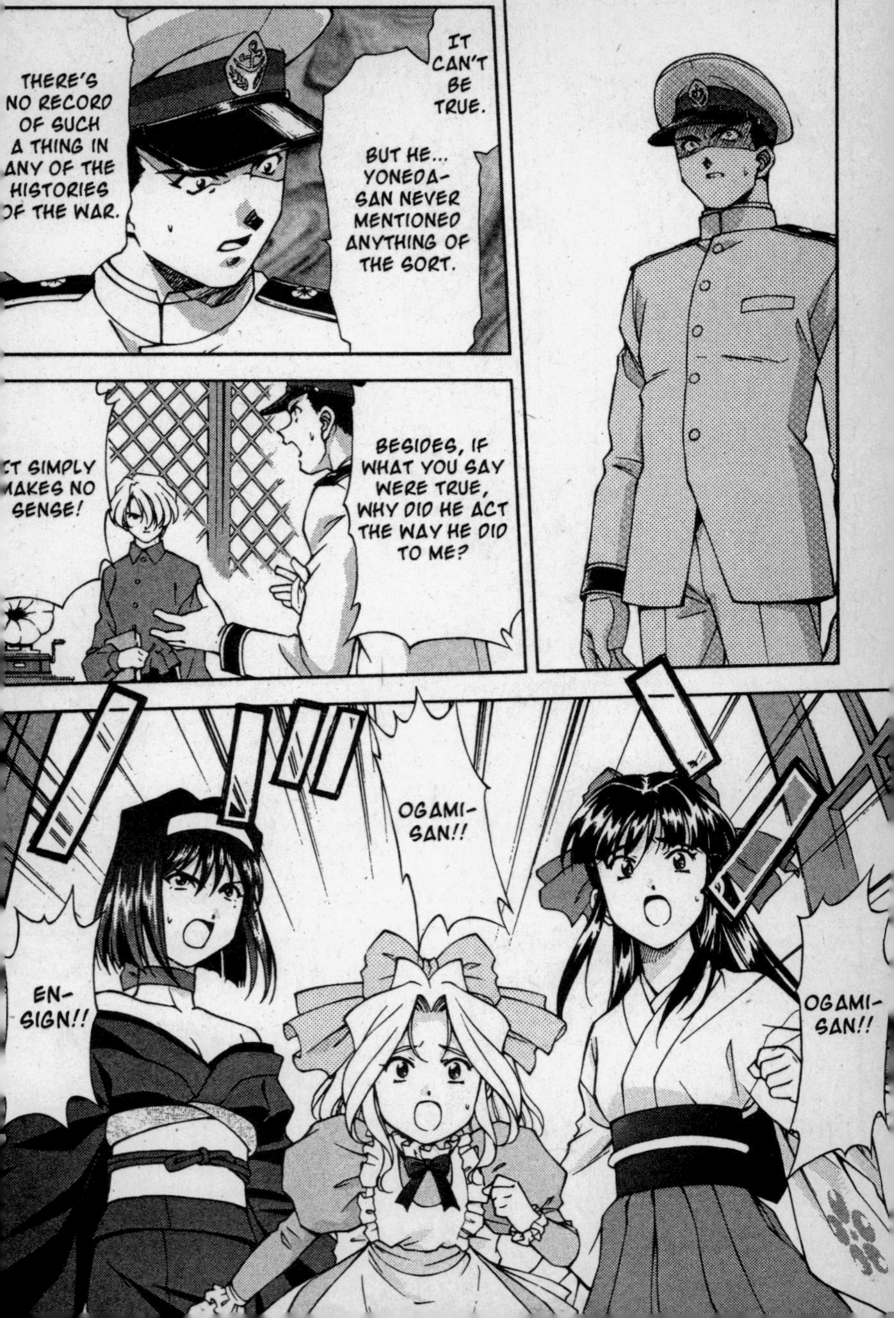
IT CAN'T BE TRUE.
BUT HE... YONEDA-SAN NEVER MENTIONED ANYTHING OF THE SORT.
THERE'S NO RECORD OF SUCH A THING IN ANY OF THE HISTORIES OF THE WAR.
BESIDES, IF WHAT YOU SAY WERE TRUE, WHY DID HE ACT THE WAY HE DID TO ME?
IT SIMPLY MAKES NO SENSE!
OGAMI-SAN!!
OGAMI-SAN!!
EN-SIGN!!

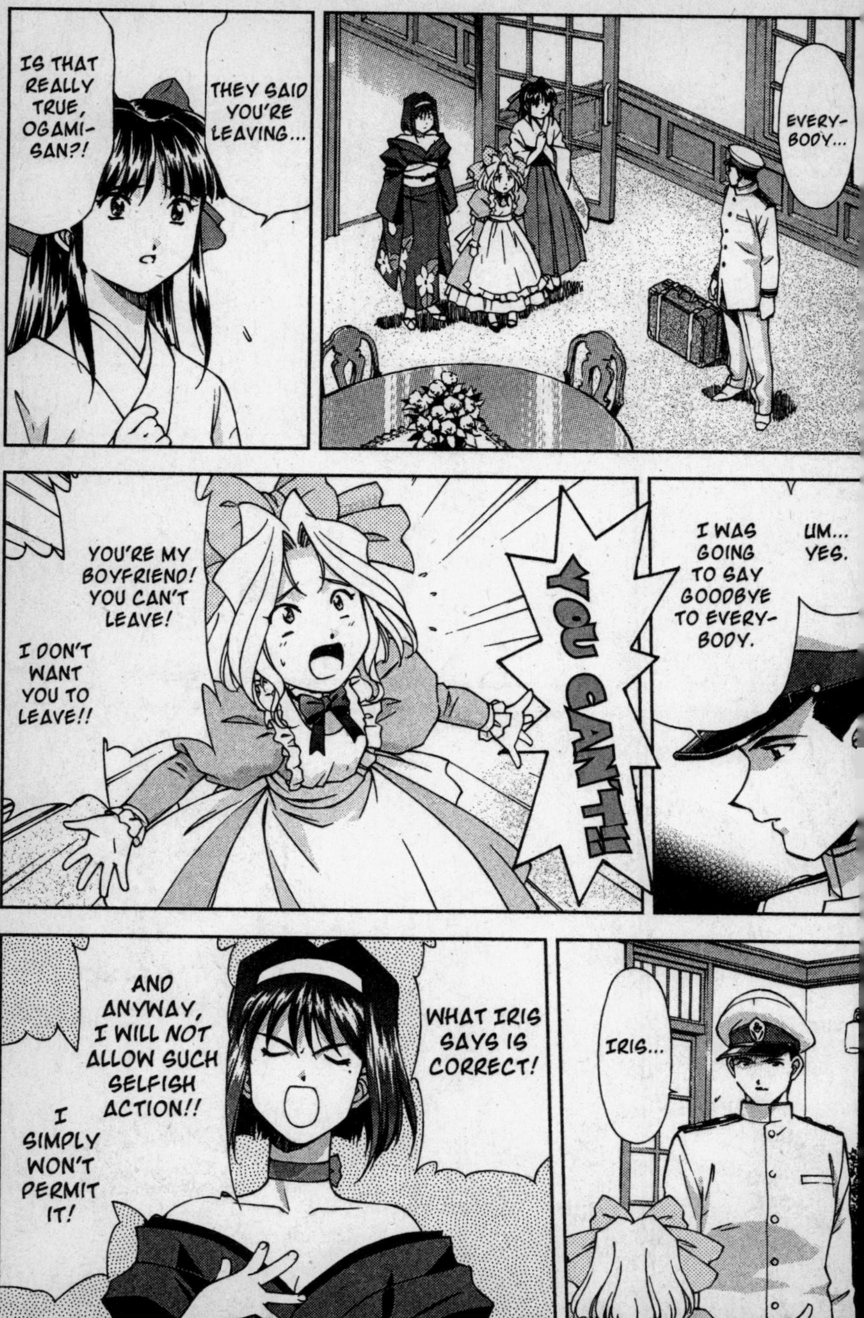
EVERY-BODY...
THEY SAID YOU'RE LEAVING...
IS THAT REALLY TRUE, OGAMI-SAN?!
UM... YES.
I WAS GOING TO SAY GOODBYE TO EVERY-BODY.
YOU CAN'T!!
YOU'RE MY BOYFRIEND! YOU CAN'T LEAVE!
I DON'T WANT YOU TO LEAVE!!
IRIS...
WHAT IRIS SAYS IS CORRECT!
AND ANYWAY, I WILL NOT ALLOW SUCH SELFISH ACTION!!
I SIMPLY WON'T PERMIT IT!

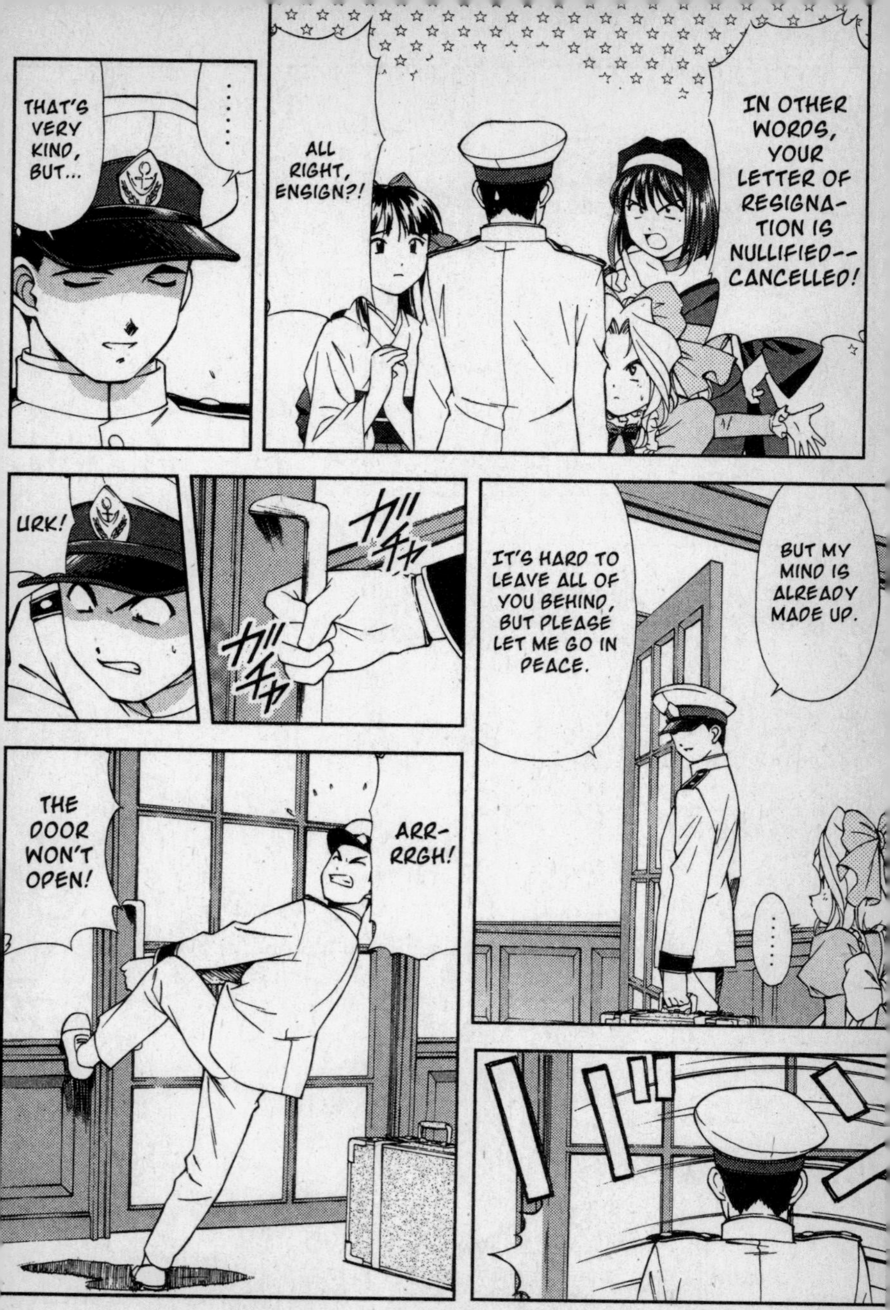
IN OTHER WORDS, YOUR LETTER OF RESIGNA-TION IS NULLIFIED--CANCELLED!
ALL RIGHT, ENSIGN?!
......
THAT'S VERY KIND, BUT...
BUT MY MIND IS ALREADY MADE UP.
IT'S HARD TO LEAVE ALL OF YOU BEHIND, BUT PLEASE LET ME GO IN PEACE.
......
ガチャ
ガチャ
URK!
ARR-RRGH!
THE DOOR WON'T OPEN!

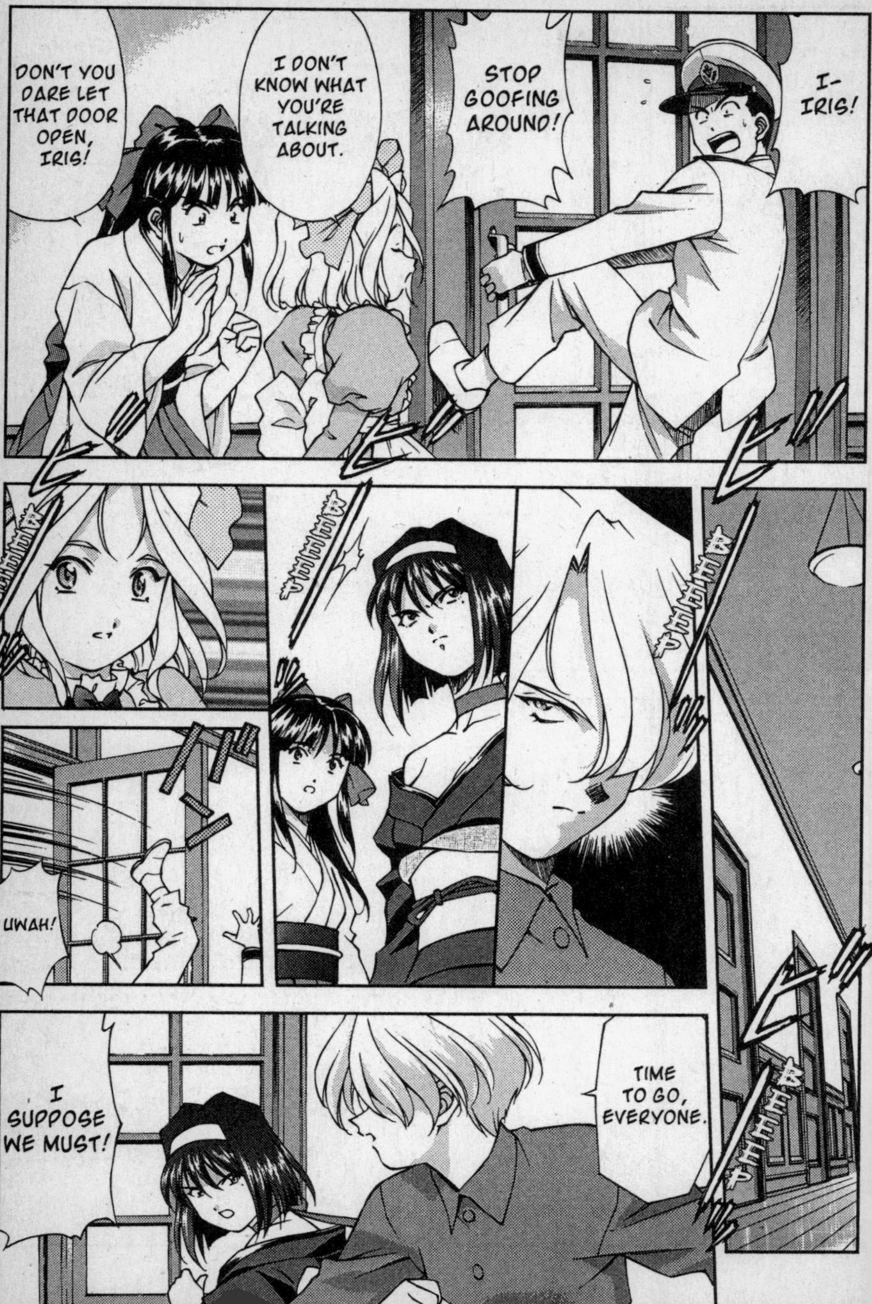

I- IRIS!
STOP GOOFING AROUND!
I DON'T KNOW WHAT YOU'RE TALKING ABOUT.
DON'T YOU DARE LET THAT DOOR OPEN, IRIS!
BEEEEP
BEEEEP
BEEEEP
UWAH!
BEEEEP
TIME TO GO, EVERYONE.
I SUPPOSE WE MUST!

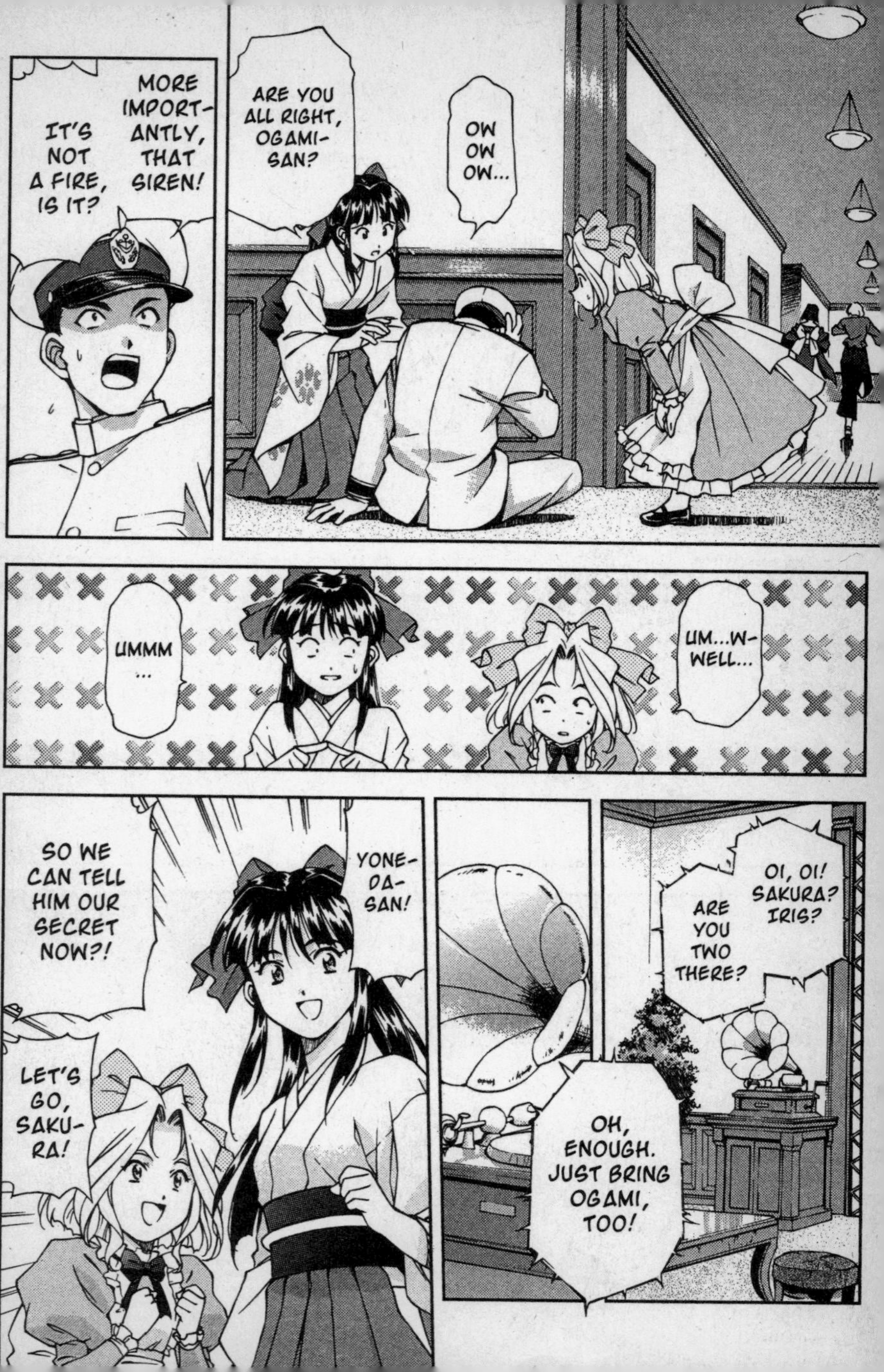
OW OW OW...
ARE YOU ALL RIGHT, OGAMI-SAN?
MORE IMPORT-ANTLY, THAT SIREN!
IT'S NOT A FIRE, IS IT?
UM...W-WELL...
UMMM ...
OI, OI! SAKURA? IRIS?
ARE YOU TWO THERE?
OH, ENOUGH. JUST BRING OGAMI, TOO!
YONE-DA-SAN!
SO WE CAN TELL HIM OUR SECRET NOW?!
LET'S GO, SAKURA!

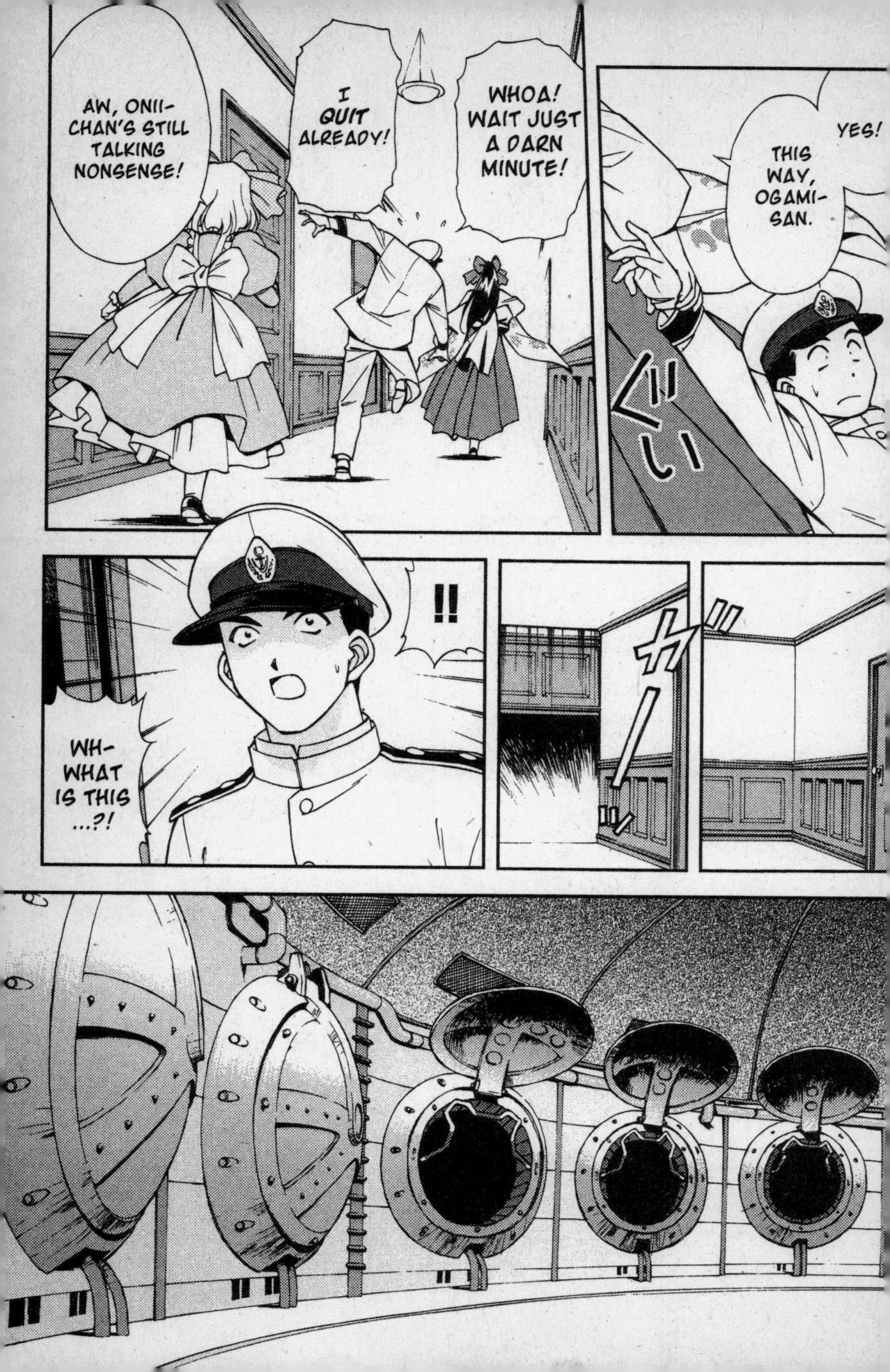
YES!
THIS WAY, OGAMI-SAN.
ぐい
WHOA! WAIT JUST A DARN MINUTE!
I QUIT ALREADY!
AW, ONII-CHAN'S STILL TALKING NONSENSE!
ガーッ
!!
WH-WHAT IS THIS ...?!

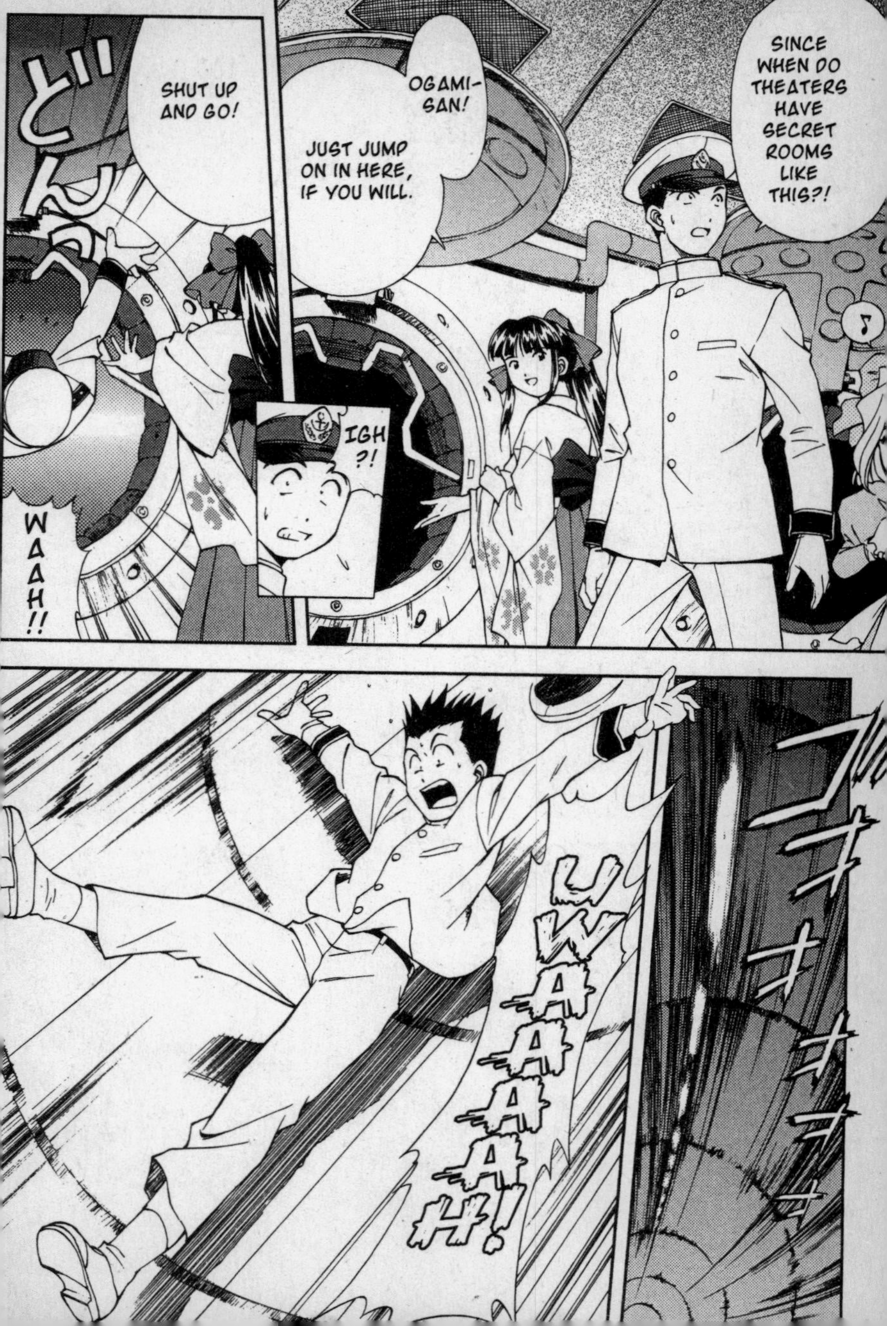
SINCE WHEN DO THEATERS HAVE SECRET ROOMS LIKE THIS?!
OGAMI-SAN!
JUST JUMP ON IN HERE, IF YOU WILL.
IGH ?!
SHUT UP AND GO!
WAAAH!!
UWAAAAH!

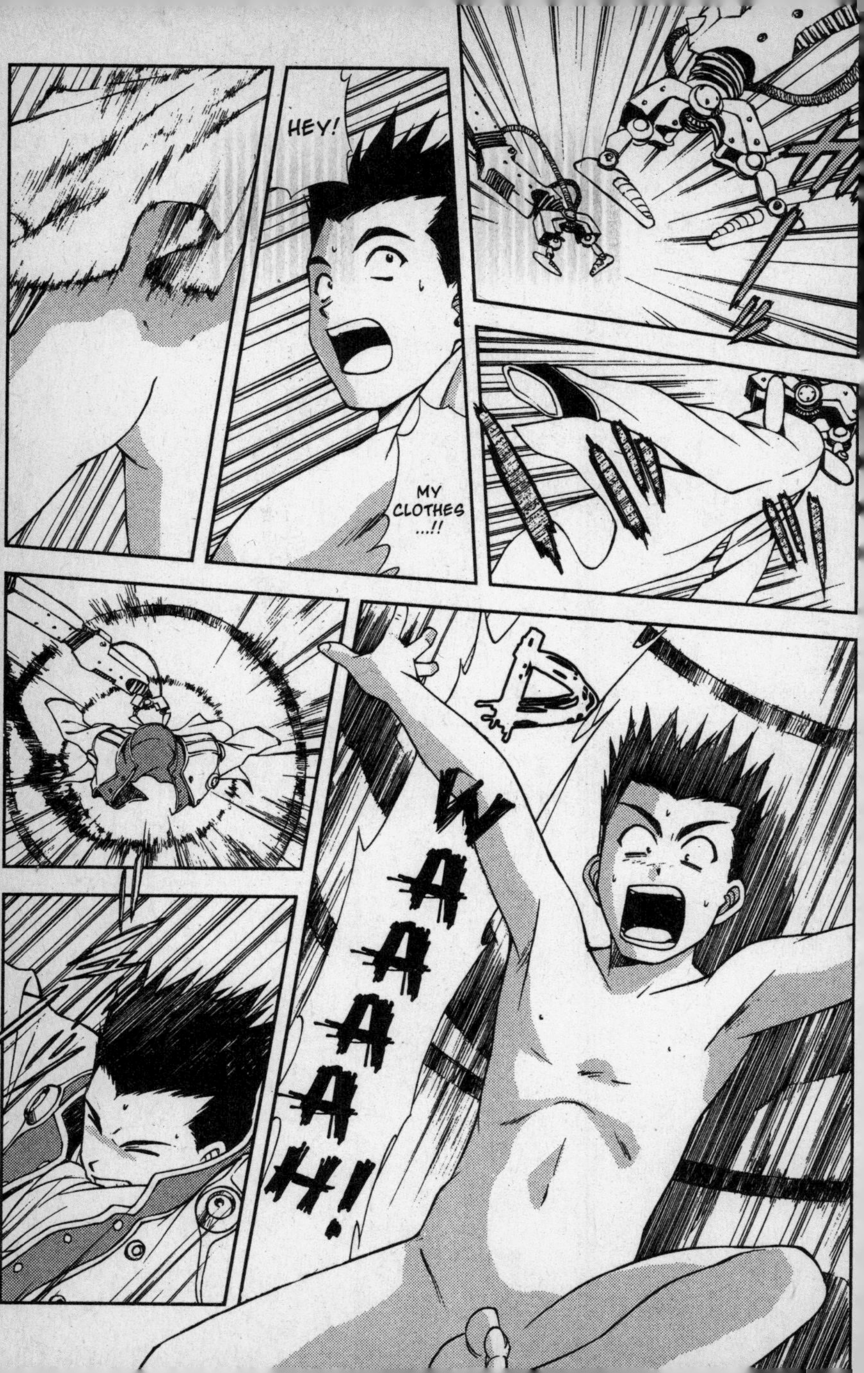
HEY!
MY CLOTHES ...!!
WAAAAAH!

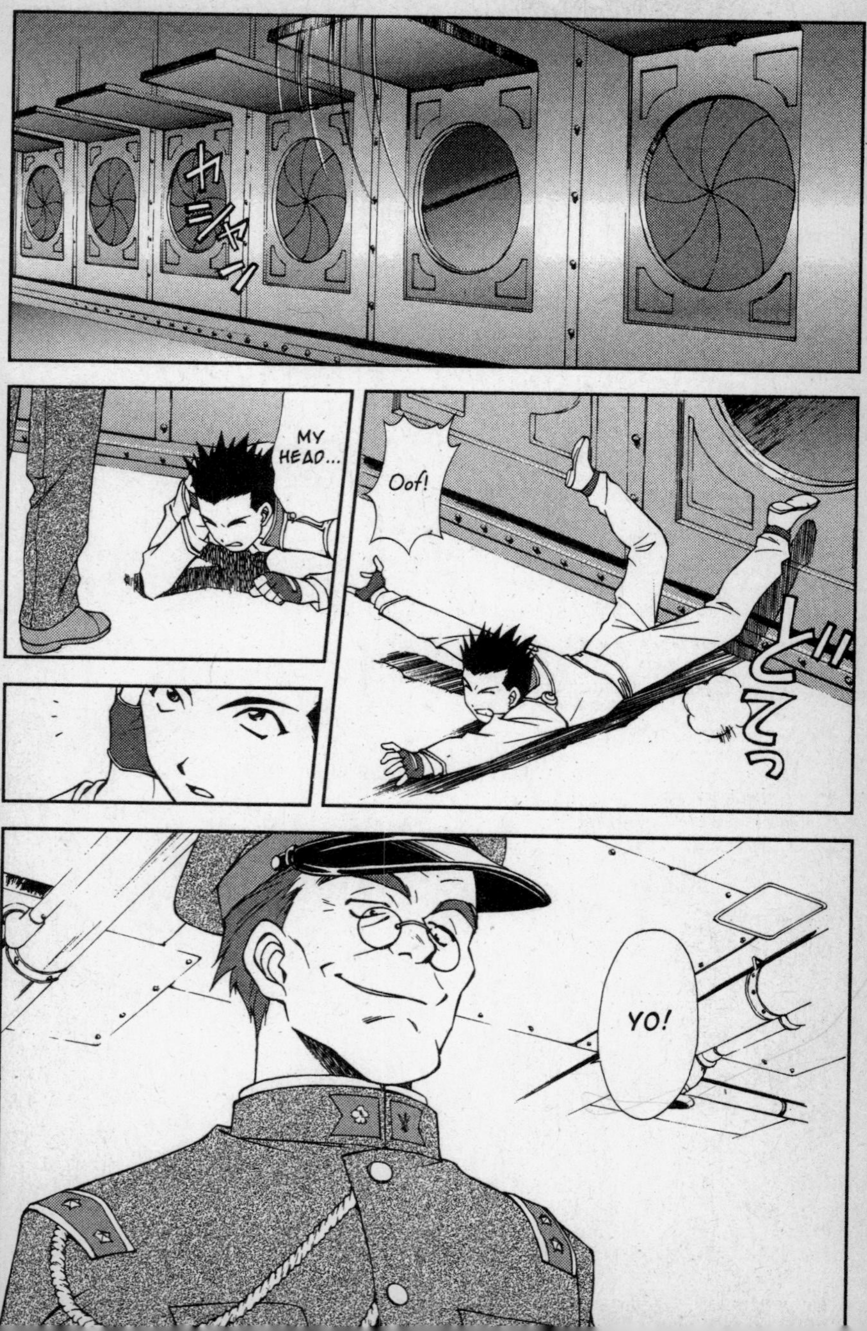

カシャン
Oof!
とてっ
MY HEAD...
YO!

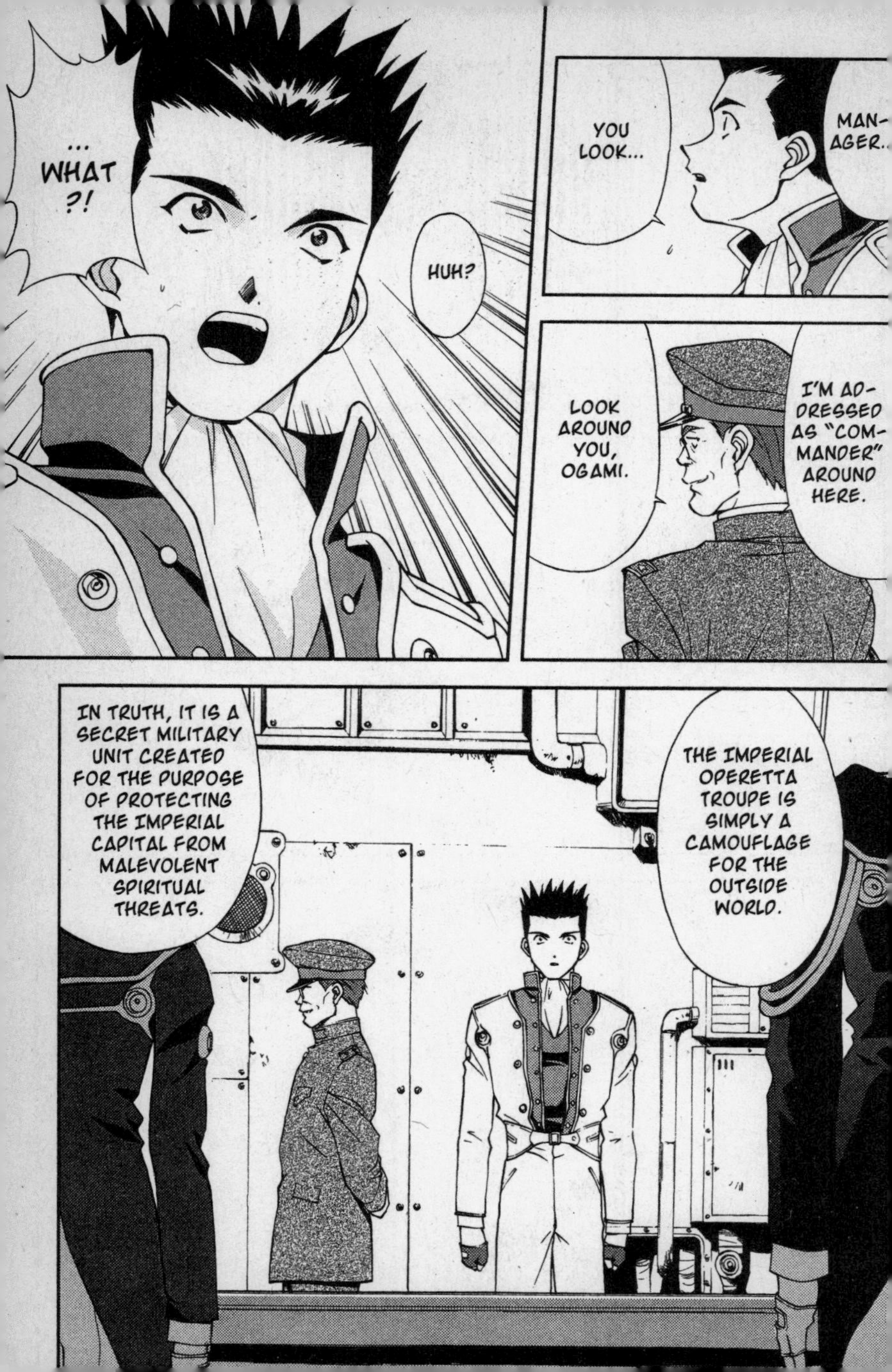
MAN-AGER..
YOU LOOK...
I'M AD-DRESSED AS "COM-MANDER" AROUND HERE.
LOOK AROUND YOU, OGAMI.
HUH?
... WHAT ?!
THE IMPERIAL OPERETTA TROUPE IS SIMPLY A CAMOUFLAGE FOR THE OUTSIDE WORLD.
IN TRUTH, IT IS A SECRET MILITARY UNIT CREATED FOR THE PURPOSE OF PROTECTING THE IMPERIAL CAPITAL FROM MALEVOLENT SPIRITUAL THREATS.

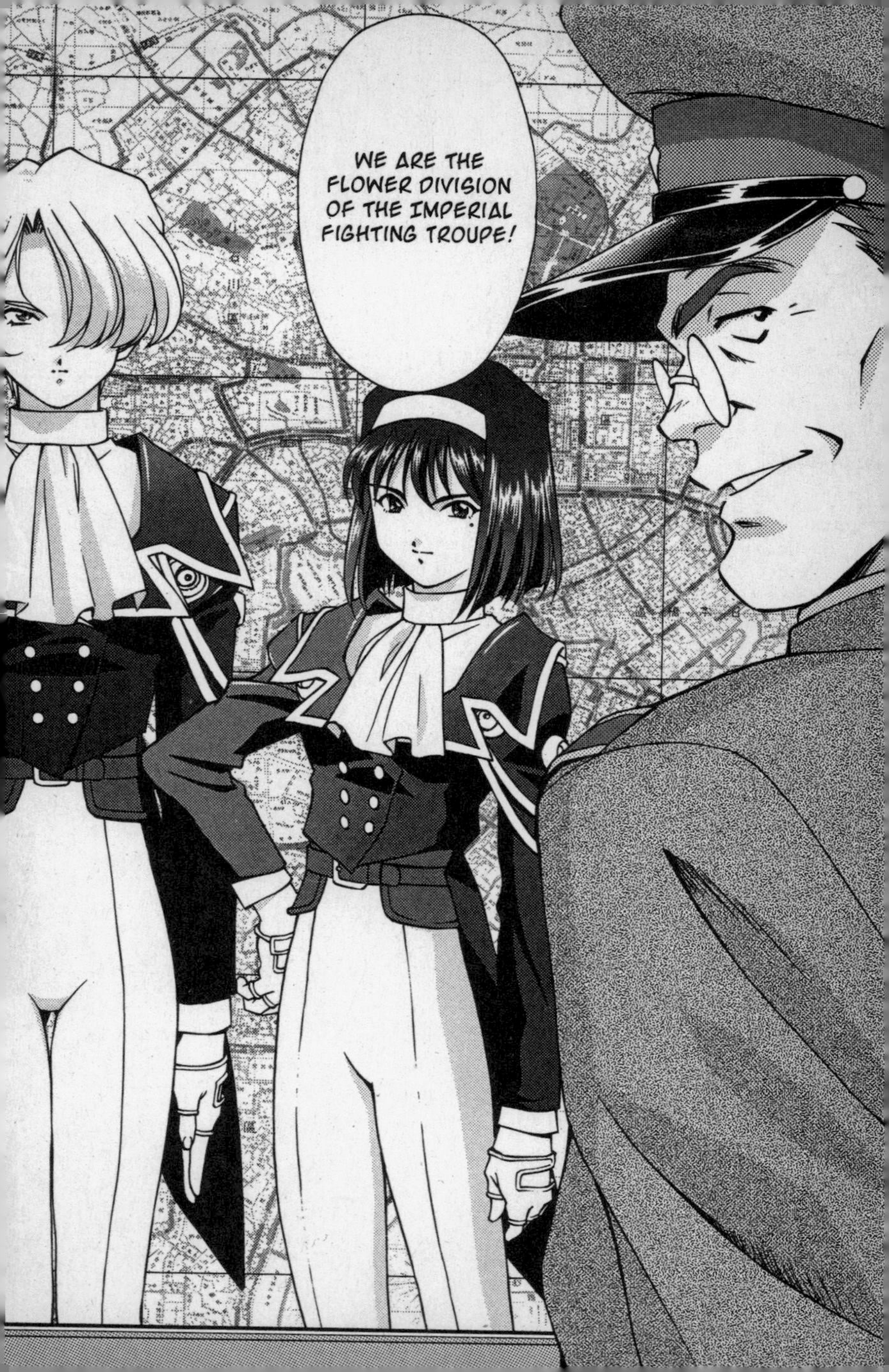
WE ARE THE FLOWER DIVISION OF THE IMPERIAL FIGHTING TROUPE!

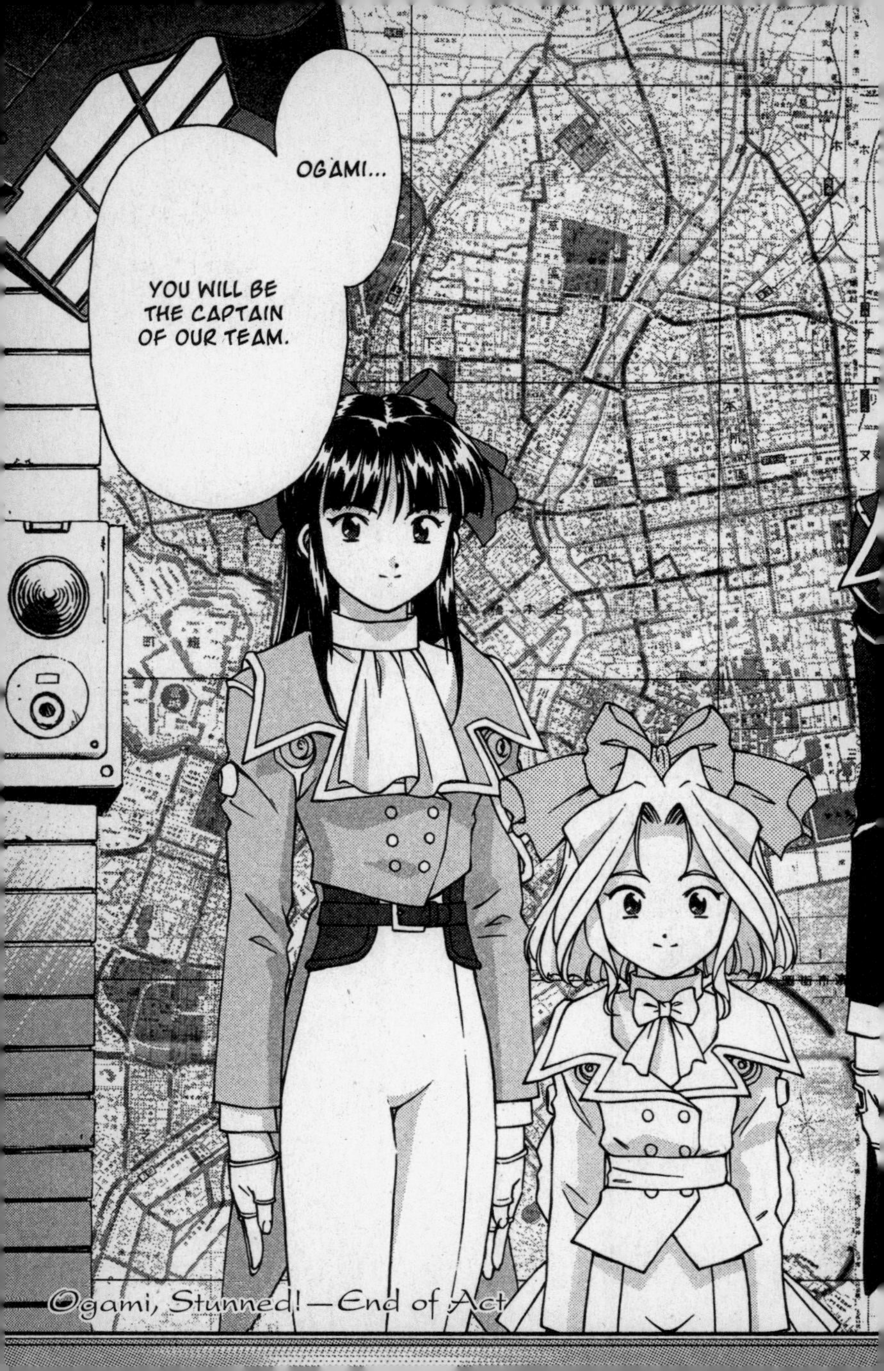
OGAMI...
YOU WILL BE THE CAPTAIN OF OUR TEAM.
Ogami, Stunned! —End of Act

織姫&レニ

Orihime and Leni

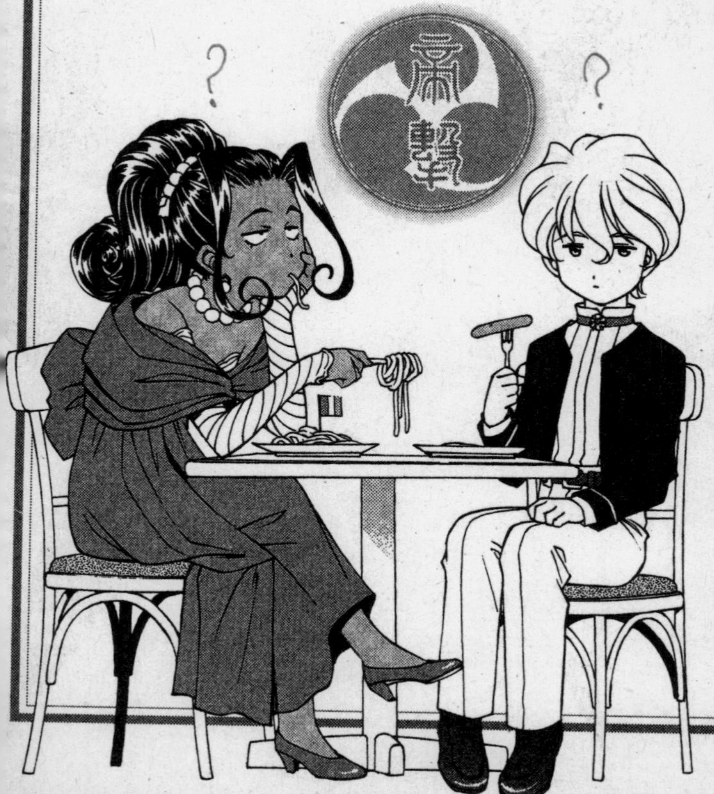

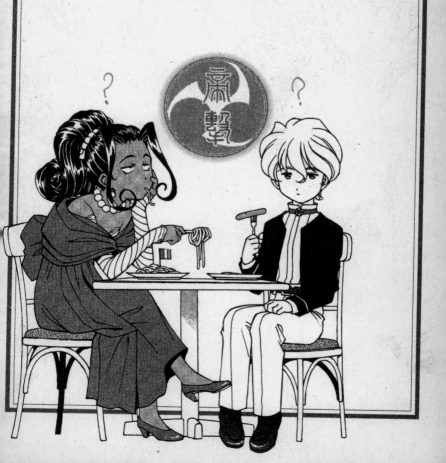

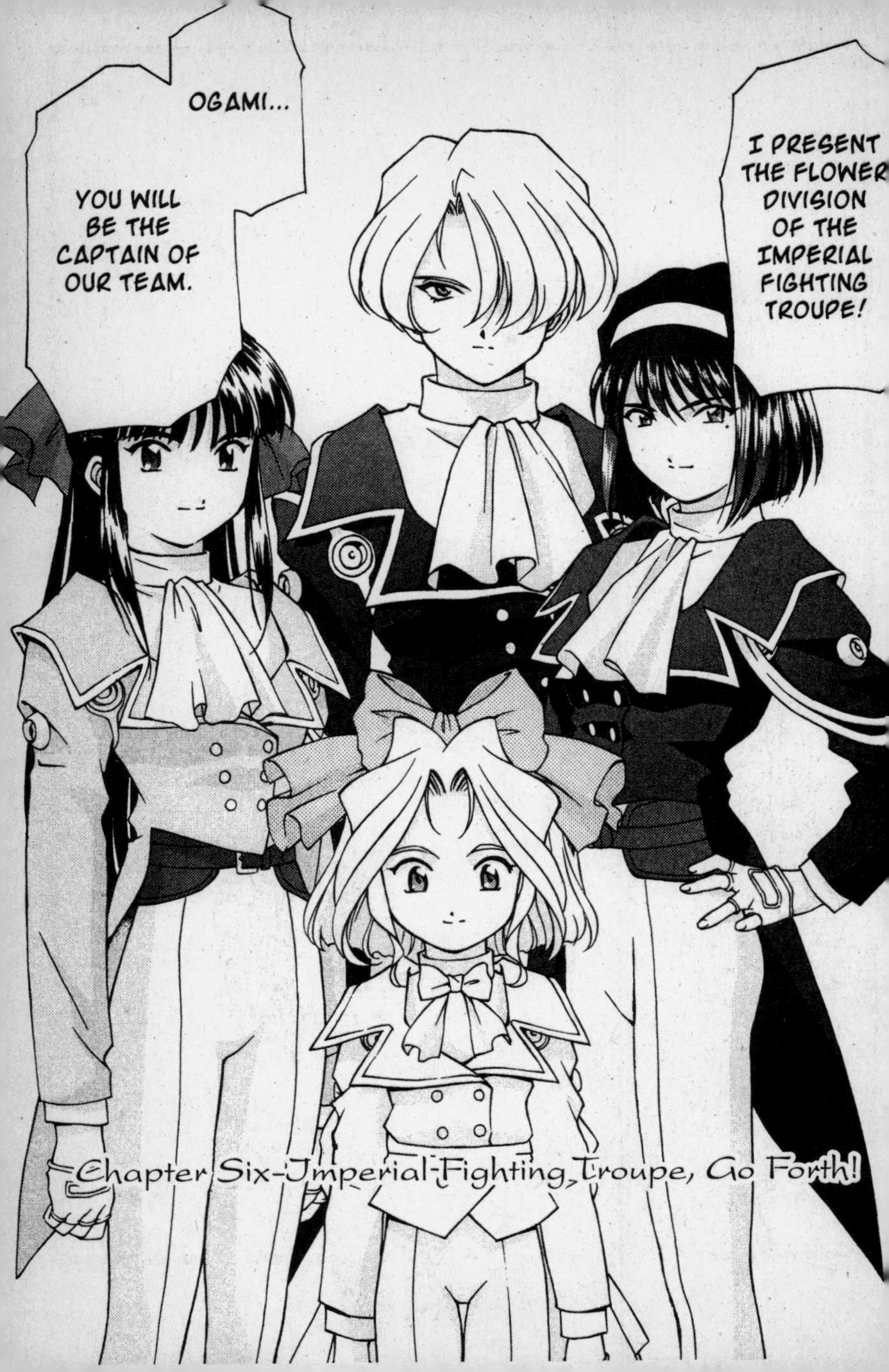
I PRESENT THE FLOWER DIVISION OF THE IMPERIAL FIGHTING TROUPE!
OGAMI...
YOU WILL BE THE CAPTAIN OF OUR TEAM.
Chapter Six-Imperial Fighting Troupe, Go Forth!

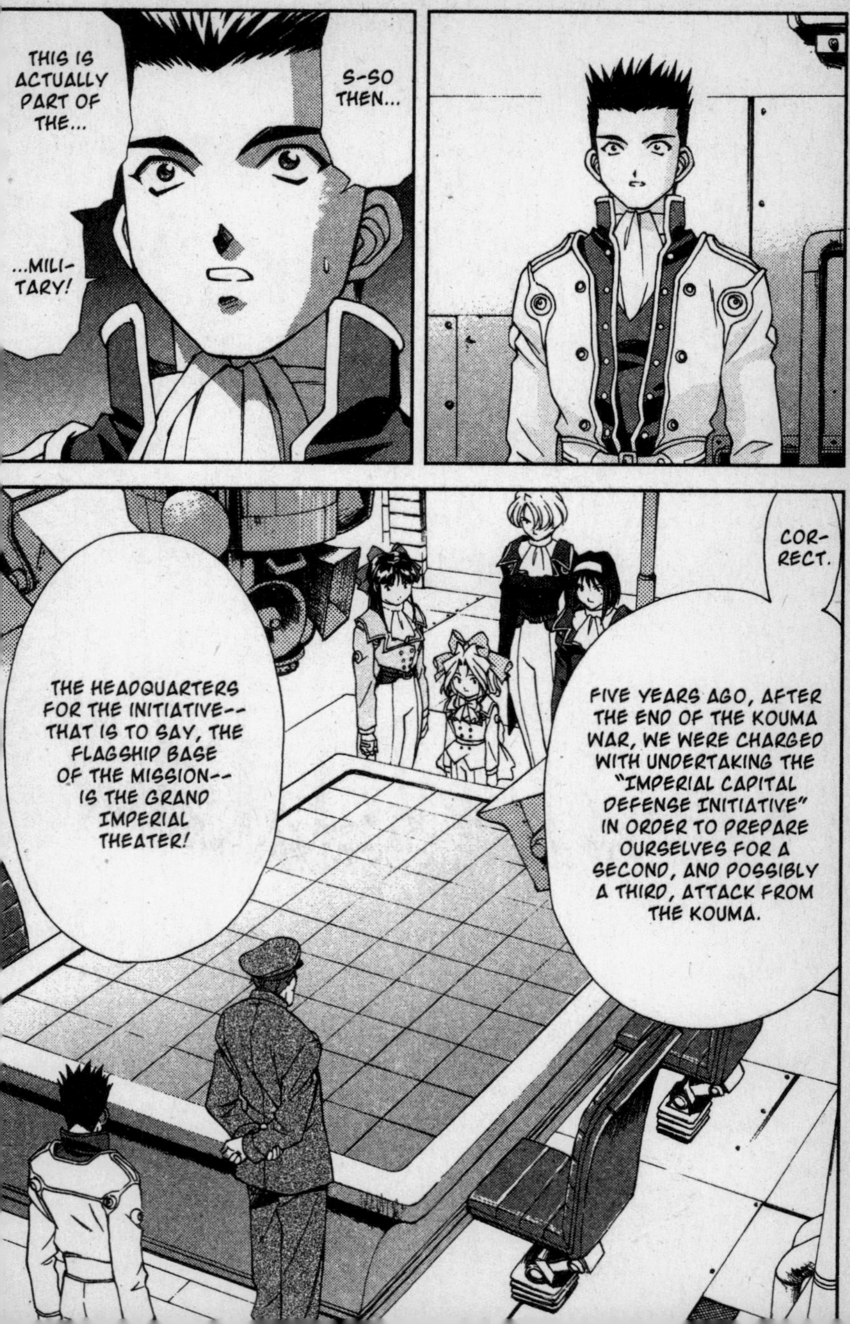
S-SO THEN...
THIS IS ACTUALLY PART OF THE...
...MILI-TARY!
COR-RECT.
FIVE YEARS AGO, AFTER THE END OF THE KOUMA WAR, WE WERE CHARGED WITH UNDERTAKING THE "IMPERIAL CAPITAL DEFENSE INITIATIVE" IN ORDER TO PREPARE OURSELVES FOR A SECOND, AND POSSIBLY A THIRD, ATTACK FROM THE KOUMA.
THE HEADQUARTERS FOR THE INITIATIVE--THAT IS TO SAY, THE FLAGSHIP BASE OF THE MISSION--IS THE GRAND IMPERIAL THEATER!

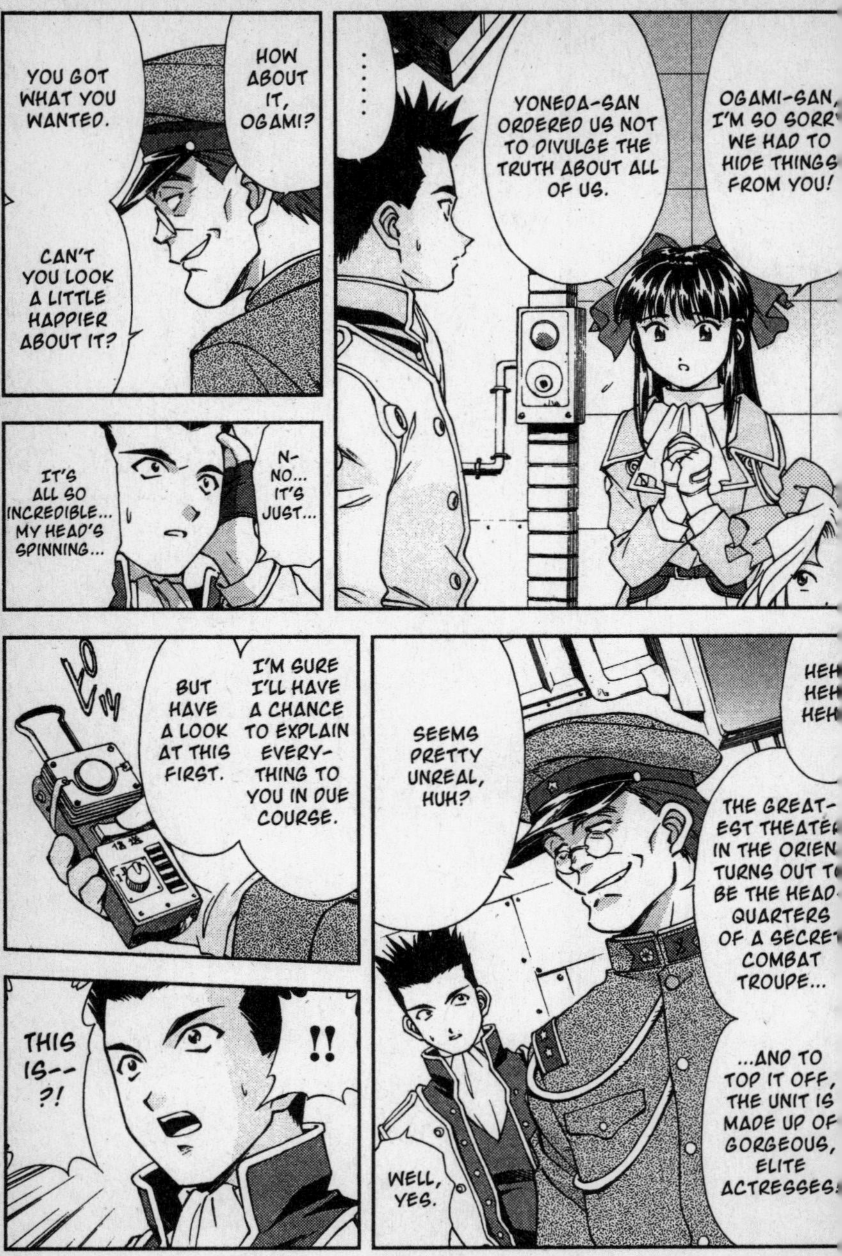
OGAMI-SAN, I'M SO SORR WE HAD TO HIDE THINGS FROM YOU!
YONEDA-SAN ORDERED US NOT TO DIVULGE THE TRUTH ABOUT ALL OF US.
......
HOW ABOUT IT, OGAMI?
YOU GOT WHAT YOU WANTED.
CAN'T YOU LOOK A LITTLE HAPPIER ABOUT IT?
N-NO... IT'S JUST...
IT'S ALL SO INCREDIBLE... MY HEAD'S SPINNING...
HEH HEH HEH
SEEMS PRETTY UNREAL, HUH?
THE GREAT-EST THEATE IN THE ORIEN TURNS OUT T BE THE HEAD-QUARTERS OF A SECRE COMBAT TROUPE...
...AND TO TOP IT OFF, THE UNIT IS MADE UP OF GORGEOUS, ELITE ACTRESSES
WELL, YES.
I'M SURE I'LL HAVE A CHANCE TO EXPLAIN EVERY-THING TO YOU IN DUE COURSE.
BUT HAVE A LOOK AT THIS FIRST.
!!
THIS IS--?!

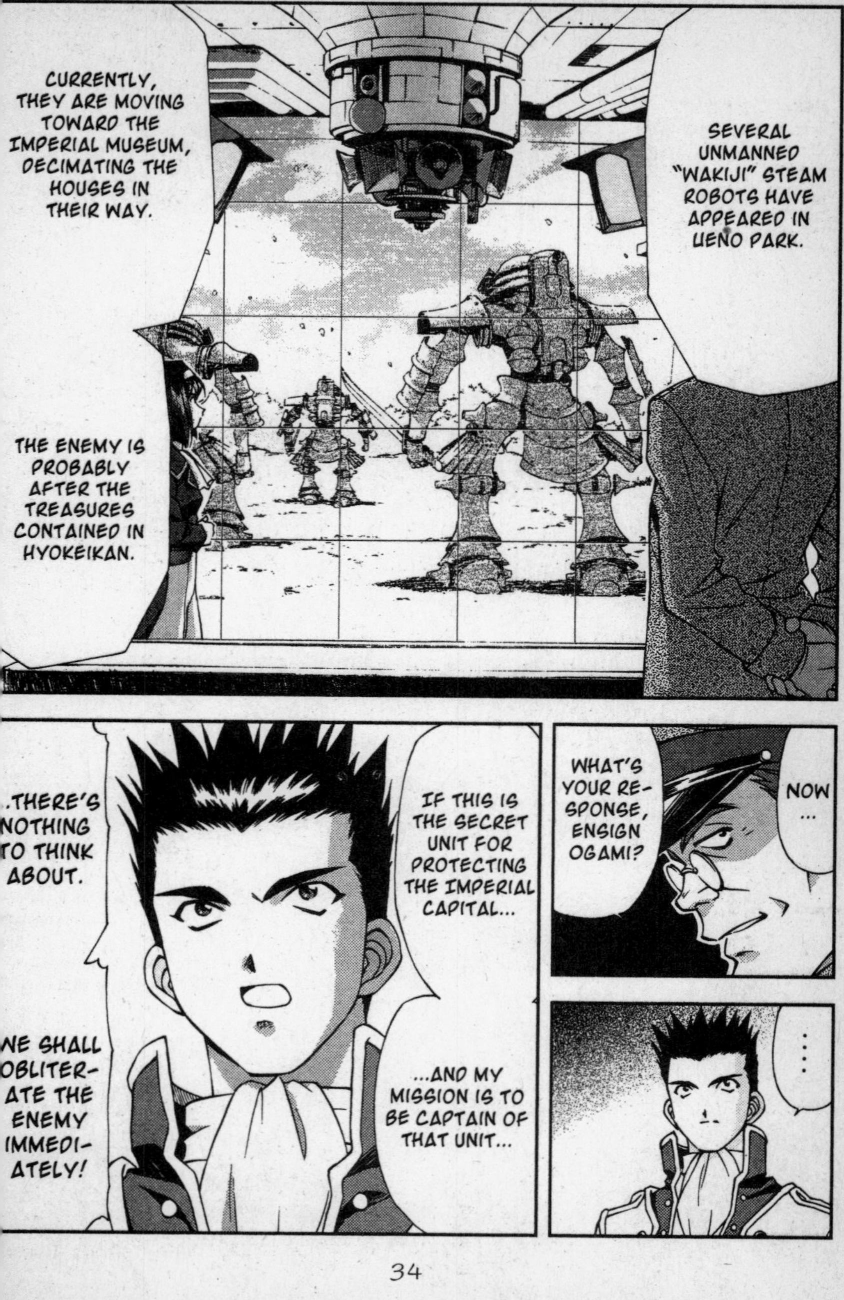
SEVERAL UNMANNED "WAKIJI" STEAM ROBOTS HAVE APPEARED IN UENO PARK.
CURRENTLY, THEY ARE MOVING TOWARD THE IMPERIAL MUSEUM, DECIMATING THE HOUSES IN THEIR WAY.
THE ENEMY IS PROBABLY AFTER THE TREASURES CONTAINED IN HYOKEIKAN.
NOW ...
WHAT'S YOUR RESPONSE, ENSIGN OGAMI?
....
IF THIS IS THE SECRET UNIT FOR PROTECTING THE IMPERIAL CAPITAL...
...AND MY MISSION IS TO BE CAPTAIN OF THAT UNIT...
.THERE'S NOTHING TO THINK ABOUT.
WE SHALL OBLITERATE THE ENEMY IMMEDIATELY!

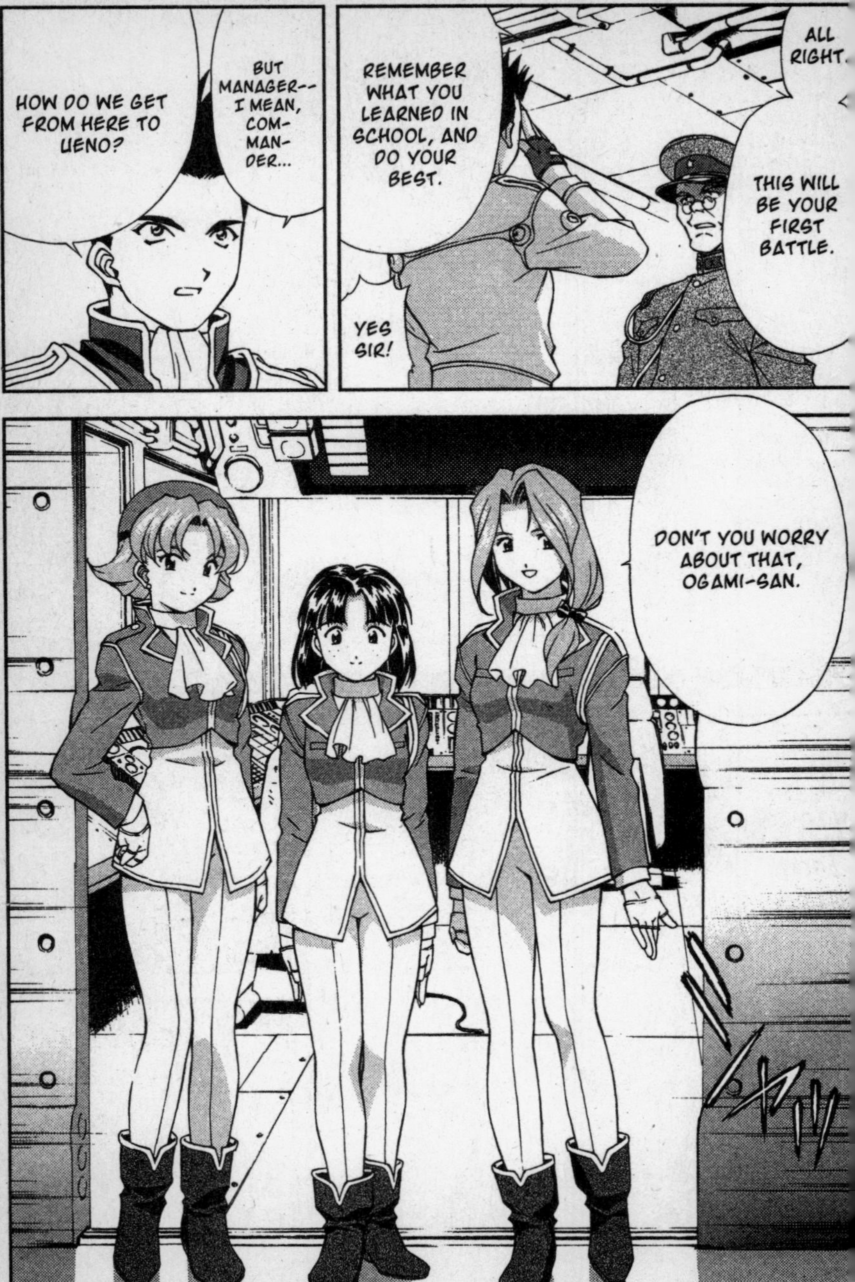
ALL RIGHT.
THIS WILL BE YOUR FIRST BATTLE.
REMEMBER WHAT YOU LEARNED IN SCHOOL, AND DO YOUR BEST.
YES SIR!
BUT MANAGER-- I MEAN, COM-MAN-DER...
HOW DO WE GET FROM HERE TO UENO?
DON'T YOU WORRY ABOUT THAT, OGAMI-SAN.

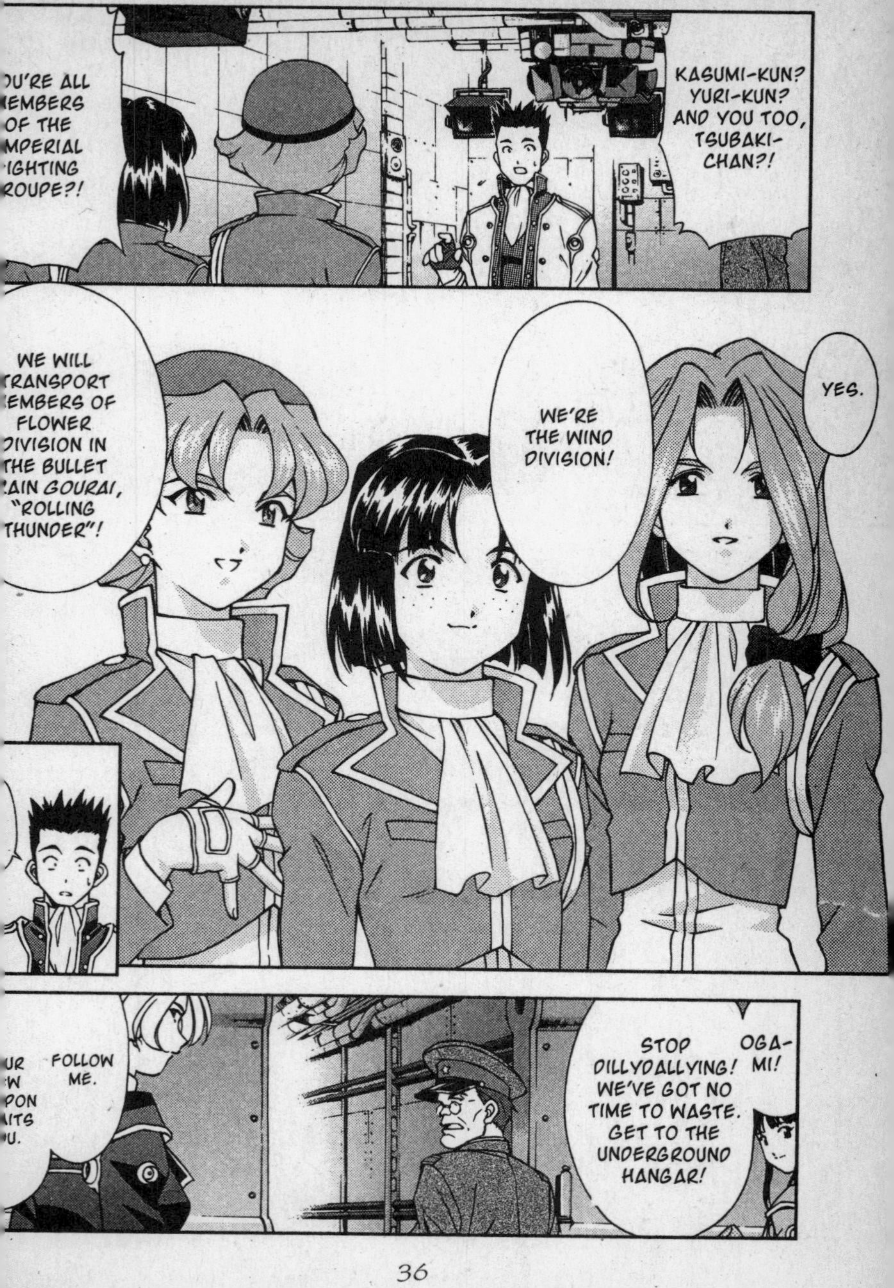
KASUMI-KUN? YURI-KUN? AND YOU TOO, TSUBAKI-CHAN?!
OU'RE ALL EMBERS OF THE MPERIAL IGHTING ROUPE?!
YES.
WE'RE THE WIND DIVISION!
WE WILL TRANSPORT EMBERS OF FLOWER DIVISION IN THE BULLET AIN GOURAI, "ROLLING THUNDER"!
OGA-MI!
STOP DILLYDALLYING! WE'VE GOT NO TIME TO WASTE. GET TO THE UNDERGROUND HANGAR!
FOLLOW ME.

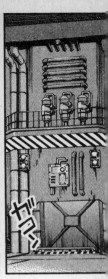

IT'S THE STEAM ROBOT FROM THE OTHER DAY!!

W- WHAT?!

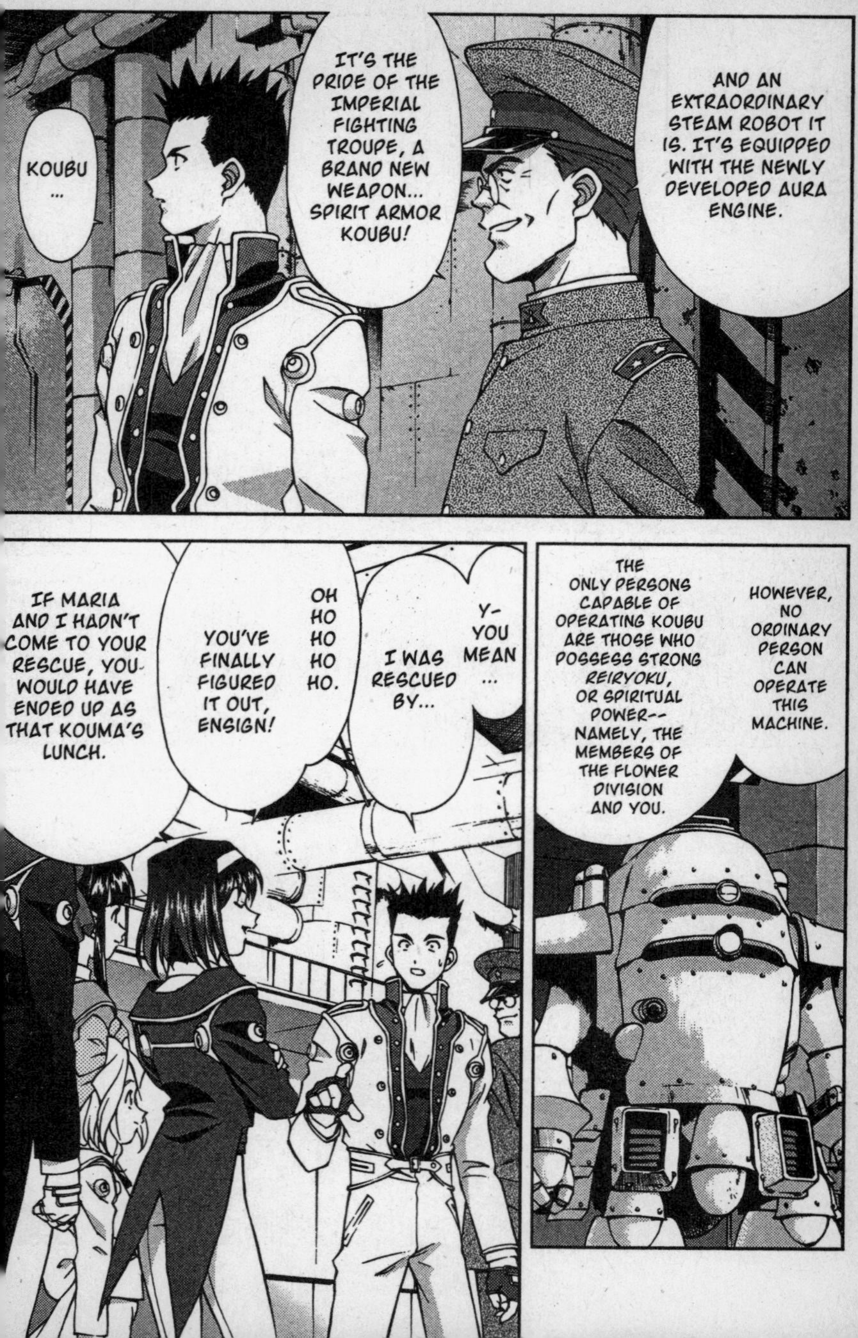
AND AN EXTRAORDINARY STEAM ROBOT IT IS. IT'S EQUIPPED WITH THE NEWLY DEVELOPED AURA ENGINE.
IT'S THE PRIDE OF THE IMPERIAL FIGHTING TROUPE, A BRAND NEW WEAPON... SPIRIT ARMOR KOUBU!
KOUBU ...
HOWEVER, NO ORDINARY PERSON CAN OPERATE THIS MACHINE.
THE ONLY PERSONS CAPABLE OF OPERATING KOUBU ARE THOSE WHO POSSESS STRONG REIRYOKU, OR SPIRITUAL POWER-- NAMELY, THE MEMBERS OF THE FLOWER DIVISION AND YOU.
Y-YOU MEAN ...
I WAS RESCUED BY...
OH HO HO HO HO.
YOU'VE FINALLY FIGURED IT OUT, ENSIGN!
IF MARIA AND I HADN'T COME TO YOUR RESCUE, YOU WOULD HAVE ENDED UP AS THAT KOUMA'S LUNCH.

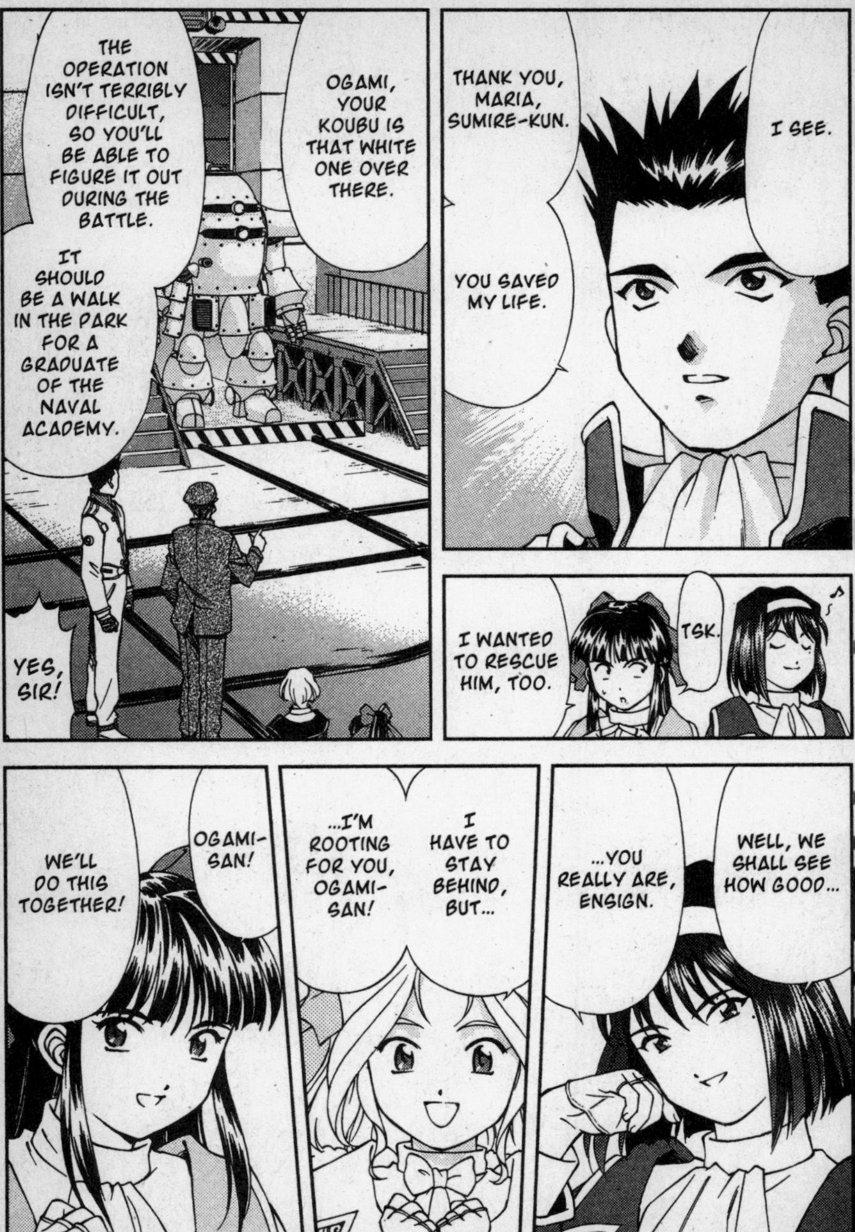
I SEE.
THANK YOU, MARIA, SUMIRE-KUN.
YOU SAVED MY LIFE.
TSK.
I WANTED TO RESCUE HIM, TOO.
OGAMI, YOUR KOUBU IS THAT WHITE ONE OVER THERE.
THE OPERATION ISN'T TERRIBLY DIFFICULT, SO YOU'LL BE ABLE TO FIGURE IT OUT DURING THE BATTLE.
IT SHOULD BE A WALK IN THE PARK FOR A GRADUATE OF THE NAVAL ACADEMY.
YES, SIR!
WELL, WE SHALL SEE HOW GOOD...
...YOU REALLY ARE, ENSIGN.
I HAVE TO STAY BEHIND, BUT...
...I'M ROOTING FOR YOU, OGAMI-SAN!
OGAMI-SAN!
WE'LL DO THIS TOGETHER!

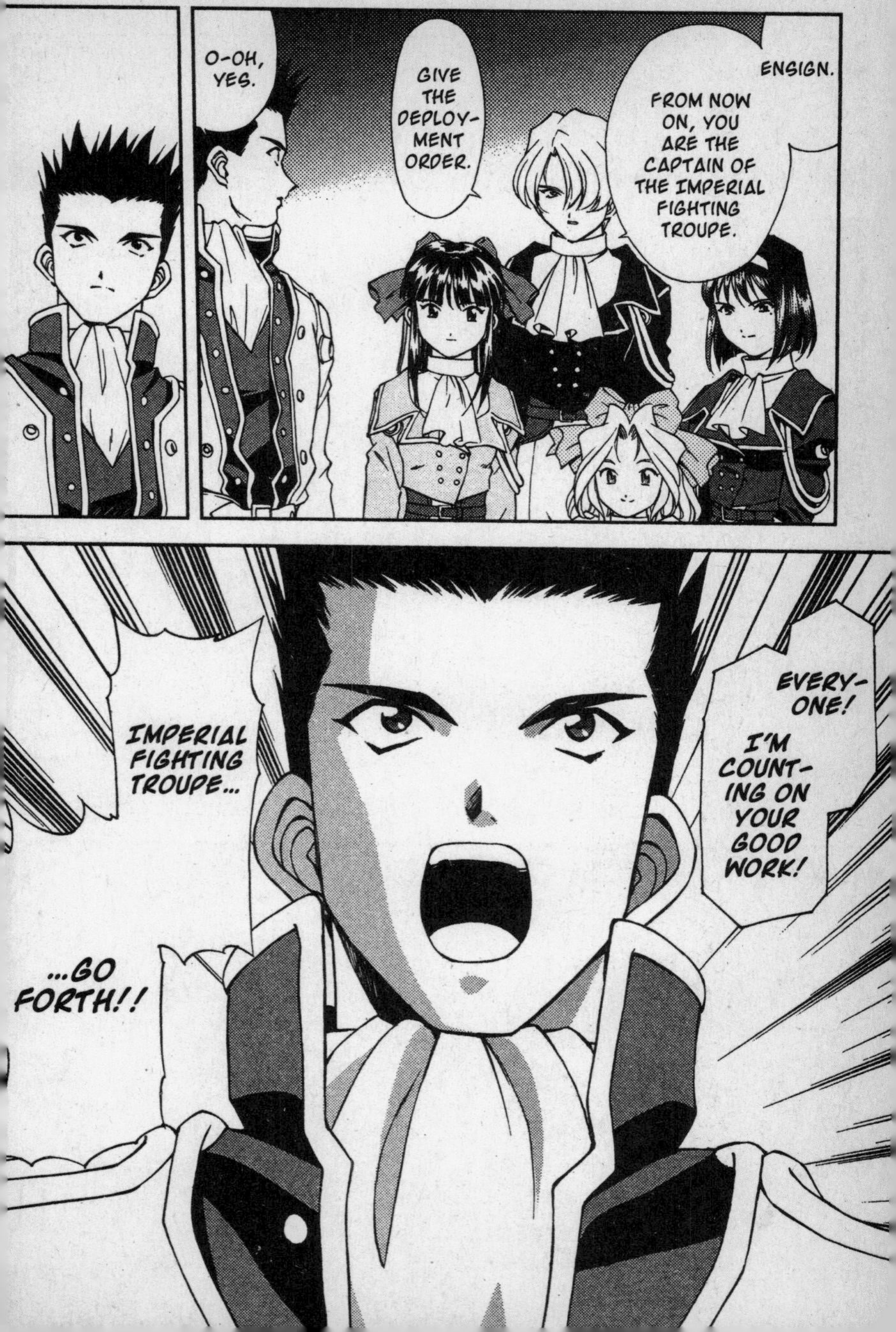
ENSIGN. FROM NOW ON, YOU ARE THE CAPTAIN OF THE IMPERIAL FIGHTING TROUPE.
GIVE THE DEPLOYMENT ORDER.
O-OH, YES.
EVERYONE! I'M COUNTING ON YOUR GOOD WORK!
IMPERIAL FIGHTING TROUPE...
...GO FORTH!!

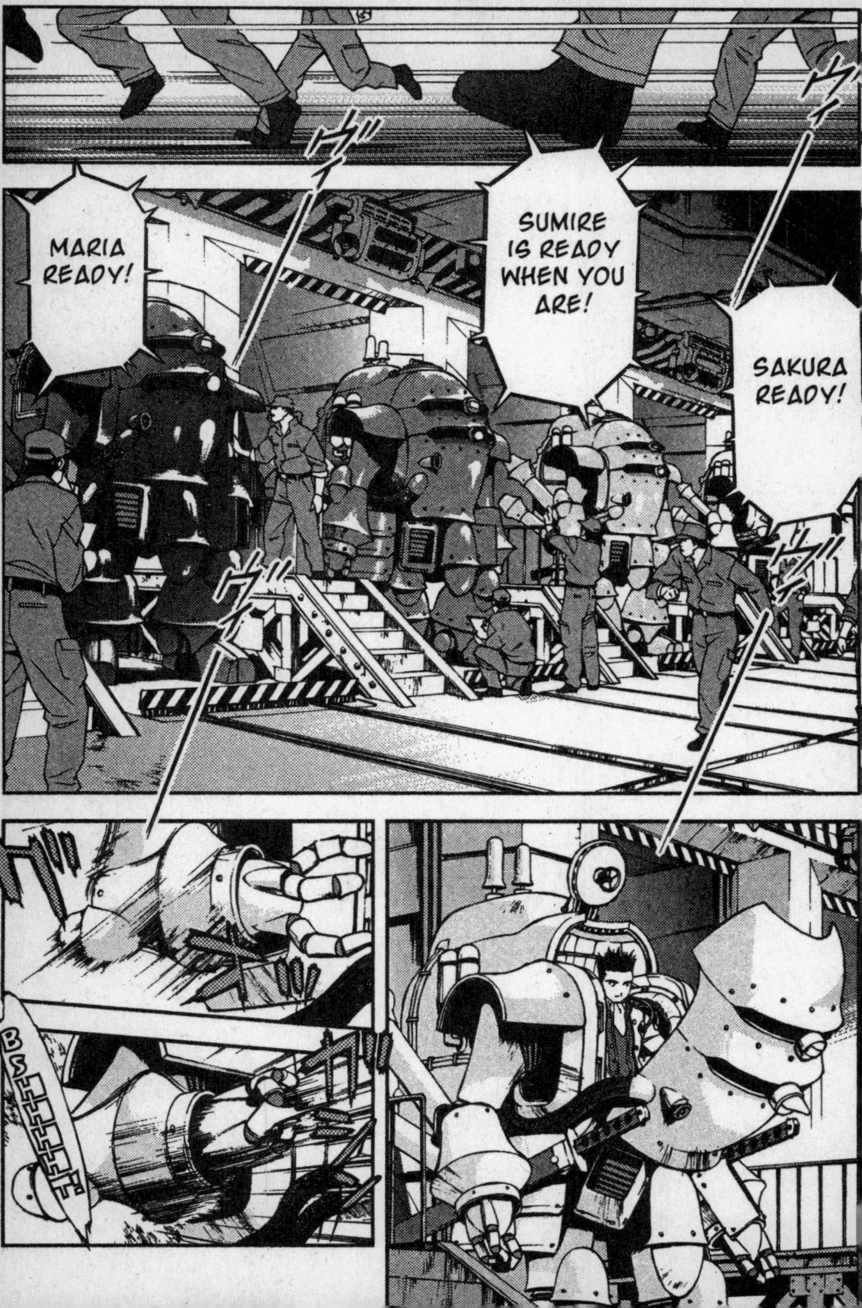
SAKURA READY!
SUMIRE IS READY WHEN YOU ARE!
MARIA READY!

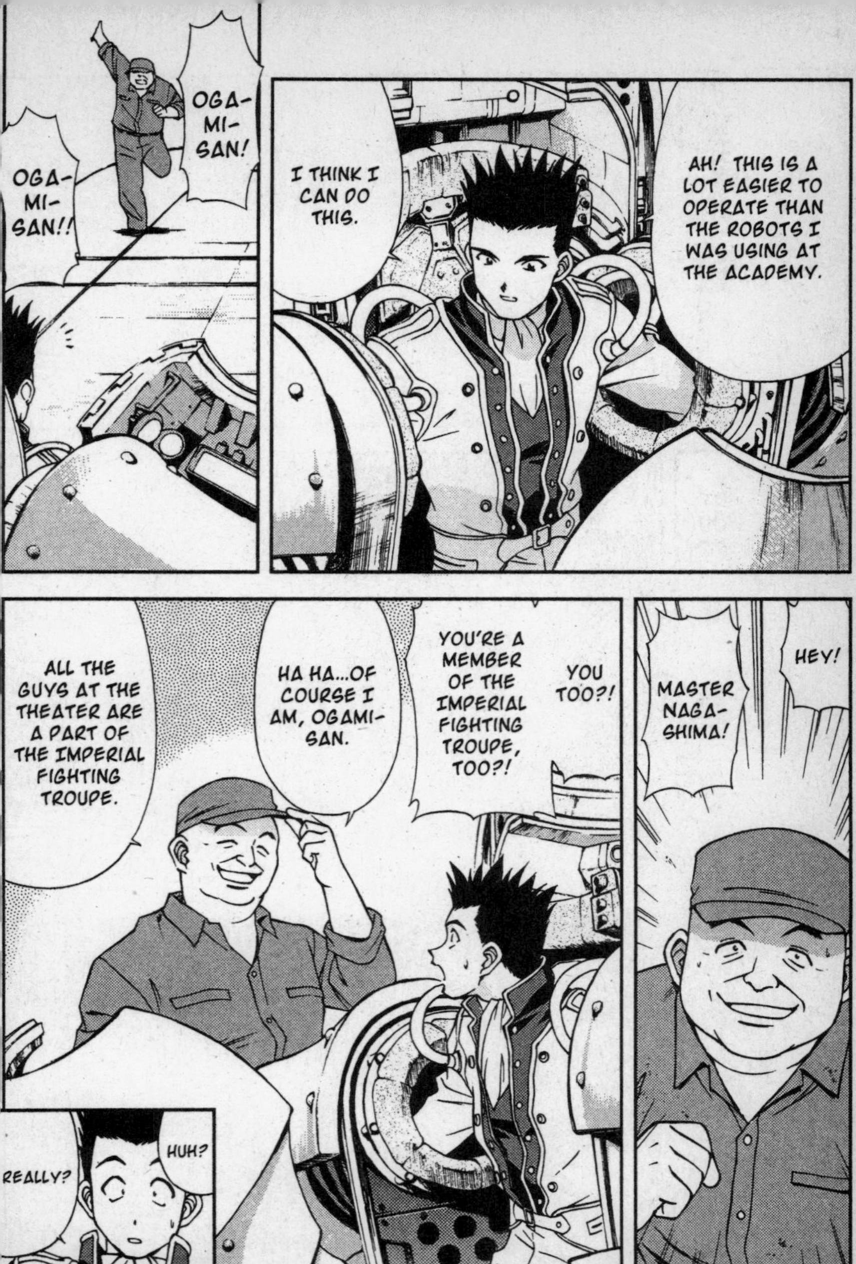
AH! THIS IS A LOT EASIER TO OPERATE THAN THE ROBOTS I WAS USING AT THE ACADEMY.
I THINK I CAN DO THIS.
OGA-MI-SAN!
OGA-MI-SAN!!
HEY!
MASTER NAGA-SHIMA!
YOU TOO?!
YOU'RE A MEMBER OF THE IMPERIAL FIGHTING TROUPE, TOO?!
HA HA...OF COURSE I AM, OGAMI-SAN.
ALL THE GUYS AT THE THEATER ARE A PART OF THE IMPERIAL FIGHTING TROUPE.
HUH?
REALLY?

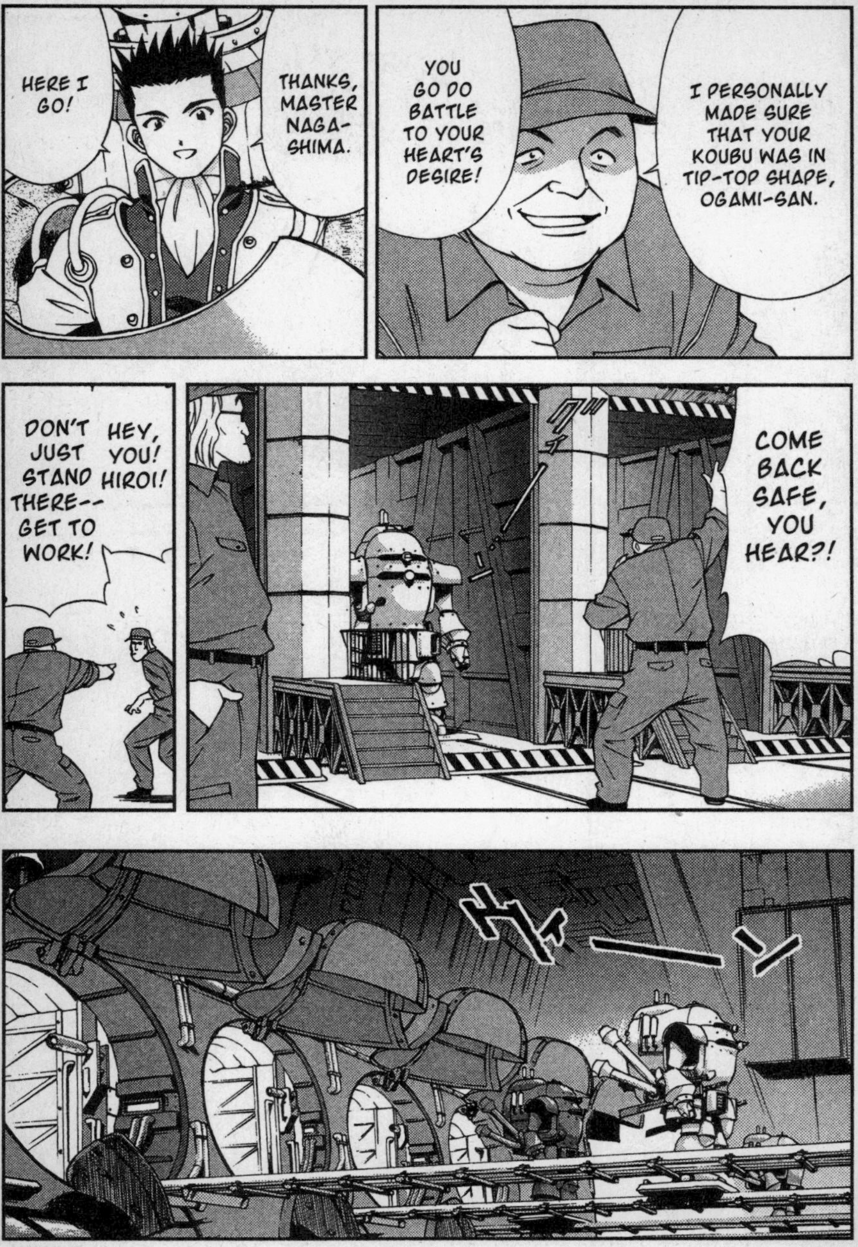
I PERSONALLY MADE SURE THAT YOUR KOUBU WAS IN TIP-TOP SHAPE, OGAMI-SAN.
YOU GO DO BATTLE TO YOUR HEART'S DESIRE!
THANKS, MASTER NAGA-SHIMA.
HERE I GO!
COME BACK SAFE, YOU HEAR?!
HEY, YOU! HIROI!
DON'T JUST STAND THERE--GET TO WORK!

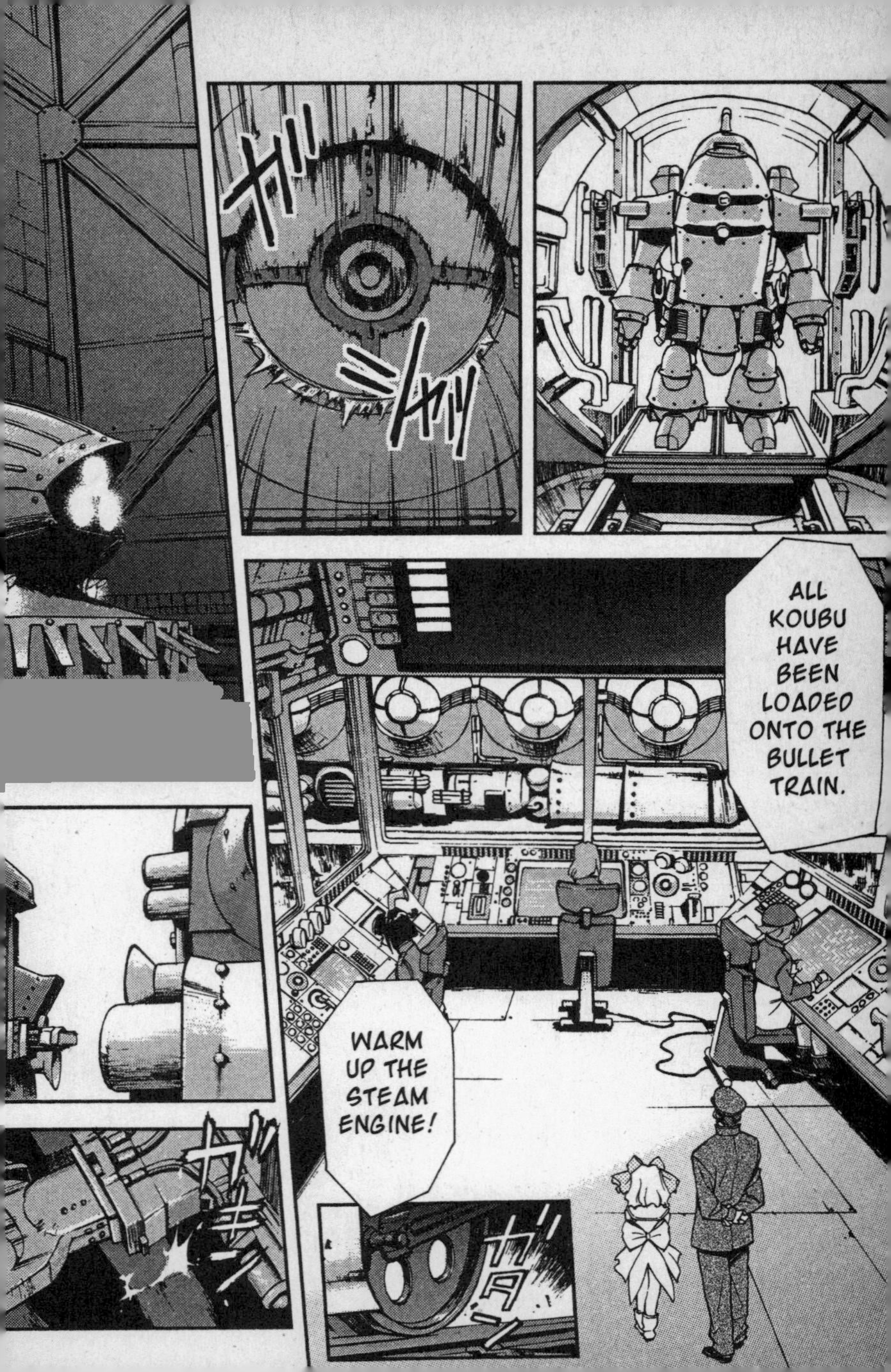
ALL KOUBU HAVE BEEN LOADED ONTO THE BULLET TRAIN.
WARM UP THE STEAM ENGINE!

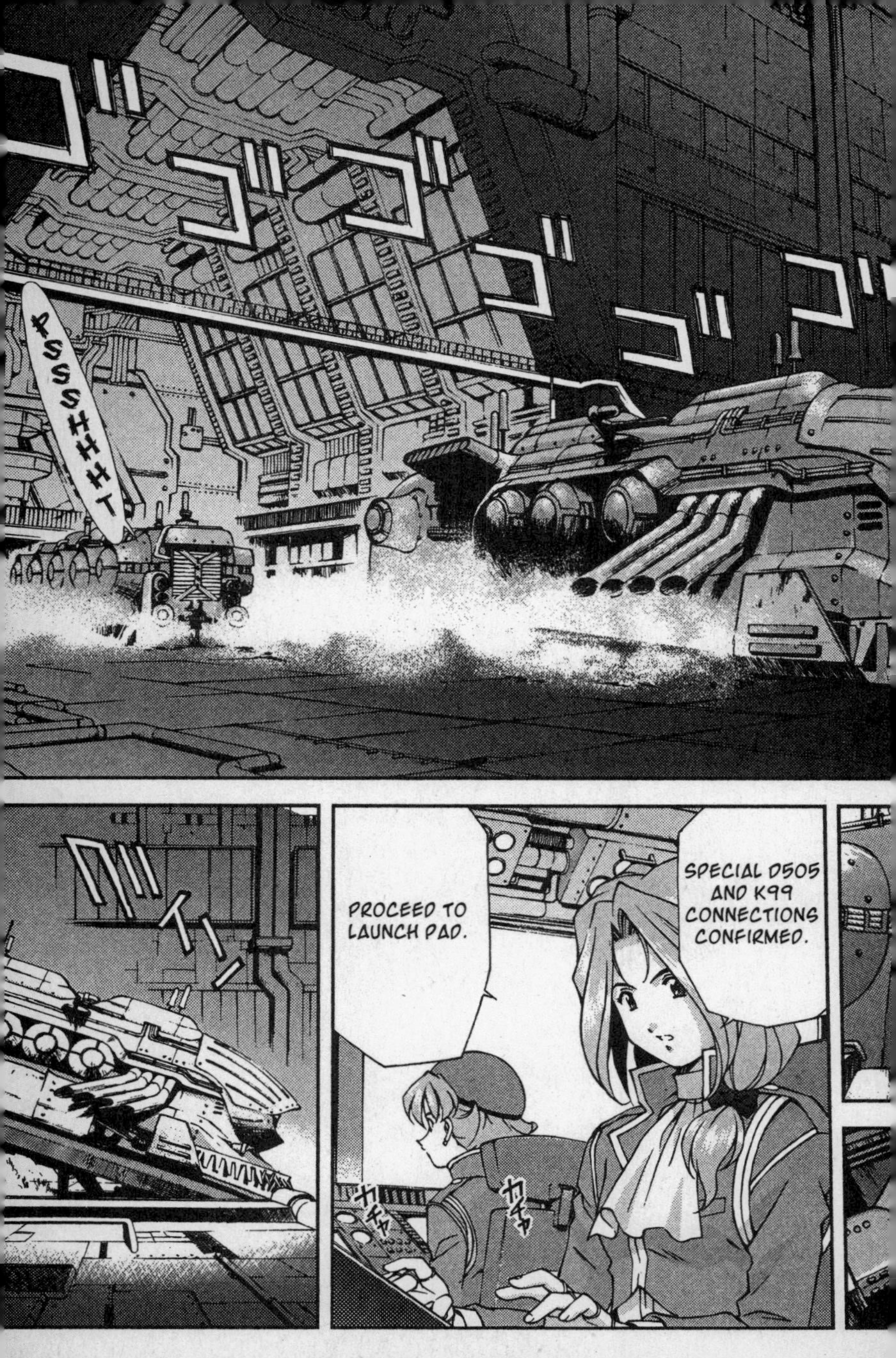
PSSSHHHT
SPECIAL D505 AND K99 CONNECTIONS CONFIRMED.
PROCEED TO LAUNCH PAD.
カチャ
カチャ

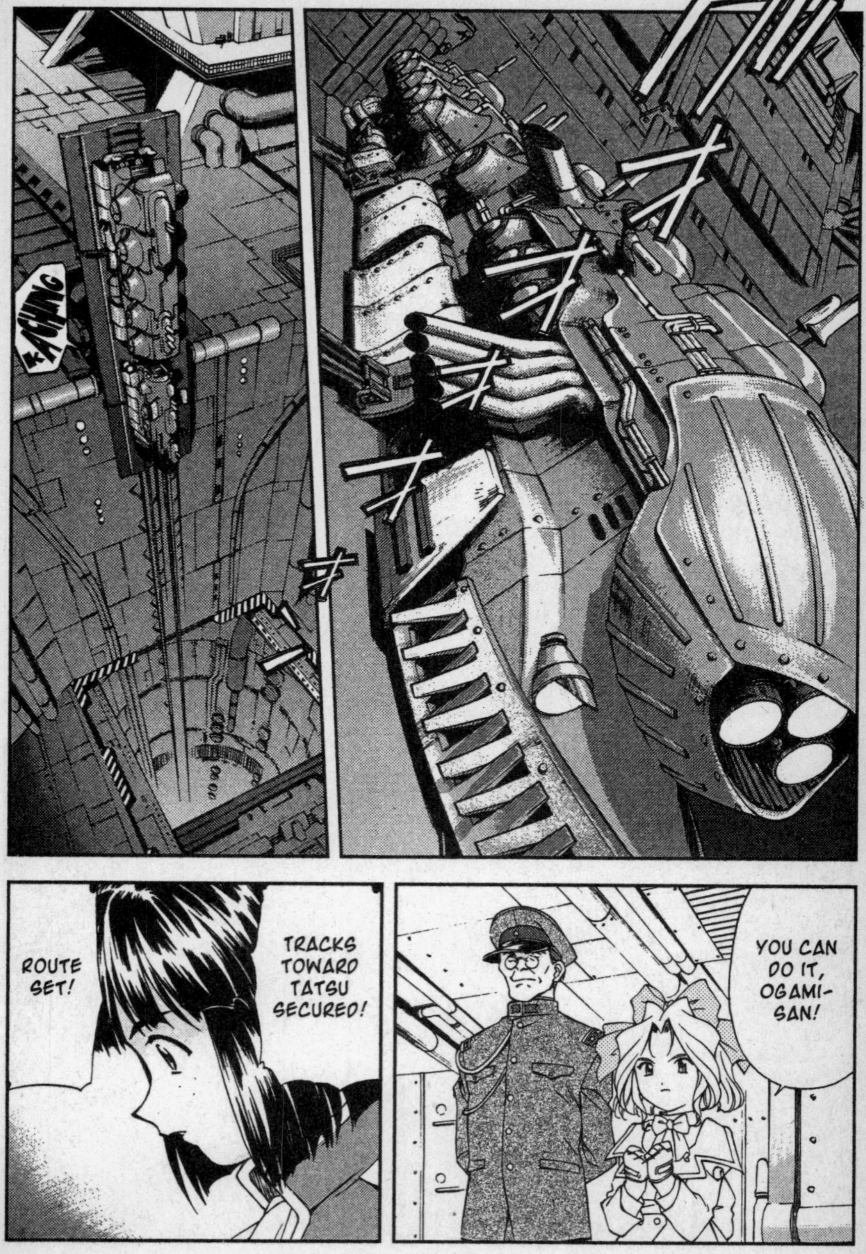
KACHING
YOU CAN DO IT, OGAMI-SAN!
TRACKS TOWARD TATSU SECURED!
ROUTE SET!

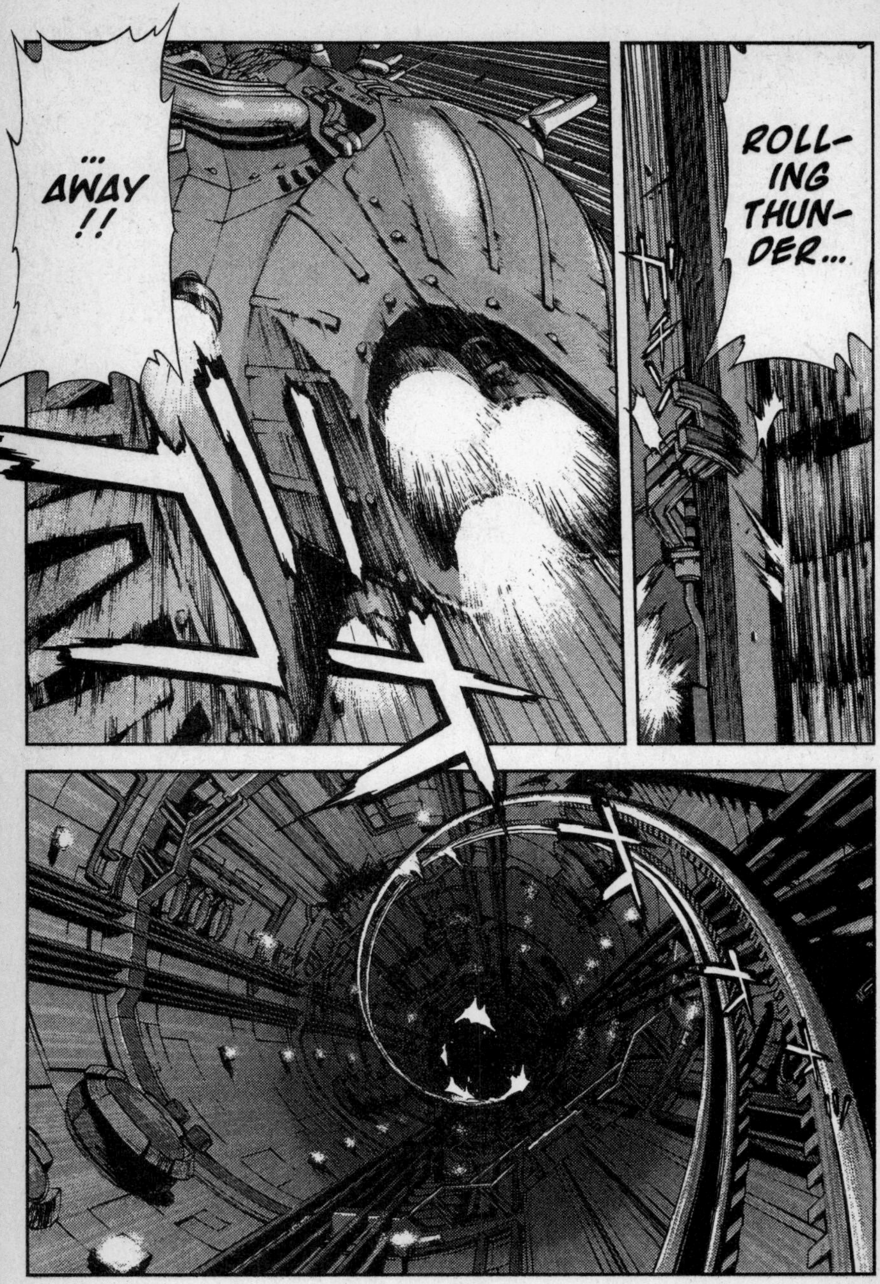
ROLL-ING THUNDER...
...AWAY!!

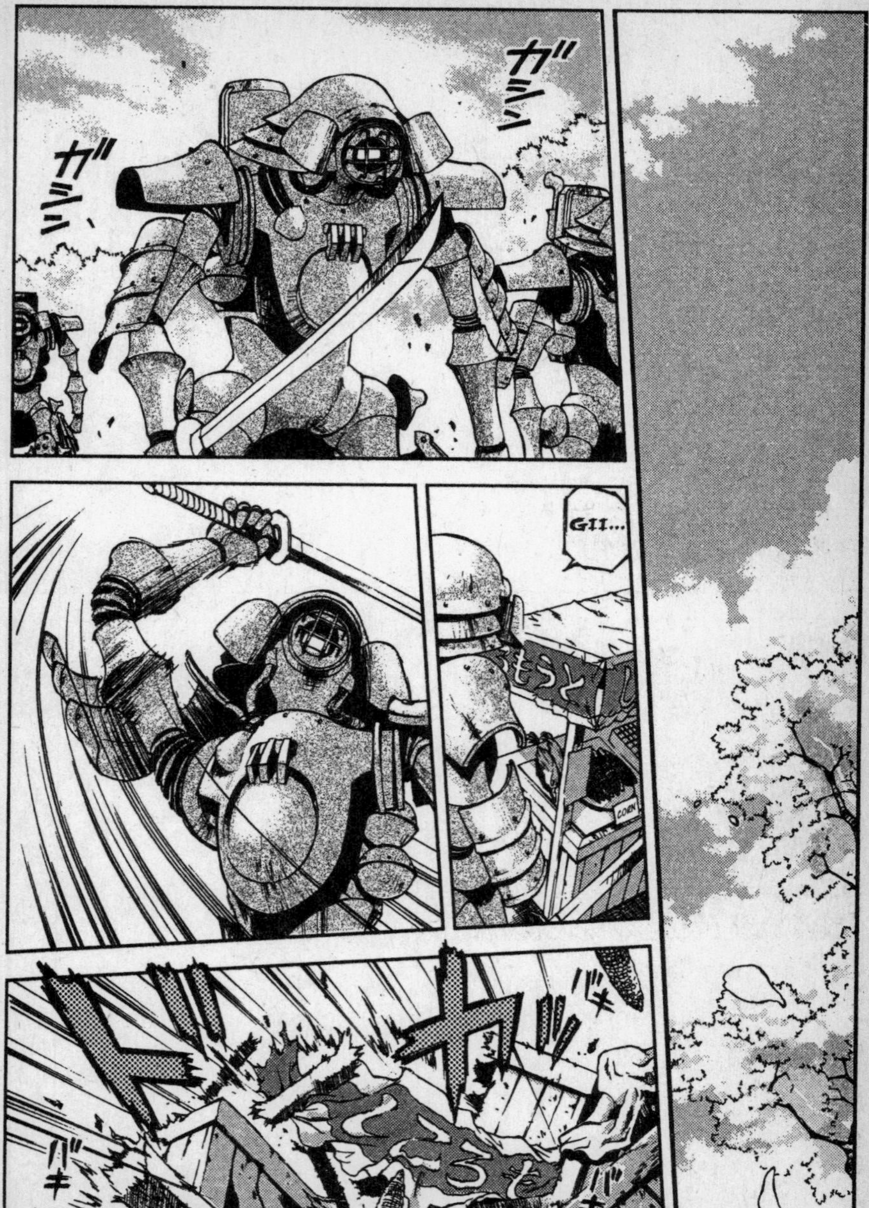
ガシン
ガシン、
GII...
ド
バキ
バキ
バキ

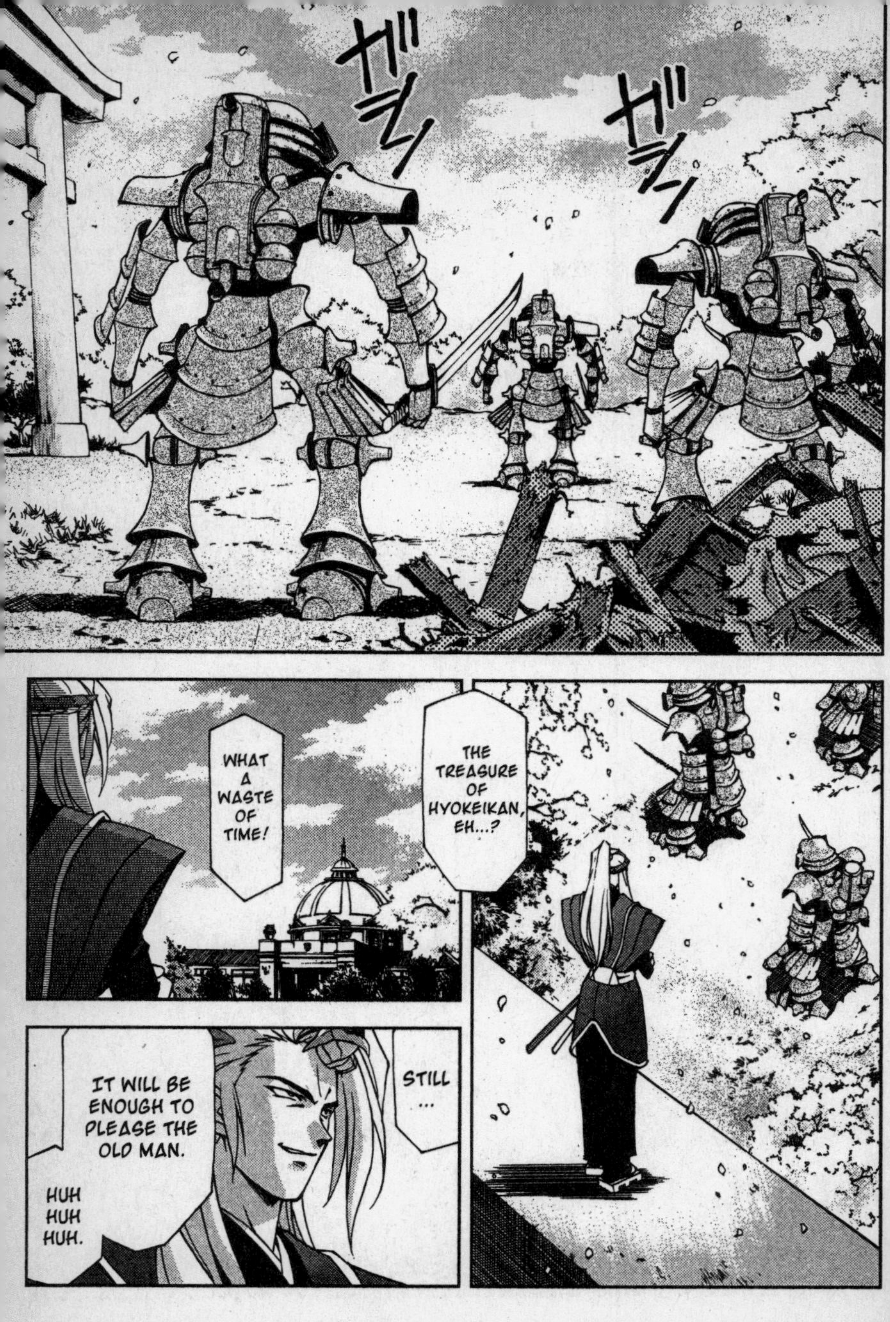
THE TREASURE OF HYOKEIKAN, EH...?
WHAT A WASTE OF TIME!
STILL ...
IT WILL BE ENOUGH TO PLEASE THE OLD MAN.
HUH HUH HUH.

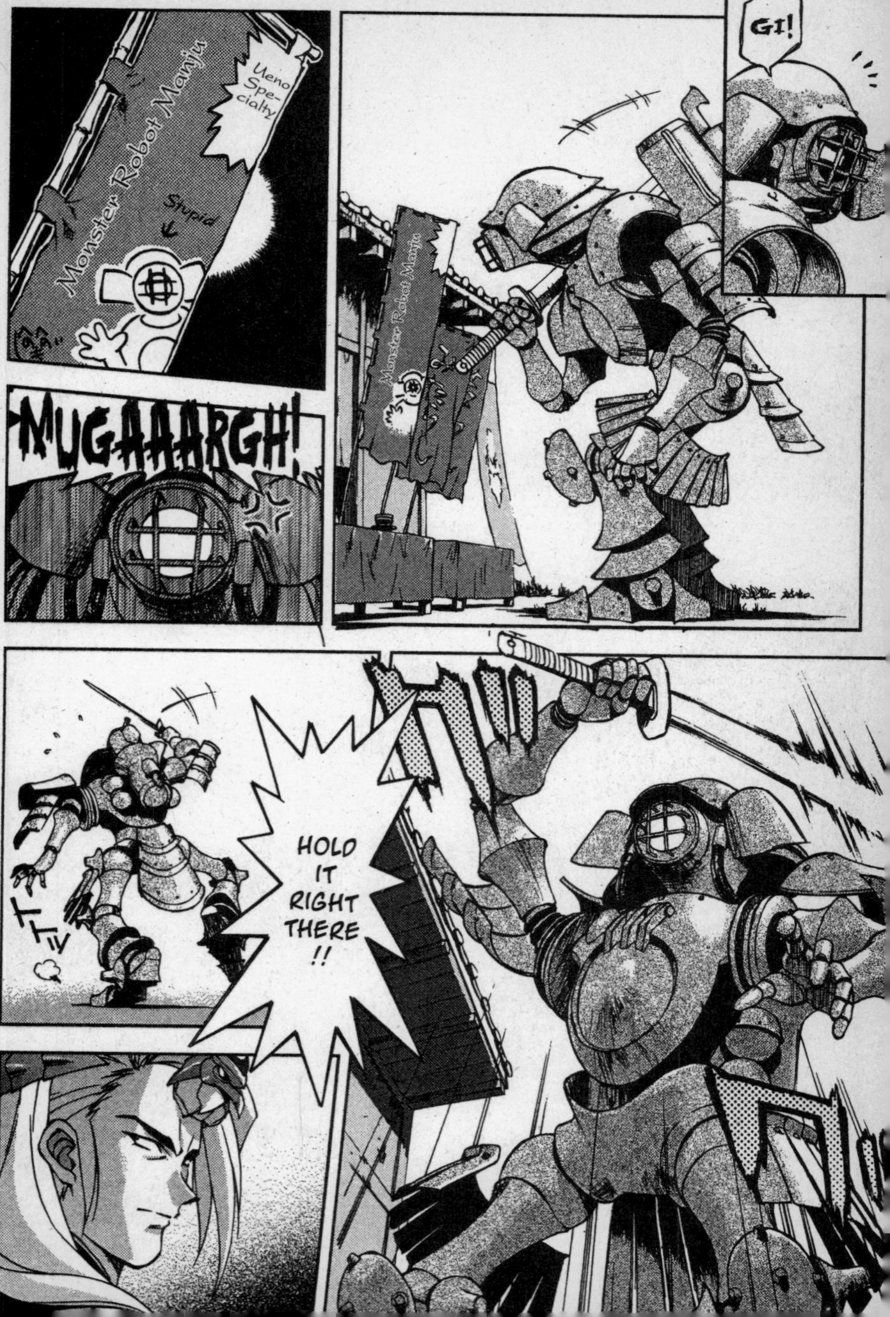
GI!
Monster Robot Manju
Ueno Spe-cialty
Monster Robot Manju
Stupid
MUGAAARGH!
HOLD IT RIGHT THERE!!

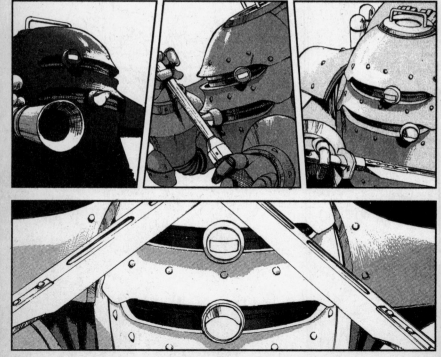

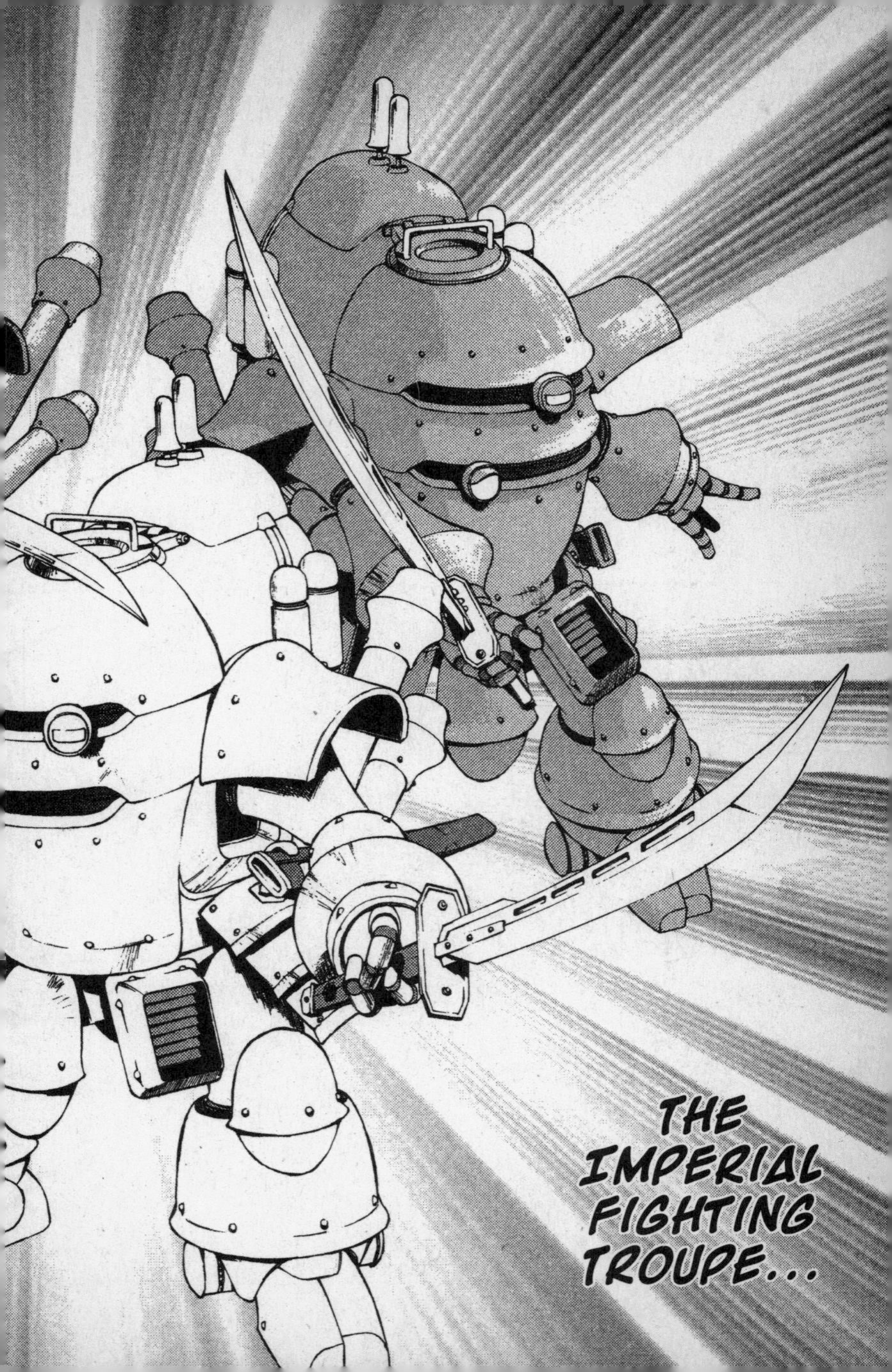
THE IMPERIAL FIGHTING TROUPE...

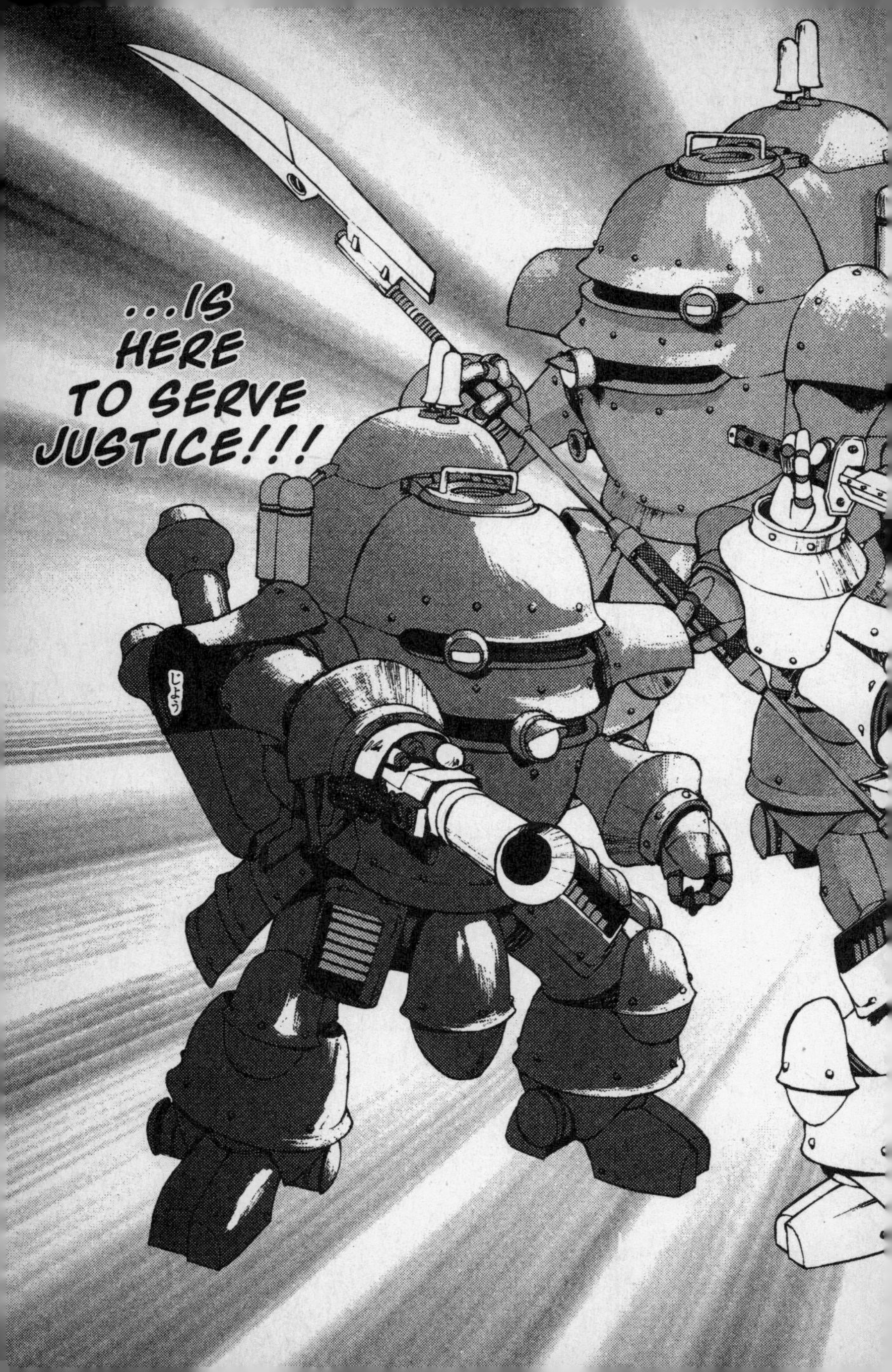
...IS HERE TO SERVE JUSTICE!!!
じょう

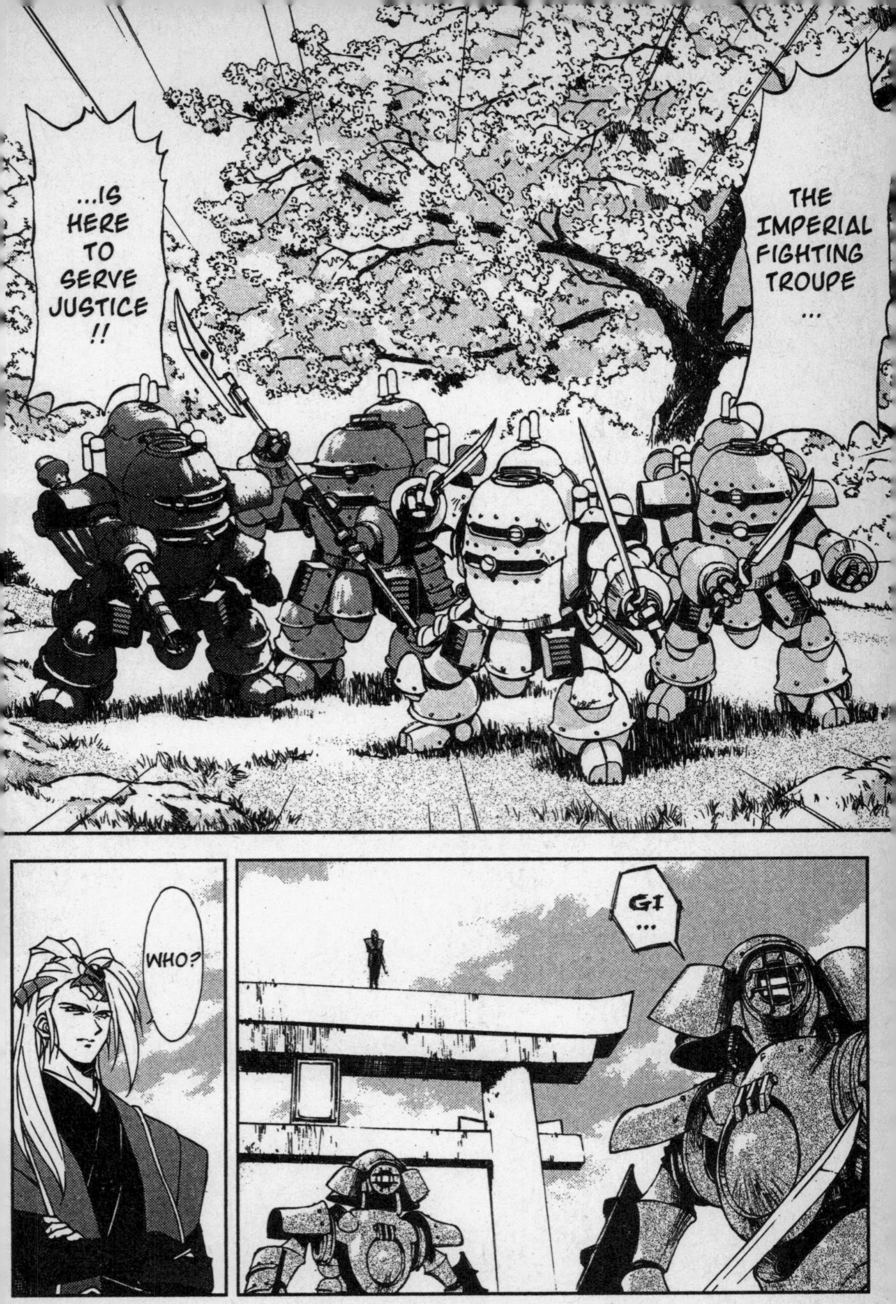
THE IMPERIAL FIGHTING TROUPE ...
...IS HERE TO SERVE JUSTICE !!
GI ...
WHO?

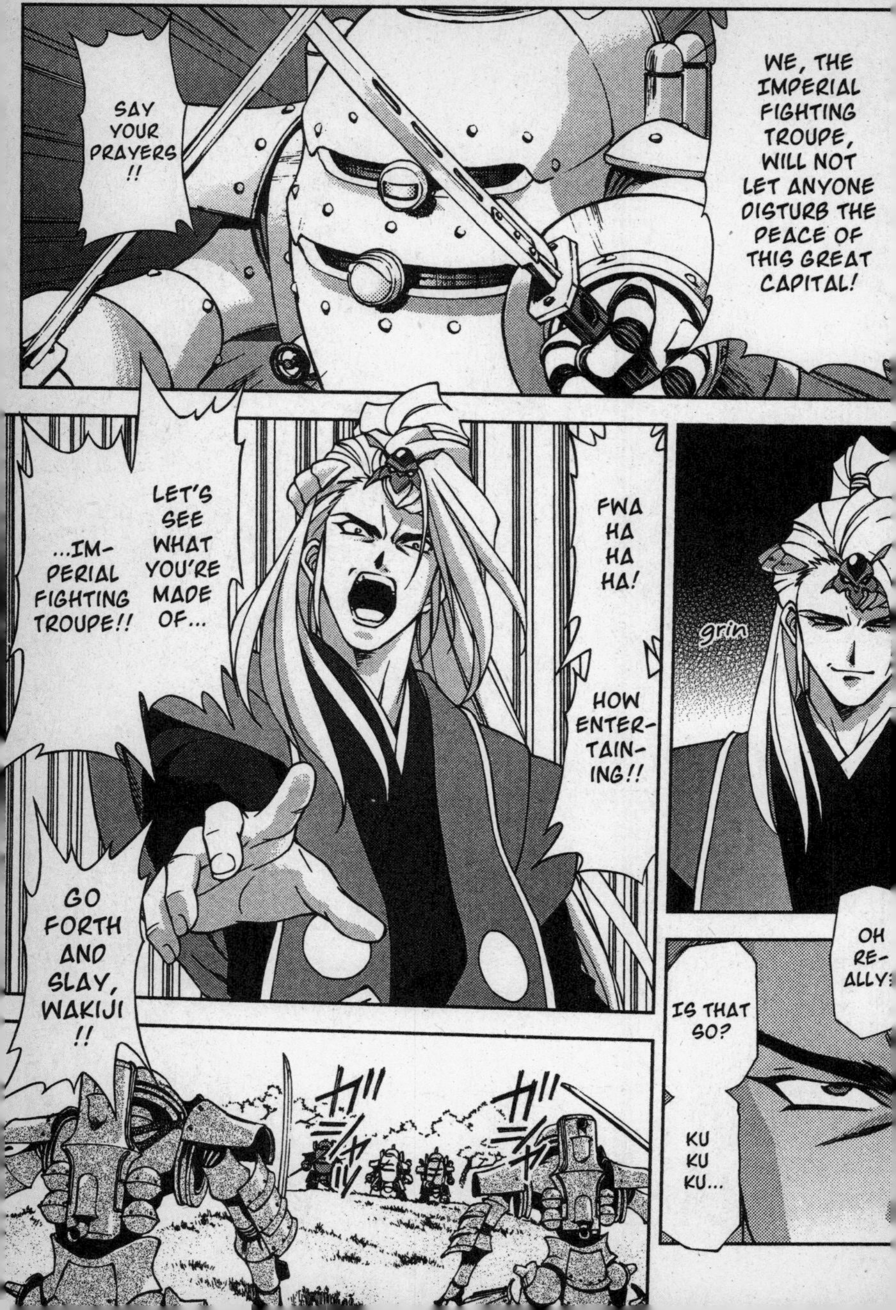
WE, THE IMPERIAL FIGHTING TROUPE, WILL NOT LET ANYONE DISTURB THE PEACE OF THIS GREAT CAPITAL!
SAY YOUR PRAYERS!!
grin
OH REALLY?
IS THAT SO?
KU KU KU...
FWA HA HA HA!
HOW ENTERTAINING!!
LET'S SEE WHAT YOU'RE MADE OF...
...IMPERIAL FIGHTING TROUPE!!
GO FORTH AND SLAY, WAKIJI!!

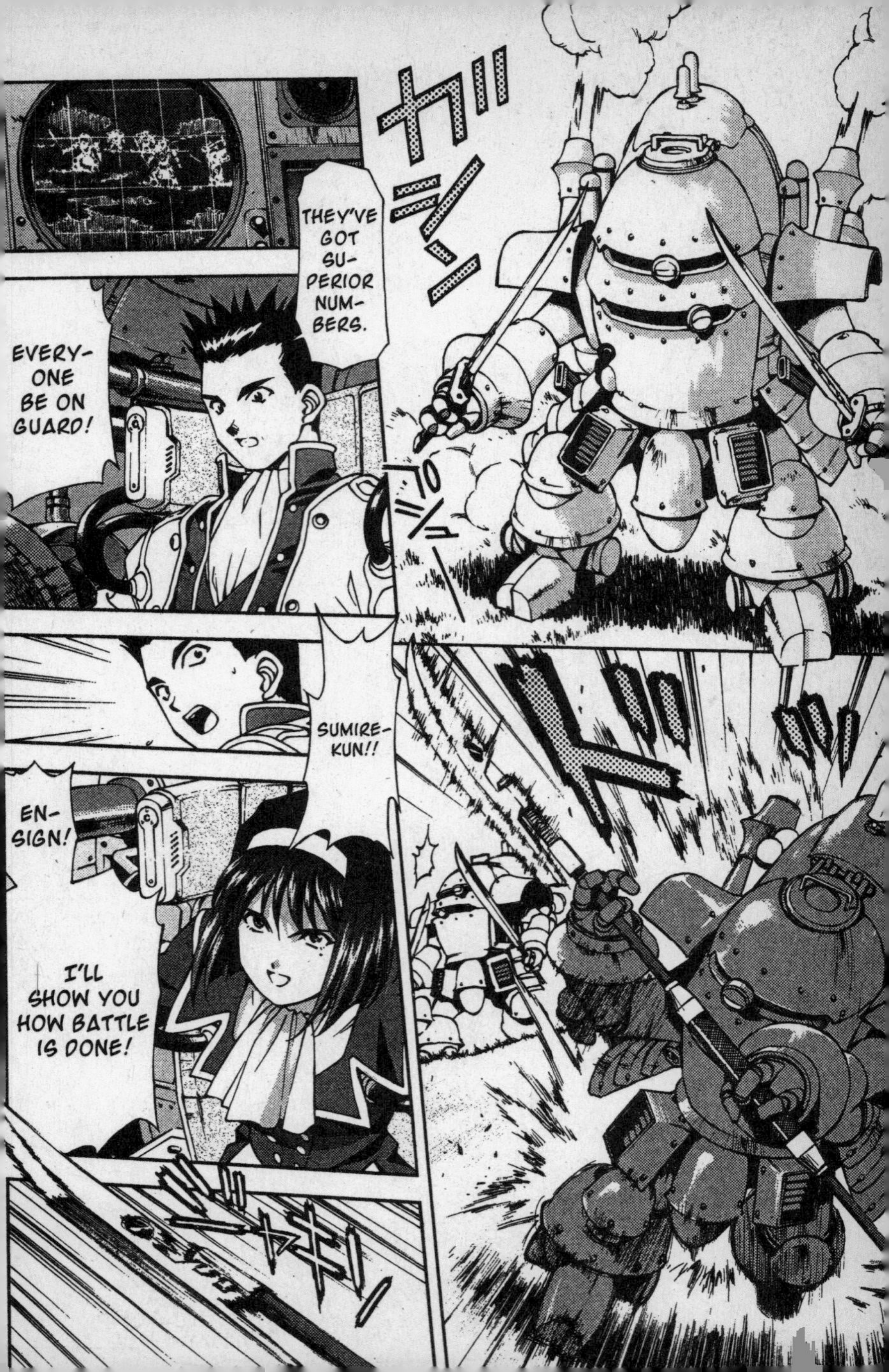
THEY'VE GOT SU-PERIOR NUM-BERS.
EVERY-ONE BE ON GUARD!
SUMIRE-KUN!!
EN-SIGN!
I'LL SHOW YOU HOW BATTLE IS DONE!

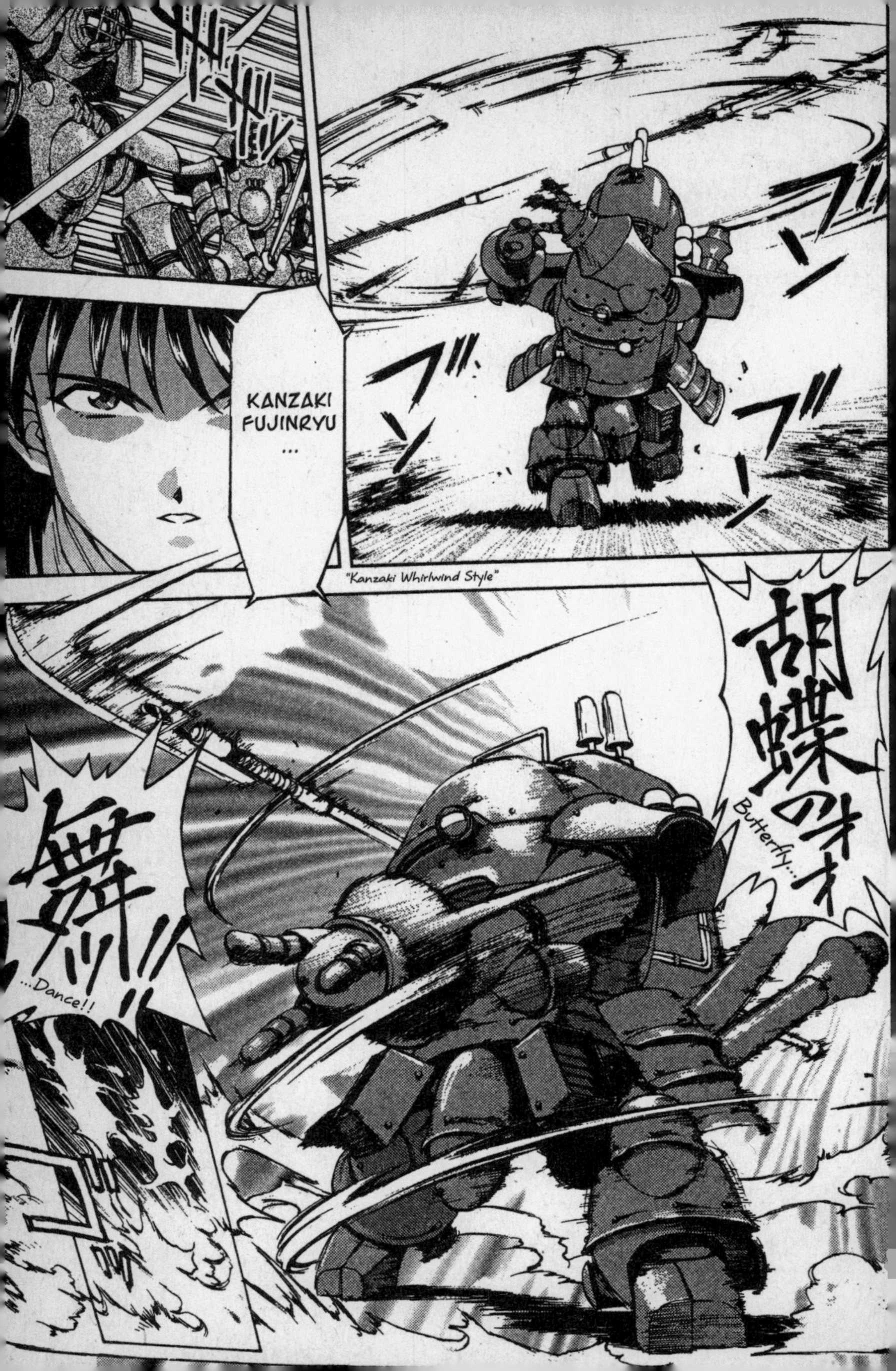

KANZAKI FUJINRYU ...
"Kanzaki Whirlwind Style"
胡蝶のオォ
Butterfly...
舞ッ!!
...Dance!!

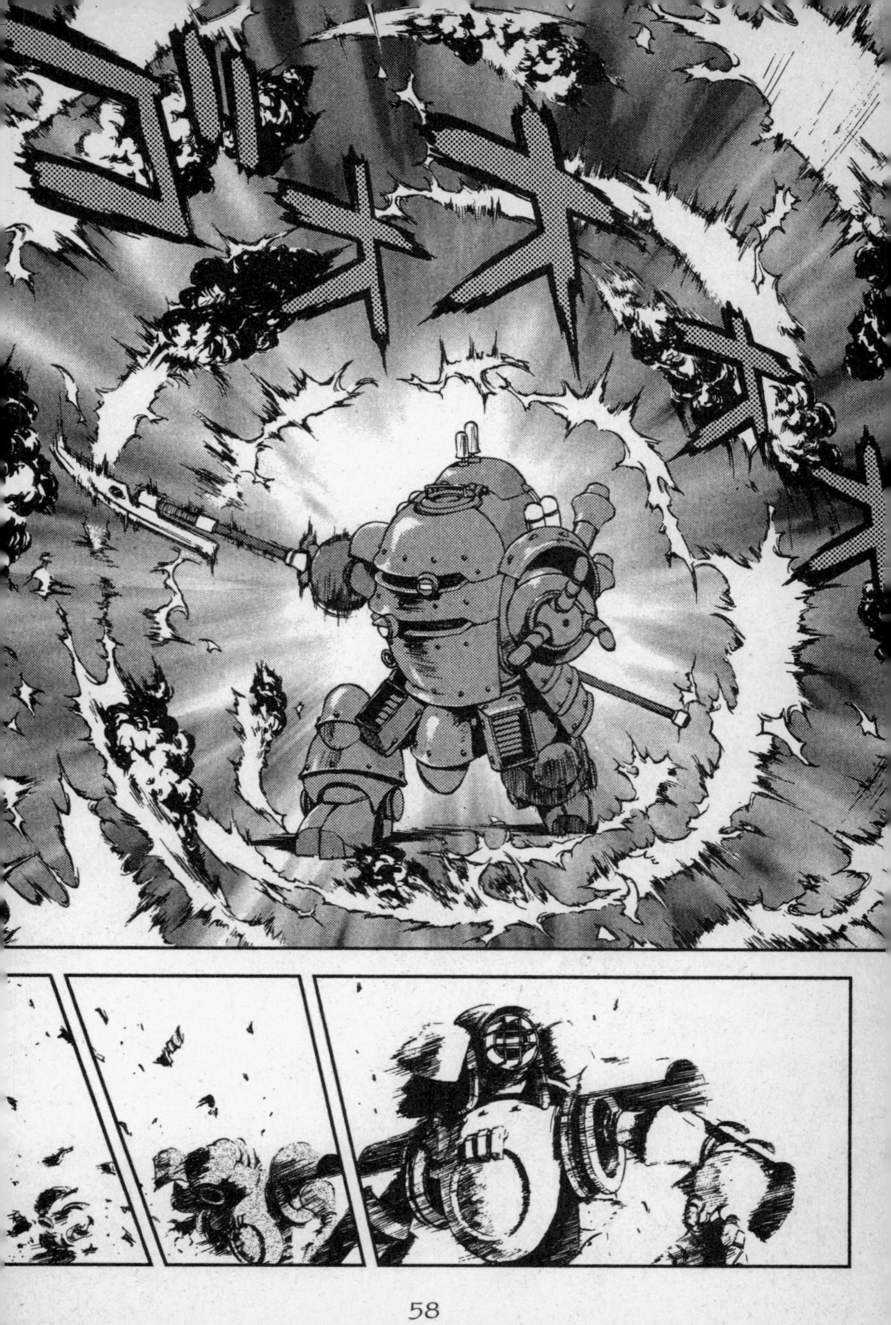

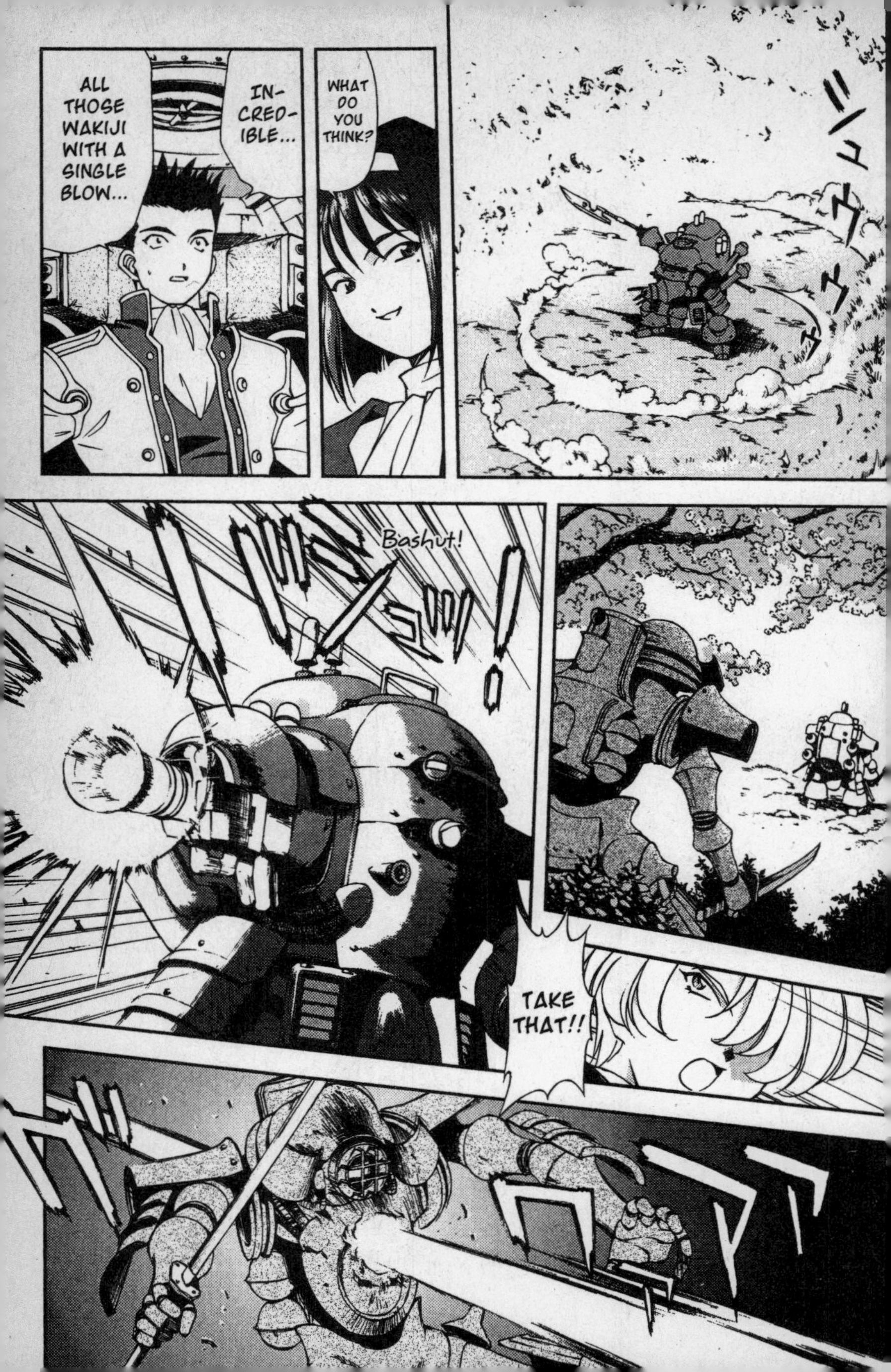

WHAT DO YOU THINK?
IN-CRED-IBLE...
ALL THOSE WAKIJI WITH A SINGLE BLOW...
Bashut!
TAKE THAT!!

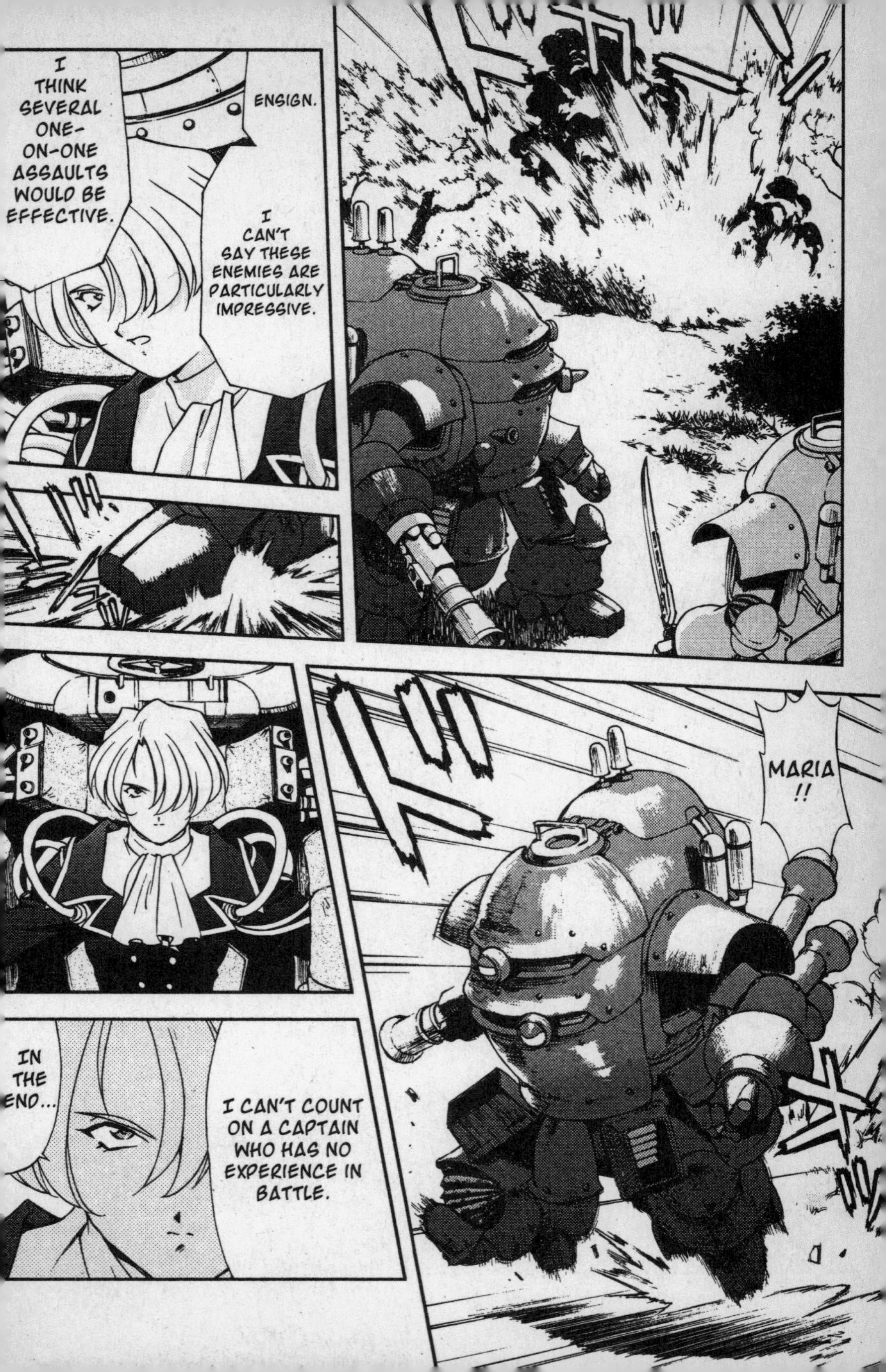
ENSIGN.
I CAN'T SAY THESE ENEMIES ARE PARTICULARLY IMPRESSIVE.
I THINK SEVERAL ONE-ON-ONE ASSAULTS WOULD BE EFFECTIVE.
MARIA!!
IN THE END...
I CAN'T COUNT ON A CAPTAIN WHO HAS NO EXPERIENCE IN BATTLE.

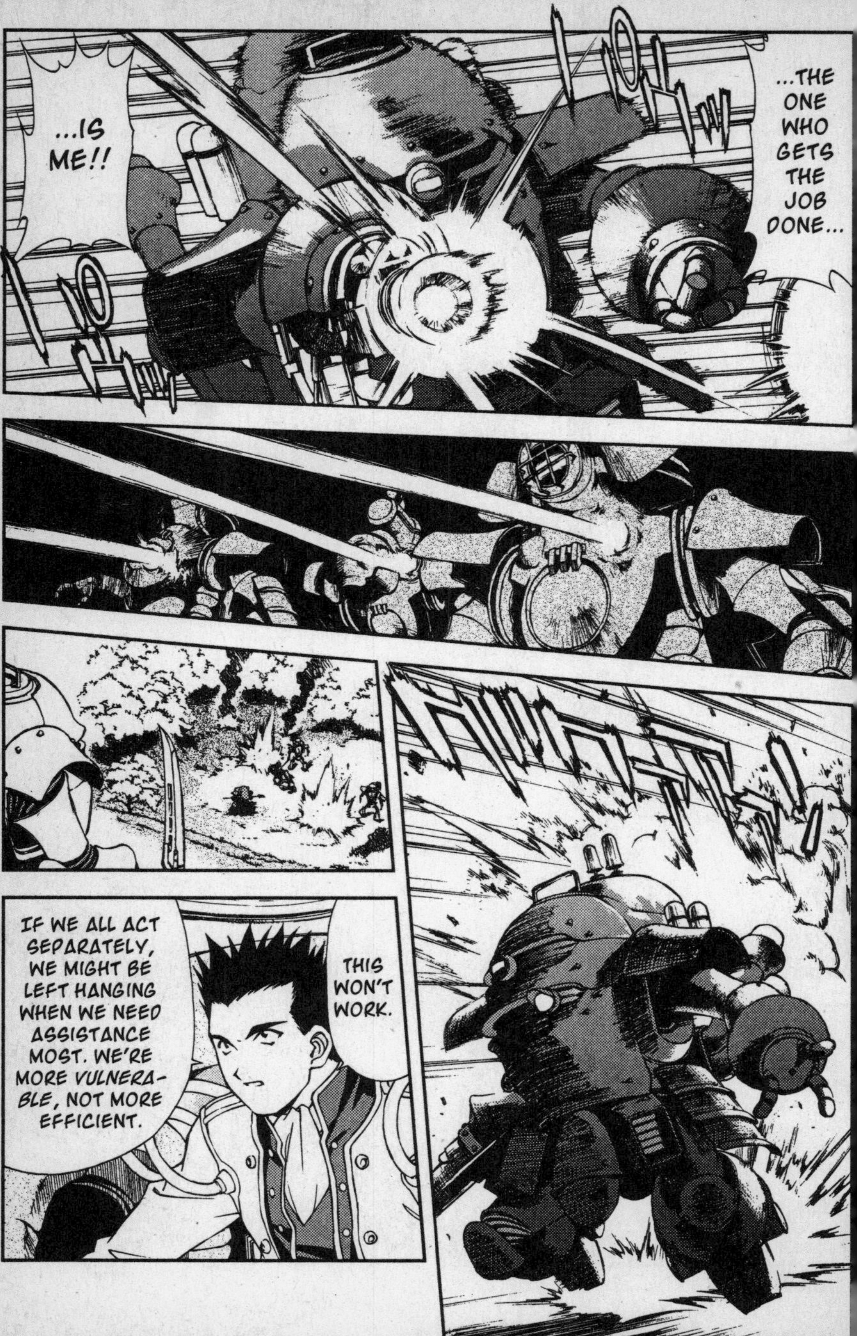
...THE ONE WHO GETS THE JOB DONE...
...IS ME!!
THIS WON'T WORK.
IF WE ALL ACT SEPARATELY, WE MIGHT BE LEFT HANGING WHEN WE NEED ASSISTANCE MOST. WE'RE MORE VULNERA-BLE, NOT MORE EFFICIENT.

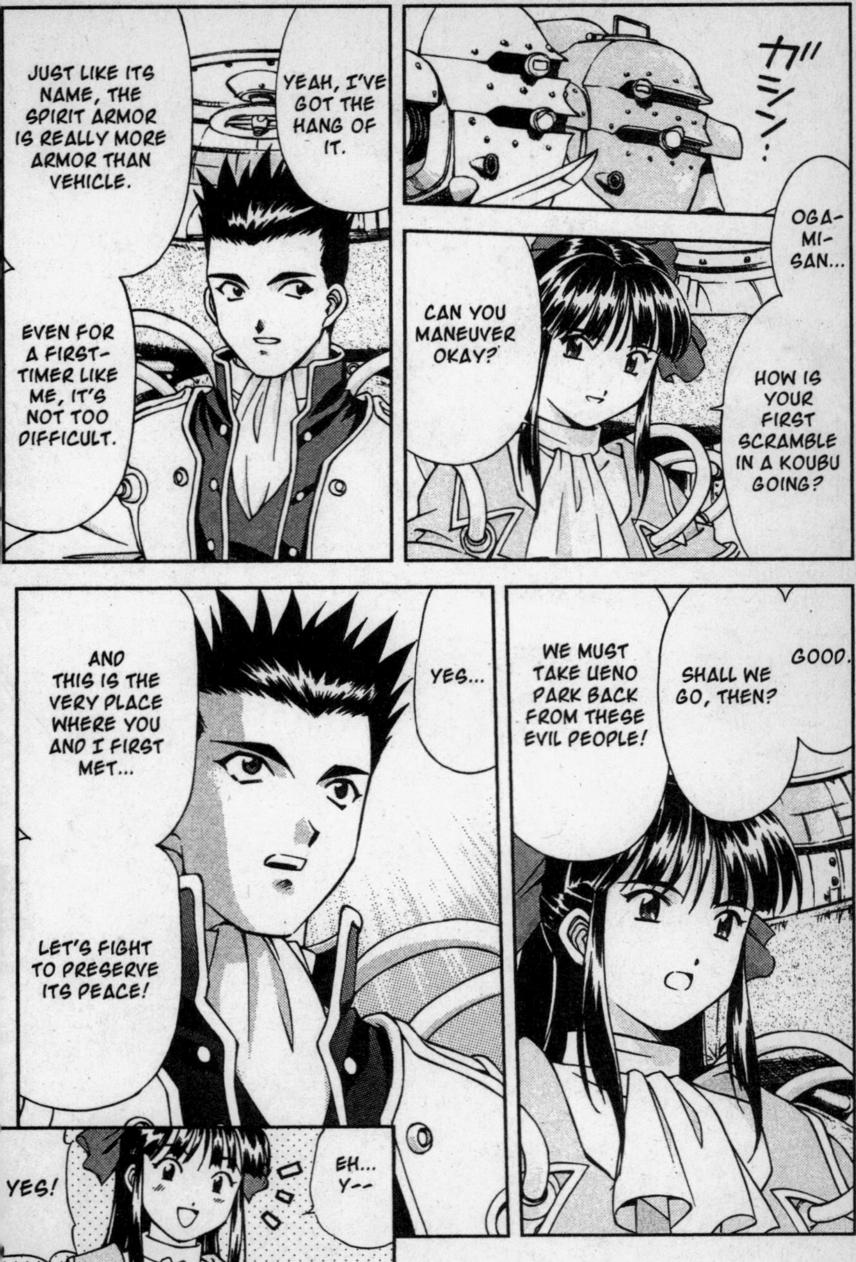
OGA-MI-SAN...
HOW IS YOUR FIRST SCRAMBLE IN A KOUBU GOING?
CAN YOU MANEUVER OKAY?
YEAH, I'VE GOT THE HANG OF IT.
JUST LIKE ITS NAME, THE SPIRIT ARMOR IS REALLY MORE ARMOR THAN VEHICLE.
EVEN FOR A FIRST-TIMER LIKE ME, IT'S NOT TOO DIFFICULT.
GOOD.
SHALL WE GO, THEN?
WE MUST TAKE UENO PARK BACK FROM THESE EVIL PEOPLE!
YES...
AND THIS IS THE VERY PLACE WHERE YOU AND I FIRST MET...
LET'S FIGHT TO PRESERVE ITS PEACE!
EH... Y--
YES!

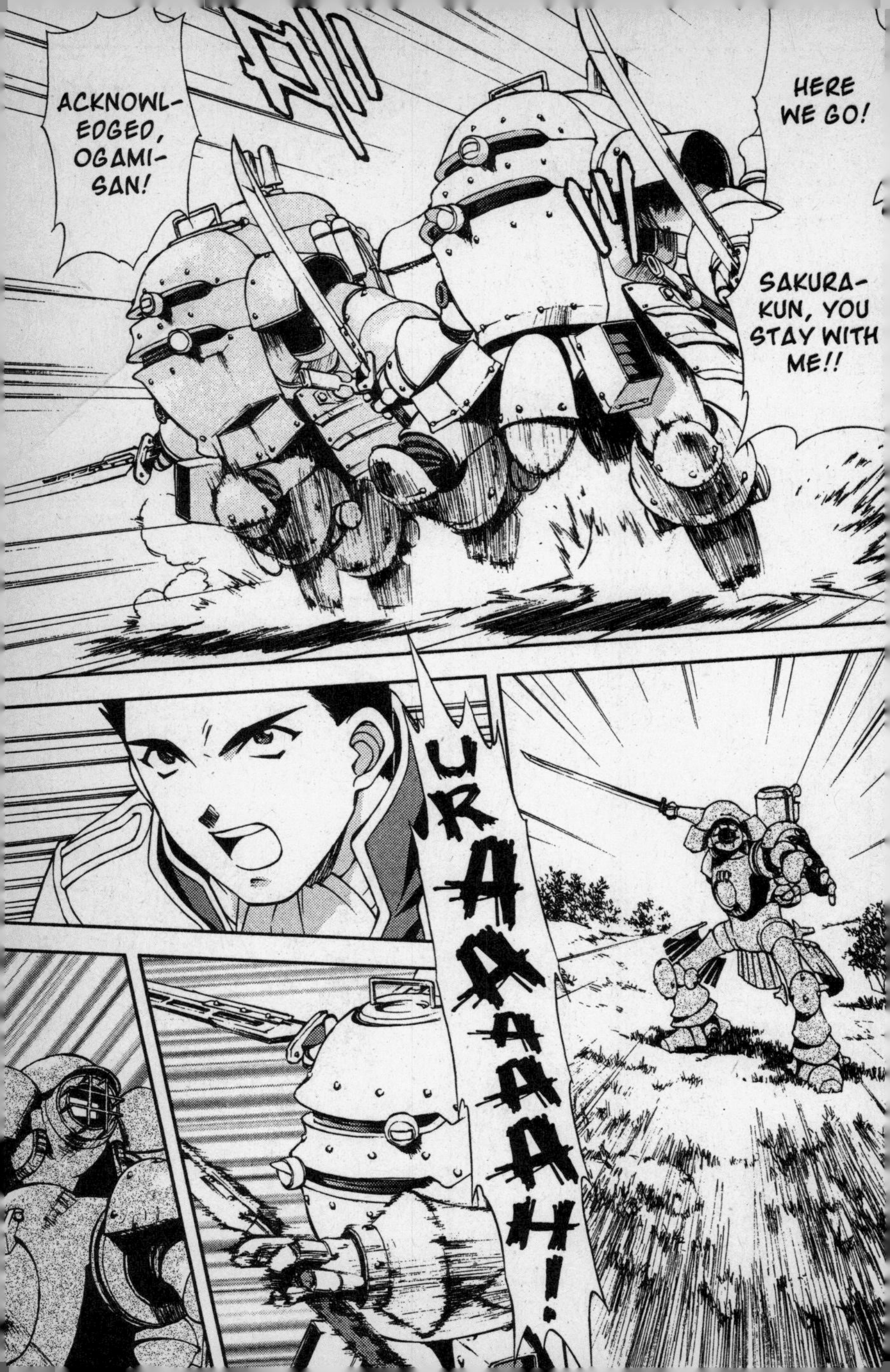
HERE WE GO!
SAKURA-KUN, YOU STAY WITH ME!!
ACKNOWLEDGED, OGAMI-SAN!
URAAAAAH!

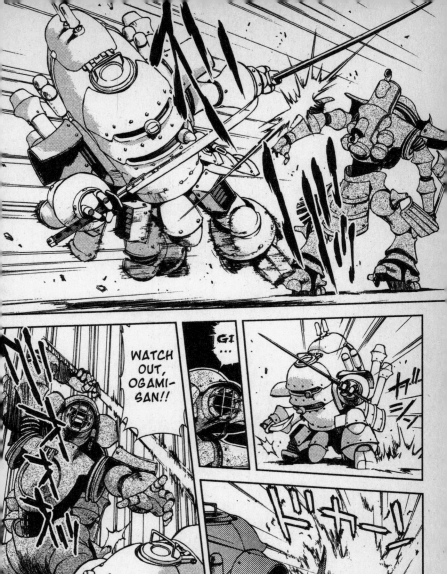

WATCH OUT, OGAMI-SAN!!

GI...

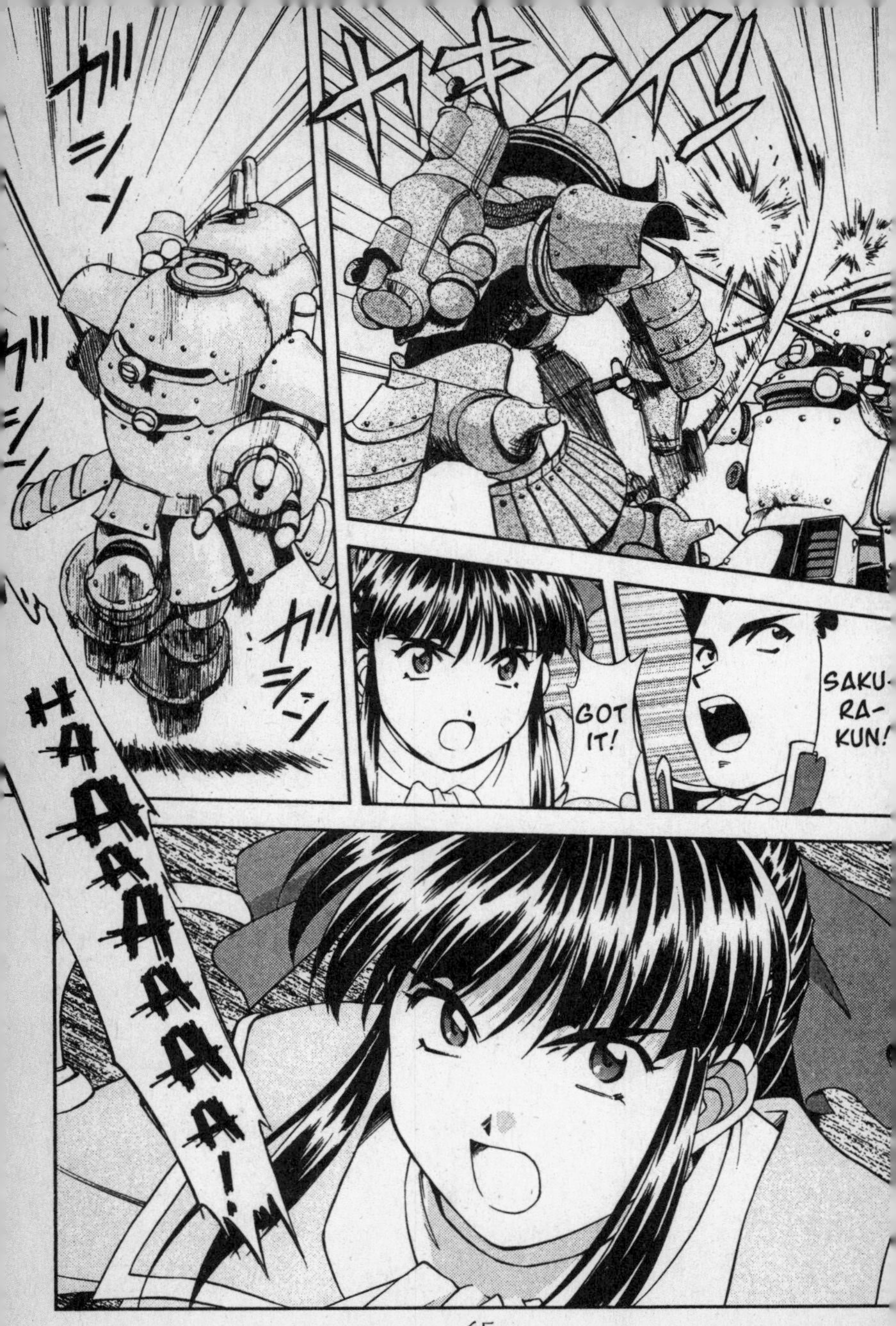
SAKU-
RA-
KUN!
GOT
IT!
HAAAAAAAAA!

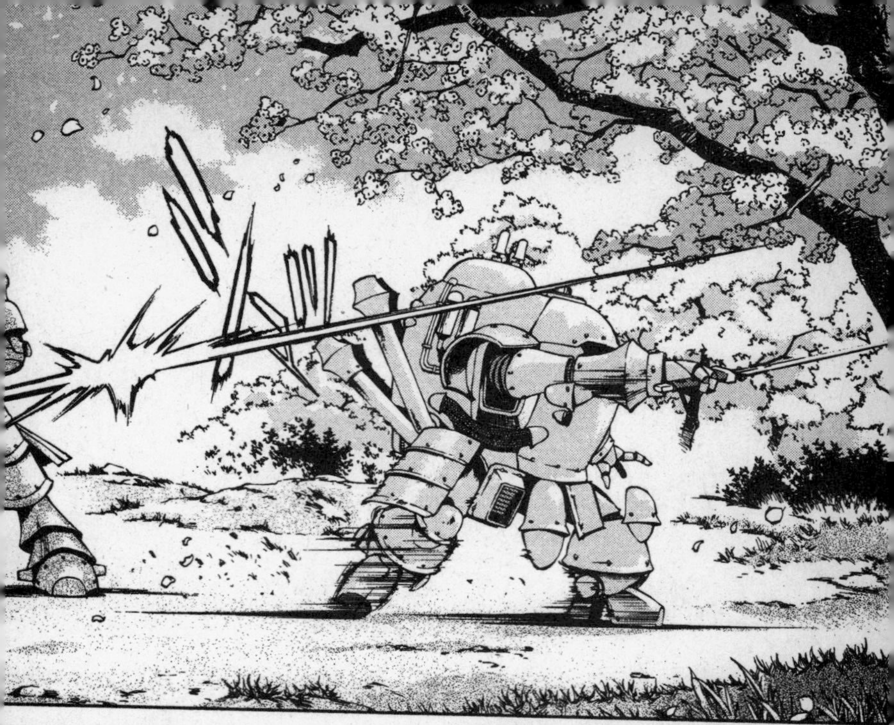

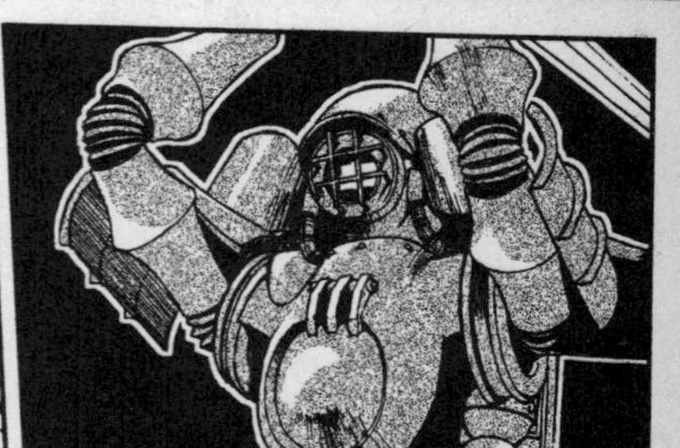

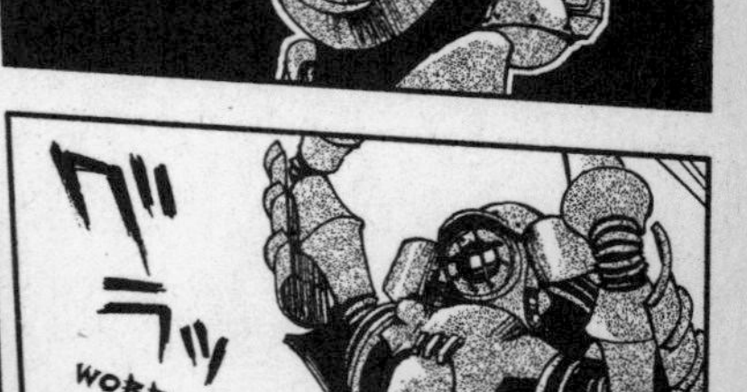
グラッ
WOBBLE

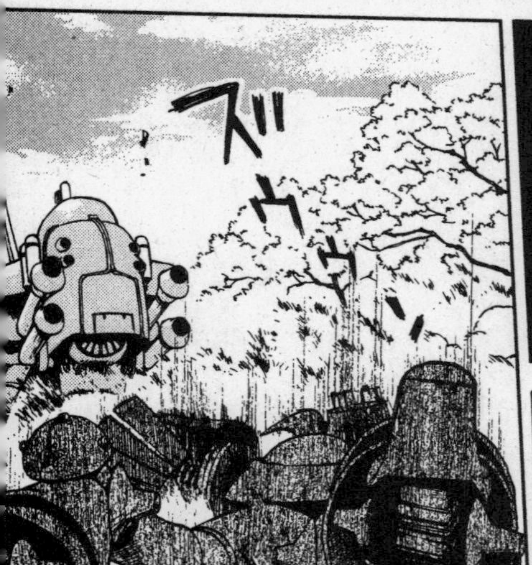

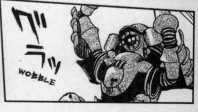

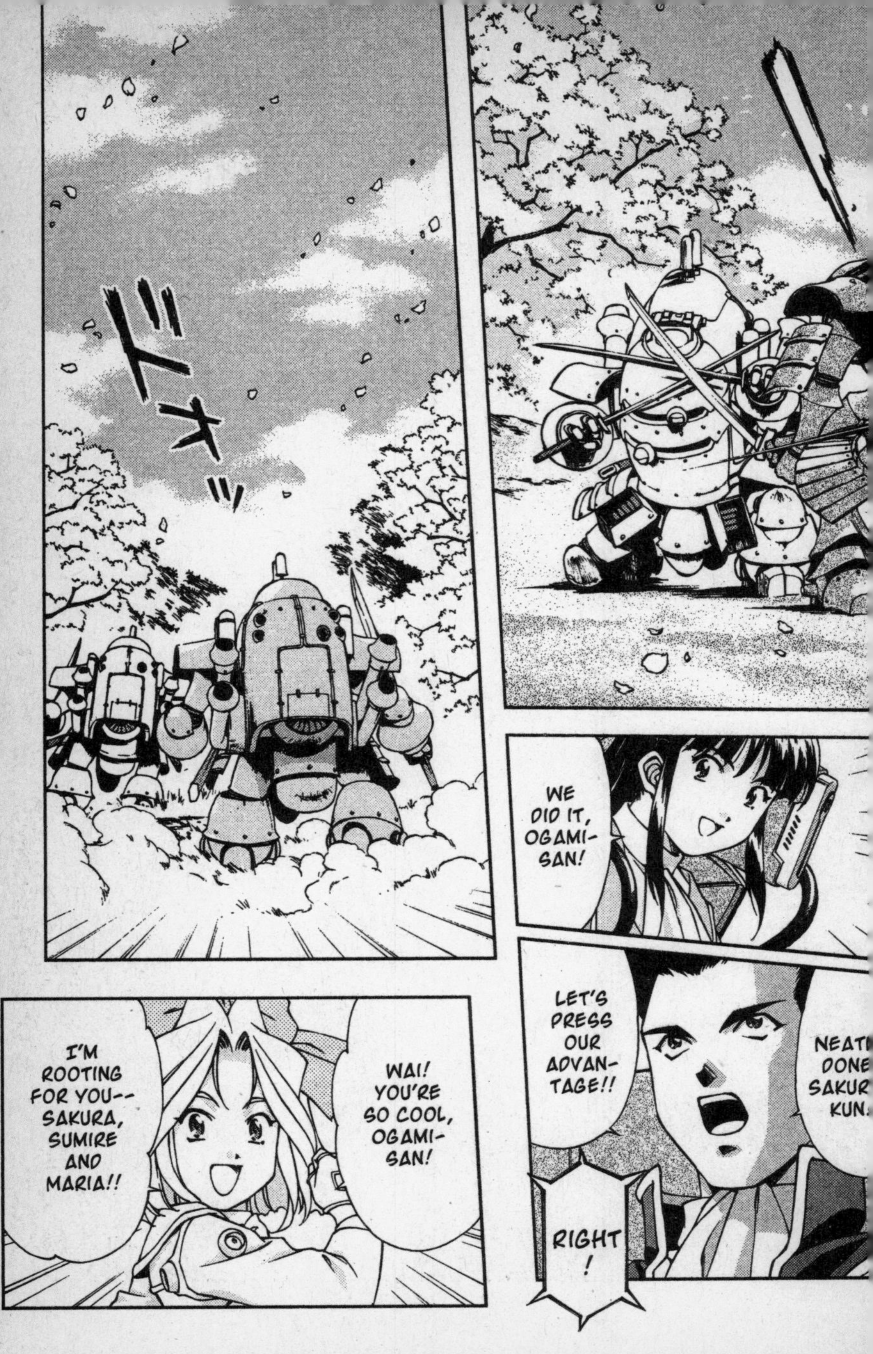
WE DID IT, OGAMI-SAN!
NEAT DONE SAKUR KUN.
LET'S PRESS OUR ADVANTAGE!!
RIGHT!
ドオッ
WAI! YOU'RE SO COOL, OGAMI-SAN!
I'M ROOTING FOR YOU--SAKURA, SUMIRE AND MARIA!!

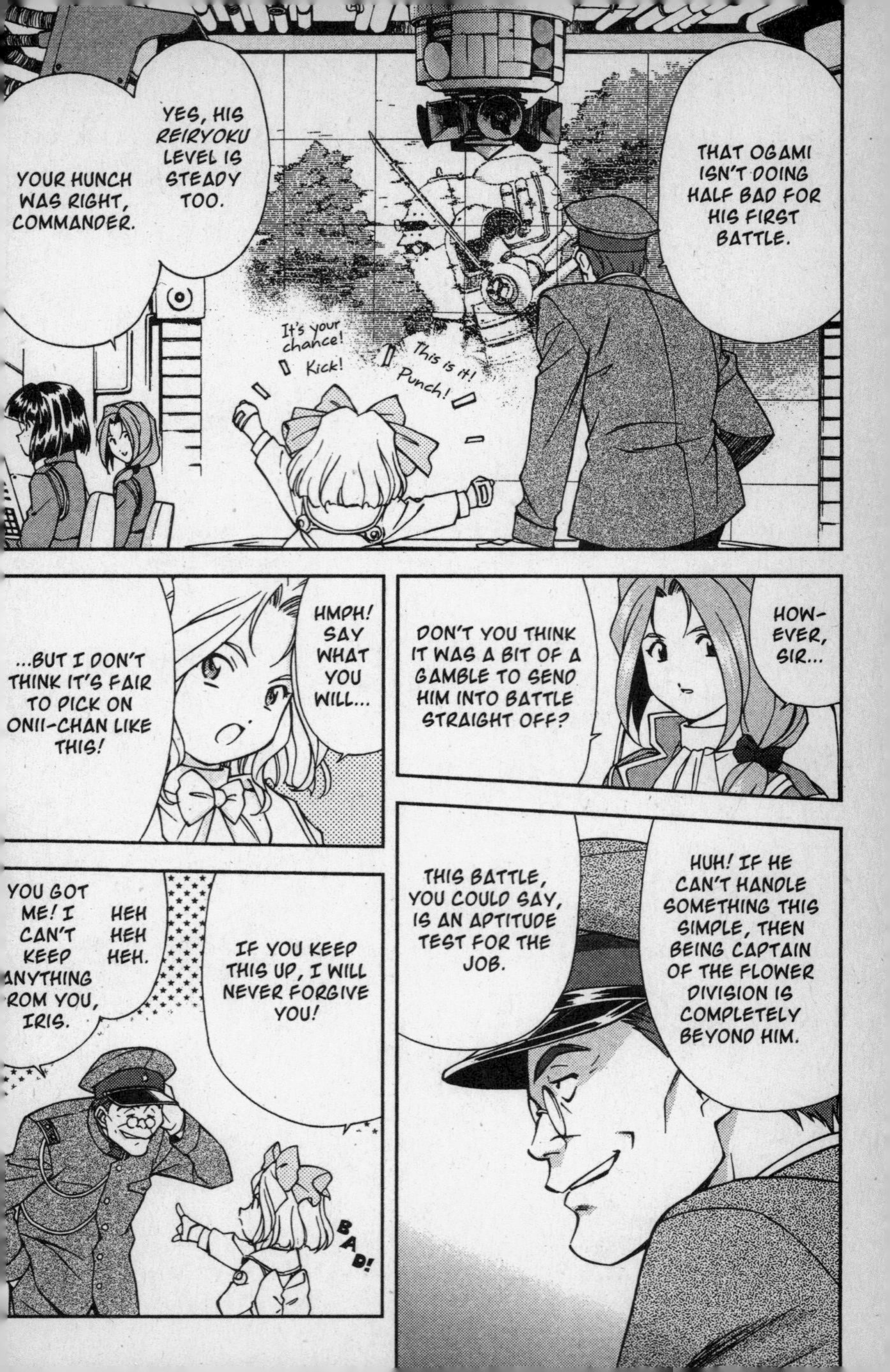
THAT OGAMI ISN'T DOING HALF BAD FOR HIS FIRST BATTLE.
YES, HIS REIRYOKU LEVEL IS STEADY TOO.
YOUR HUNCH WAS RIGHT, COMMANDER.
This is it! Punch!
It's your chance! Kick!
HOW-EVER, SIR...
DON'T YOU THINK IT WAS A BIT OF A GAMBLE TO SEND HIM INTO BATTLE STRAIGHT OFF?
HMPH! SAY WHAT YOU WILL...
...BUT I DON'T THINK IT'S FAIR TO PICK ON ONII-CHAN LIKE THIS!
HUH! IF HE CAN'T HANDLE SOMETHING THIS SIMPLE, THEN BEING CAPTAIN OF THE FLOWER DIVISION IS COMPLETELY BEYOND HIM.
THIS BATTLE, YOU COULD SAY, IS AN APTITUDE TEST FOR THE JOB.
IF YOU KEEP THIS UP, I WILL NEVER FORGIVE YOU!
HEH HEH HEH.
YOU GOT ME! I CAN'T KEEP ANYTHING ROM YOU, IRIS.
BAD!

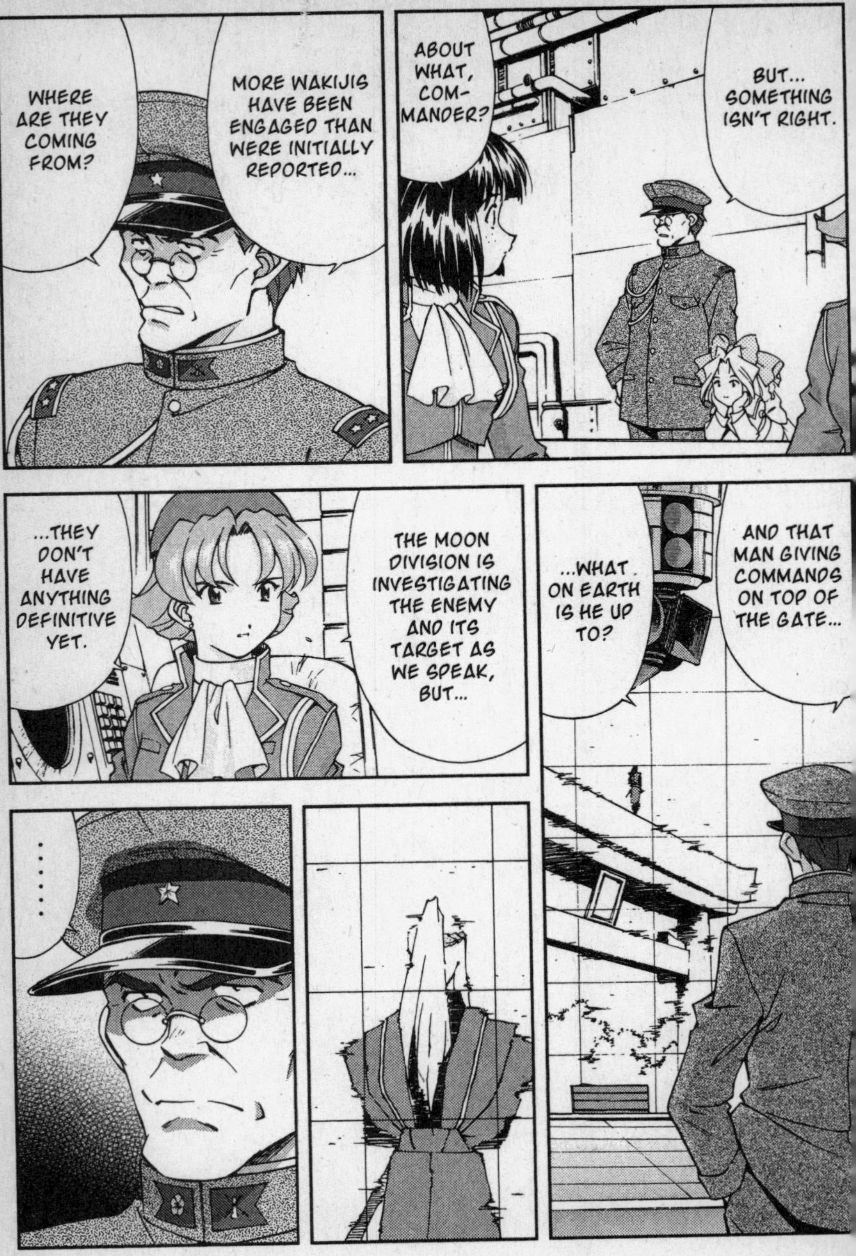
BUT... SOMETHING ISN'T RIGHT.
ABOUT WHAT, COM-MANDER?
MORE WAKIJIS HAVE BEEN ENGAGED THAN WERE INITIALLY REPORTED...
WHERE ARE THEY COMING FROM?
AND THAT MAN GIVING COMMANDS ON TOP OF THE GATE...
...WHAT ON EARTH IS HE UP TO?
THE MOON DIVISION IS INVESTIGATING THE ENEMY AND ITS TARGET AS WE SPEAK, BUT...
...THEY DON'T HAVE ANYTHING DEFINITIVE YET.
......

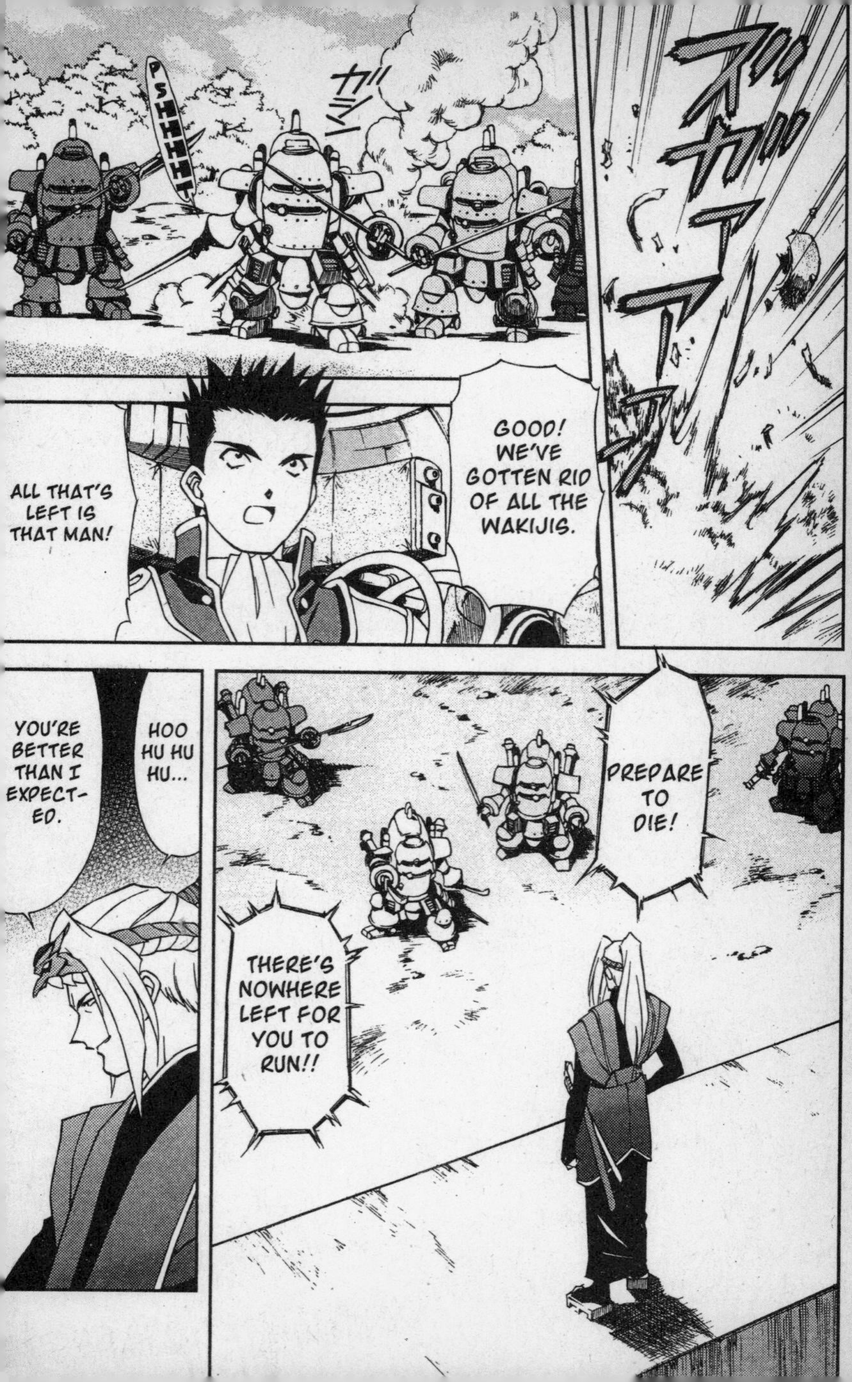
PSHHHHHT
GOOD! WE'VE GOTTEN RID OF ALL THE WAKIJIS.
ALL THAT'S LEFT IS THAT MAN!
PREPARE TO DIE!
THERE'S NOWHERE LEFT FOR YOU TO RUN!!
HOO HU HU HU...
YOU'RE BETTER THAN I EXPECTED.

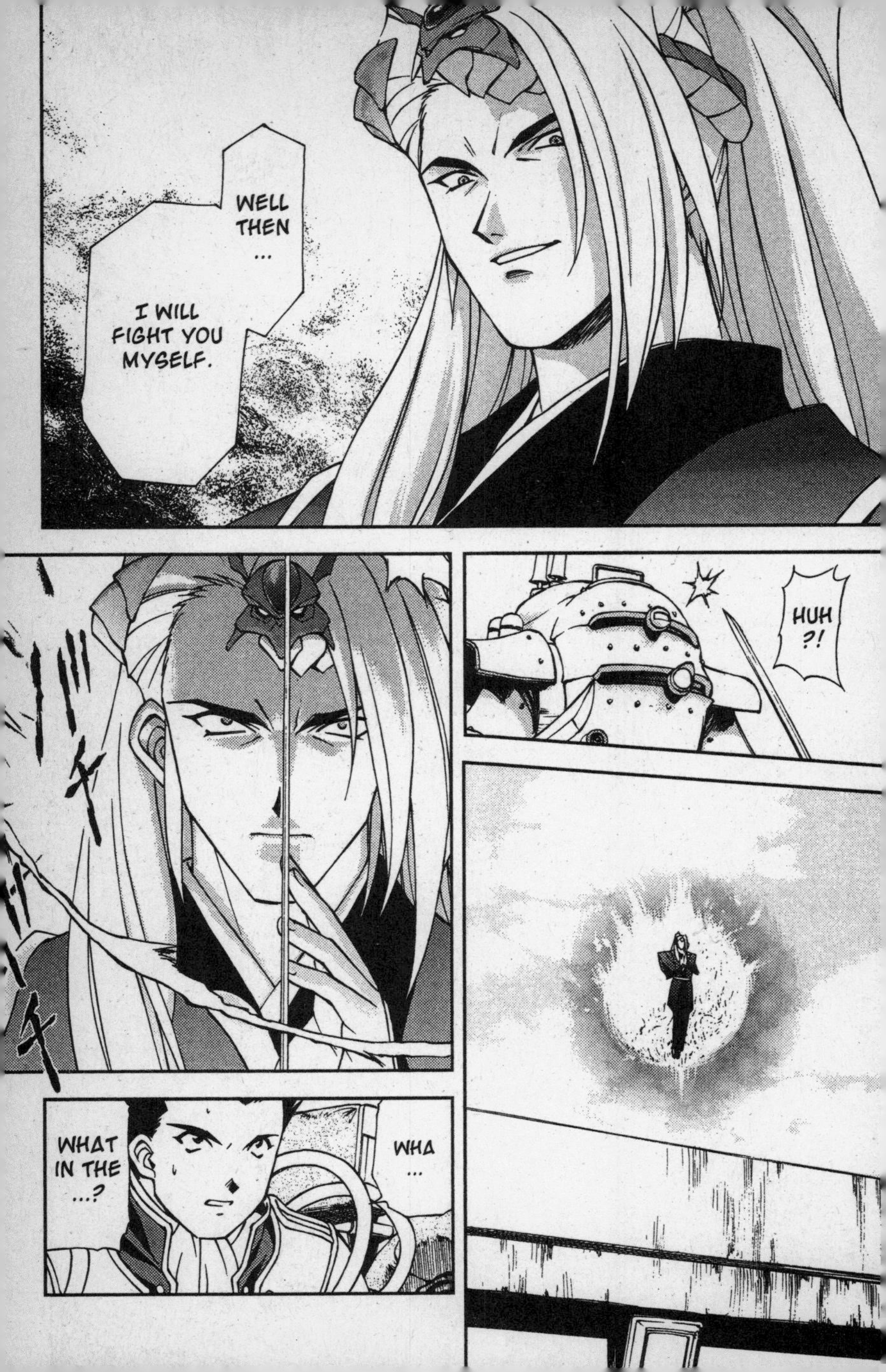
WELL THEN ...
I WILL FIGHT YOU MYSELF.
HUH ?!
WHA ...
WHAT IN THE ...?

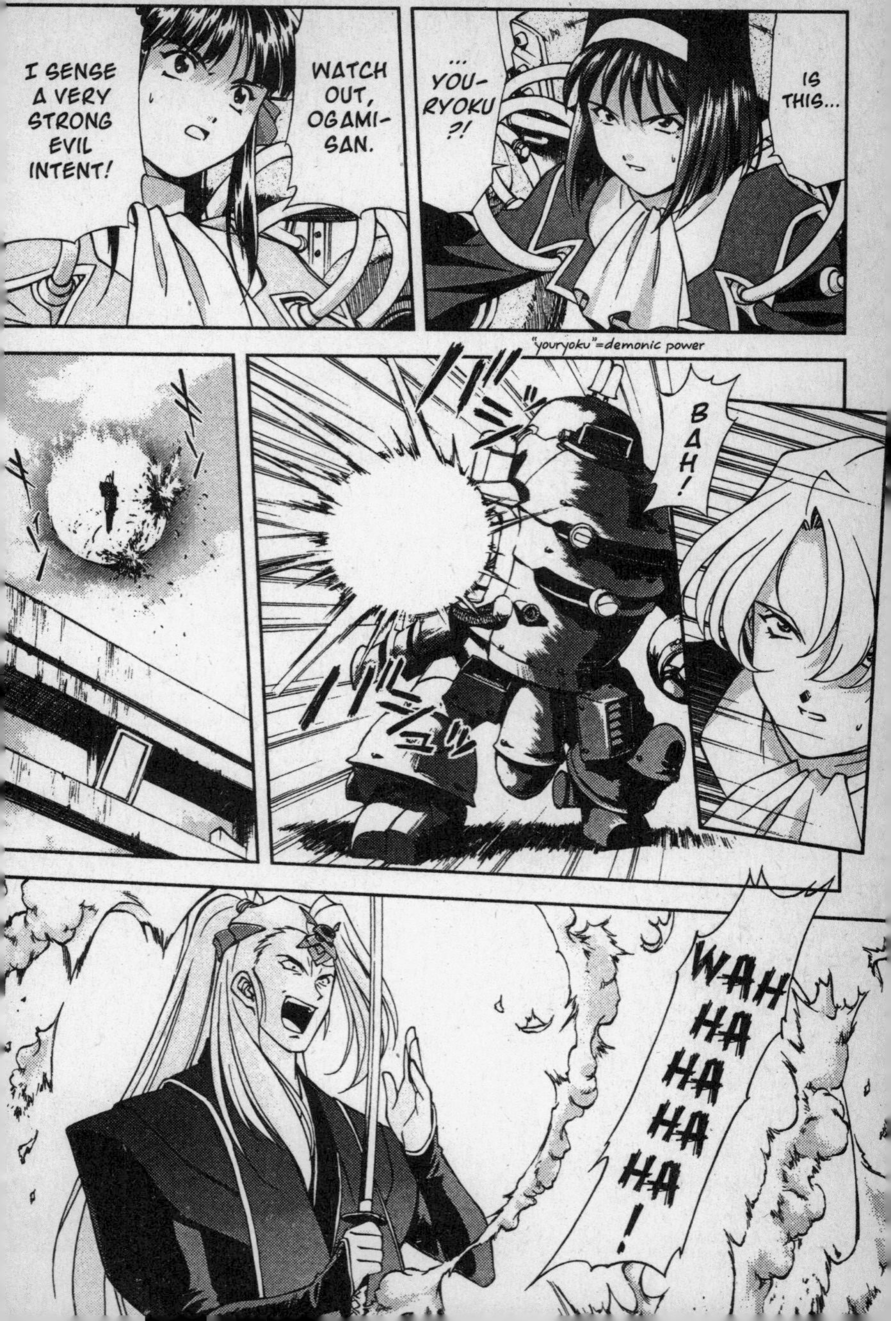
IS THIS...
... YOU-RYOKU ?!
WATCH OUT, OGAMI-SAN.
I SENSE A VERY STRONG EVIL INTENT!
"youryoku"=demonic power
BAH!
WAH HA HA HA HA HA!

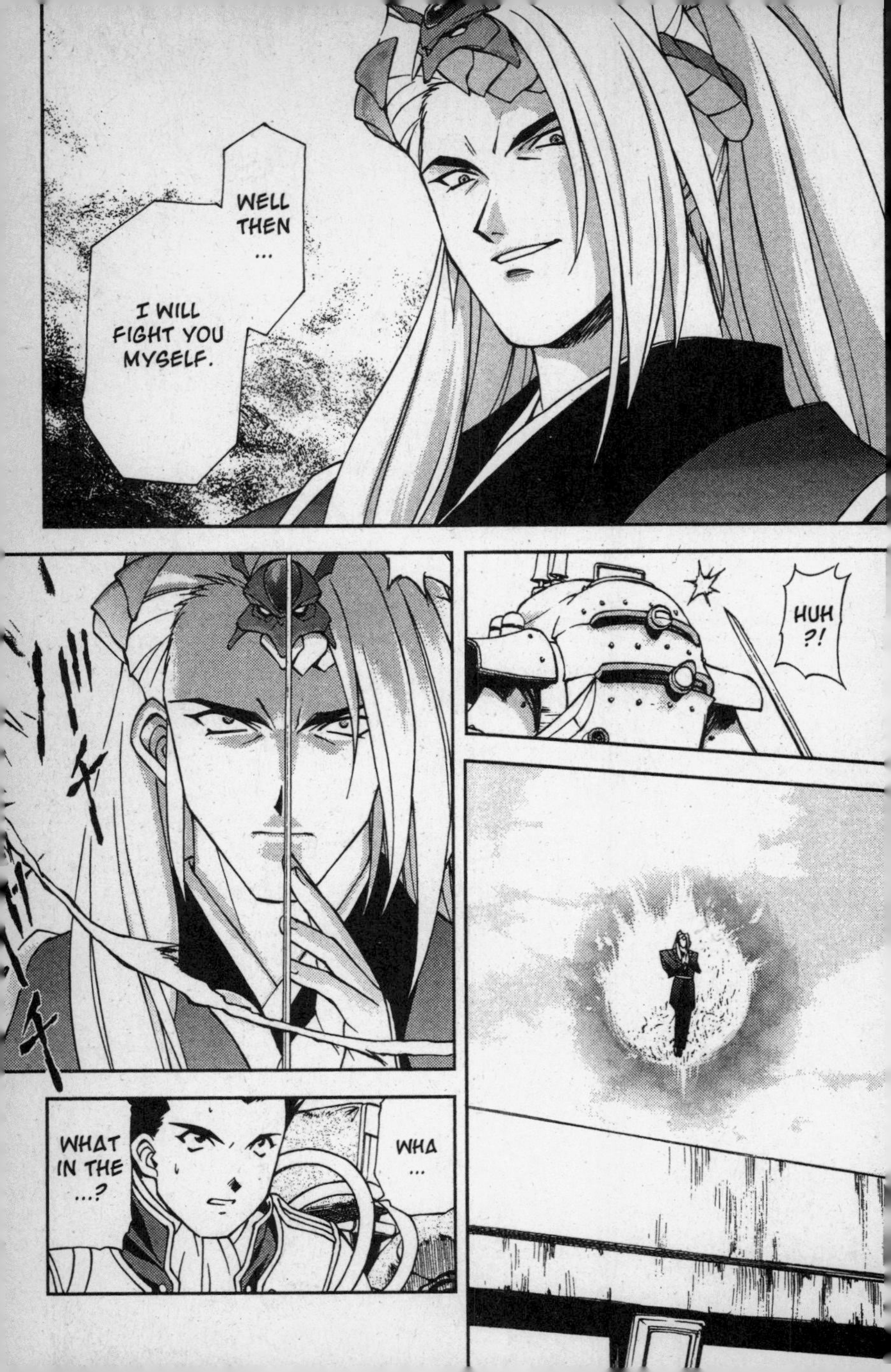
WELL THEN ...
I WILL FIGHT YOU MYSELF.
HUH ?!
WHA ...
WHAT IN THE ...?

"youryoku"=demonic power

I SUMMON...

DEMON-DRIVEN SOLDIER KAMUI!

!!

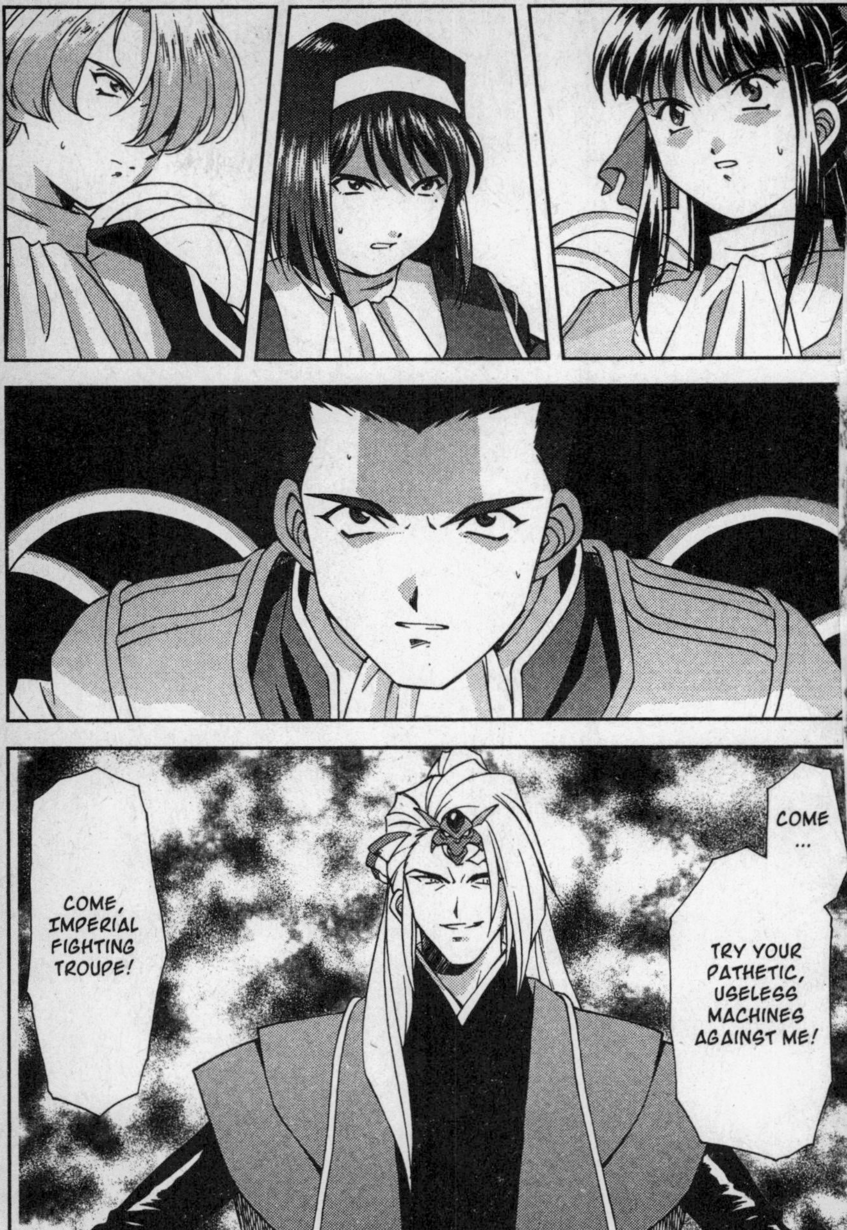
COME ...
TRY YOUR PATHETIC, USELESS MACHINES AGAINST ME!
COME, IMPERIAL FIGHTING TROUPE!

COME,
IMPERIAL
FIGHTING
TROUPE!!

COME
...

TRY YOUR
PATHETIC,
USELESS
MACHINES
AGAINST
ME!

GRR
...

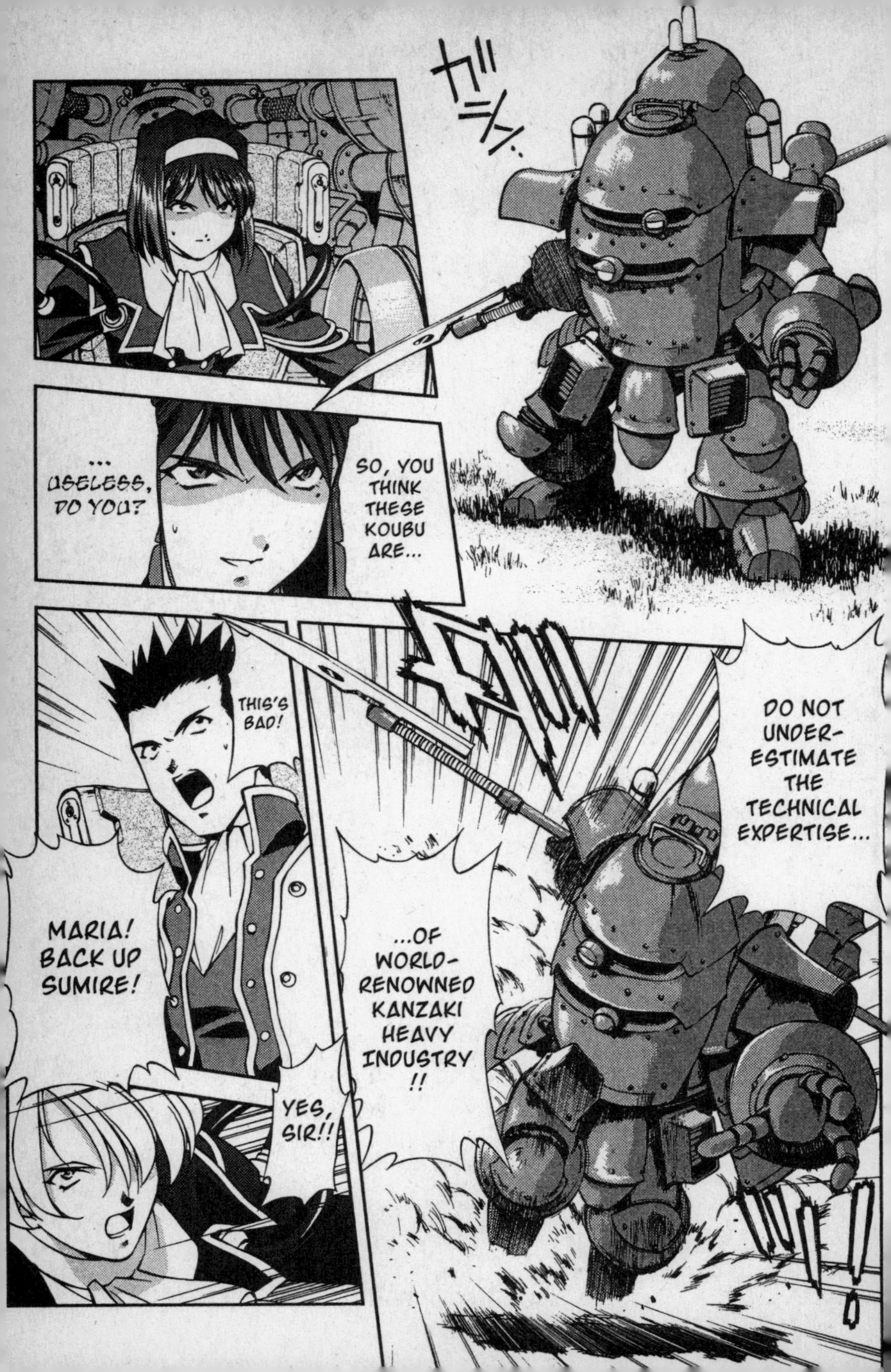
SO, YOU THINK THESE KOUBU ARE...
...USELESS, DO YOU?
DO NOT UNDER-ESTIMATE THE TECHNICAL EXPERTISE...
...OF WORLD-RENOWNED KANZAKI HEAVY INDUSTRY !!
THIS'S BAD!
MARIA! BACK UP SUMIRE!
YES, SIR!!

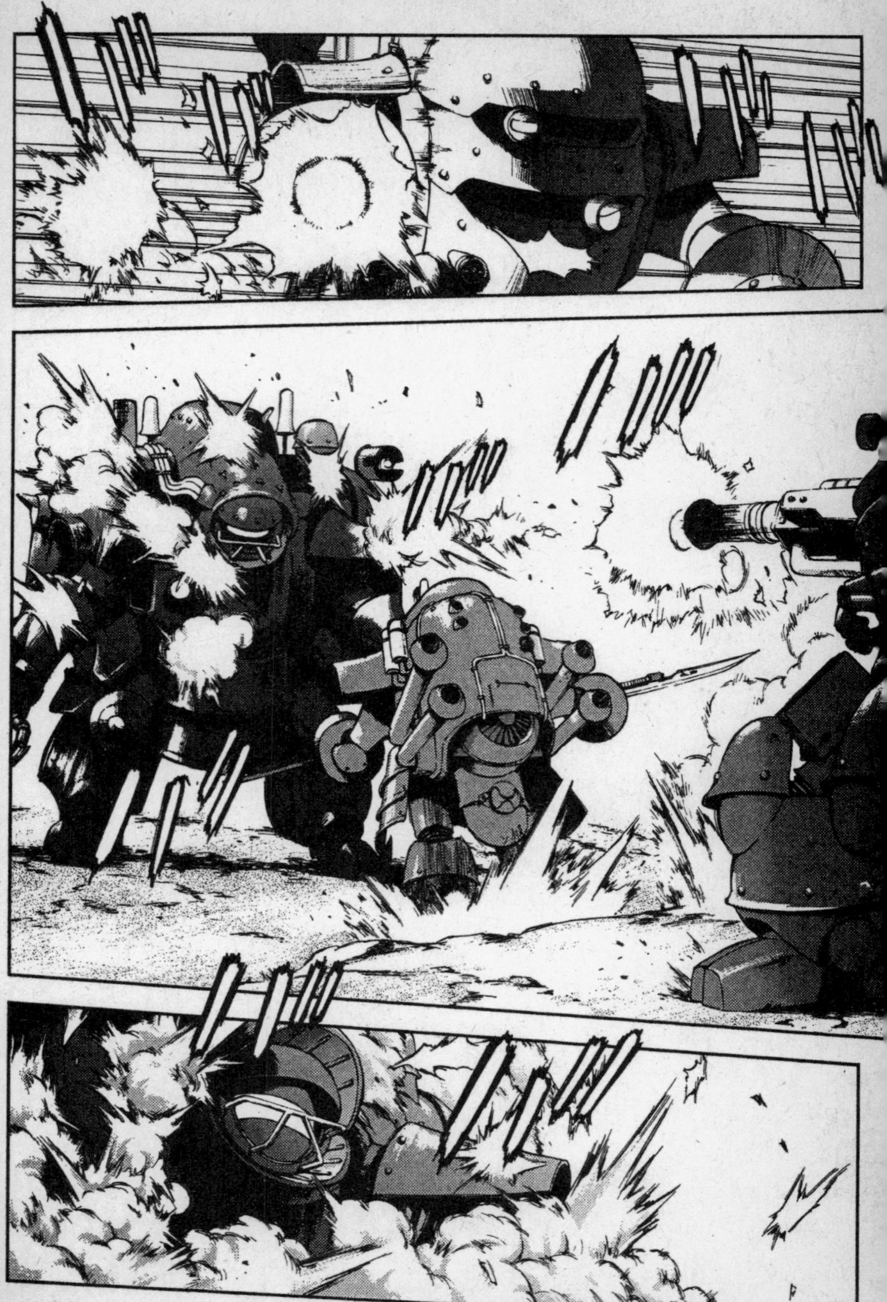

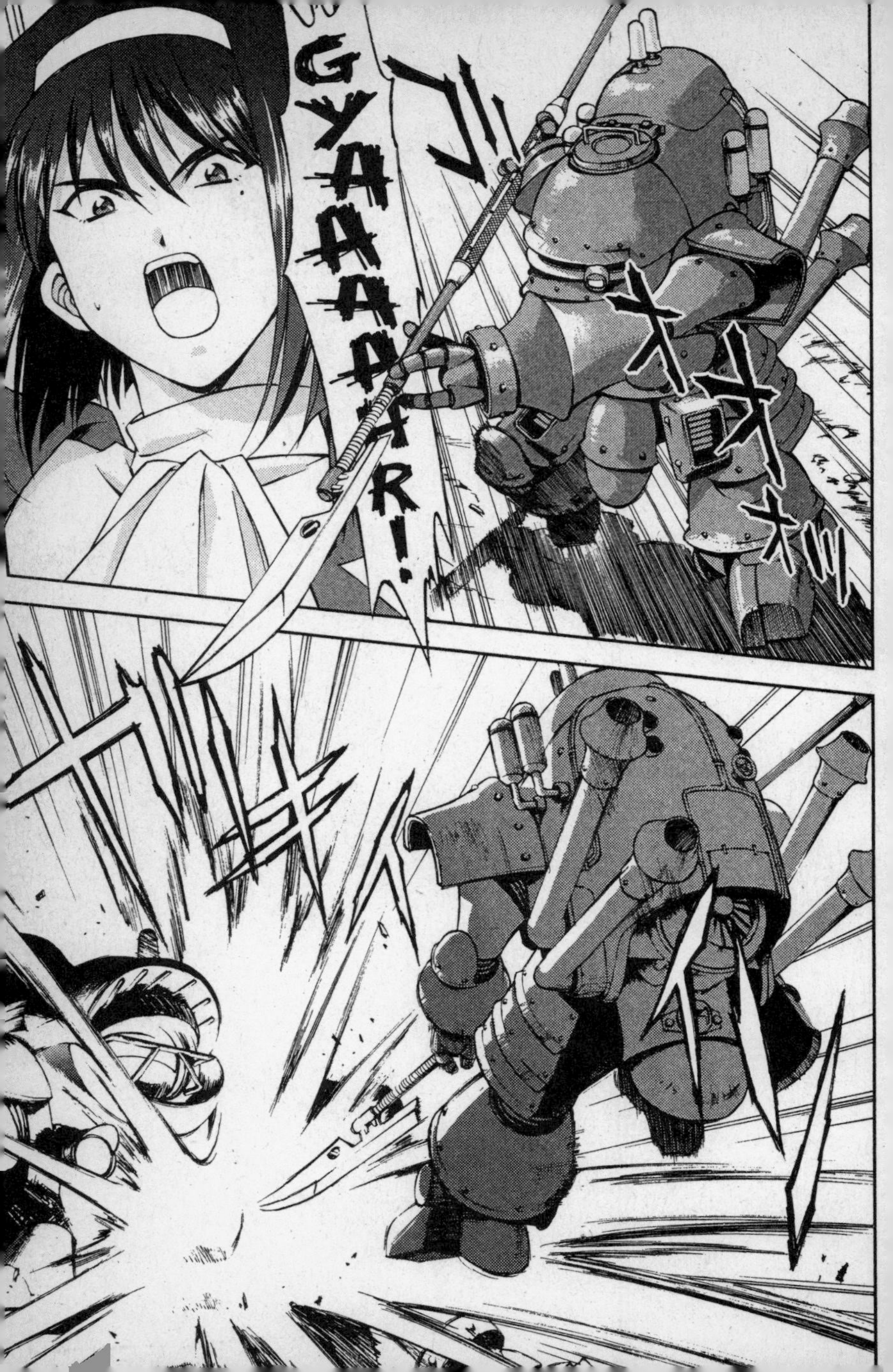
GYAAAAAR!

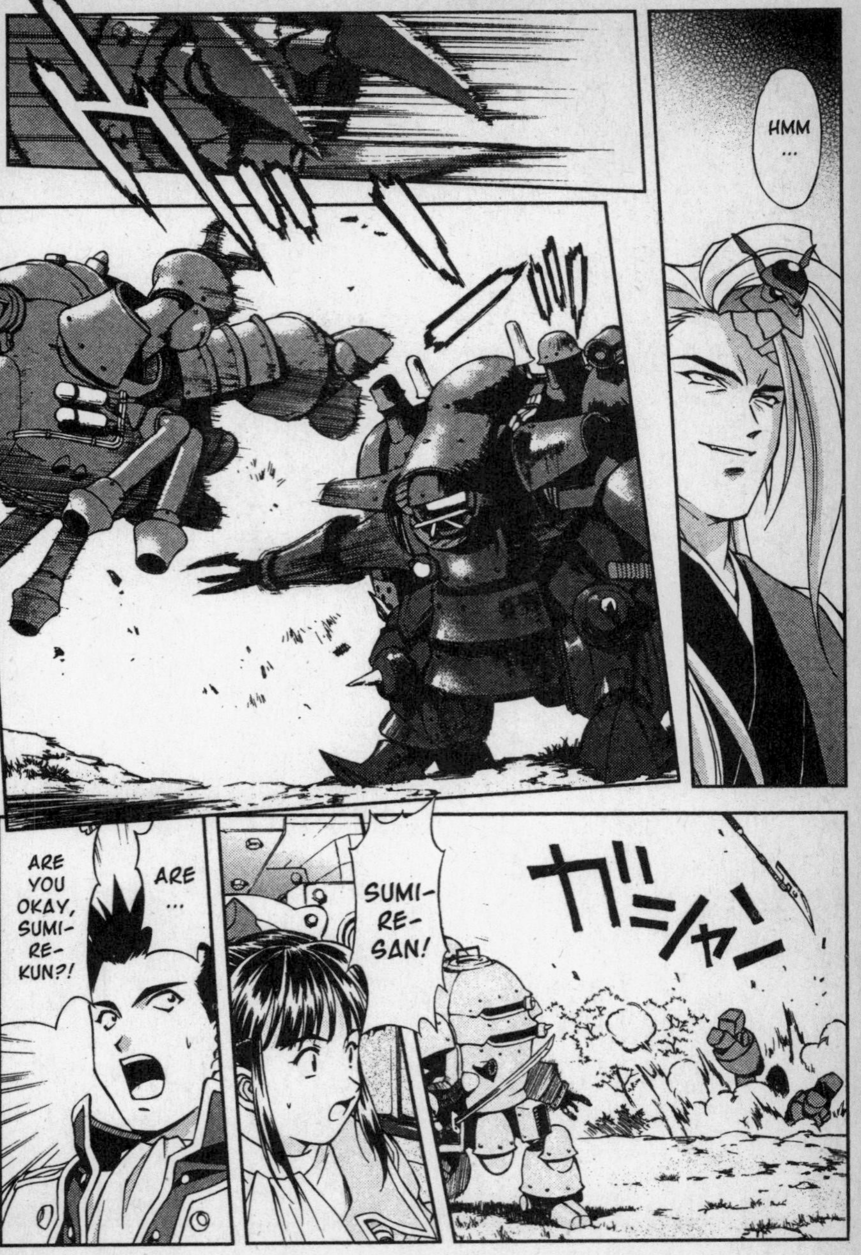
HMM ...
ガシャン
SUMI-RE-SAN!
ARE ...
ARE YOU OKAY, SUMI-RE-KUN?!

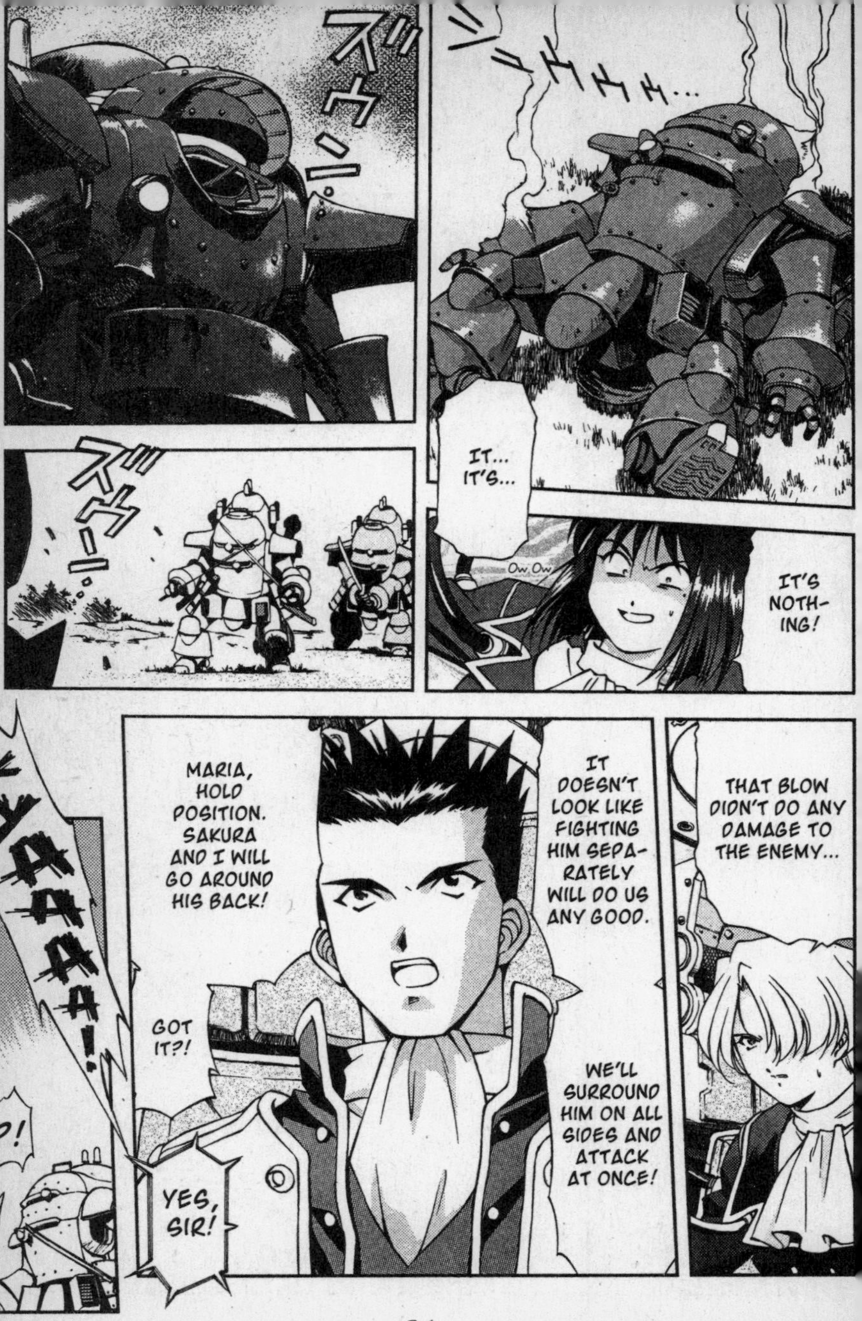
IT... IT'S...
Ow Ow
IT'S NOTH-ING!
THAT BLOW DIDN'T DO ANY DAMAGE TO THE ENEMY...
IT DOESN'T LOOK LIKE FIGHTING HIM SEPA-RATELY WILL DO US ANY GOOD.
WE'LL SURROUND HIM ON ALL SIDES AND ATTACK AT ONCE!
MARIA, HOLD POSITION. SAKURA AND I WILL GO AROUND HIS BACK!
GOT IT?!
YES, SIR!
KYAAAA!!
?!

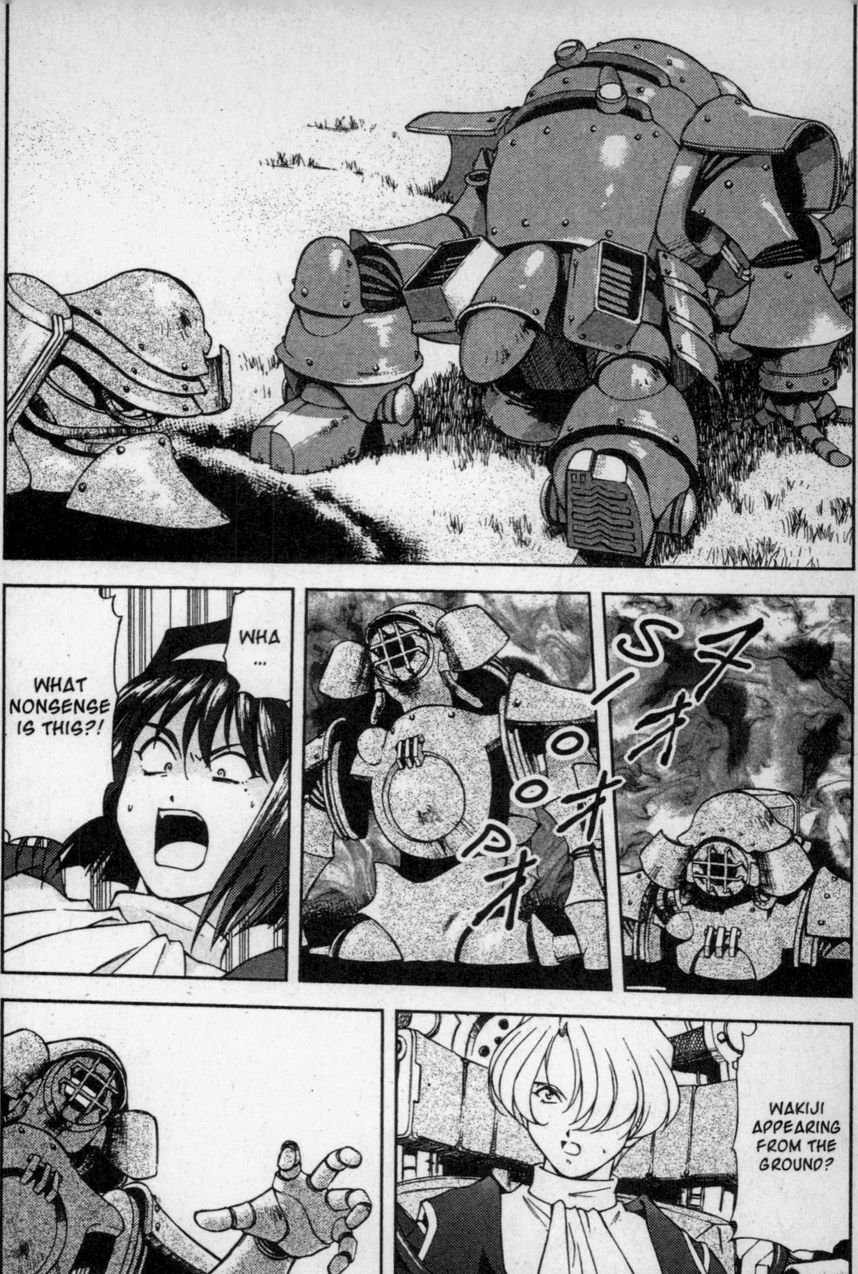
SOOP
スーオオオ
WHA ...
WHAT NONSENSE IS THIS?!
WAKIJI APPEARING FROM THE GROUND?

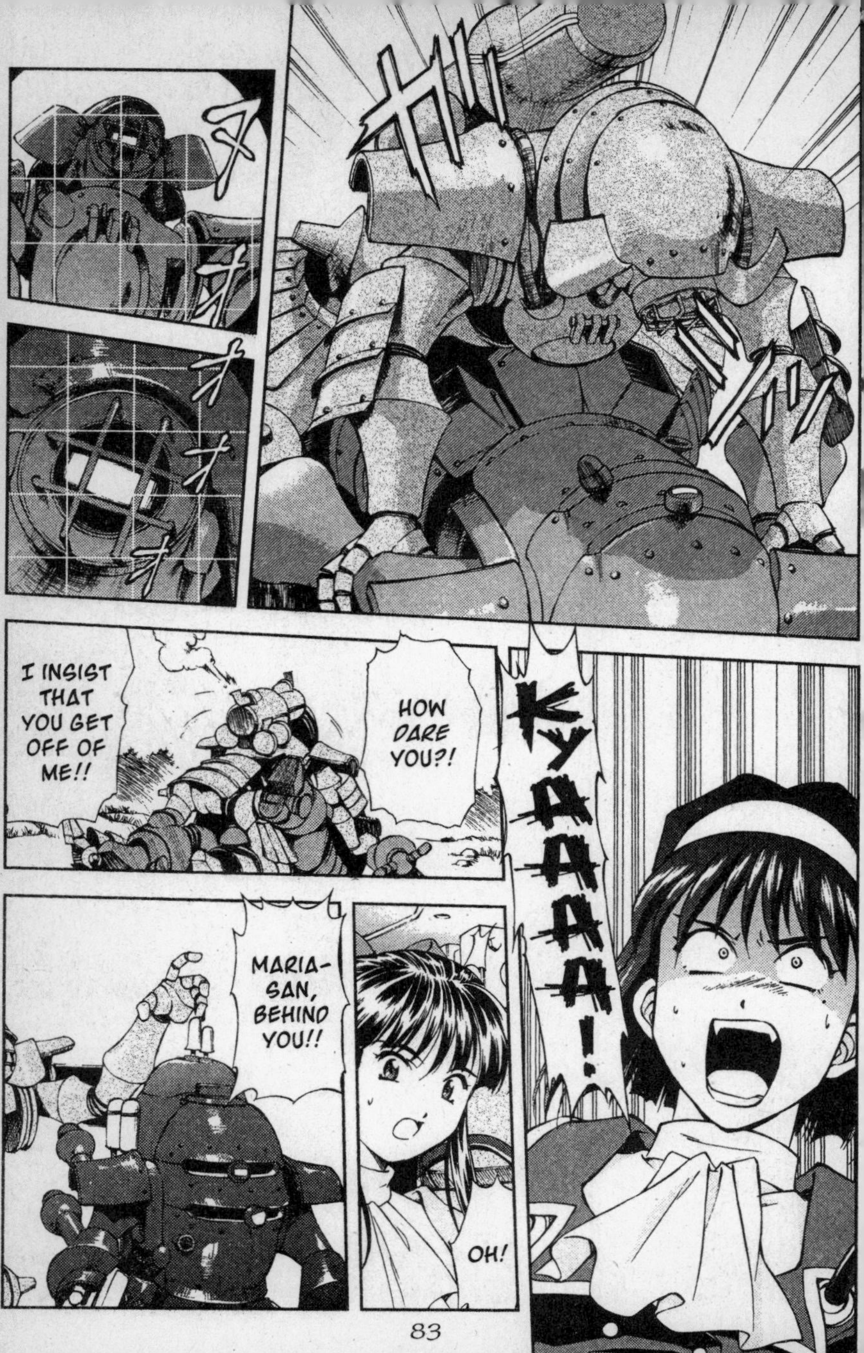
KYAAAA!
HOW DARE YOU?!
I INSIST THAT YOU GET OFF OF ME!!
OH!
MARIA-SAN, BEHIND YOU!!

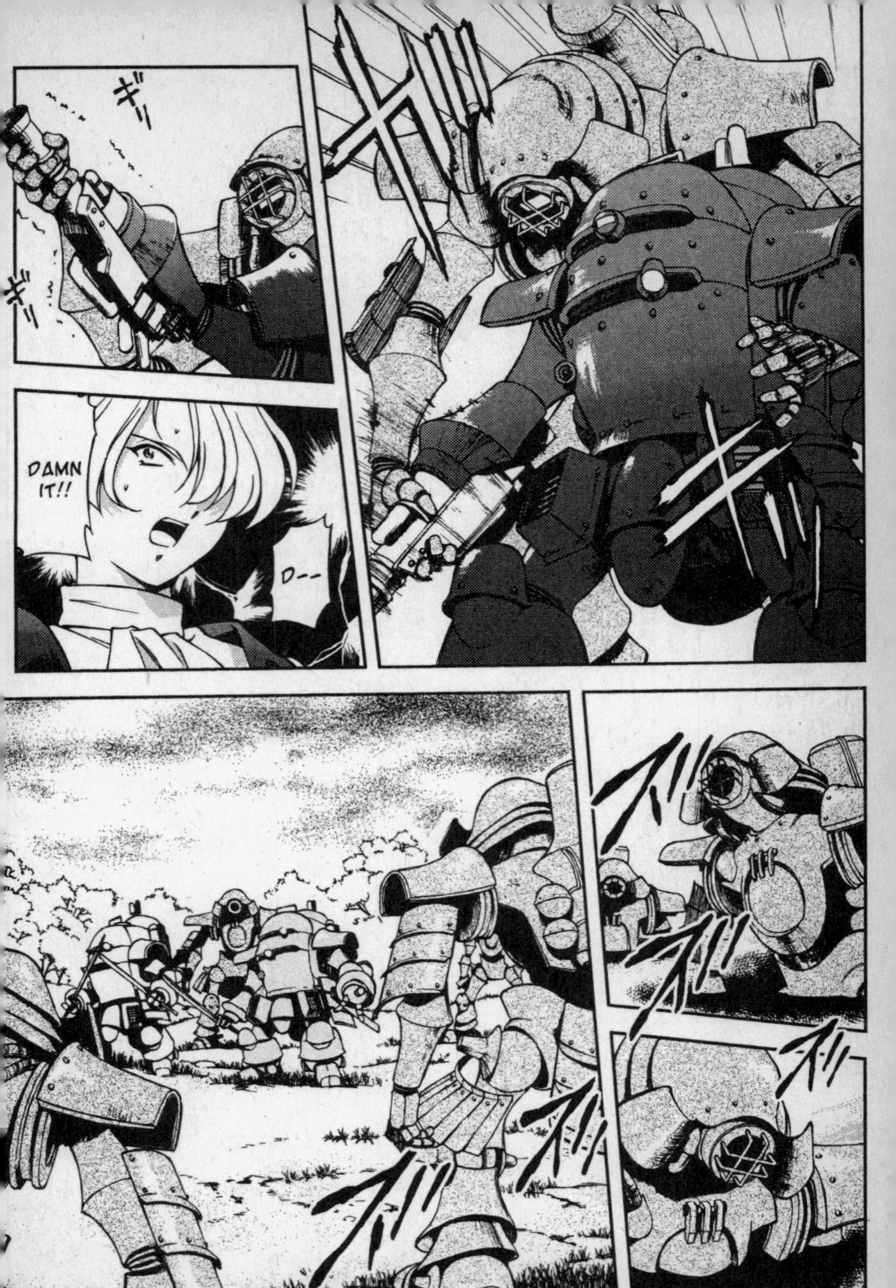
ギリ
ギリ
DAMN IT!!
D--

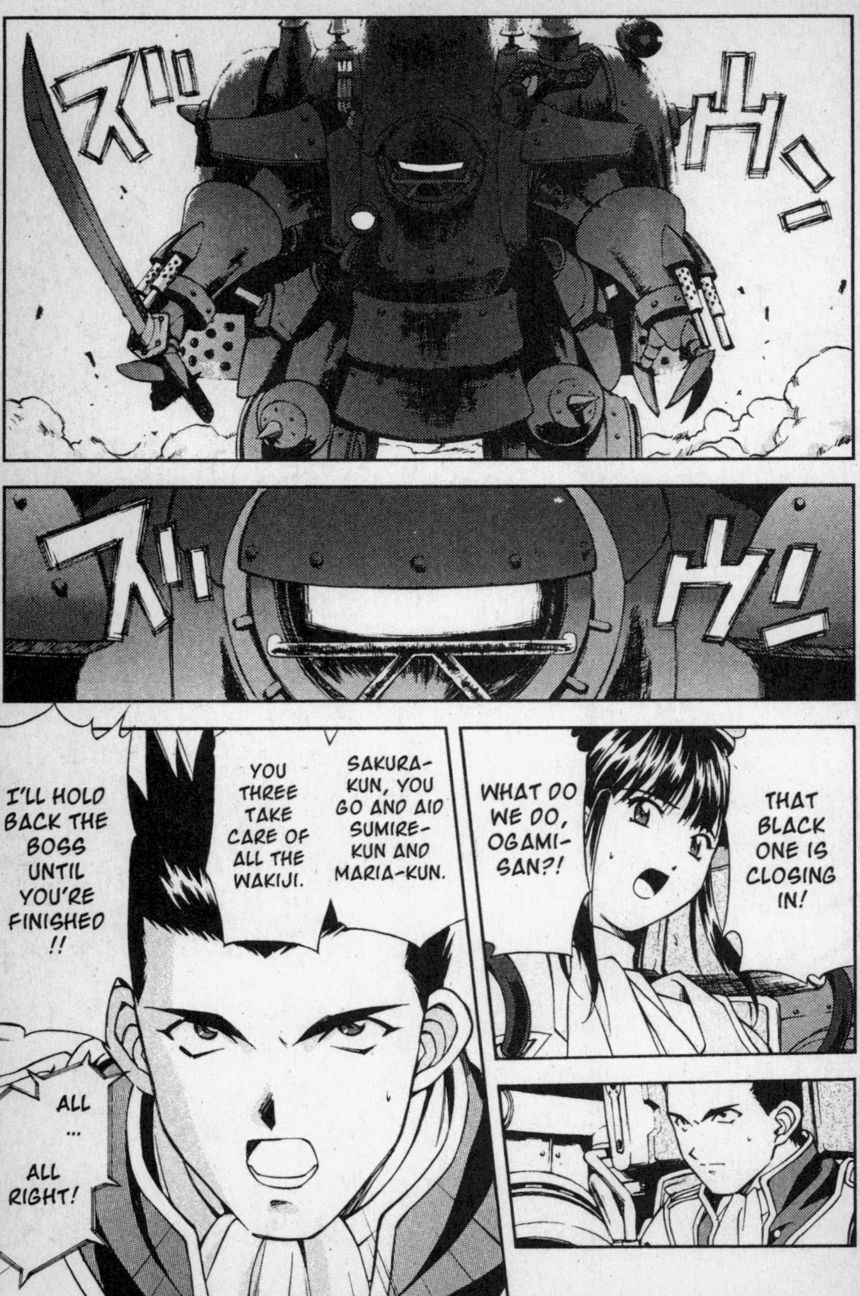
THAT BLACK ONE IS CLOSING IN!
WHAT DO WE DO, OGAMI-SAN?!
SAKURA-KUN, YOU GO AND AID SUMIRE-KUN AND MARIA-KUN.
YOU THREE TAKE CARE OF ALL THE WAKIJI.
I'LL HOLD BACK THE BOSS UNTIL YOU'RE FINISHED!!
ALL ... ALL RIGHT!

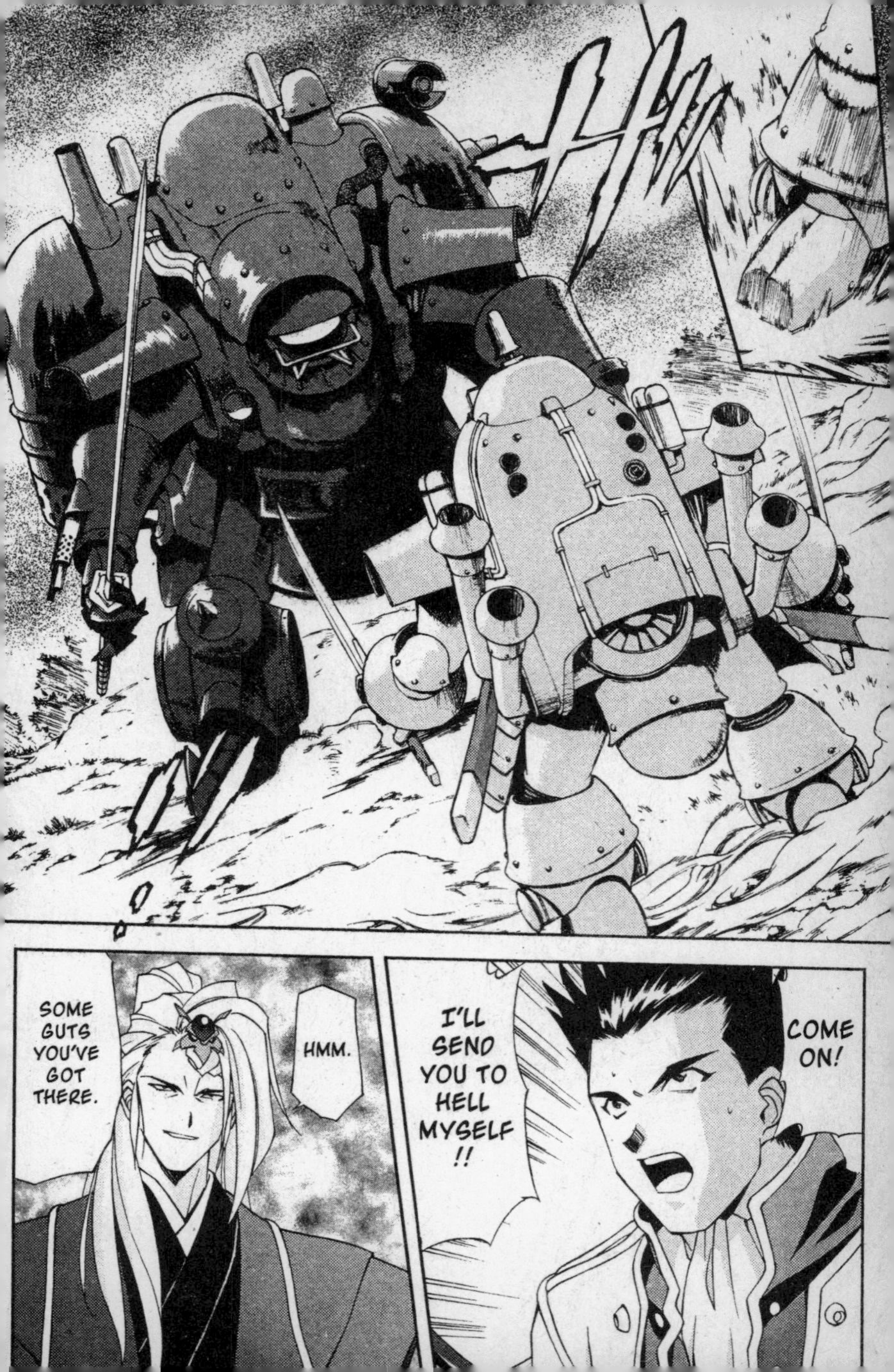
COME ON!
I'LL SEND YOU TO HELL MYSELF!!
HMM.
SOME GUTS YOU'VE GOT THERE.

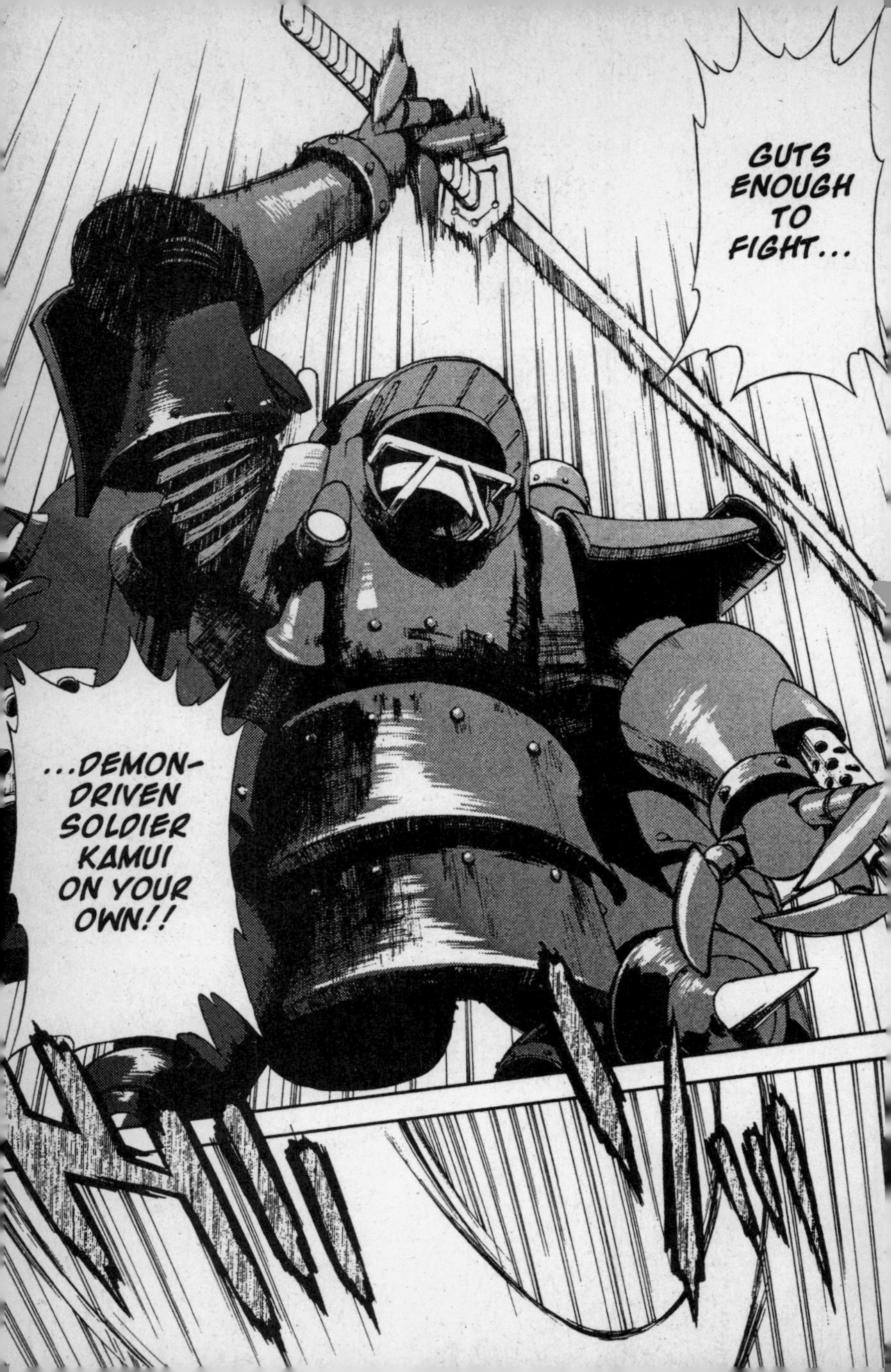
GUTS ENOUGH TO FIGHT...
...DEMON-DRIVEN SOLDIER KAMUI ON YOUR OWN!!

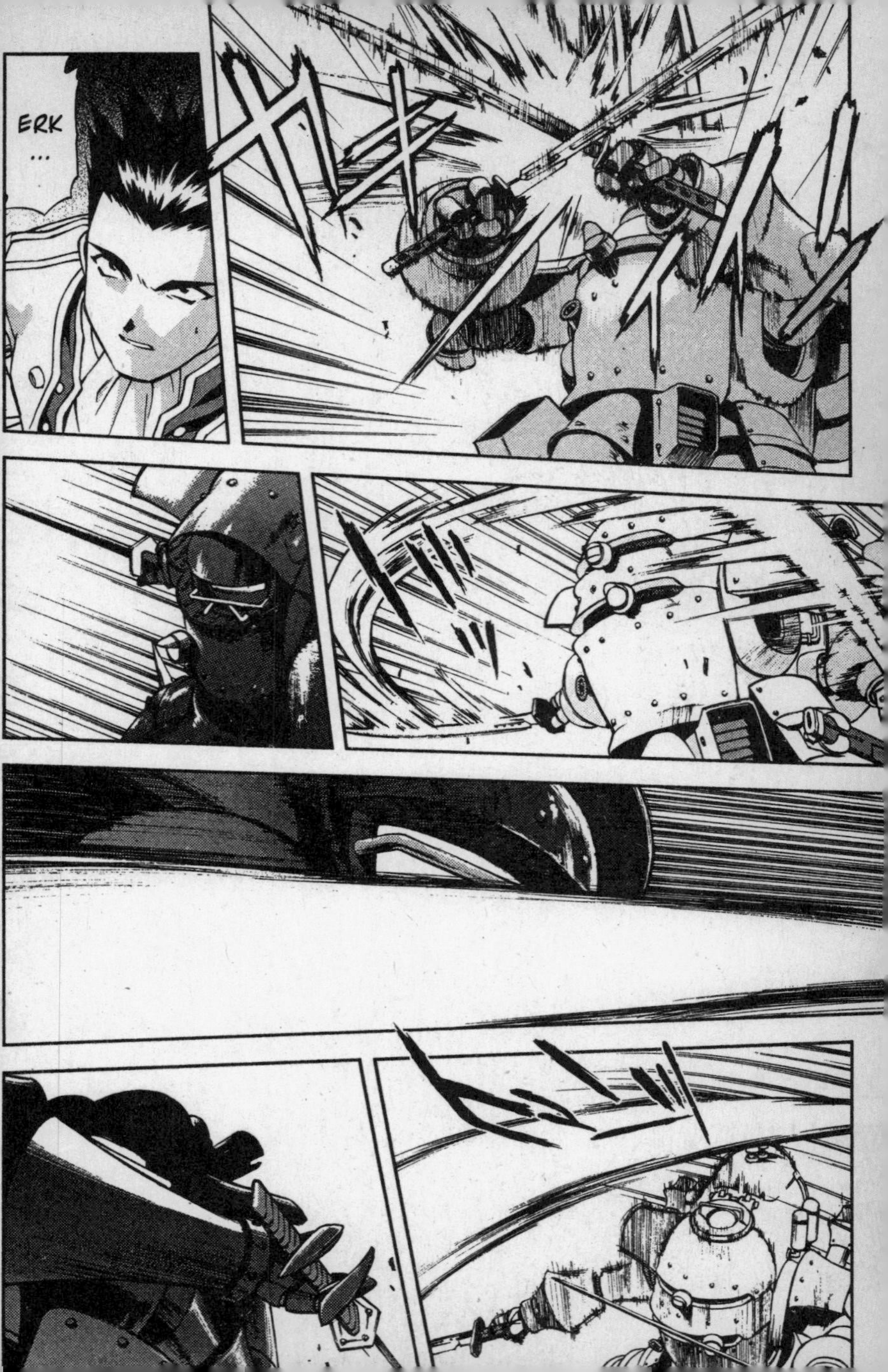
ERK
...

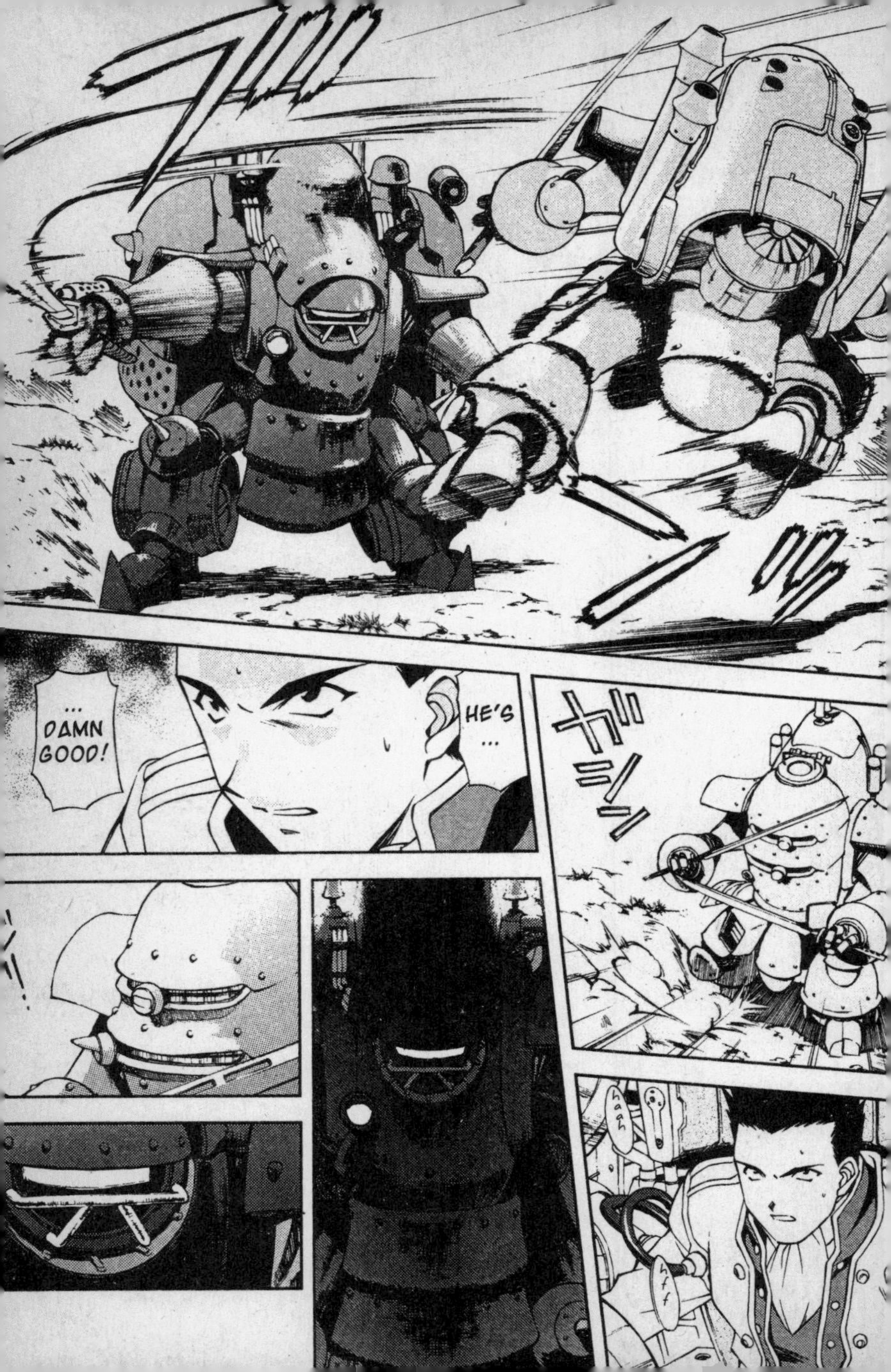
HE'S ...
... DAMN GOOD!
haah
hff

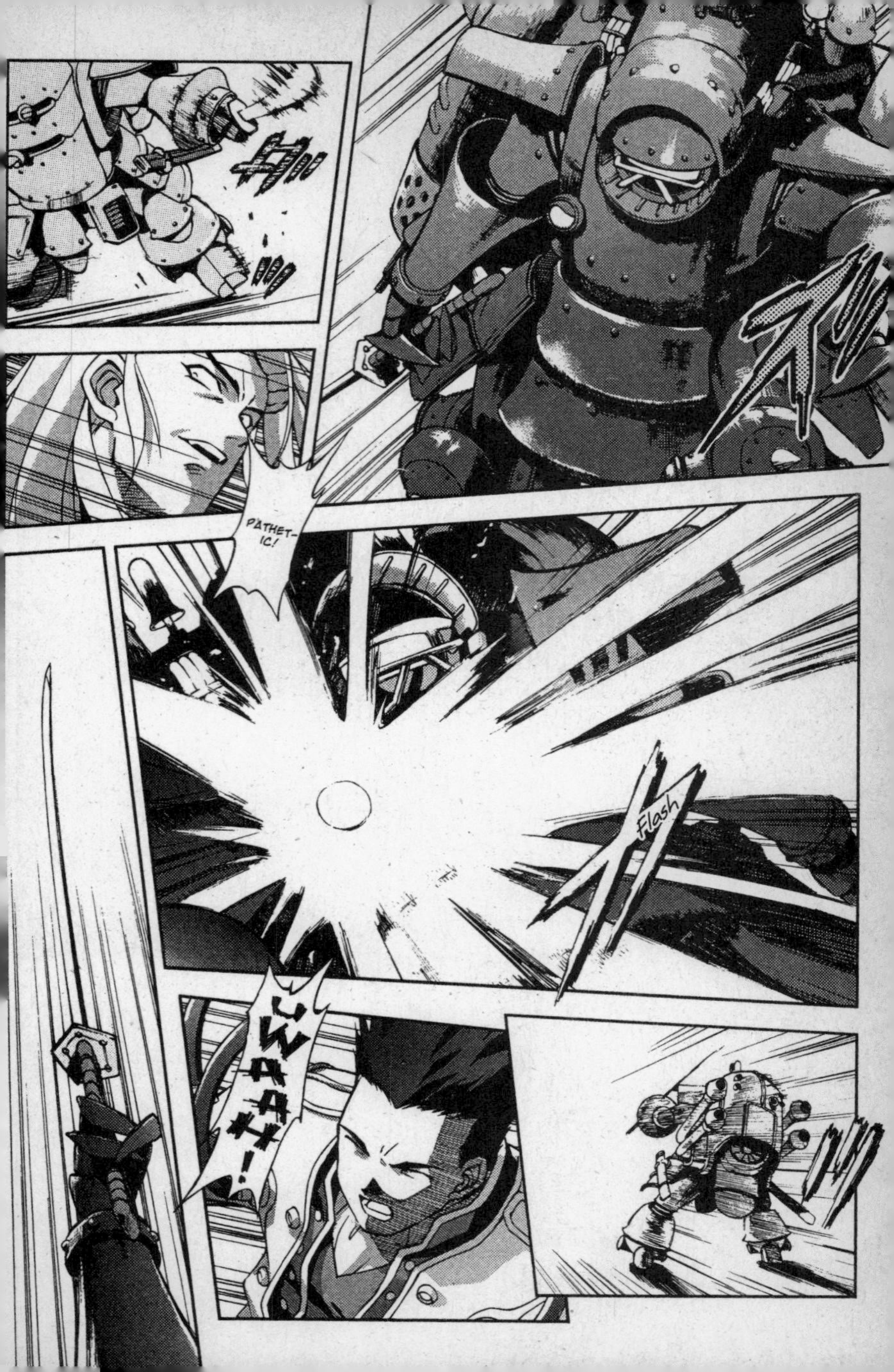
PATHET-IC!
Flash
UWAAH!

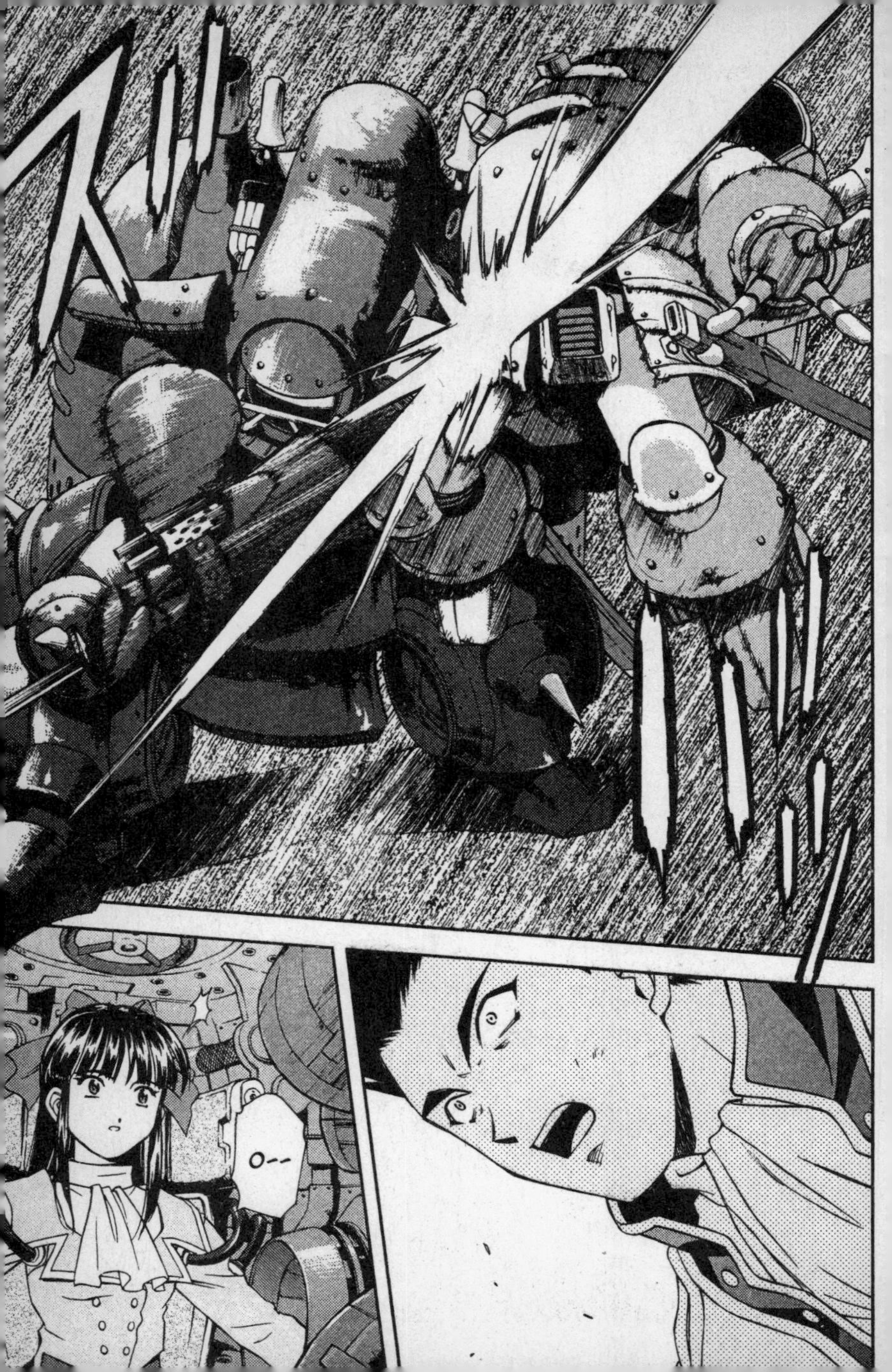
O--

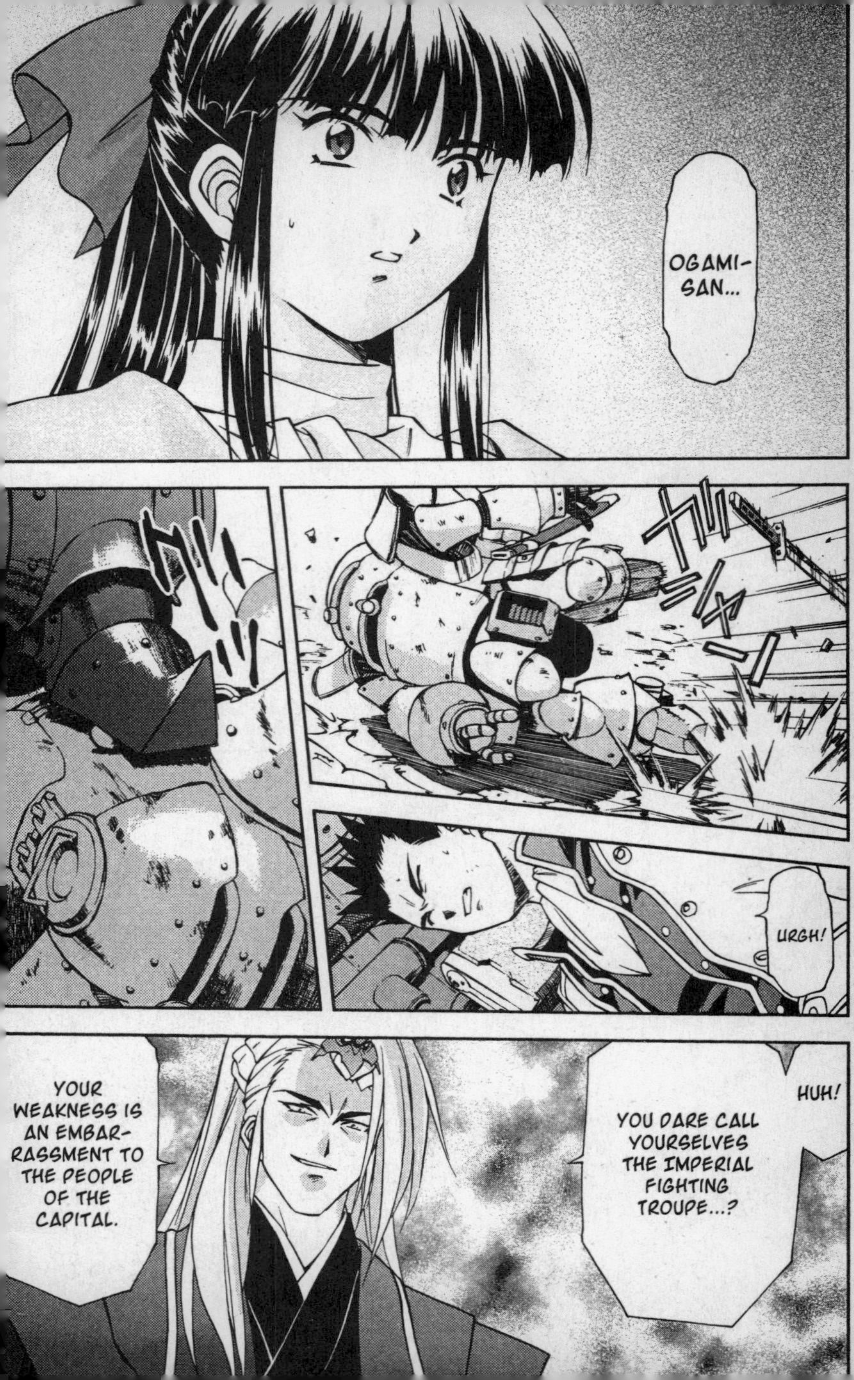
OGAMI-SAN...
URGH!
HUH!
YOU DARE CALL YOURSELVES THE IMPERIAL FIGHTING TROUPE...?
YOUR WEAKNESS IS AN EMBARRASSMENT TO THE PEOPLE OF THE CAPITAL.

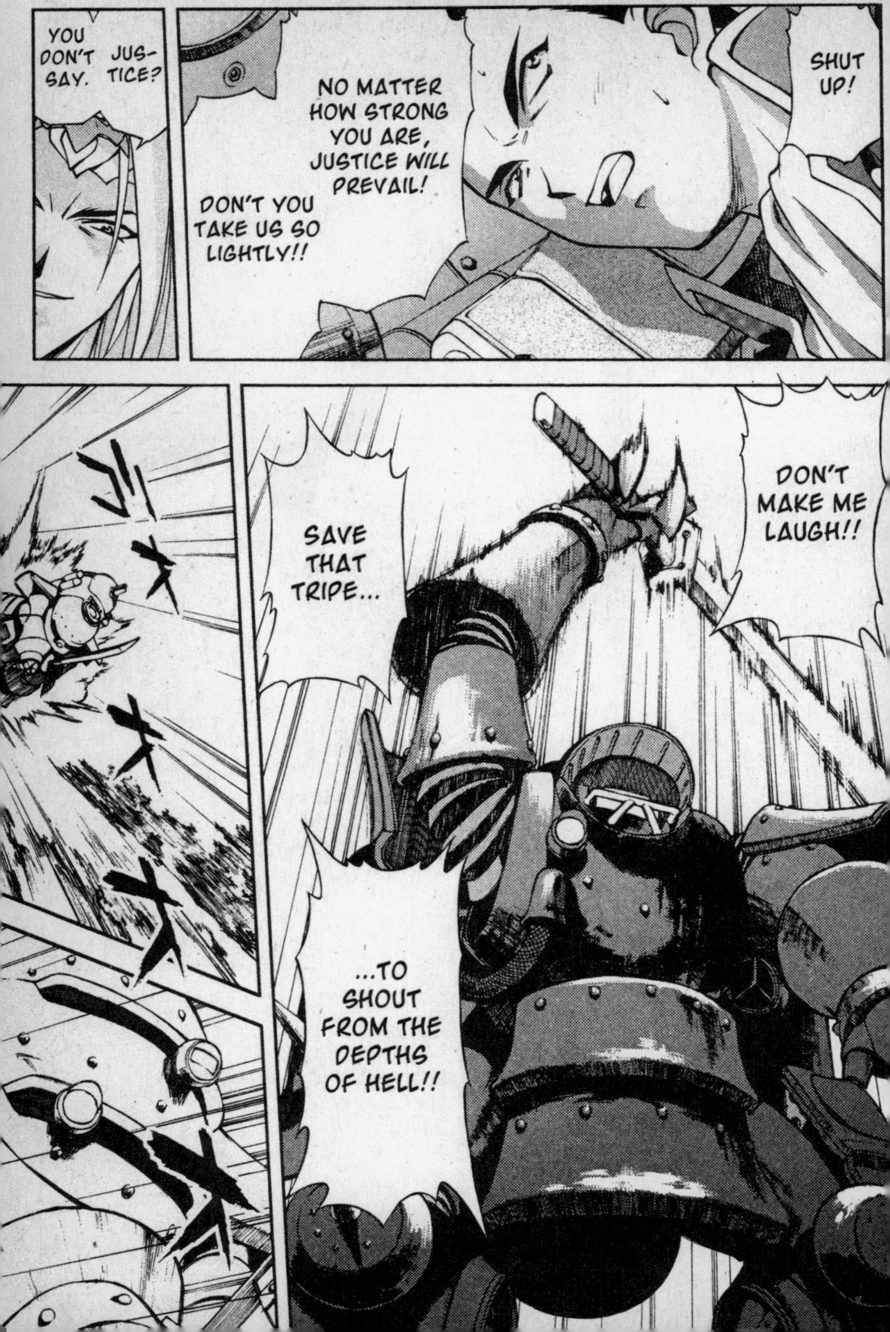
SHUT UP!
NO MATTER HOW STRONG YOU ARE, JUSTICE WILL PREVAIL!
DON'T YOU TAKE US SO LIGHTLY!!
JUS-TICE?
YOU DON'T SAY.
DON'T MAKE ME LAUGH!!
SAVE THAT TRIPE...
...TO SHOUT FROM THE DEPTHS OF HELL!!

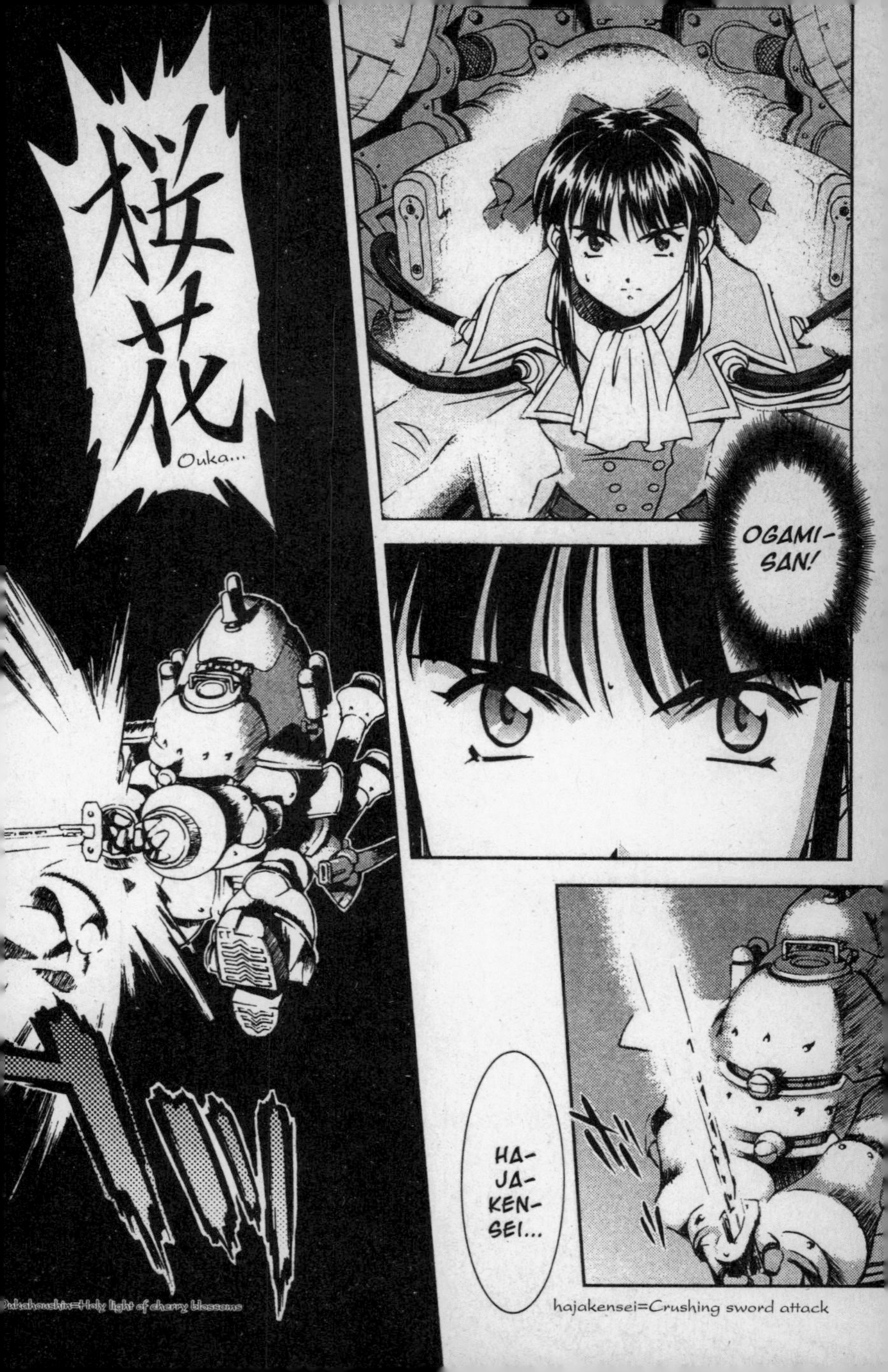
OGAMI-SAN!
HA-JA-KEN-SEI...
hajakensei=Crushing sword attack
桜花
Ouka...
Oukahoushin=Holy light of cherry blossoms

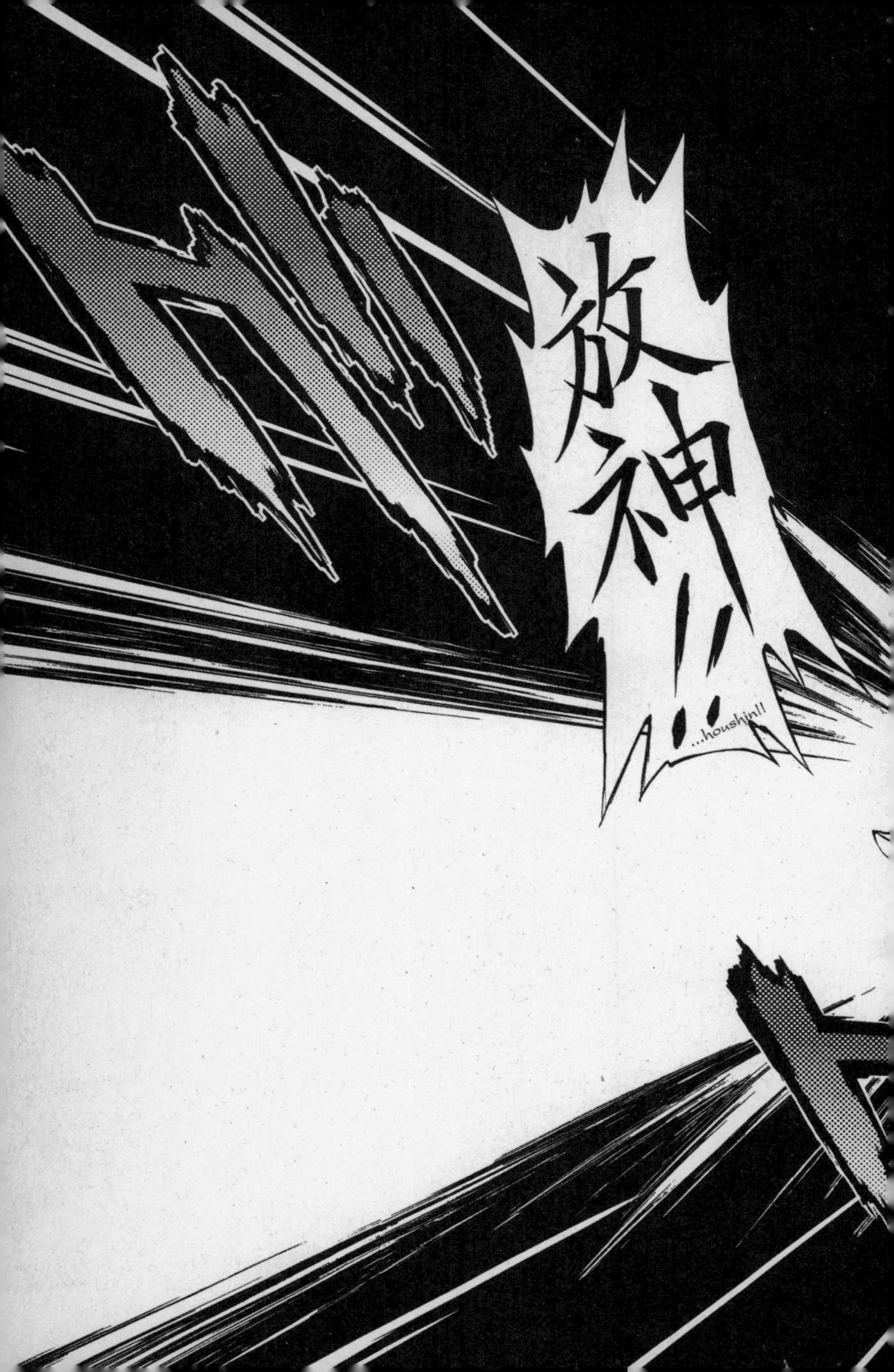

放神!!!
...houshin!!

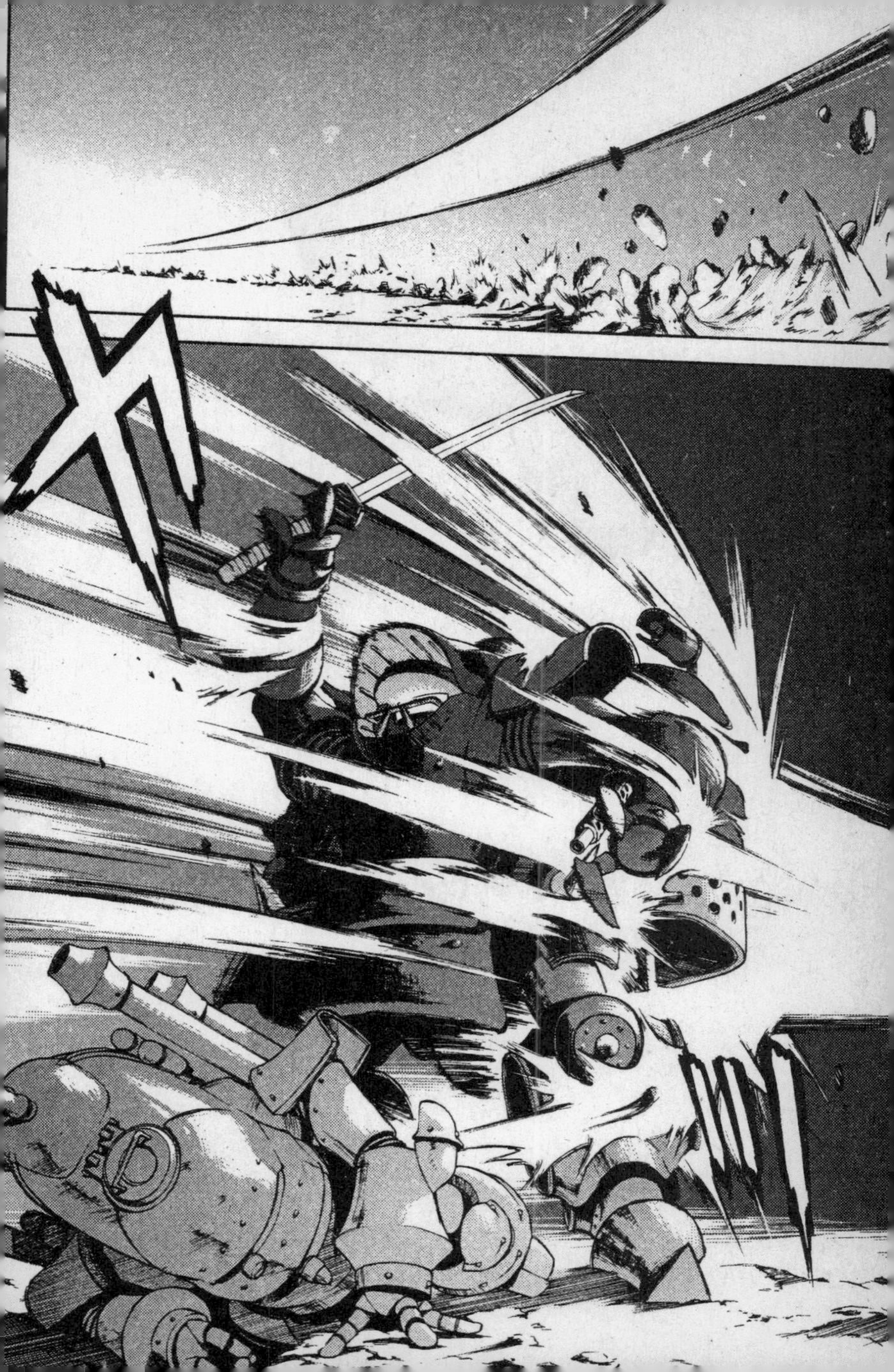

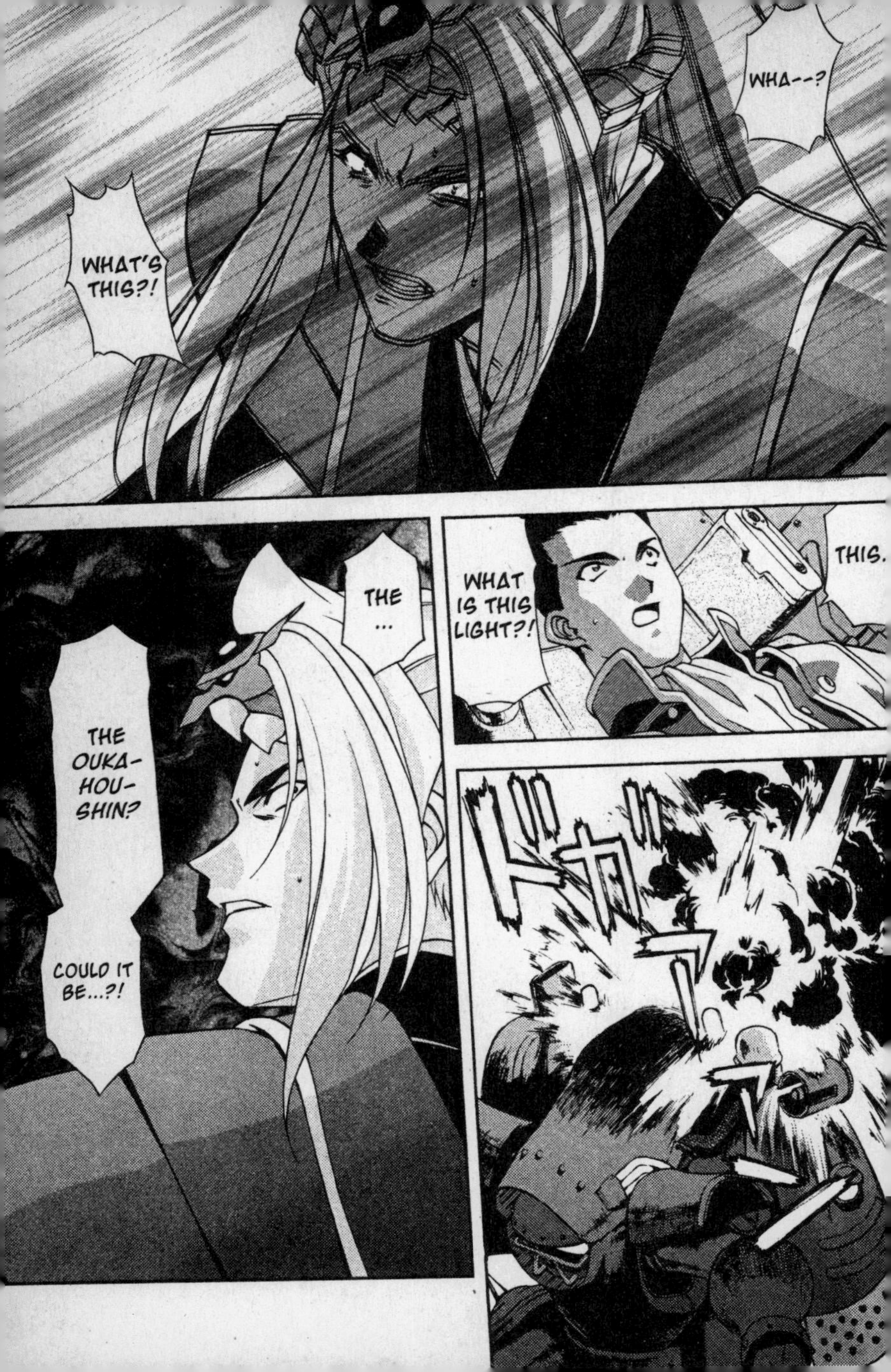
WHA--?
WHAT'S THIS?!
THIS.
WHAT IS THIS LIGHT?!
THE ...
THE OUKA-HOUSHIN?
COULD IT BE...?!

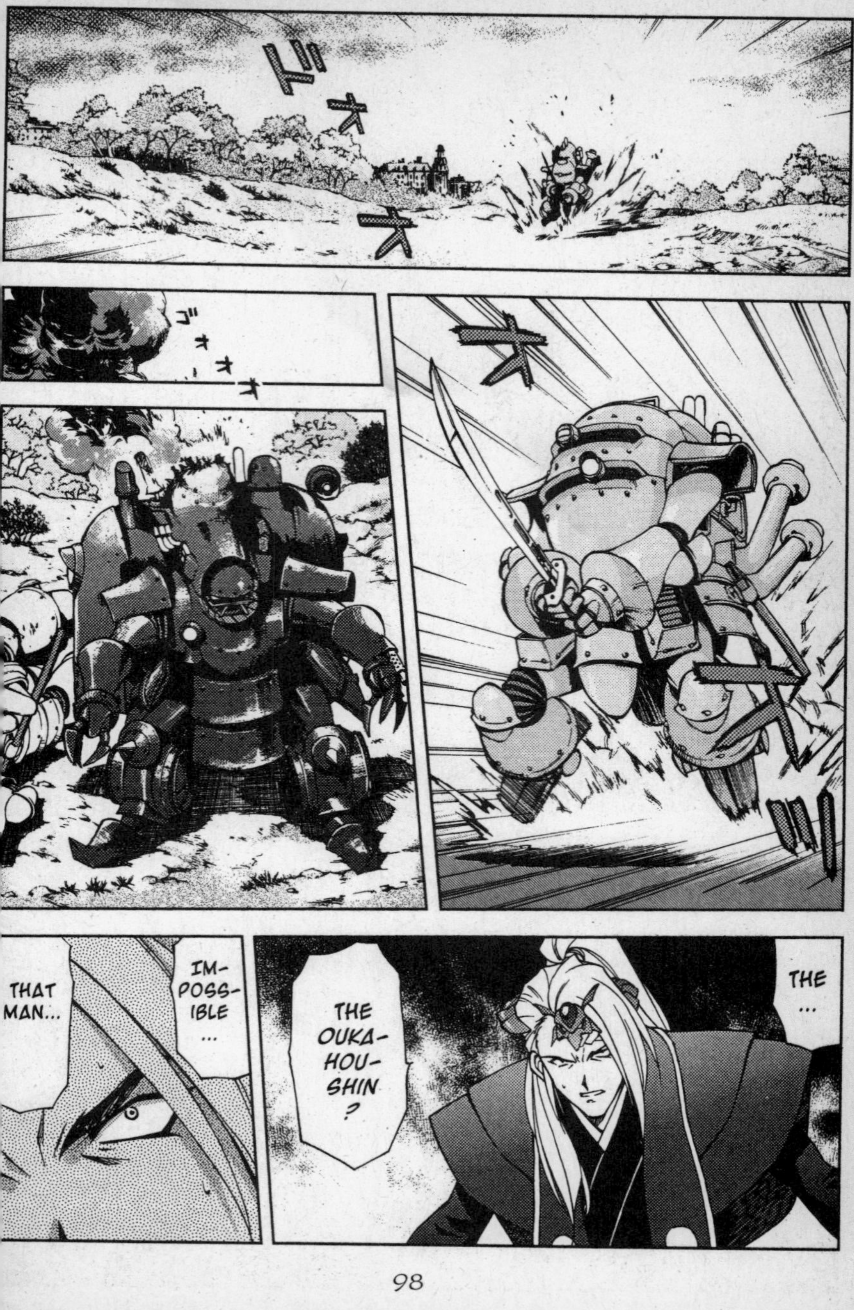
THE ...
THE OUKA-HOUSHIN ?
IM-POSS-IBLE ...
THAT MAN...

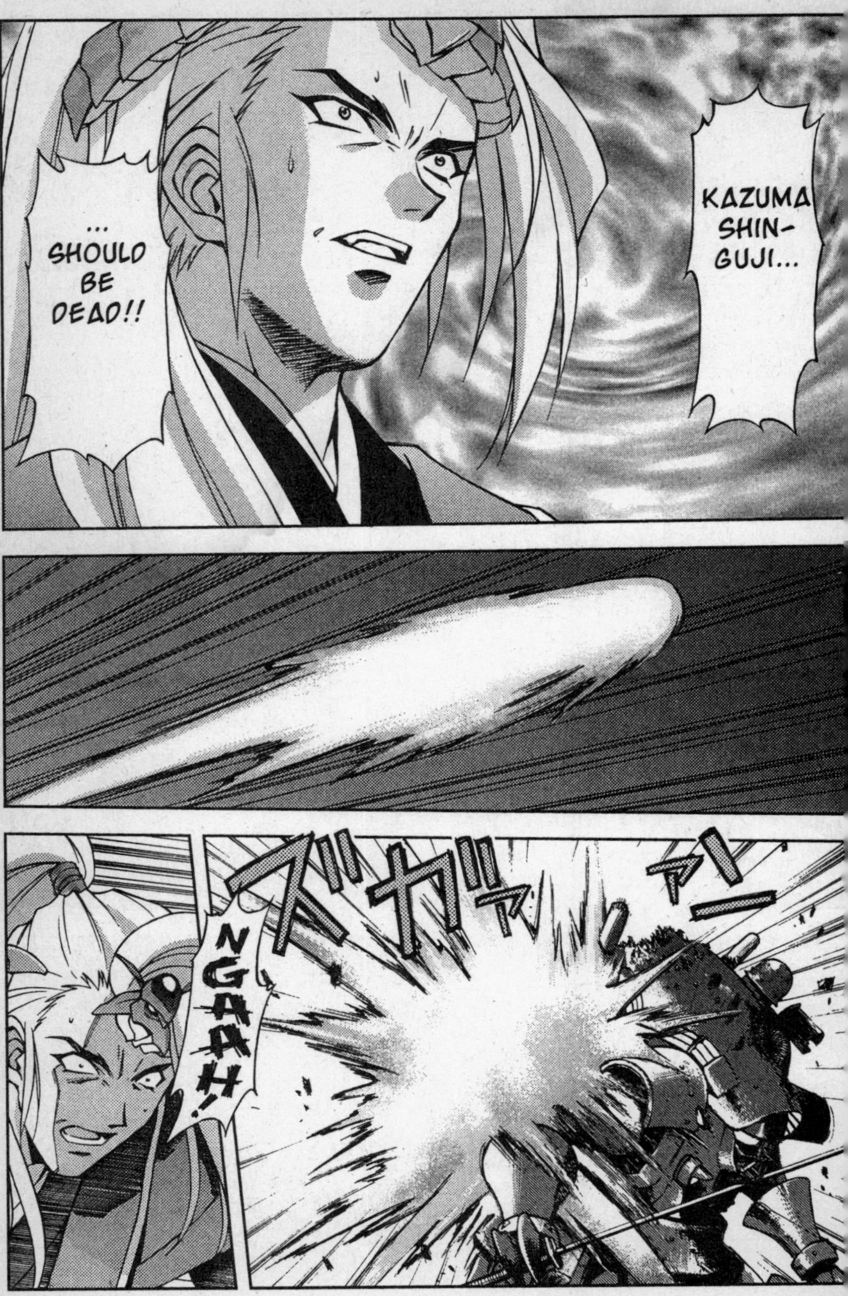
KAZUMA SHIN-GUJI...
... SHOULD BE DEAD!!
NGAH!

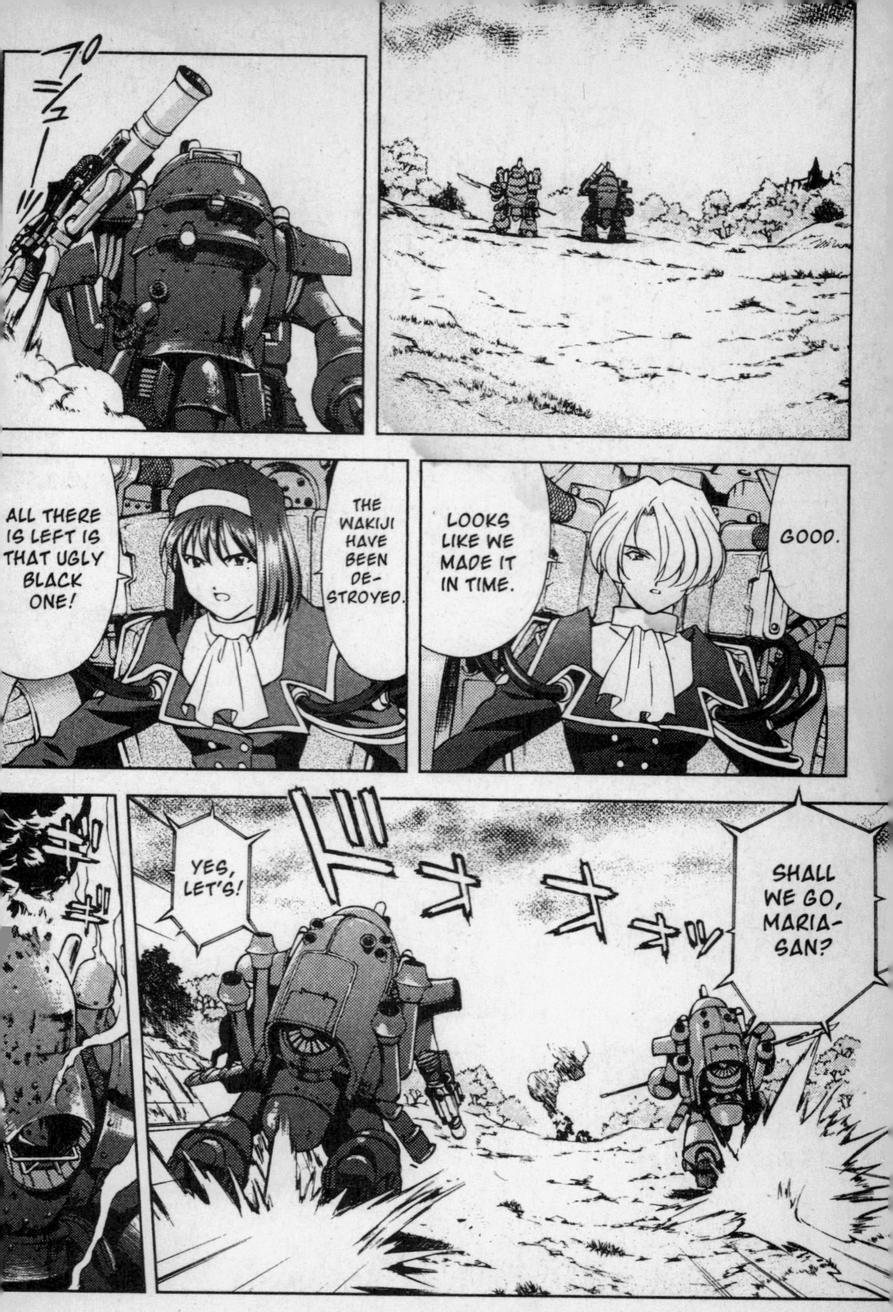
GOOD.
LOOKS LIKE WE MADE IT IN TIME.
THE WAKIJI HAVE BEEN DE-STROYED.
ALL THERE IS LEFT IS THAT UGLY BLACK ONE!
SHALL WE GO, MARIA-SAN?
YES, LET'S!

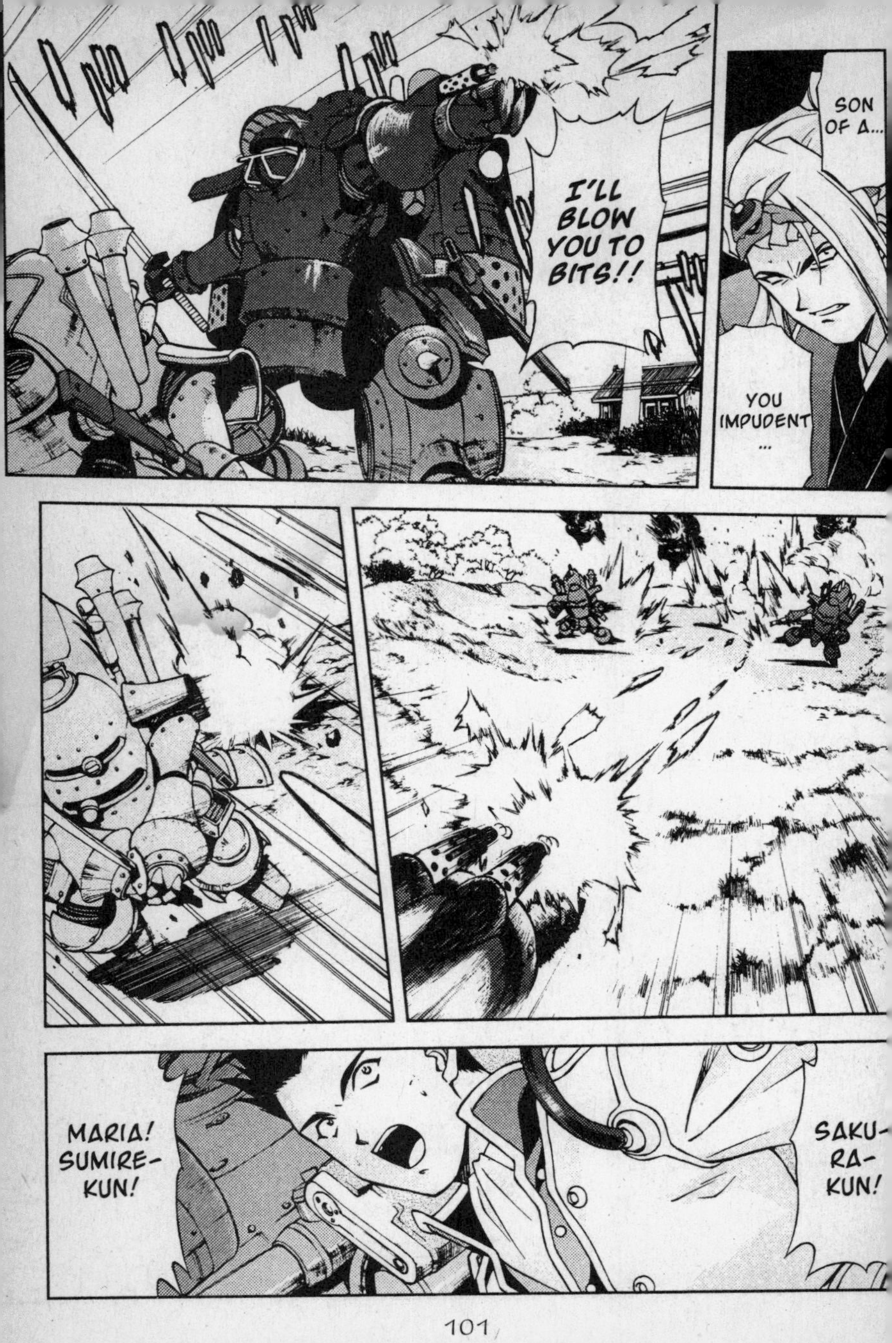
SON OF A...
YOU IMPUDENT ...
I'LL BLOW YOU TO BITS!!
SAKU-RA-KUN!
MARIA! SUMIRE-KUN!

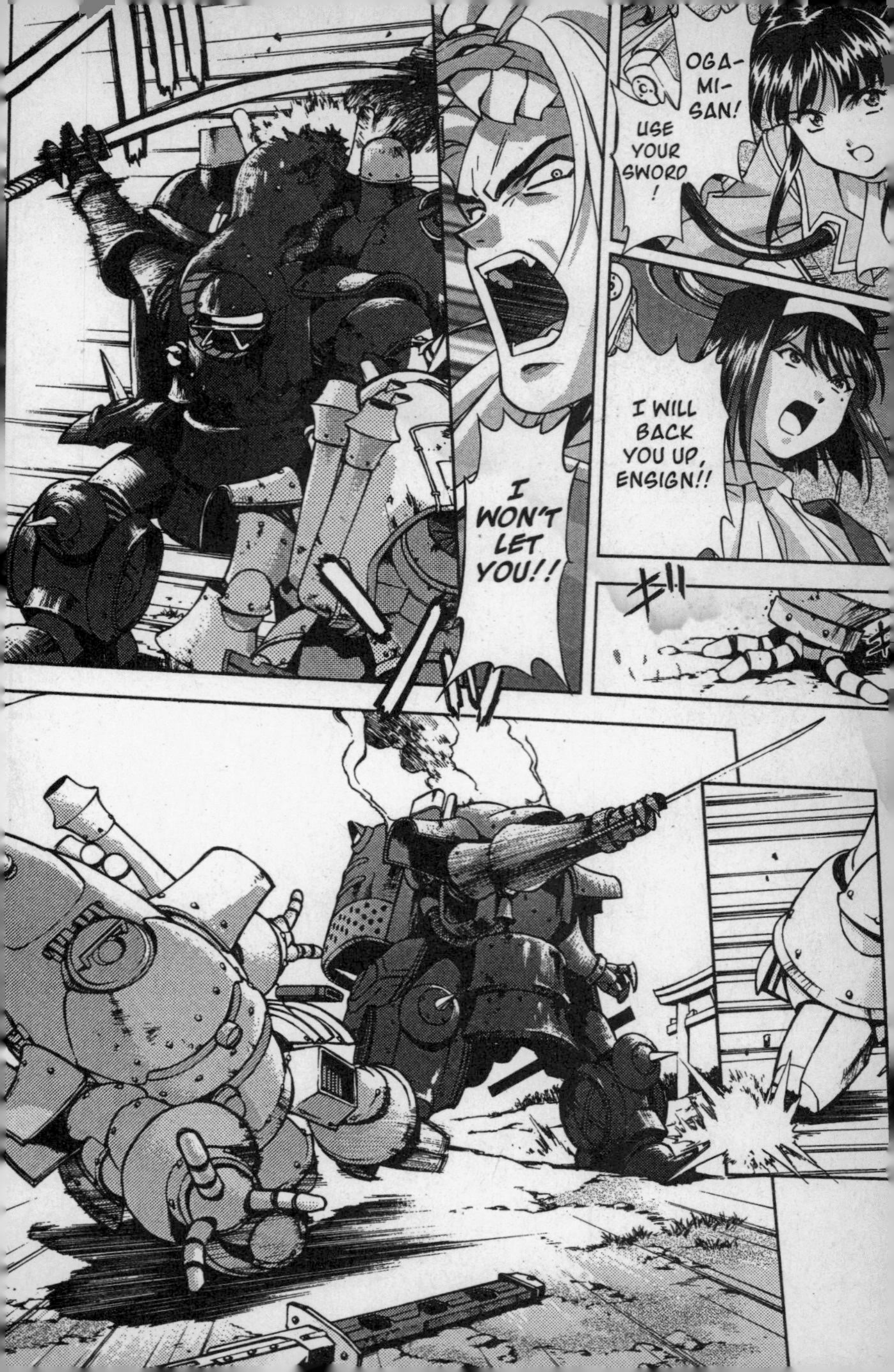
OGA-MI-SAN!
USE YOUR SWORD!
I WILL BACK YOU UP, ENSIGN!!
I WON'T LET YOU!!

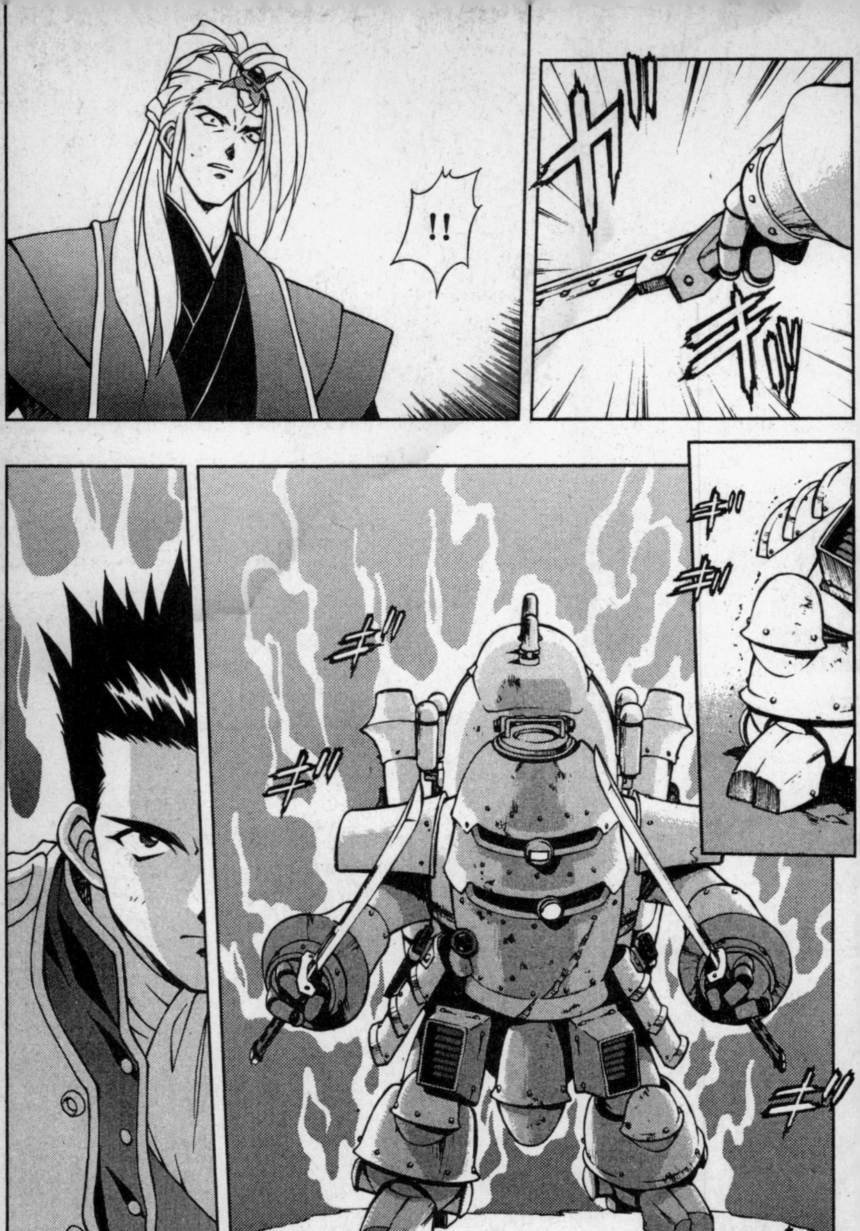
!!

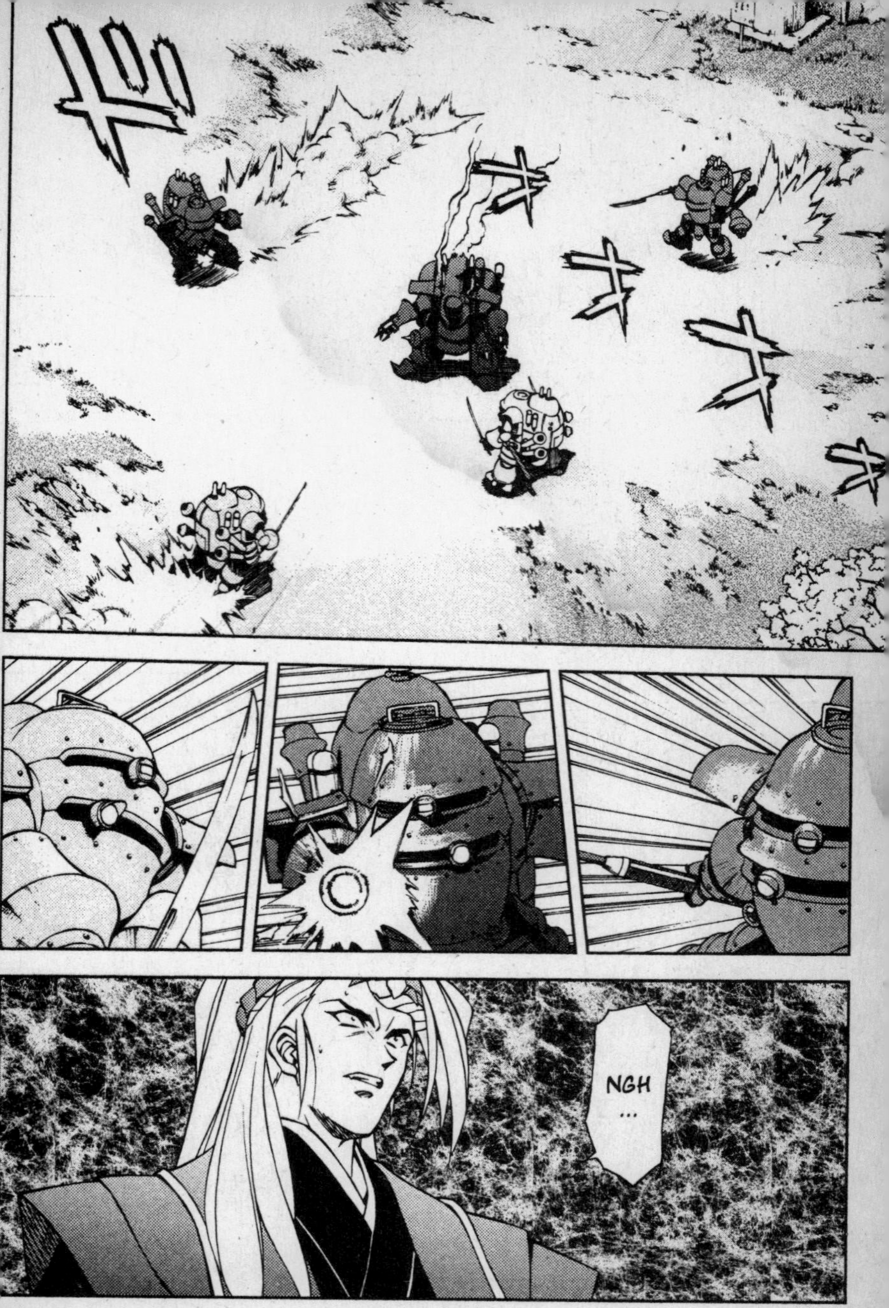
NGH ...

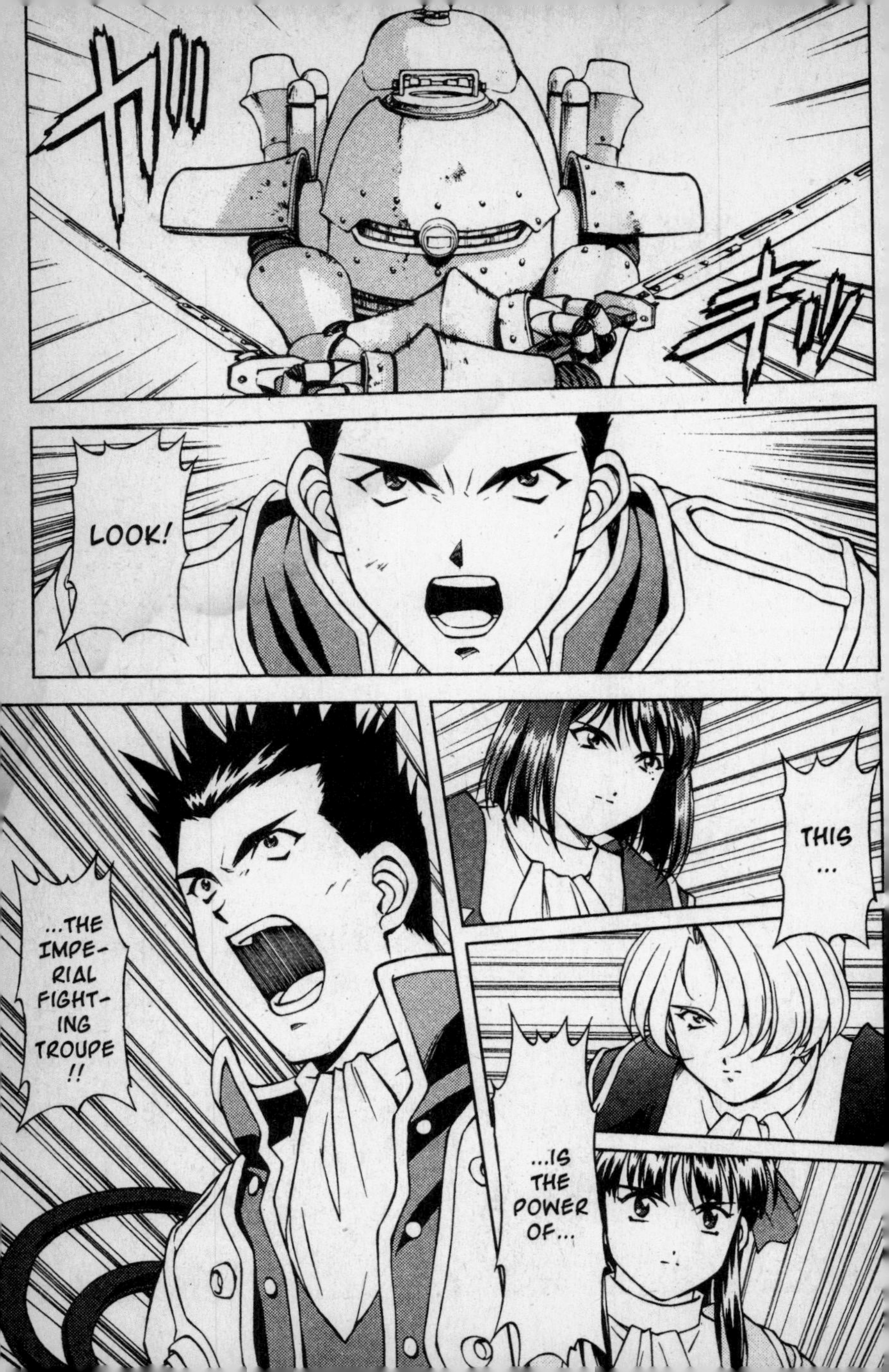
LOOK!
THIS ...
...IS THE POWER OF...
...THE IMPE-RIAL FIGHT-ING TROUPE !!

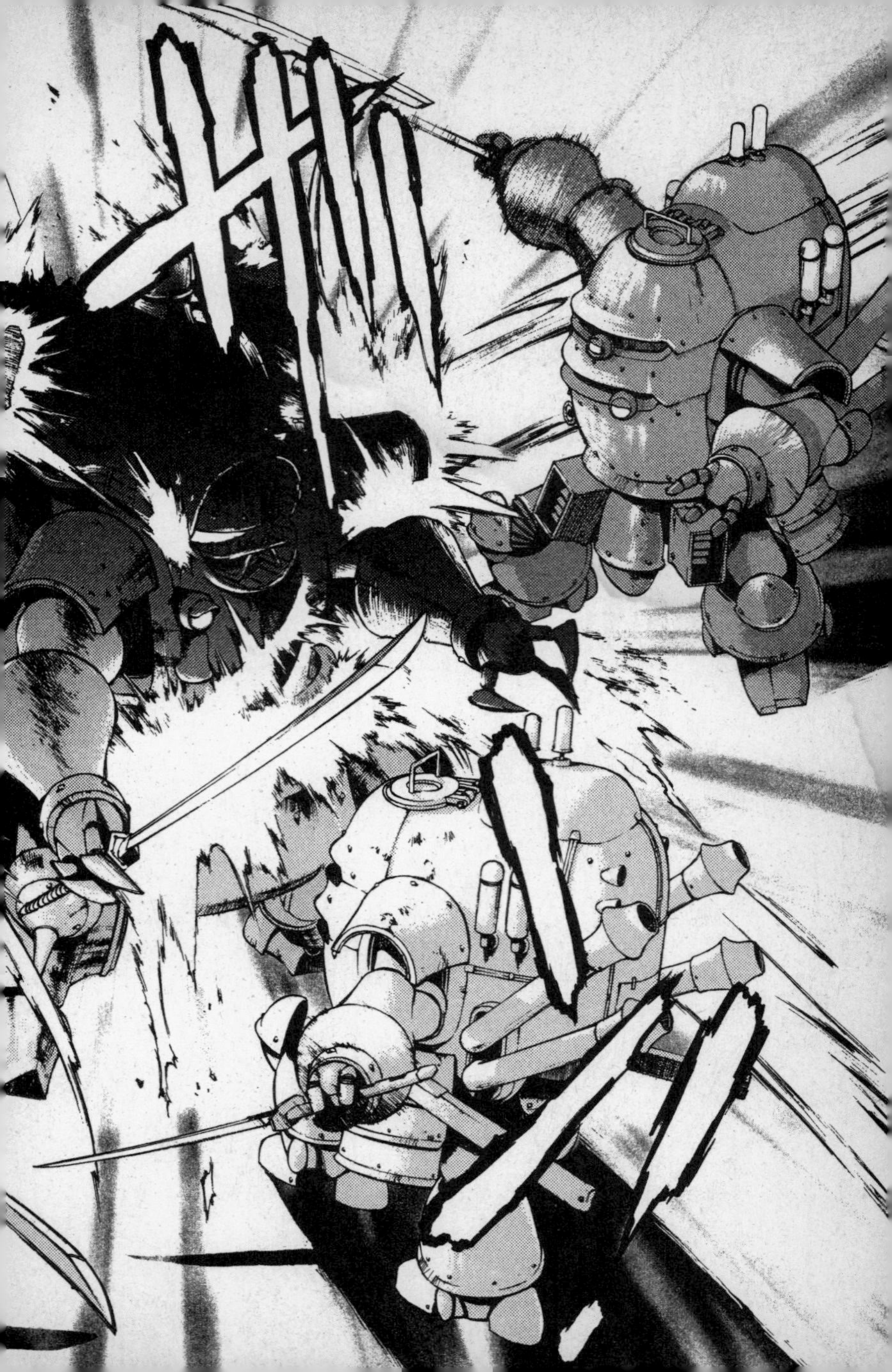

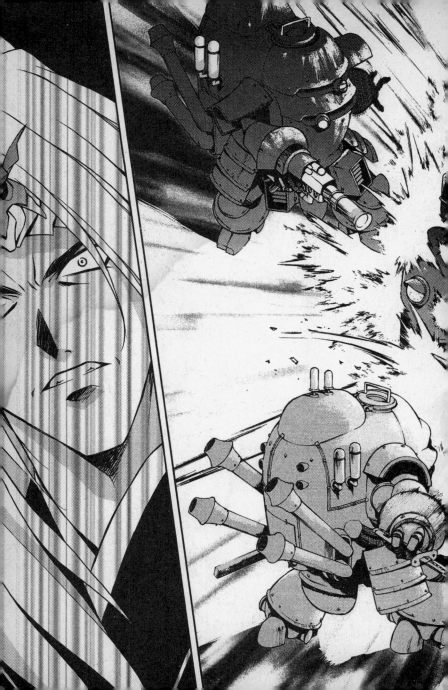

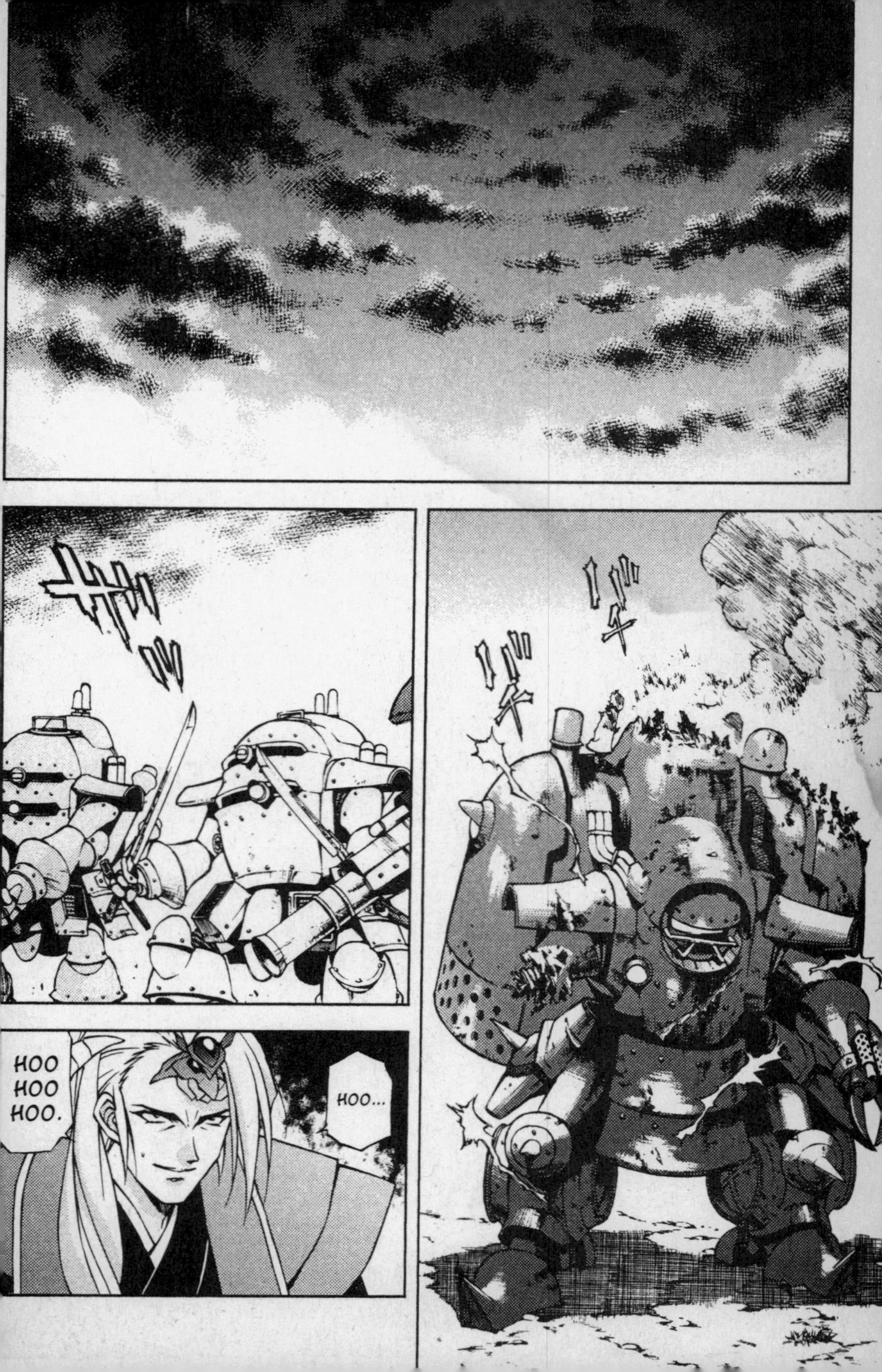
HOO...
HOO HOO HOO.

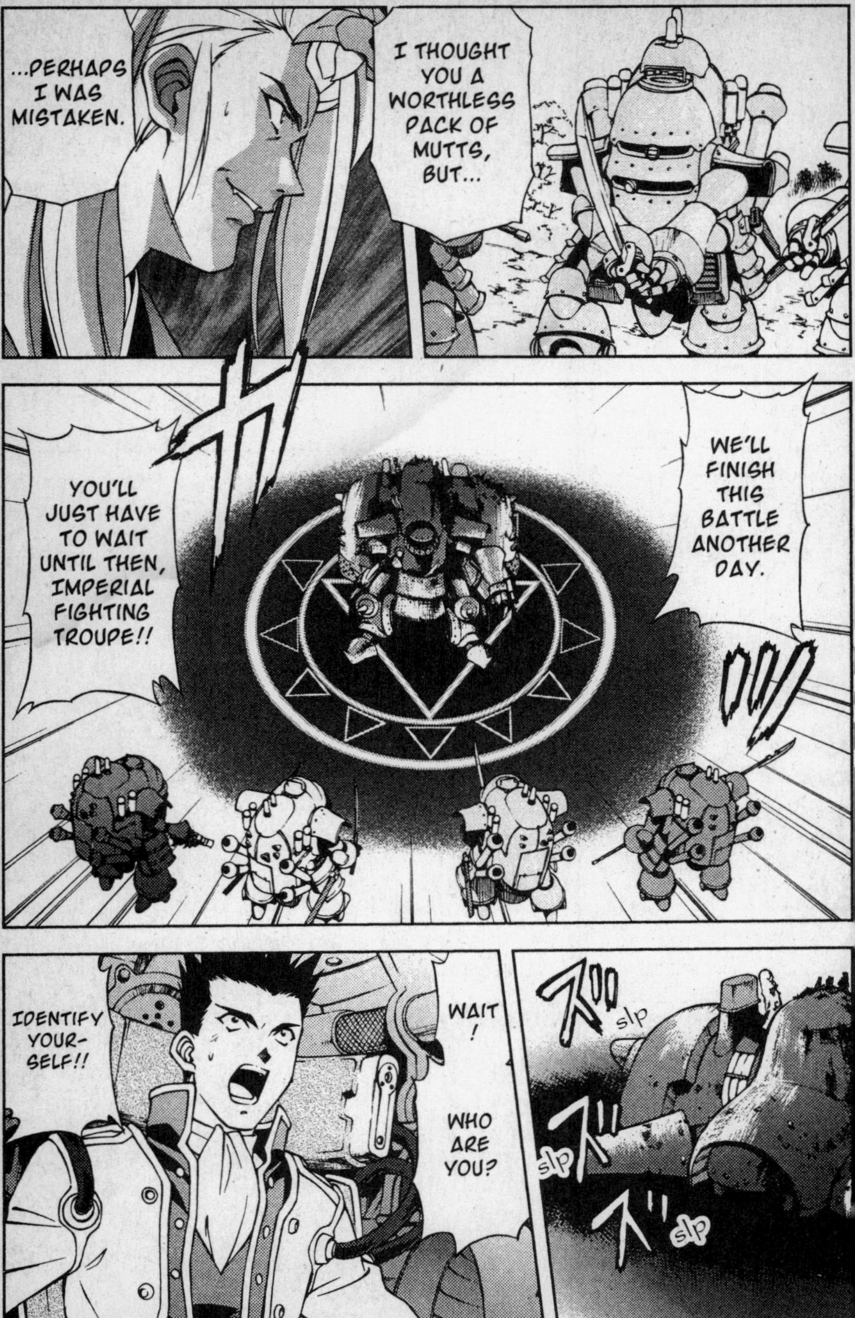
I THOUGHT YOU A WORTHLESS PACK OF MUTTS, BUT...
...PERHAPS I WAS MISTAKEN.
WE'LL FINISH THIS BATTLE ANOTHER DAY.
YOU'LL JUST HAVE TO WAIT UNTIL THEN, IMPERIAL FIGHTING TROUPE!!
slp
slp
slp
WAIT!
WHO ARE YOU?
IDENTIFY YOUR-SELF!!

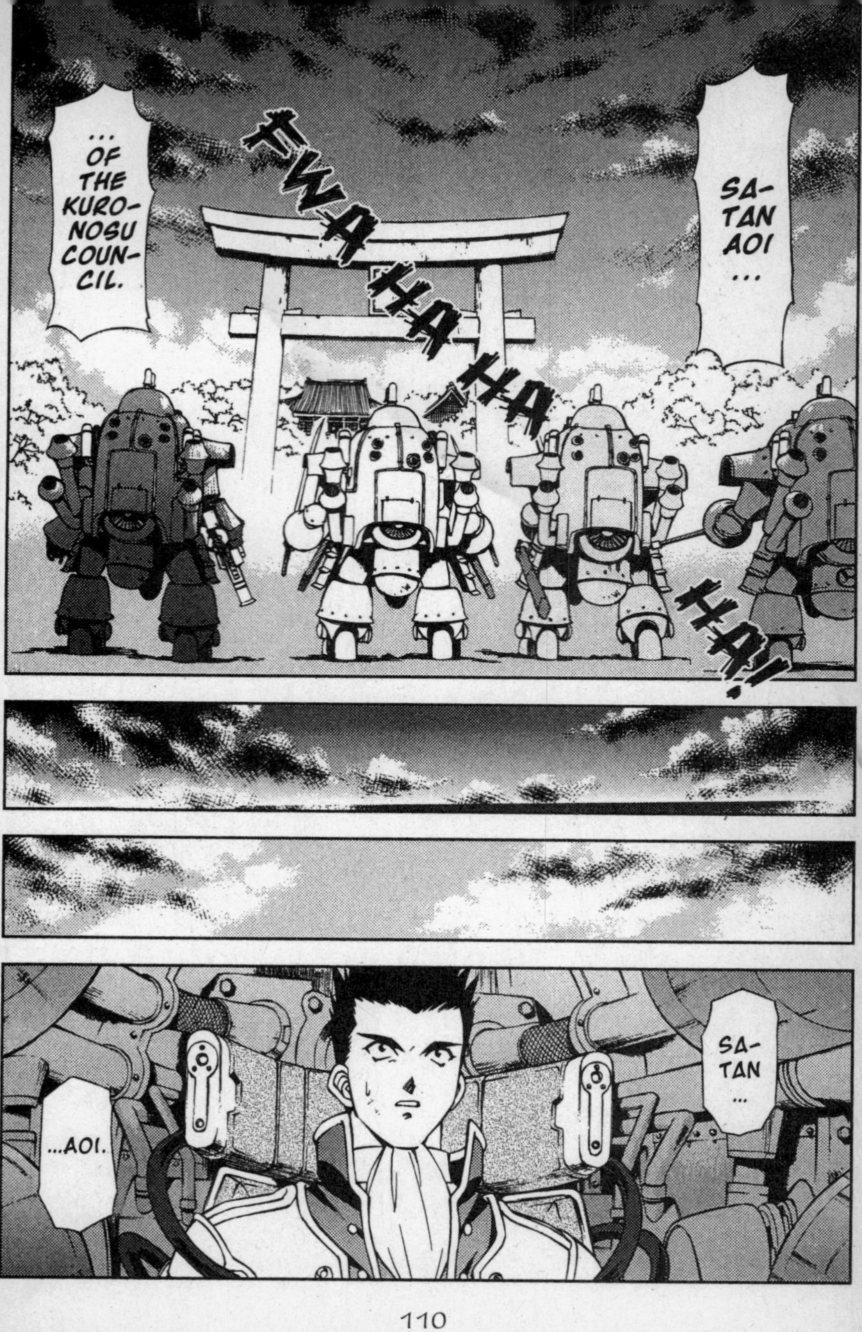
SA-TAN AOI ...
... OF THE KURO-NOSU COUN-CIL.
FWA HA HA HA HA!!
SA-TAN ...
...AOI.

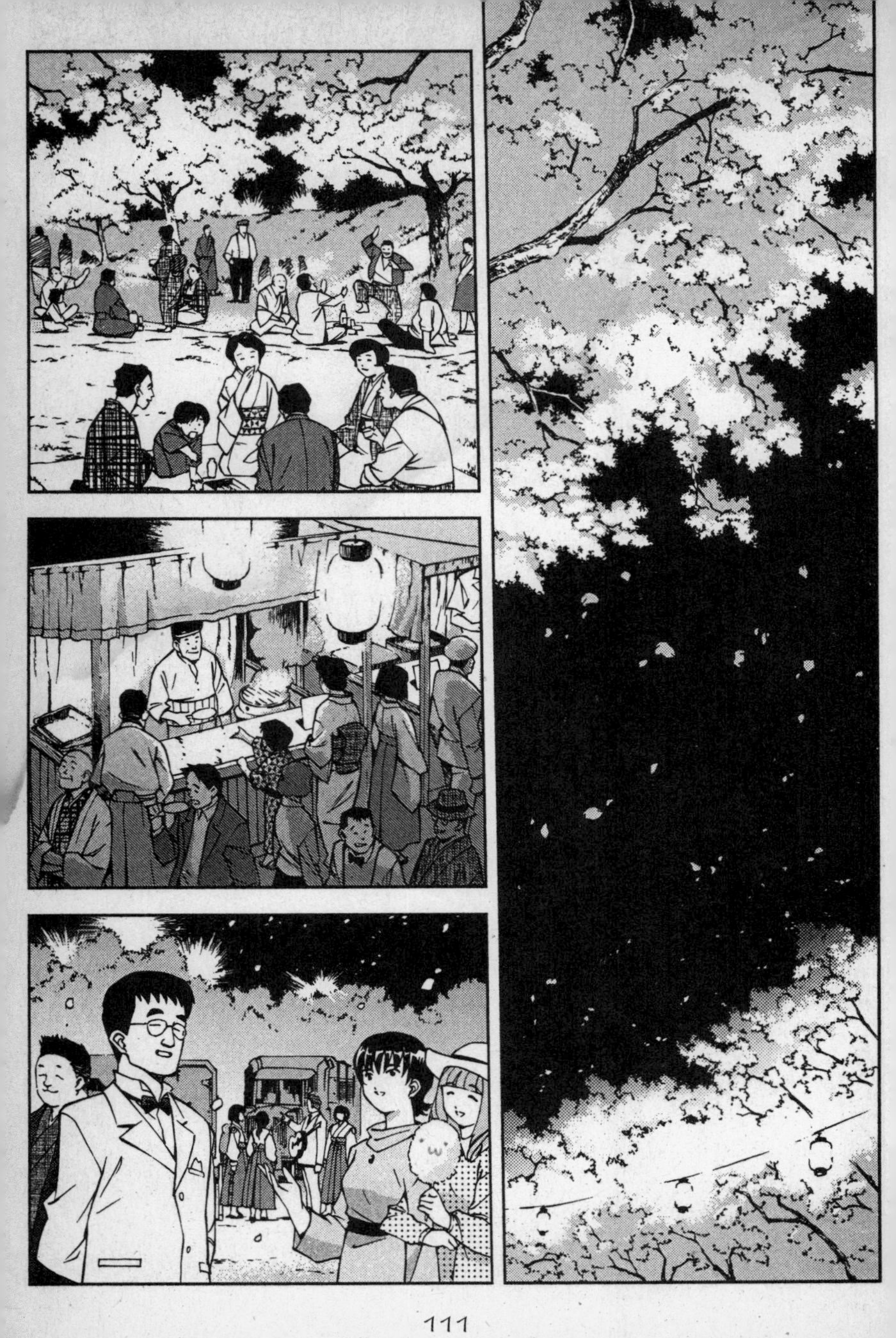

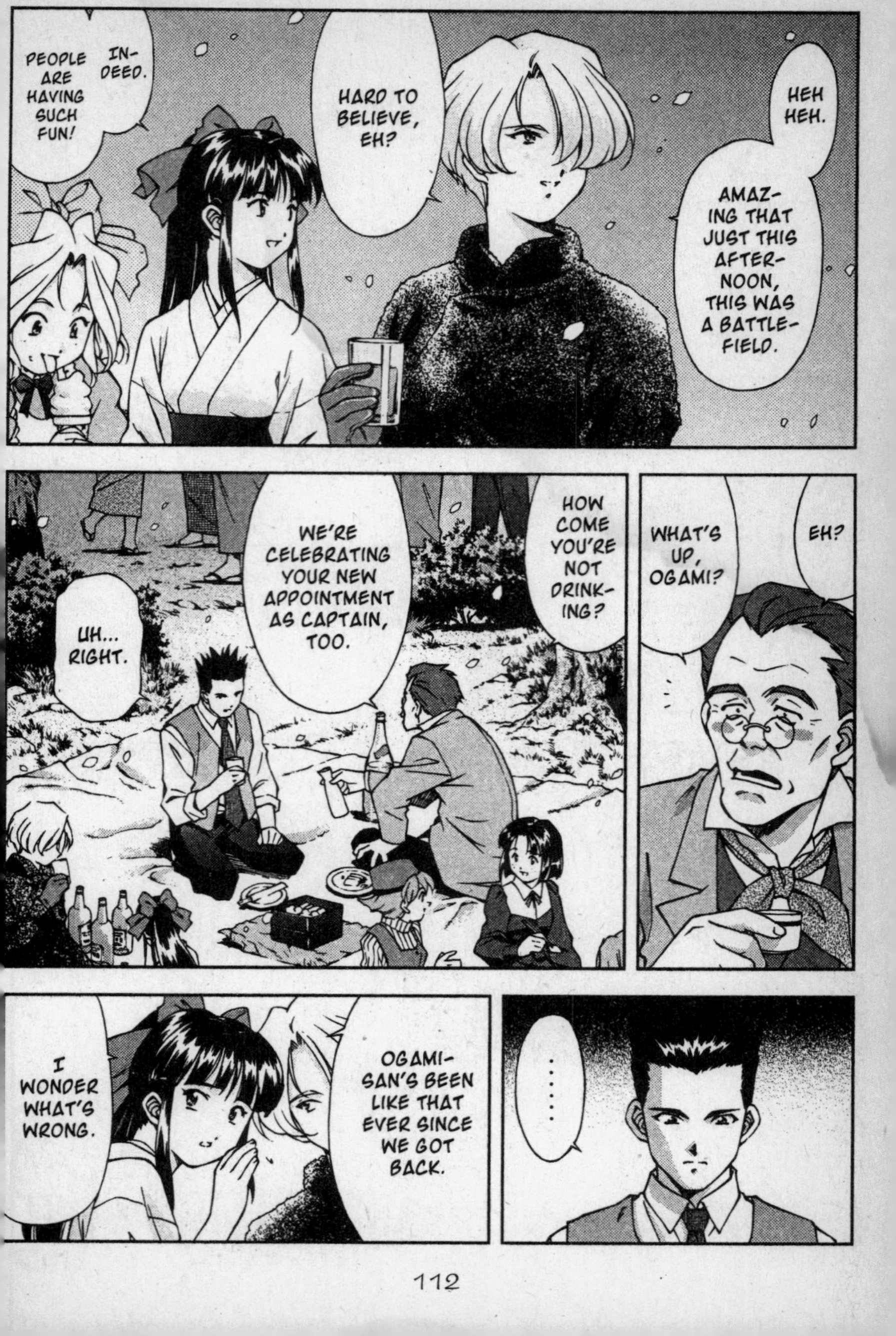
HEH HEH.
AMAZ-ING THAT JUST THIS AFTER-NOON, THIS WAS A BATTLE-FIELD.
HARD TO BELIEVE, EH?
IN-DEED.
PEOPLE ARE HAVING SUCH FUN!
EH?
WHAT'S UP, OGAMI?
HOW COME YOU'RE NOT DRINK-ING?
WE'RE CELEBRATING YOUR NEW APPOINTMENT AS CAPTAIN, TOO.
UH... RIGHT.
......
OGAMI-SAN'S BEEN LIKE THAT EVER SINCE WE GOT BACK.
I WONDER WHAT'S WRONG.

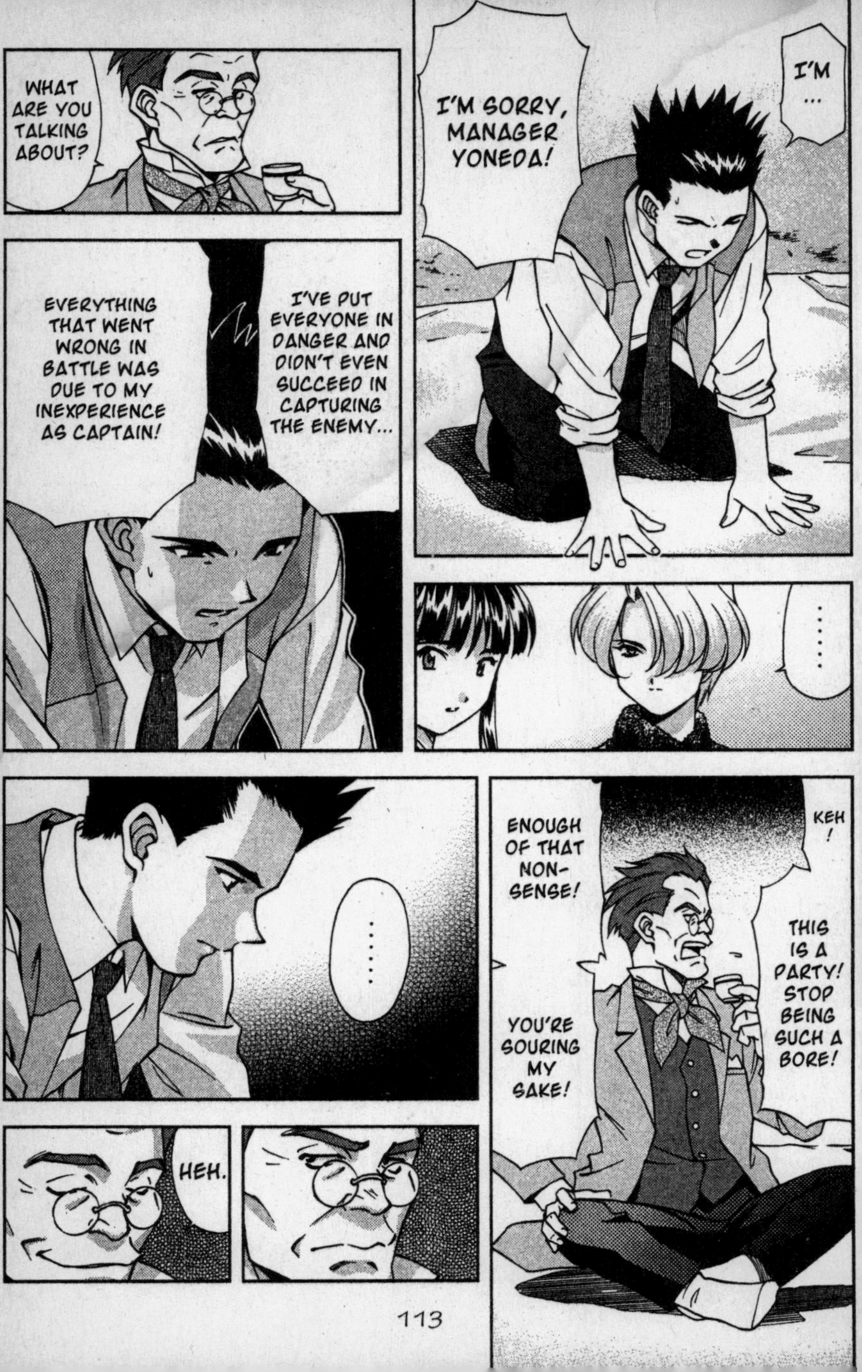

I'M ...
I'M SORRY, MANAGER YONEDA!
WHAT ARE YOU TALKING ABOUT?
I'VE PUT EVERYONE IN DANGER AND DIDN'T EVEN SUCCEED IN CAPTURING THE ENEMY...
EVERYTHING THAT WENT WRONG IN BATTLE WAS DUE TO MY INEXPERIENCE AS CAPTAIN!
......
KEH!
ENOUGH OF THAT NON-SENSE!
THIS IS A PARTY! STOP BEING SUCH A BORE!
YOU'RE SOURING MY SAKE!
......
HEH.

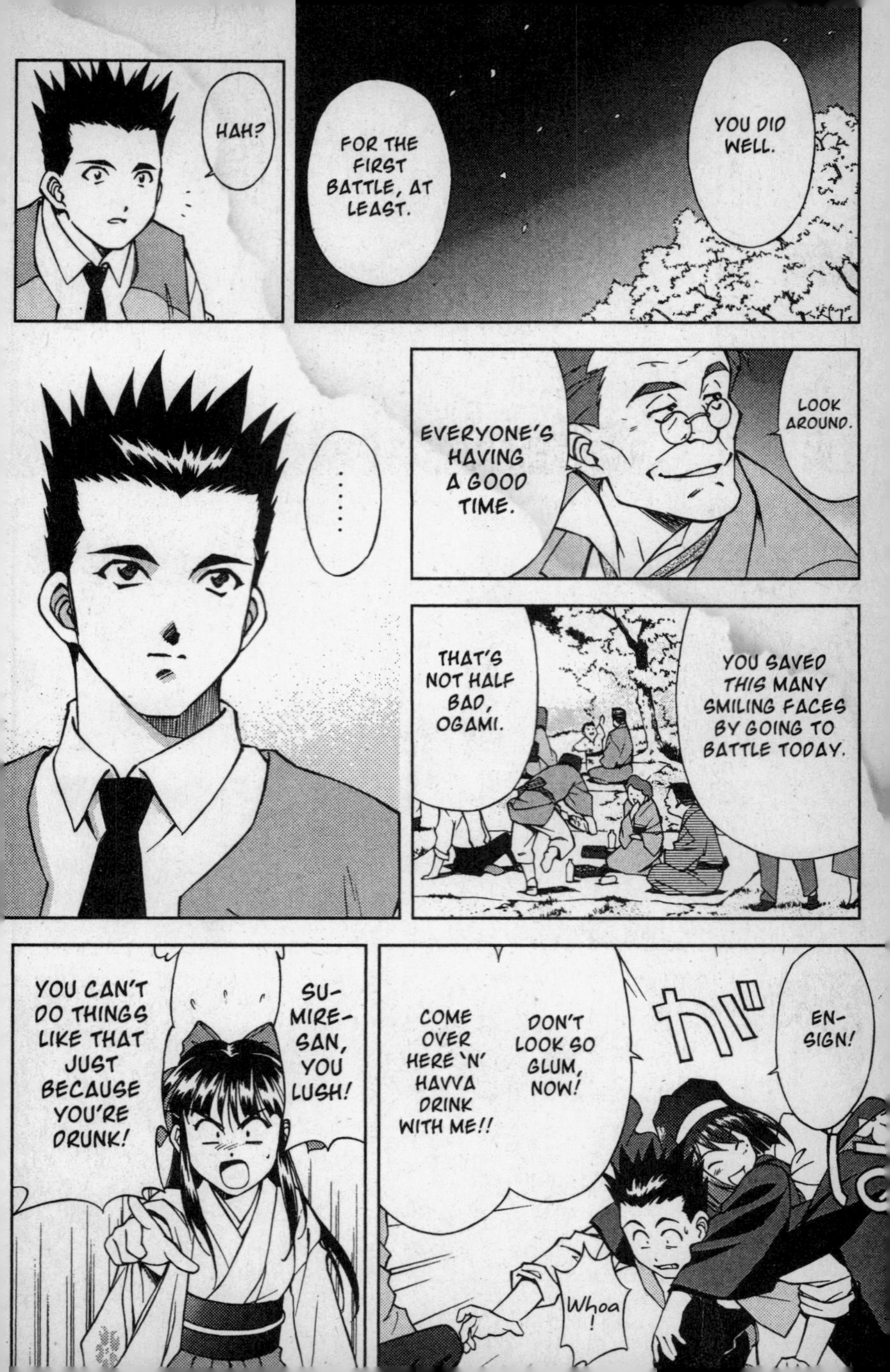
YOU DID WELL.
FOR THE FIRST BATTLE, AT LEAST.
HAH?
LOOK AROUND.
EVERYONE'S HAVING A GOOD TIME.
YOU SAVED THIS MANY SMILING FACES BY GOING TO BATTLE TODAY.
THAT'S NOT HALF BAD, OGAMI.
......
EN-SIGN!
ガ
DON'T LOOK SO GLUM, NOW!
COME OVER HERE 'N' HAVVA DRINK WITH ME!!
Whoa!
SU-MIRE-SAN, YOU LUSH!
YOU CAN'T DO THINGS LIKE THAT JUST BECAUSE YOU'RE DRUNK!

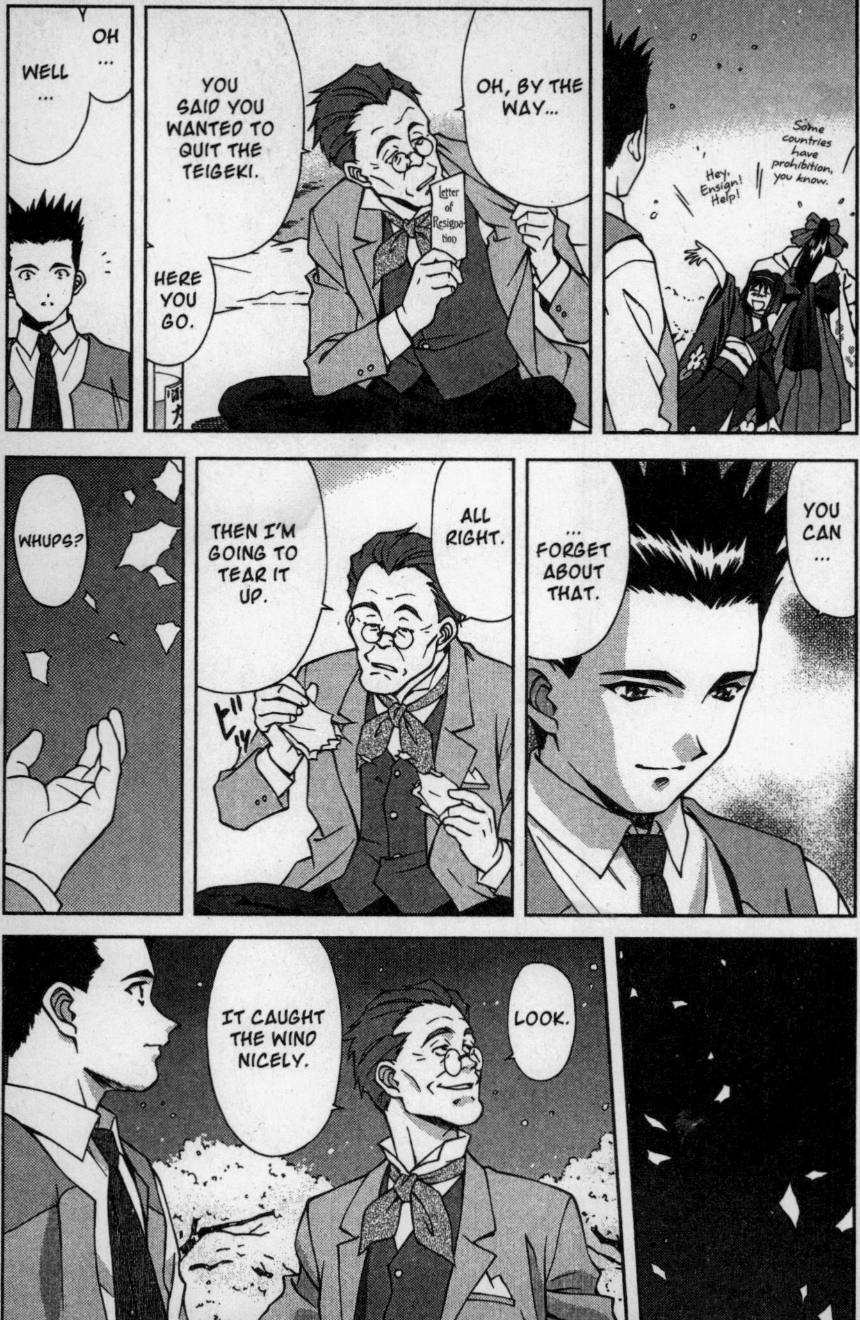
Some countries have prohibition, you know.
Hey, Ensign! Help!
OH, BY THE WAY...
YOU SAID YOU WANTED TO QUIT THE TEIGEKI.
Letter of Resignation
HERE YOU GO.
OH ...
WELL ...
YOU CAN ...
... FORGET ABOUT THAT.
ALL RIGHT.
THEN I'M GOING TO TEAR IT UP.
WHUPS?
LOOK.
IT CAUGHT THE WIND NICELY.

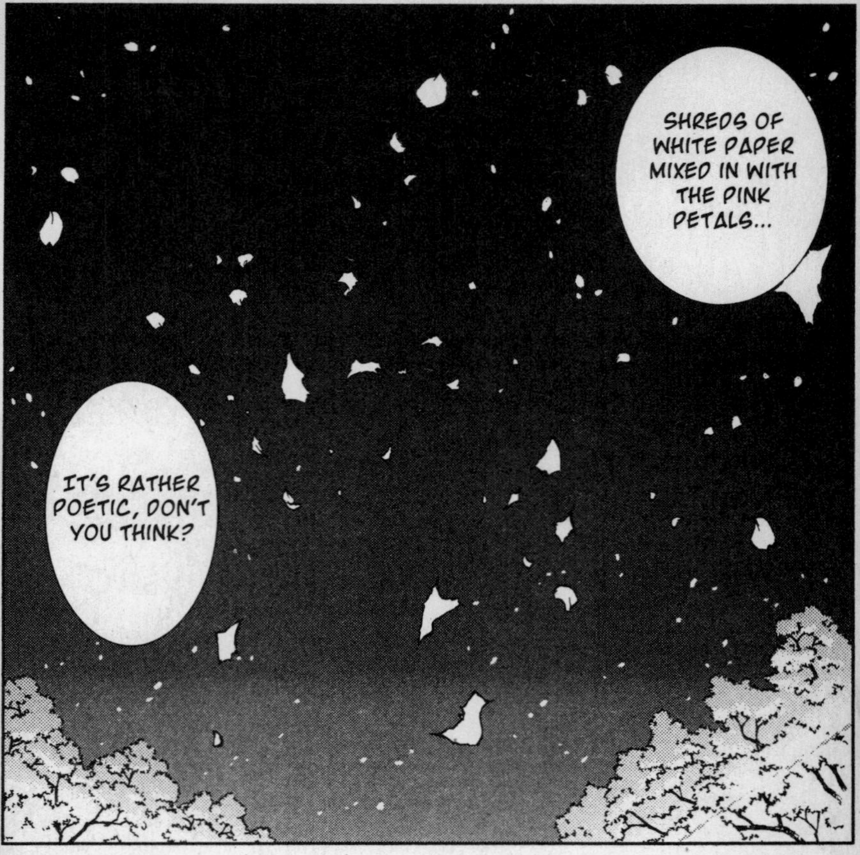
SHREDS OF WHITE PAPER MIXED IN WITH THE PINK PETALS...
IT'S RATHER POETIC, DON'T YOU THINK?

Imperial Fighting Troupe, Go Forth—End of Act

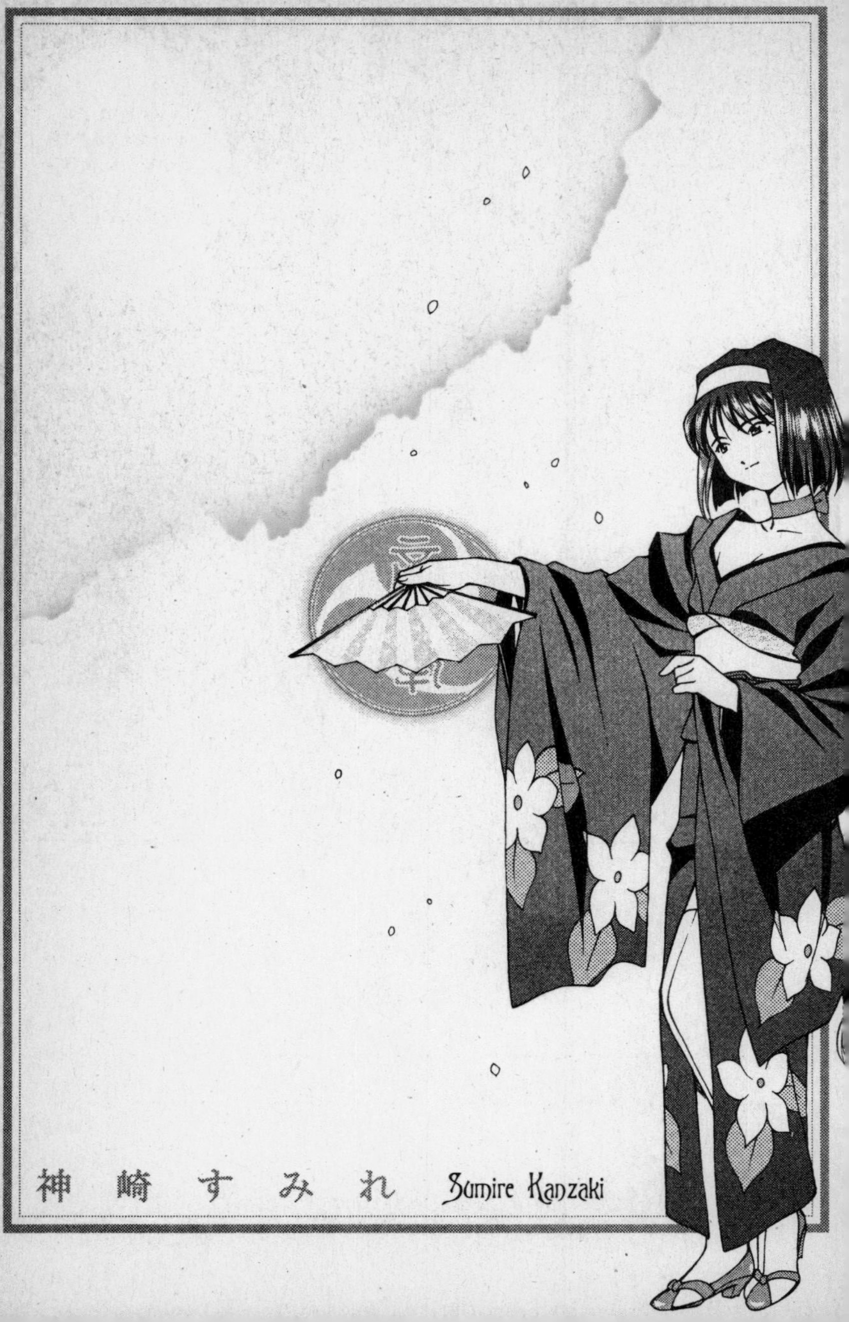
神 崎 す み れ Sumire Kanzaki

さくら＆アイリス Sakura and Iris

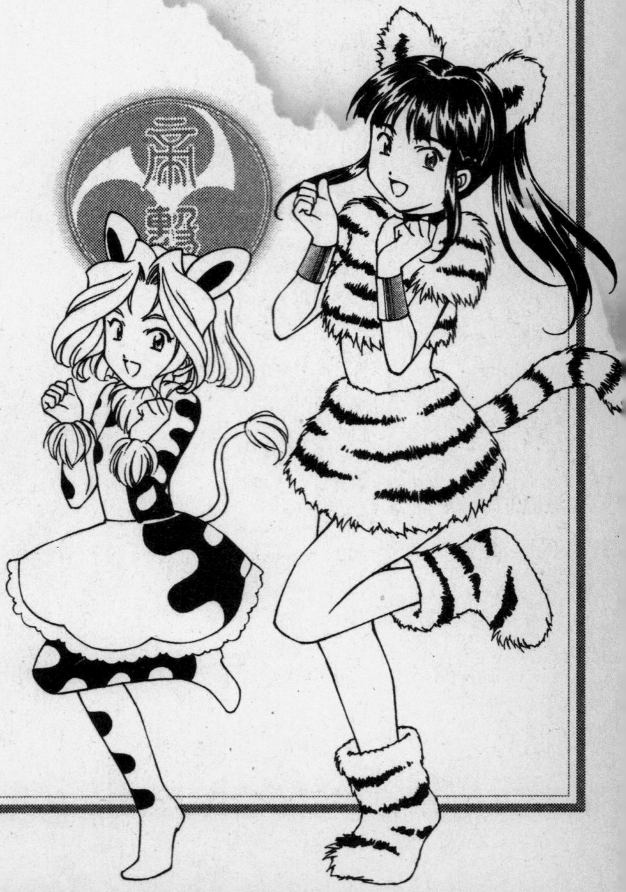

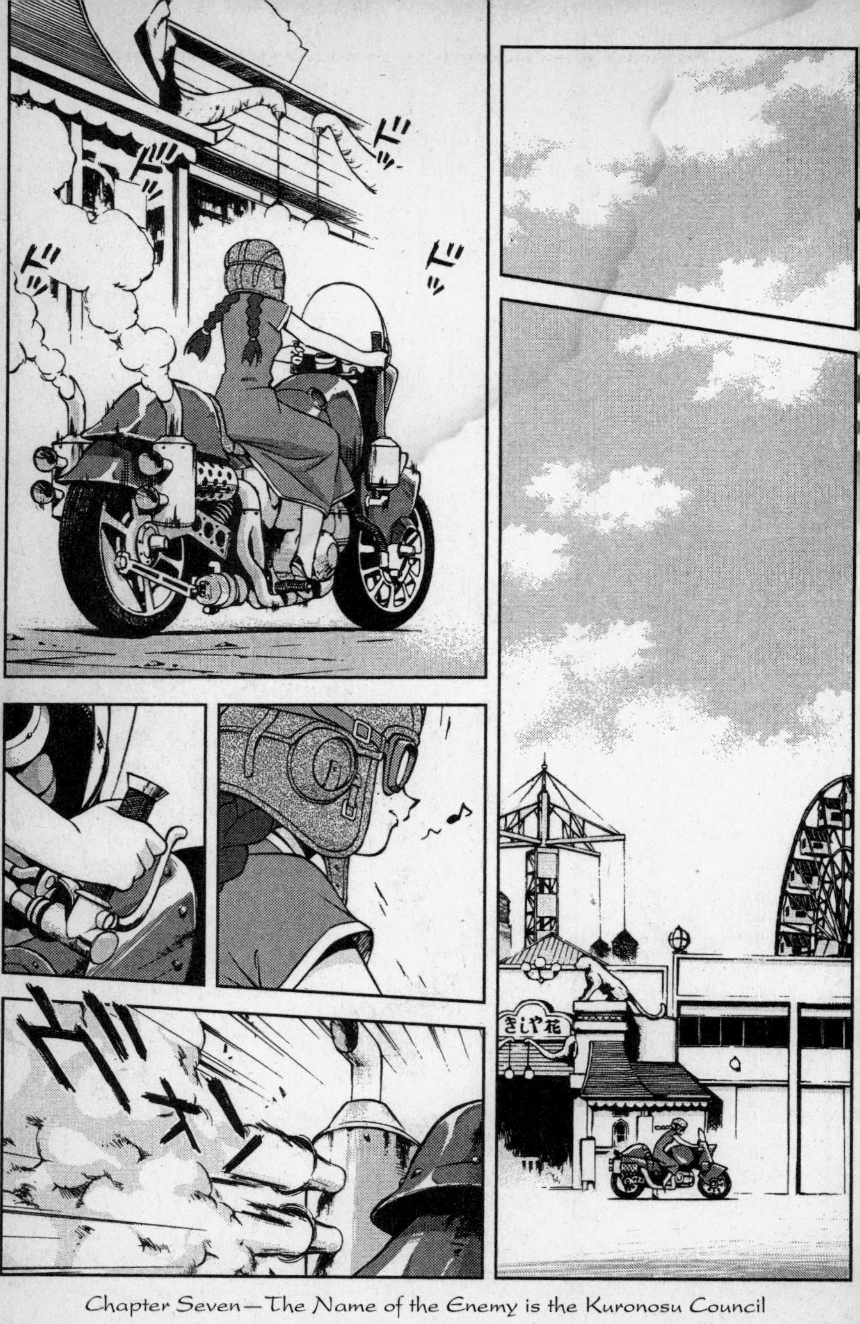
花やしき

Chapter Seven—The Name of the Enemy is the Kuronosu Council

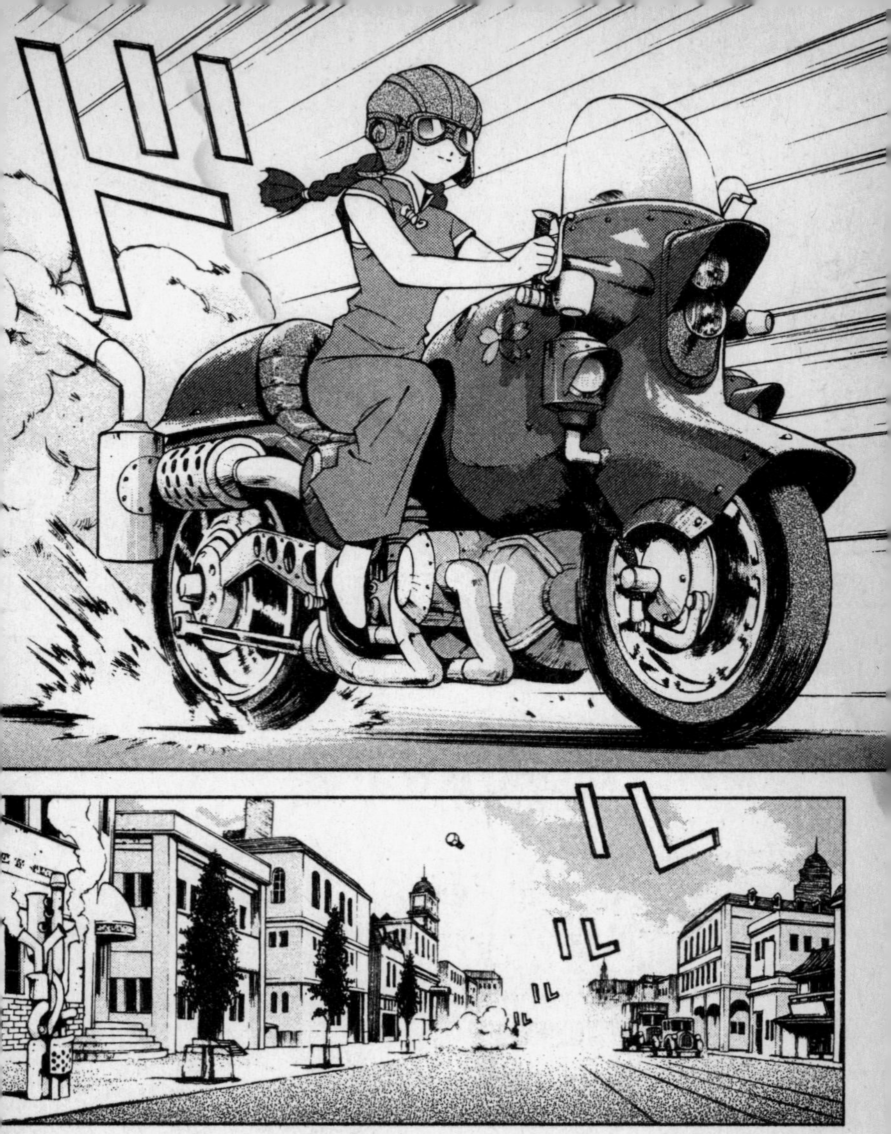
ド
ル
ル
ル
ル
DINK

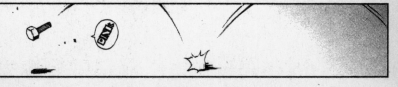

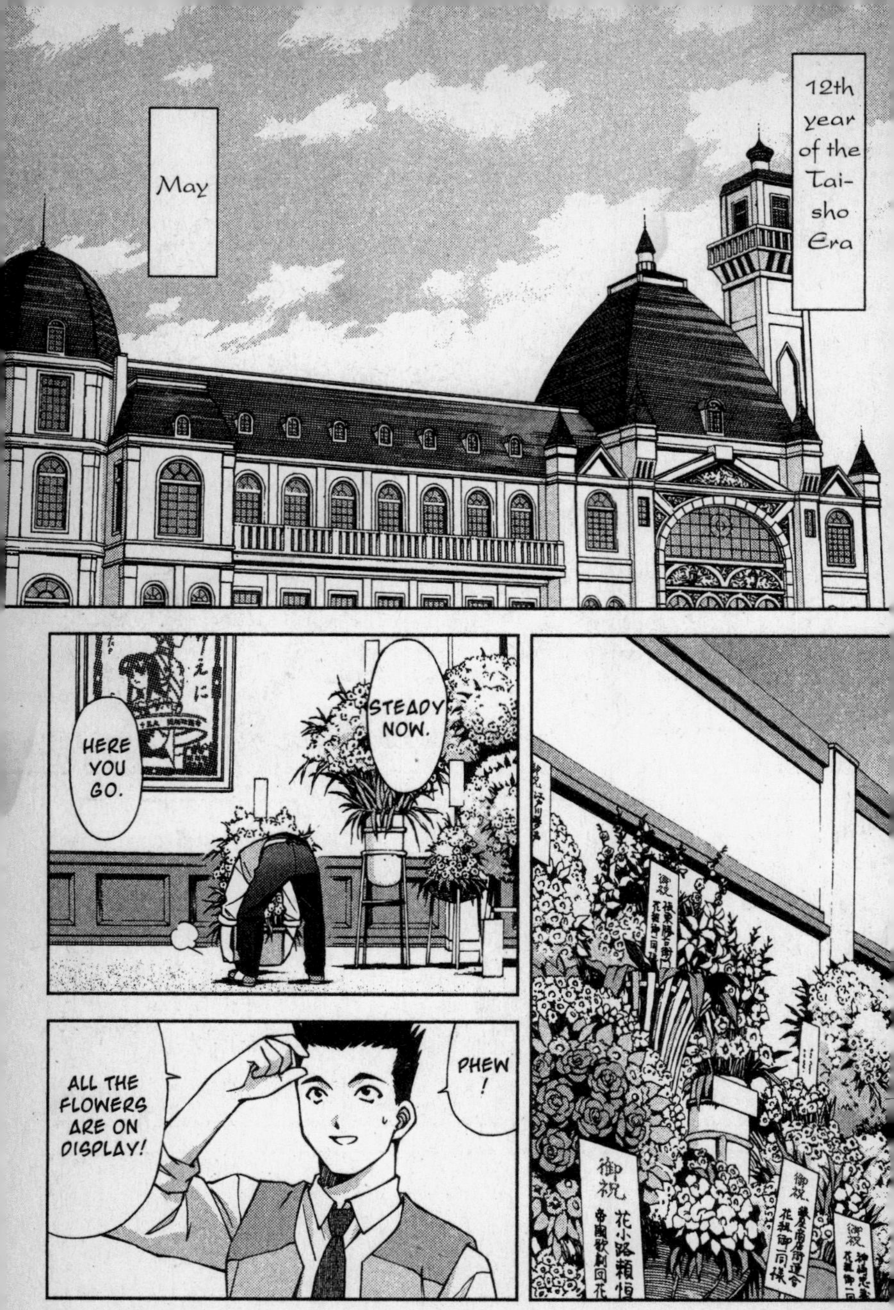

12th year of the Tai-sho Era
May
御祝
花小路頼恒
STEADY NOW.
HERE YOU GO.
PHEW!
ALL THE FLOWERS ARE ON DISPLAY!

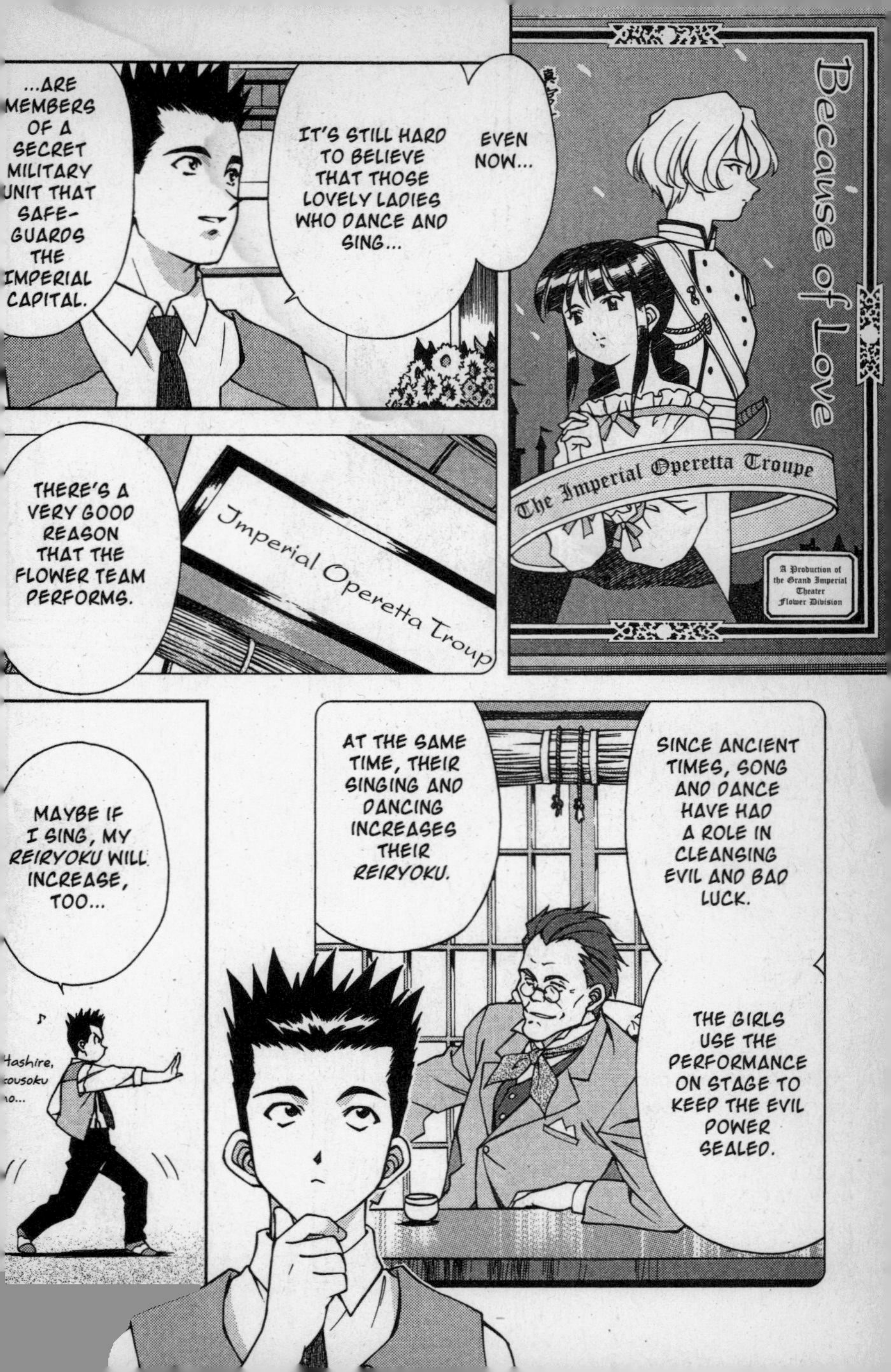
Because of Love
The Imperial Operetta Troupe
A Production of the Grand Imperial Theater Flower Division
EVEN NOW...
IT'S STILL HARD TO BELIEVE THAT THOSE LOVELY LADIES WHO DANCE AND SING...
...ARE MEMBERS OF A SECRET MILITARY UNIT THAT SAFE-GUARDS THE IMPERIAL CAPITAL.
Imperial Operetta Troup
THERE'S A VERY GOOD REASON THAT THE FLOWER TEAM PERFORMS.
SINCE ANCIENT TIMES, SONG AND DANCE HAVE HAD A ROLE IN CLEANSING EVIL AND BAD LUCK.
THE GIRLS USE THE PERFORMANCE ON STAGE TO KEEP THE EVIL POWER SEALED.
AT THE SAME TIME, THEIR SINGING AND DANCING INCREASES THEIR REIRYOKU.
MAYBE IF I SING, MY REIRYOKU WILL INCREASE, TOO...
Hashire, kousoku no...

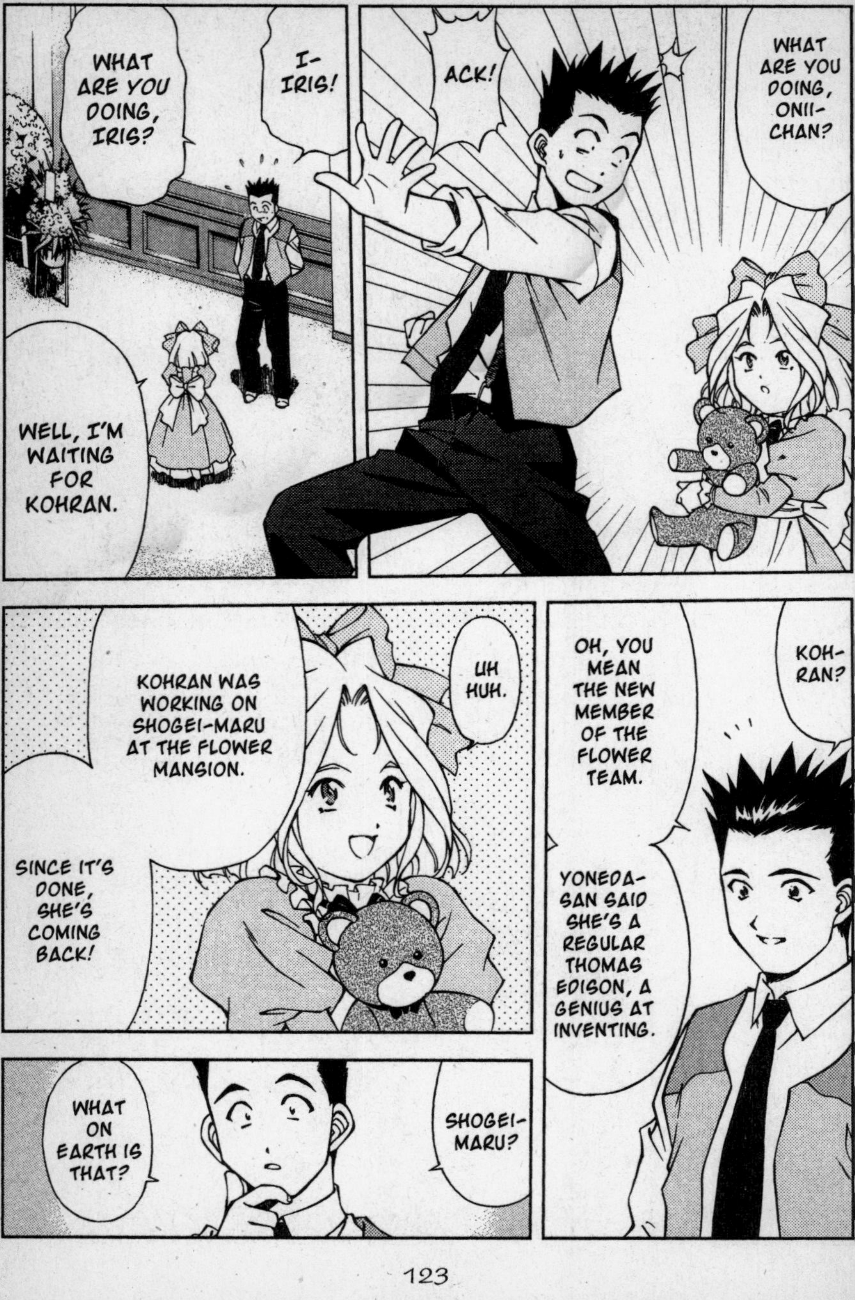

WHAT ARE YOU DOING, ONII-CHAN?
ACK!
I- IRIS!
WHAT ARE YOU DOING, IRIS?
WELL, I'M WAITING FOR KOHRAN.
KOH-RAN?
OH, YOU MEAN THE NEW MEMBER OF THE FLOWER TEAM.
YONEDA-SAN SAID SHE'S A REGULAR THOMAS EDISON, A GENIUS AT INVENTING.
UH HUH.
KOHRAN WAS WORKING ON SHOGEI-MARU AT THE FLOWER MANSION.
SINCE IT'S DONE, SHE'S COMING BACK!
SHOGEI-MARU?
WHAT ON EARTH IS THAT?

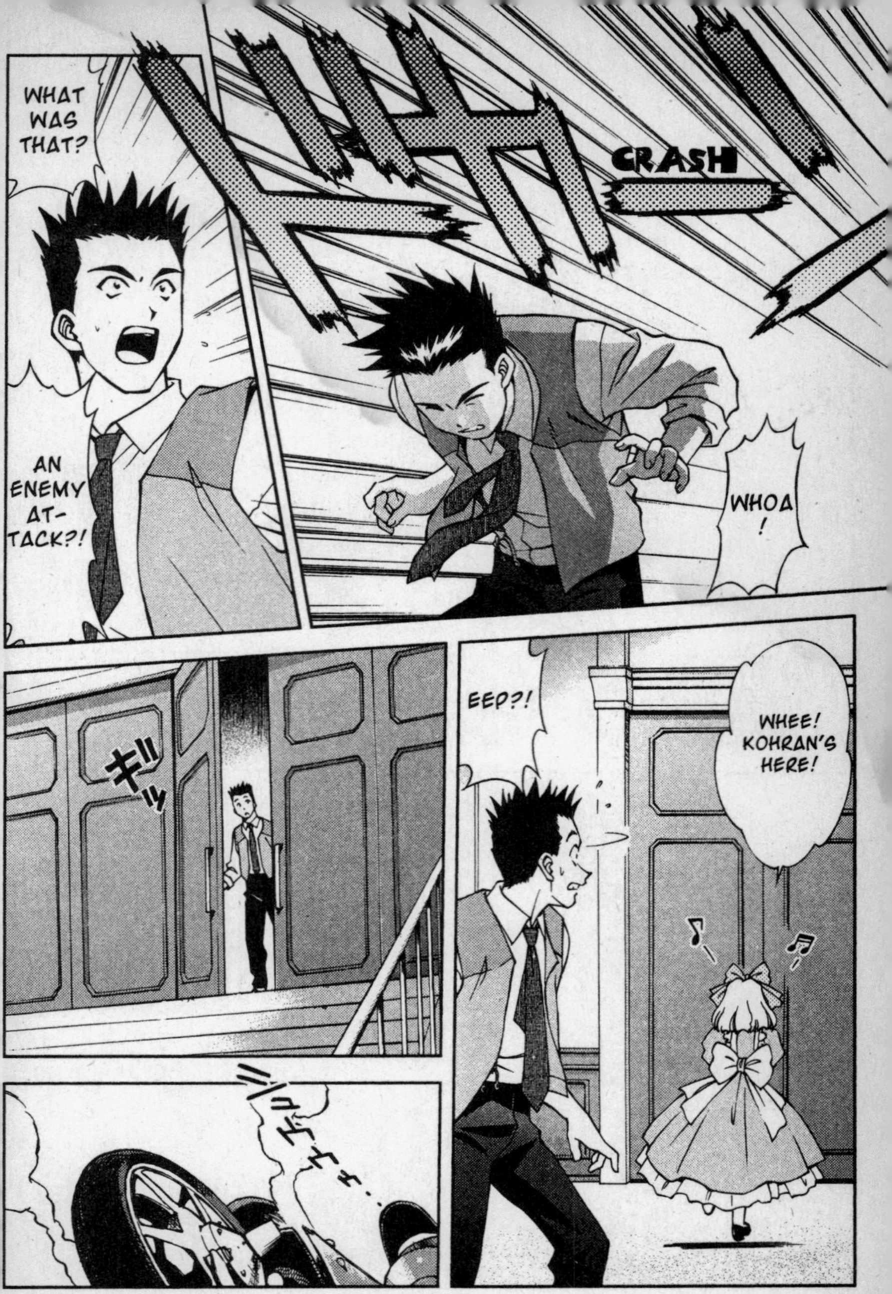
CRASH
WHOA!
WHAT WAS THAT?
AN ENEMY AT-TACK?!
WHEE! KOHRAN'S HERE!
EEP?!
ギッ

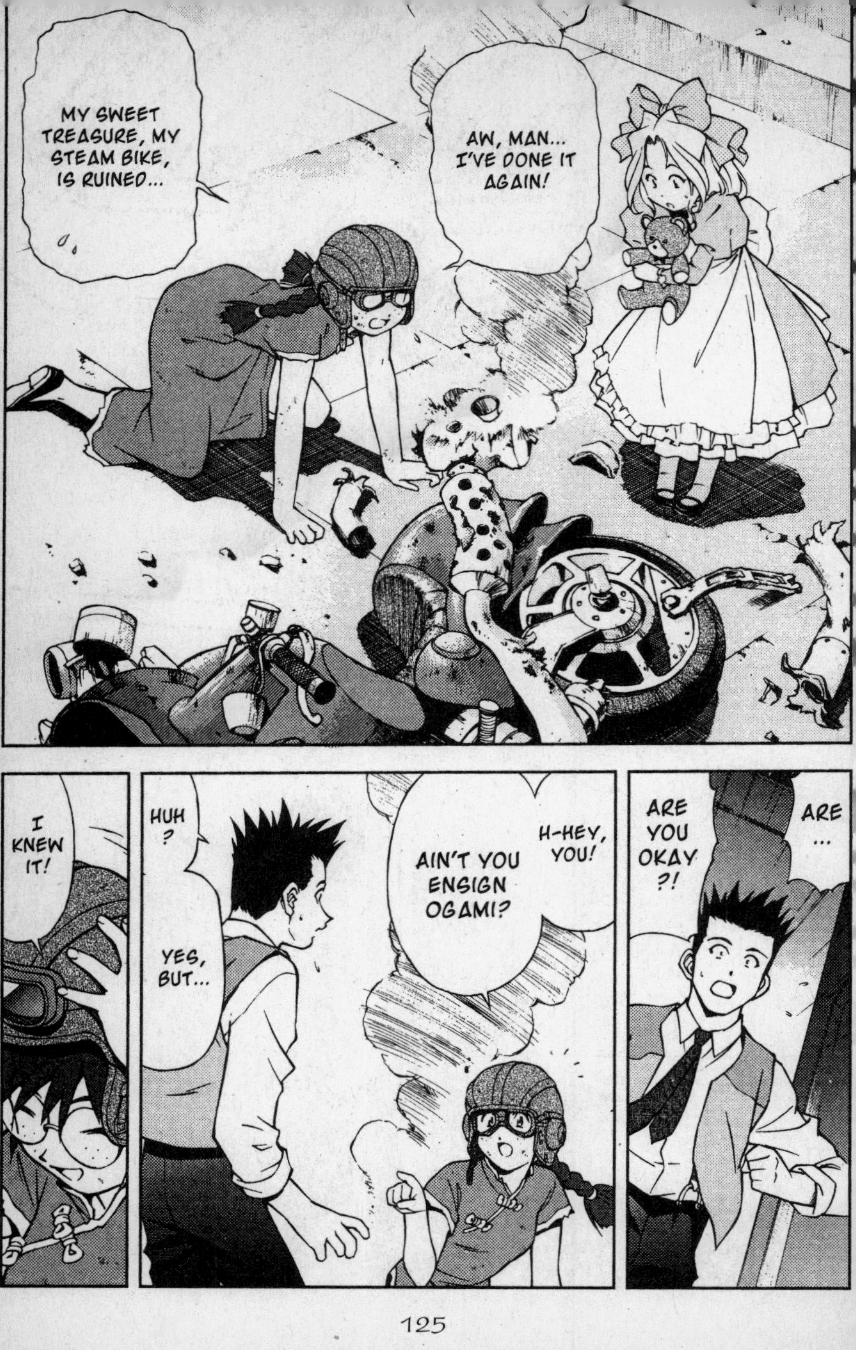
AW, MAN... I'VE DONE IT AGAIN!
MY SWEET TREASURE, MY STEAM BIKE, IS RUINED...
ARE ...
ARE YOU OKAY ?!
H-HEY, YOU!
AIN'T YOU ENSIGN OGAMI?
HUH ?
YES, BUT...
I KNEW IT!

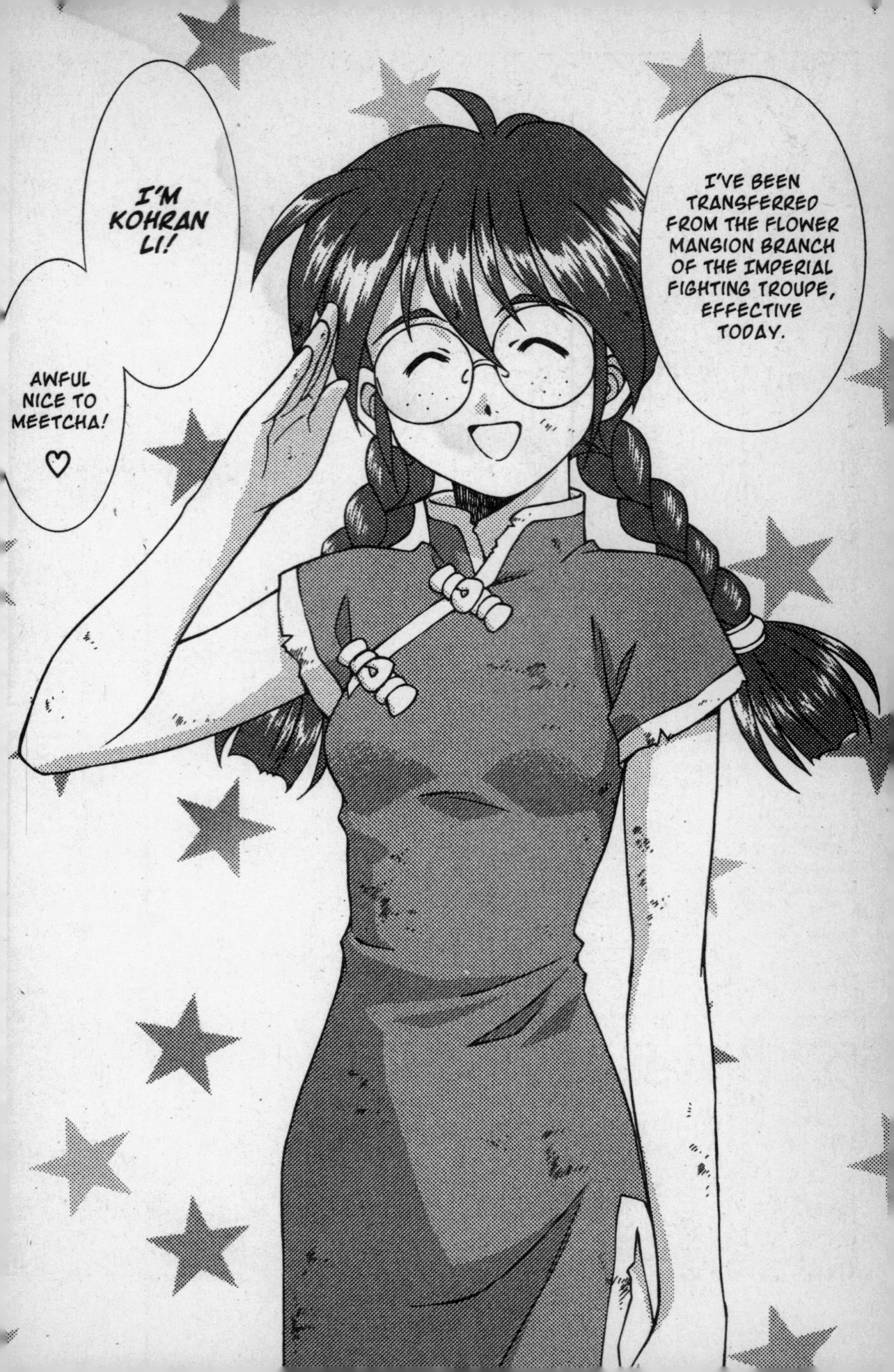
I'VE BEEN TRANSFERRED FROM THE FLOWER MANSION BRANCH OF THE IMPERIAL FIGHTING TROUPE, EFFECTIVE TODAY.
I'M KOHRAN LI!
AWFUL NICE TO MEETCHA! ♡

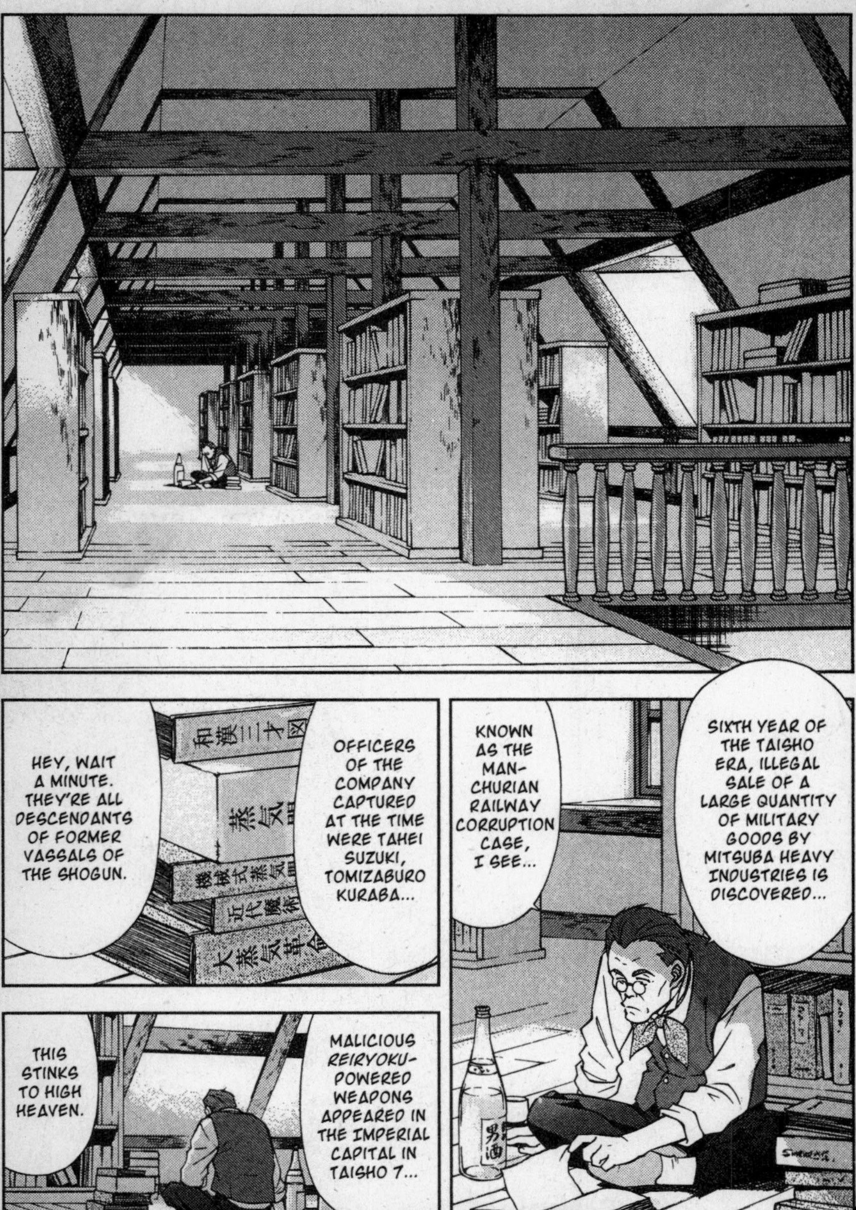
SIXTH YEAR OF THE TAISHO ERA, ILLEGAL SALE OF A LARGE QUANTITY OF MILITARY GOODS BY MITSUBA HEAVY INDUSTRIES IS DISCOVERED...
KNOWN AS THE MAN-CHURIAN RAILWAY CORRUPTION CASE, I SEE...
OFFICERS OF THE COMPANY CAPTURED AT THE TIME WERE TAHEI SUZUKI, TOMIZABURO KURABA...
HEY, WAIT A MINUTE. THEY'RE ALL DESCENDANTS OF FORMER VASSALS OF THE SHOGUN.
MALICIOUS REIRYOKU-POWERED WEAPONS APPEARED IN THE IMPERIAL CAPITAL IN TAISHO 7...
THIS STINKS TO HIGH HEAVEN.

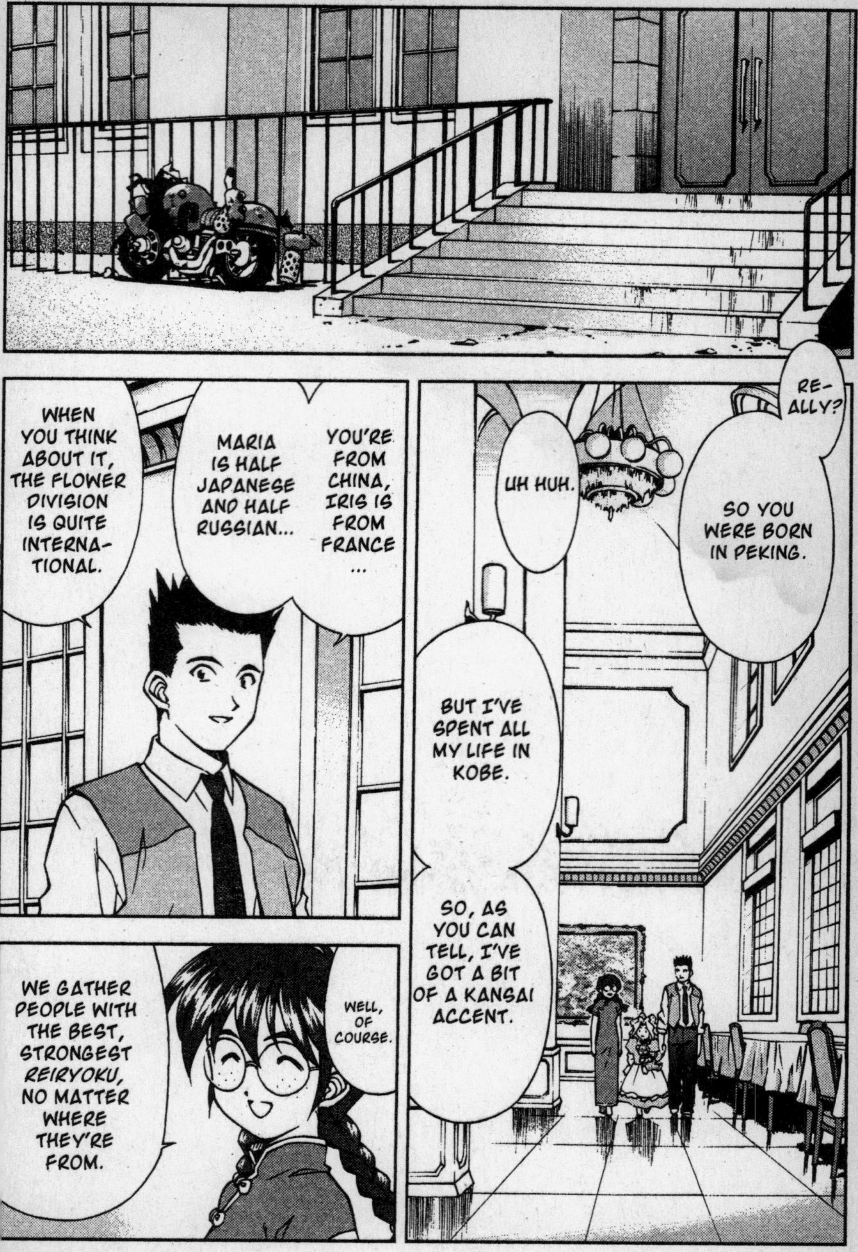

RE-ALLY?
SO YOU WERE BORN IN PEKING.
UH HUH.
BUT I'VE SPENT ALL MY LIFE IN KOBE.
SO, AS YOU CAN TELL, I'VE GOT A BIT OF A KANSAI ACCENT.
YOU'RE FROM CHINA, IRIS IS FROM FRANCE ...
MARIA IS HALF JAPANESE AND HALF RUSSIAN...
WHEN YOU THINK ABOUT IT, THE FLOWER DIVISION IS QUITE INTERNA-TIONAL.
WELL, OF COURSE.
WE GATHER PEOPLE WITH THE BEST, STRONGEST *REIRYOKU*, NO MATTER WHERE THEY'RE FROM.

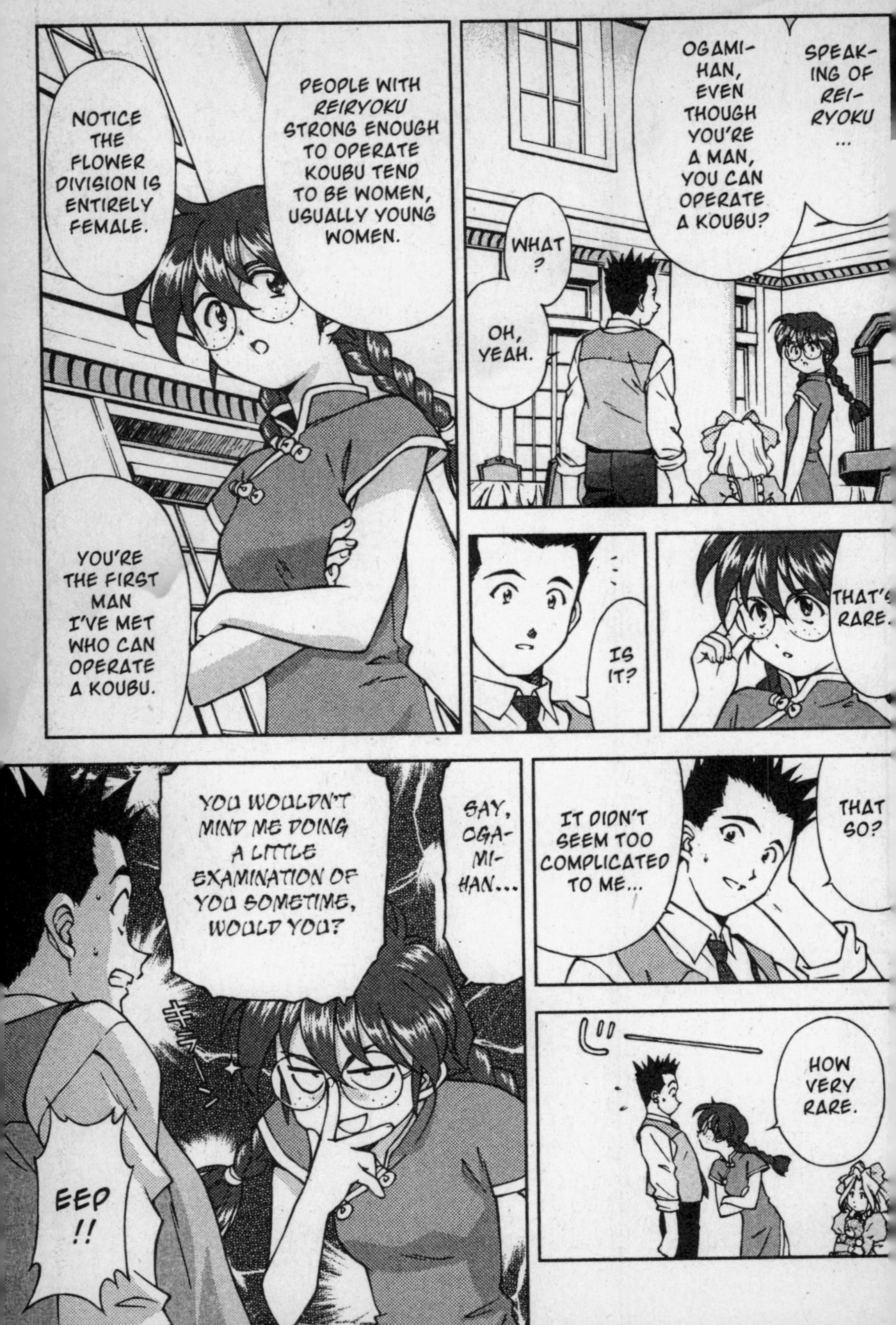

SPEAKING OF REIRYOKU...
OGAMI-HAN, EVEN THOUGH YOU'RE A MAN, YOU CAN OPERATE A KOUBU?
WHAT?
OH, YEAH.
THAT'S RARE.
IS IT?
PEOPLE WITH REIRYOKU STRONG ENOUGH TO OPERATE KOUBU TEND TO BE WOMEN, USUALLY YOUNG WOMEN.
NOTICE THE FLOWER DIVISION IS ENTIRELY FEMALE.
YOU'RE THE FIRST MAN I'VE MET WHO CAN OPERATE A KOUBU.
THAT SO?
IT DIDN'T SEEM TOO COMPLICATED TO ME...
HOW VERY RARE.
じ—
SAY, OGAMI-HAN...
YOU WOULDN'T MIND ME DOING A LITTLE EXAMINATION OF YOU SOMETIME, WOULD YOU?
EEP!!

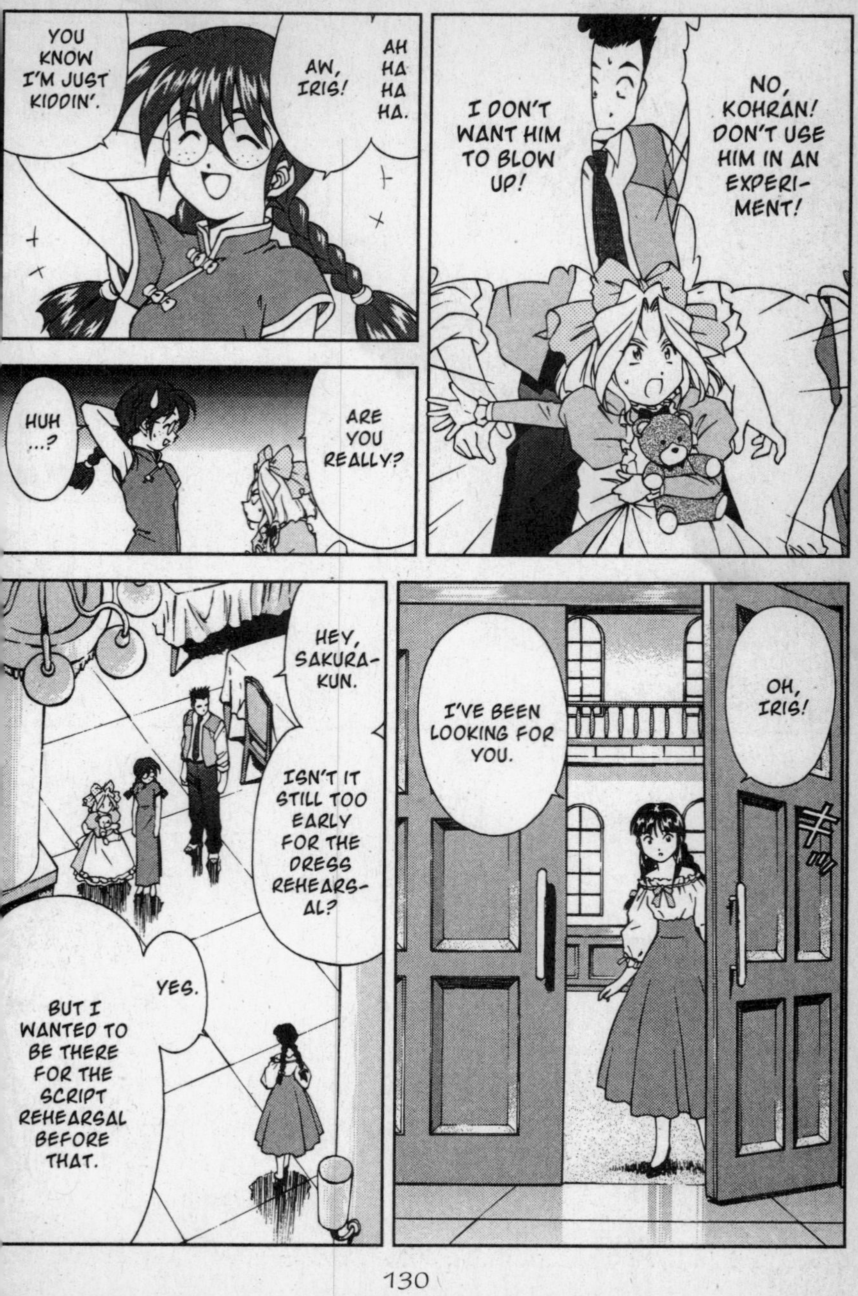
NO, KOHRAN! DON'T USE HIM IN AN EXPERIMENT!
I DON'T WANT HIM TO BLOW UP!
AH HA HA HA.
AW, IRIS!
YOU KNOW I'M JUST KIDDIN'.
ARE YOU REALLY?
HUH ...?
OH, IRIS!
I'VE BEEN LOOKING FOR YOU.
HEY, SAKURA-KUN.
ISN'T IT STILL TOO EARLY FOR THE DRESS REHEARSAL?
YES.
BUT I WANTED TO BE THERE FOR THE SCRIPT REHEARSAL BEFORE THAT.

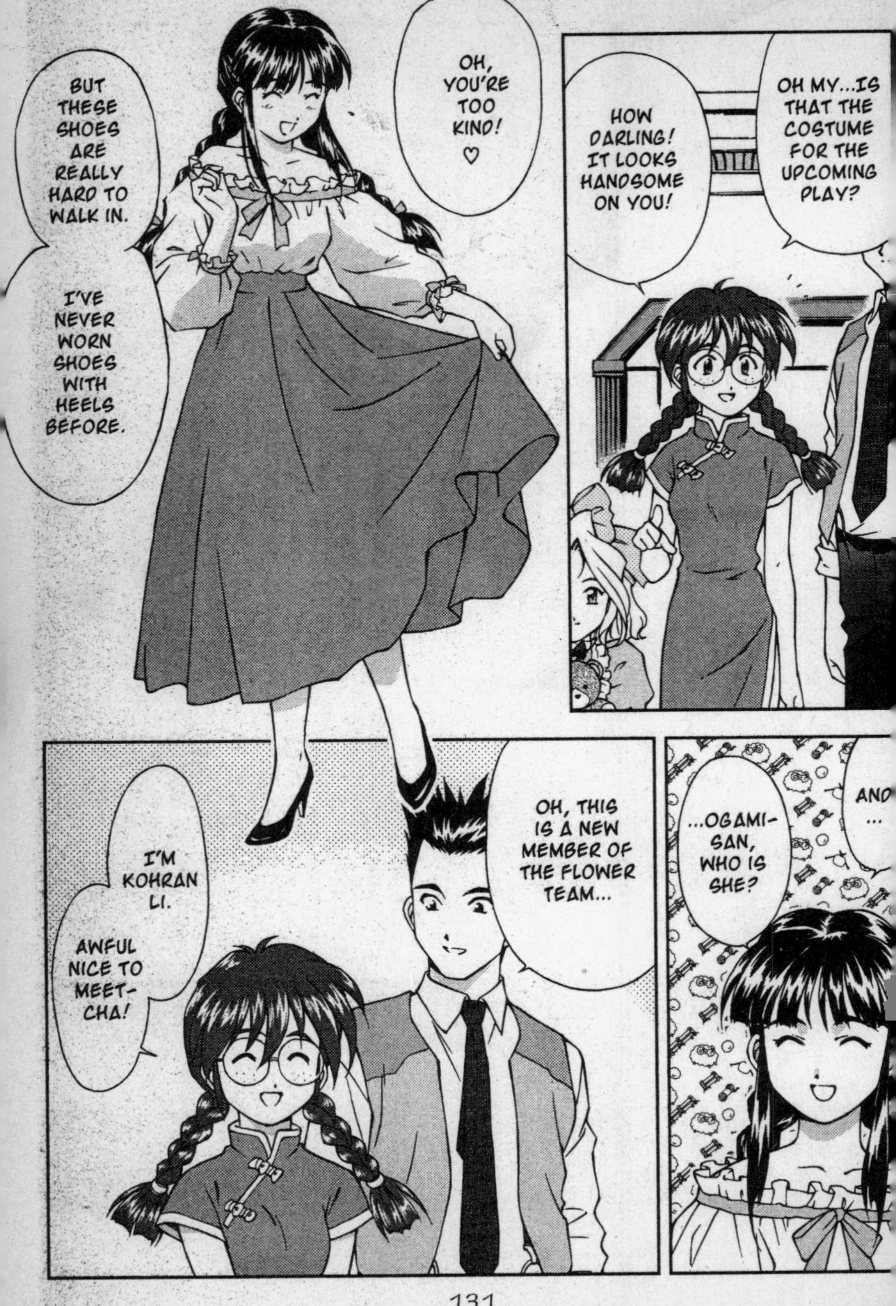
OH MY...IS THAT THE COSTUME FOR THE UPCOMING PLAY?
HOW DARLING! IT LOOKS HANDSOME ON YOU!
OH, YOU'RE TOO KIND! ♡
BUT THESE SHOES ARE REALLY HARD TO WALK IN.
I'VE NEVER WORN SHOES WITH HEELS BEFORE.
AND ...
...OGAMI-SAN, WHO IS SHE?
OH, THIS IS A NEW MEMBER OF THE FLOWER TEAM...
I'M KOHRAN LI.
AWFUL NICE TO MEET-CHA!

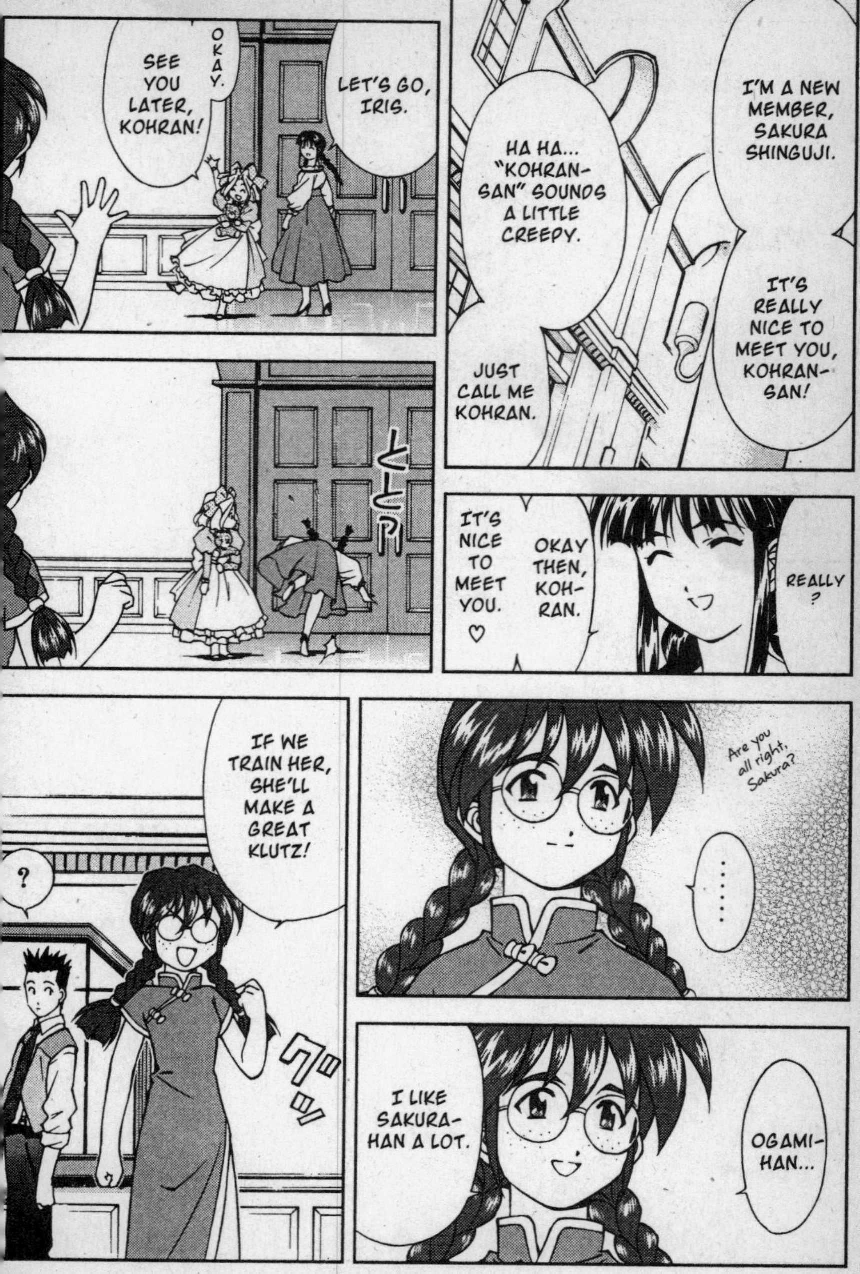
I'M A NEW MEMBER, SAKURA SHINGUJI.
IT'S REALLY NICE TO MEET YOU, KOHRAN-SAN!
HA HA... "KOHRAN-SAN" SOUNDS A LITTLE CREEPY.
JUST CALL ME KOHRAN.
REALLY?
OKAY THEN, KOH-RAN.
IT'S NICE TO MEET YOU. ♡
LET'S GO, IRIS.
OKAY.
SEE YOU LATER, KOHRAN!
とと
Are you all right, Sakura?
......
OGAMI-HAN...
I LIKE SAKURA-HAN A LOT.
IF WE TRAIN HER, SHE'LL MAKE A GREAT KLUTZ!
?

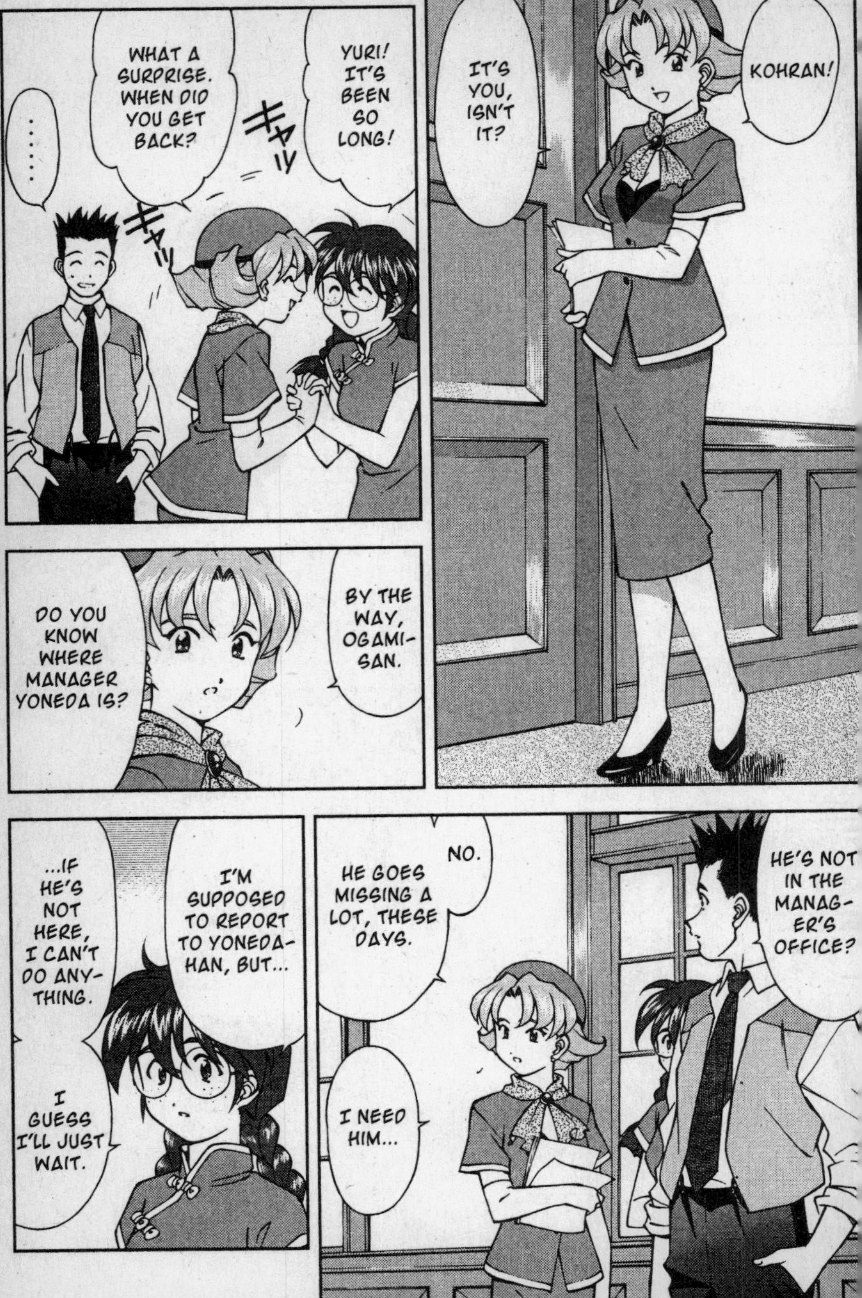
KOHRAN!
IT'S YOU, ISN'T IT?
YURI! IT'S BEEN SO LONG!
WHAT A SURPRISE. WHEN DID YOU GET BACK?
......
BY THE WAY, OGAMI-SAN.
DO YOU KNOW WHERE MANAGER YONEDA IS?
HE'S NOT IN THE MANAGER'S OFFICE?
NO.
HE GOES MISSING A LOT, THESE DAYS.
I NEED HIM...
I'M SUPPOSED TO REPORT TO YONEDA-HAN, BUT...
...IF HE'S NOT HERE, I CAN'T DO ANYTHING.
I GUESS I'LL JUST WAIT.

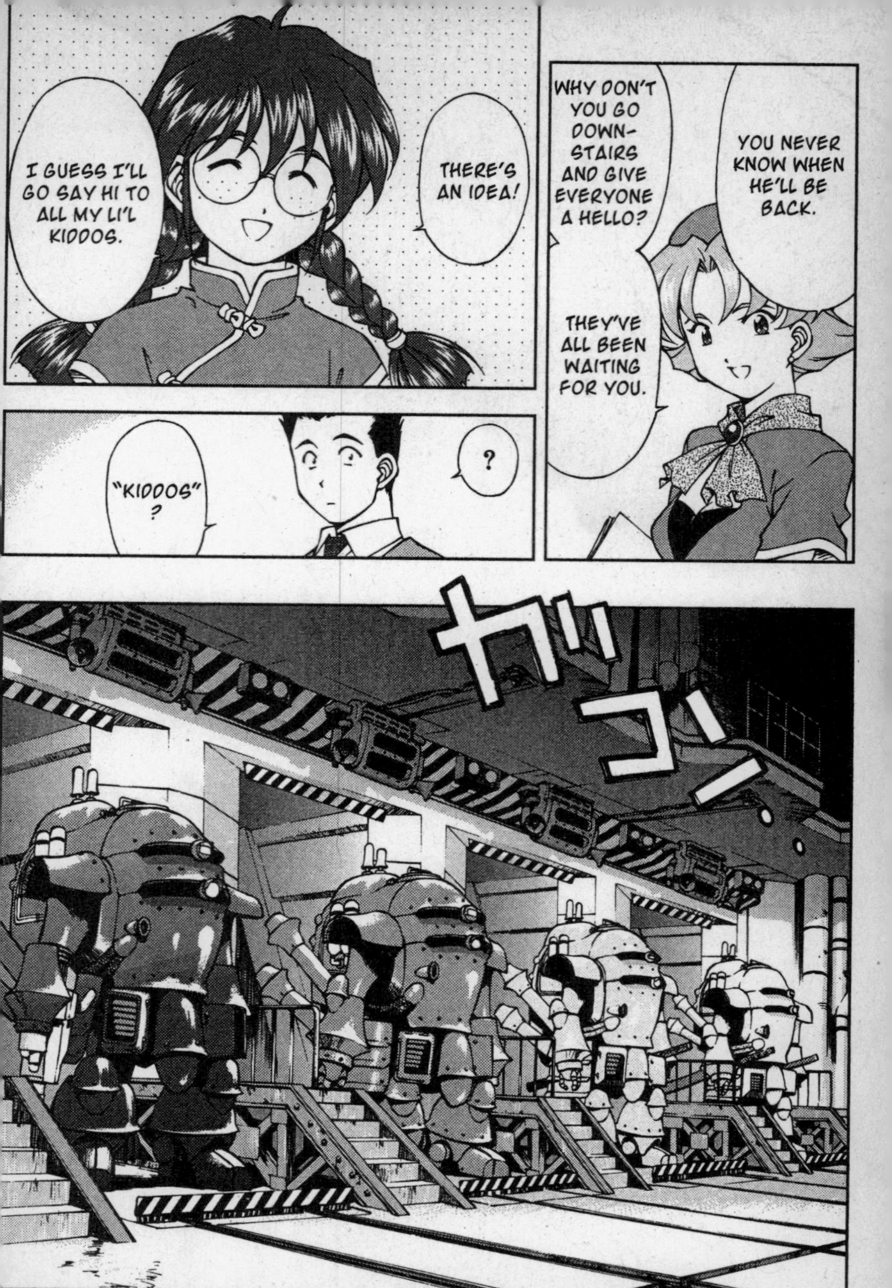
YOU NEVER KNOW WHEN HE'LL BE BACK.
WHY DON'T YOU GO DOWN-STAIRS AND GIVE EVERYONE A HELLO?
THEY'VE ALL BEEN WAITING FOR YOU.
THERE'S AN IDEA!
I GUESS I'LL GO SAY HI TO ALL MY LI'L KIDDOS.
?
"KIDDOS" ?
ガッコン

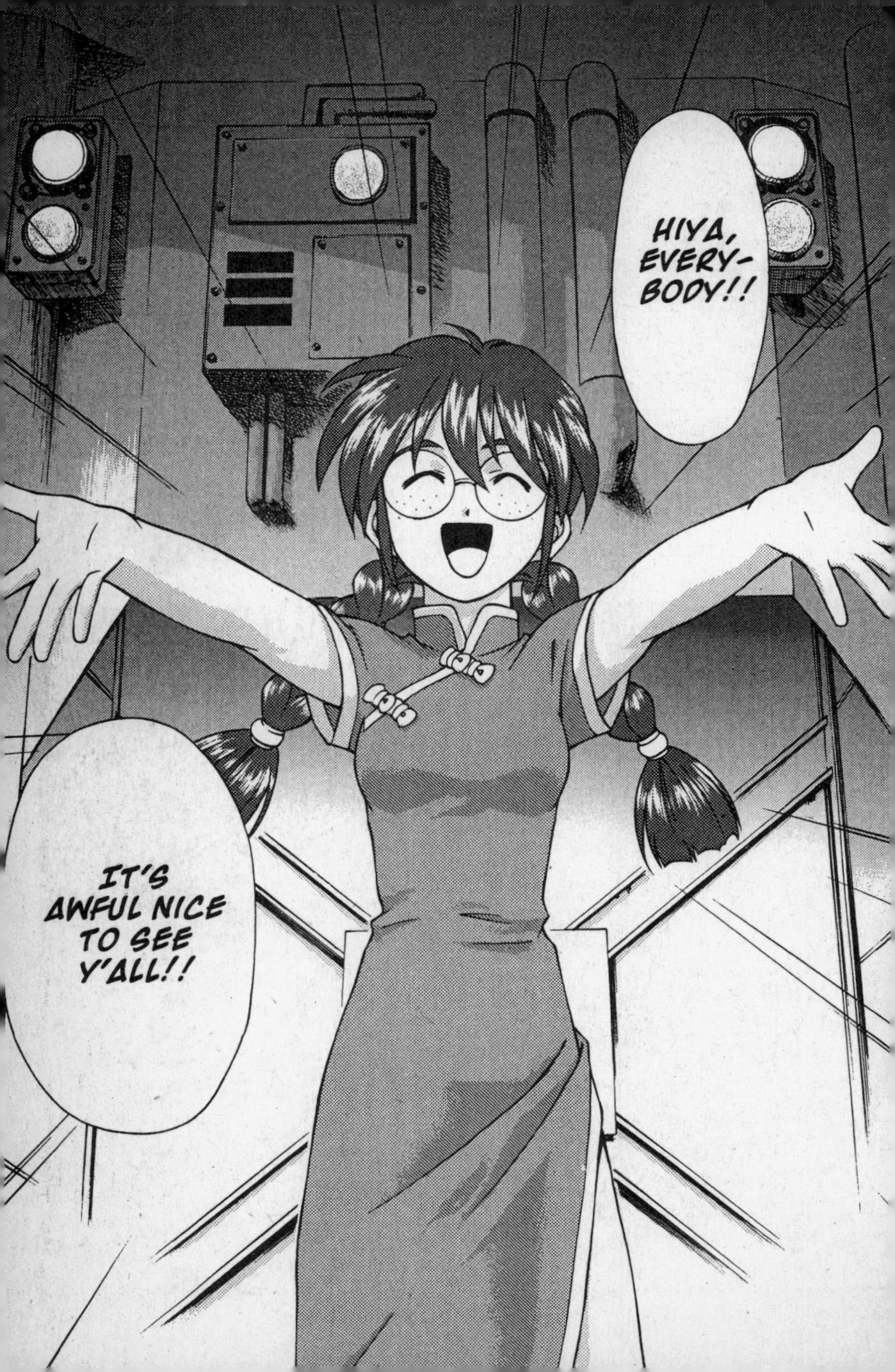
HIYA, EVERY-BODY!!
IT'S AWFUL NICE TO SEE Y'ALL!!

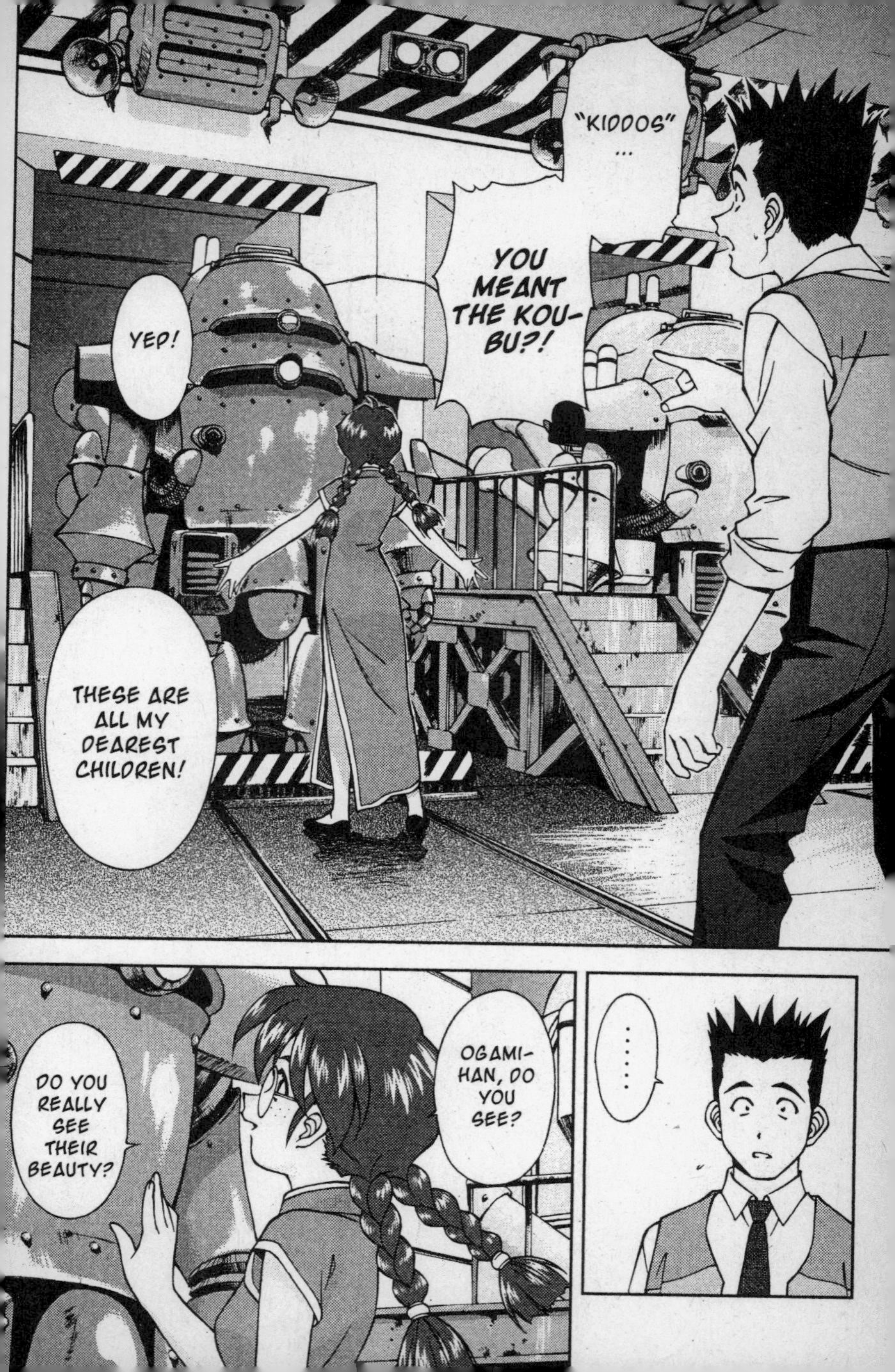
"KIDDOS" ...
YOU MEANT THE KOU-BU?!
YEP!
THESE ARE ALL MY DEAREST CHILDREN!
......
OGAMI-HAN, DO YOU SEE?
DO YOU REALLY SEE THEIR BEAUTY?

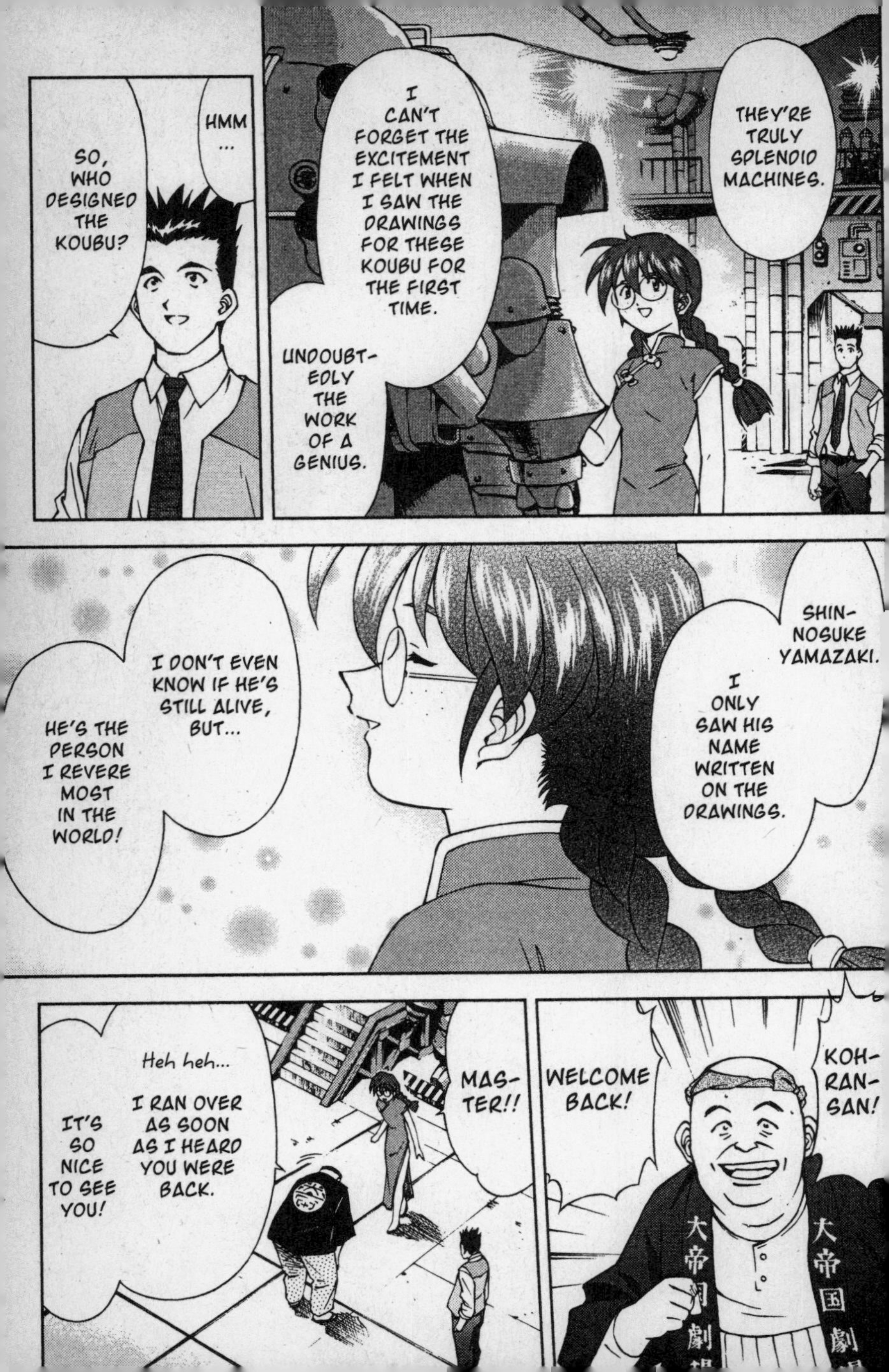
THEY'RE TRULY SPLENDID MACHINES.
I CAN'T FORGET THE EXCITEMENT I FELT WHEN I SAW THE DRAWINGS FOR THESE KOUBU FOR THE FIRST TIME.
UNDOUBT-EDLY THE WORK OF A GENIUS.
HMM...
SO, WHO DESIGNED THE KOUBU?
SHIN-NOSUKE YAMAZAKI.
I ONLY SAW HIS NAME WRITTEN ON THE DRAWINGS.
I DON'T EVEN KNOW IF HE'S STILL ALIVE, BUT...
HE'S THE PERSON I REVERE MOST IN THE WORLD!
KOH-RAN-SAN!
WELCOME BACK!
MAS-TER!!
Heh heh...
I RAN OVER AS SOON AS I HEARD YOU WERE BACK.
IT'S SO NICE TO SEE YOU!

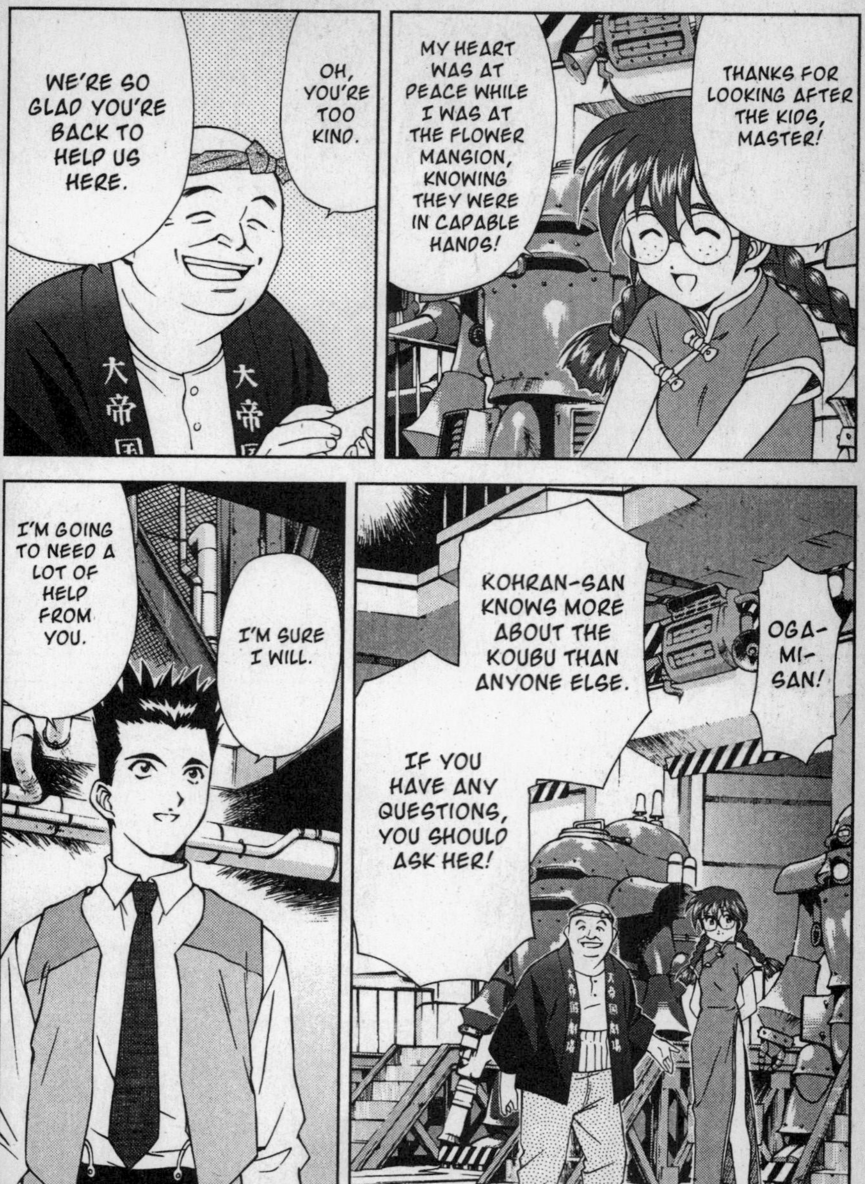
THANKS FOR LOOKING AFTER THE KIDS, MASTER!
MY HEART WAS AT PEACE WHILE I WAS AT THE FLOWER MANSION, KNOWING THEY WERE IN CAPABLE HANDS!
WE'RE SO GLAD YOU'RE BACK TO HELP US HERE.
OH, YOU'RE TOO KIND.
大帝国
大帝国
OGA-MI-SAN!
KOHRAN-SAN KNOWS MORE ABOUT THE KOUBU THAN ANYONE ELSE.
IF YOU HAVE ANY QUESTIONS, YOU SHOULD ASK HER!
I'M GOING TO NEED A LOT OF HELP FROM YOU.
I'M SURE I WILL.

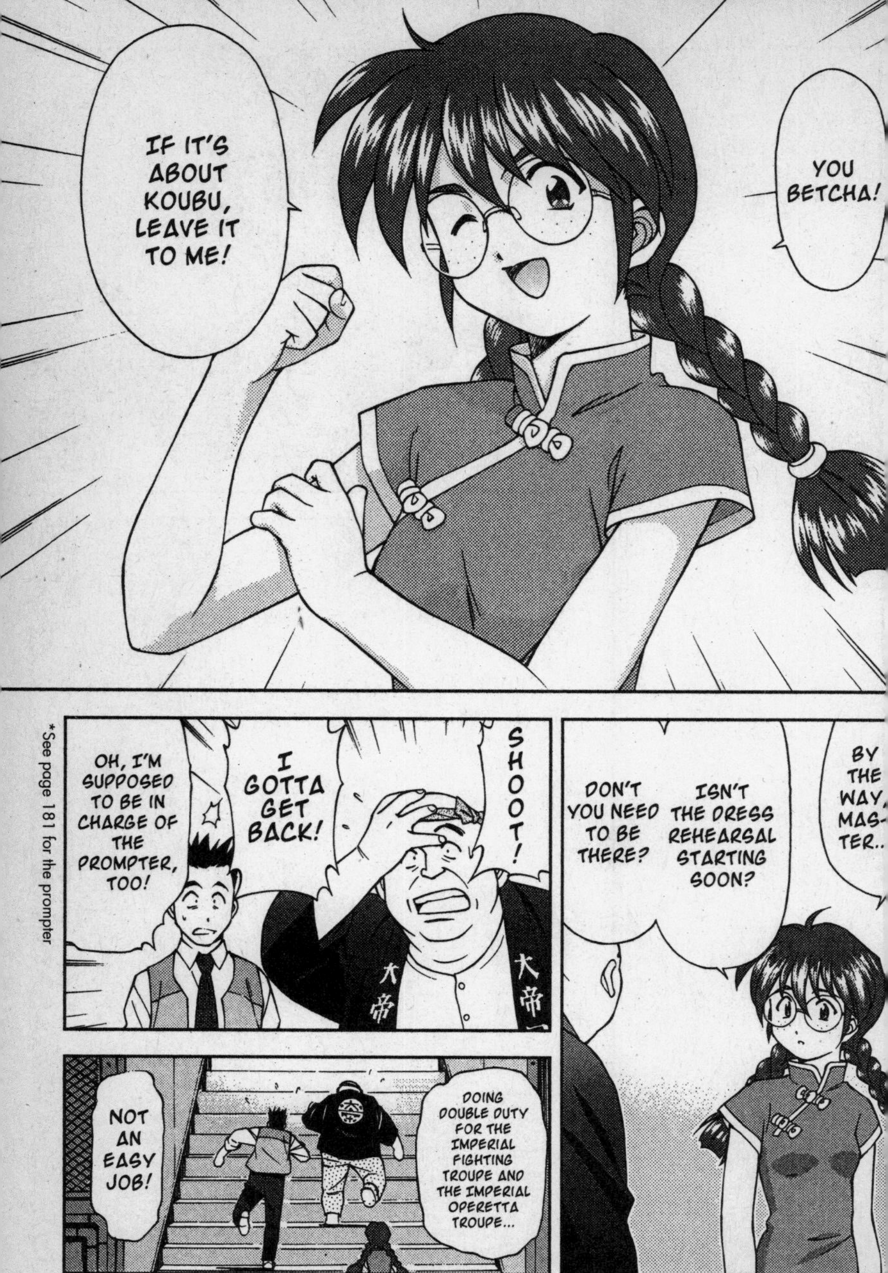
YOU BETCHA!
IF IT'S ABOUT KOUBU, LEAVE IT TO ME!
BY THE WAY, MASTER...
ISN'T THE DRESS REHEARSAL STARTING SOON?
DON'T YOU NEED TO BE THERE?
SHOOT!
I GOTTA GET BACK!
OH, I'M SUPPOSED TO BE IN CHARGE OF THE PROMPTER, TOO!
DOING DOUBLE DUTY FOR THE IMPERIAL FIGHTING TROUPE AND THE IMPERIAL OPERETTA TROUPE...
NOT AN EASY JOB!

*See page 181 for the prompter

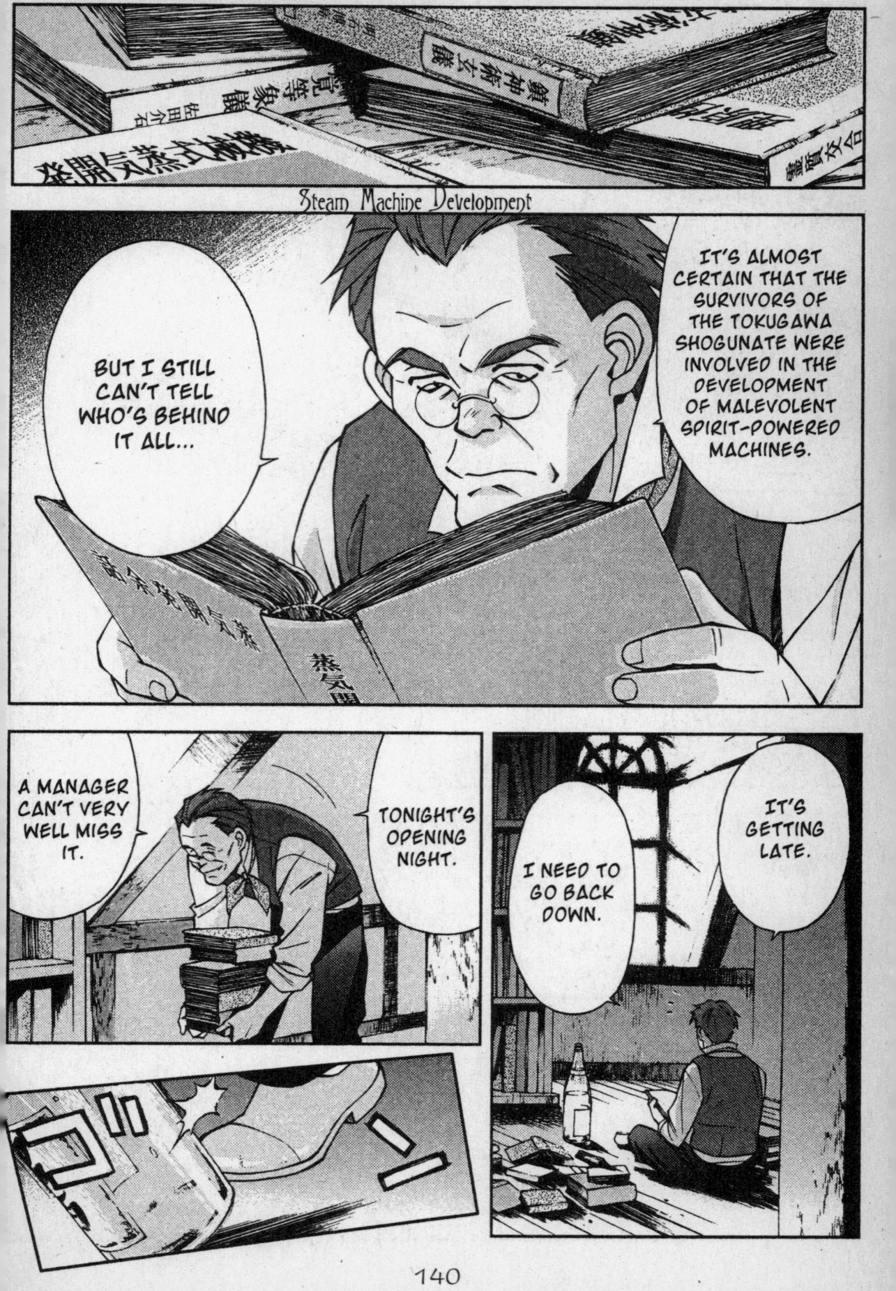
Steam Machine Development
IT'S ALMOST CERTAIN THAT THE SURVIVORS OF THE TOKUGAWA SHOGUNATE WERE INVOLVED IN THE DEVELOPMENT OF MALEVOLENT SPIRIT-POWERED MACHINES.
BUT I STILL CAN'T TELL WHO'S BEHIND IT ALL...
IT'S GETTING LATE.
I NEED TO GO BACK DOWN.
TONIGHT'S OPENING NIGHT.
A MANAGER CAN'T VERY WELL MISS IT.

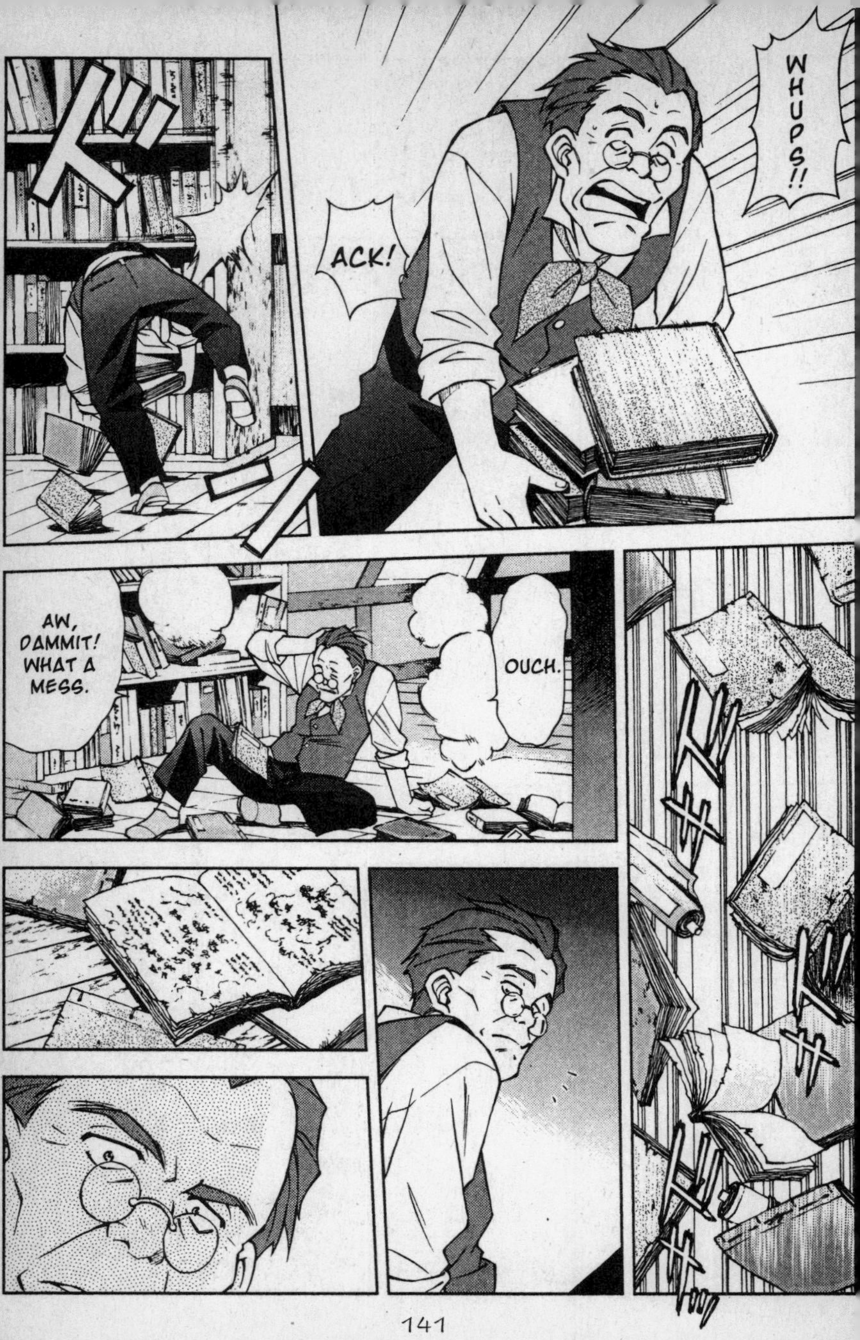
WHUPS!!
ACK!
ドッ
OUCH.
AW, DAMMIT! WHAT A MESS.

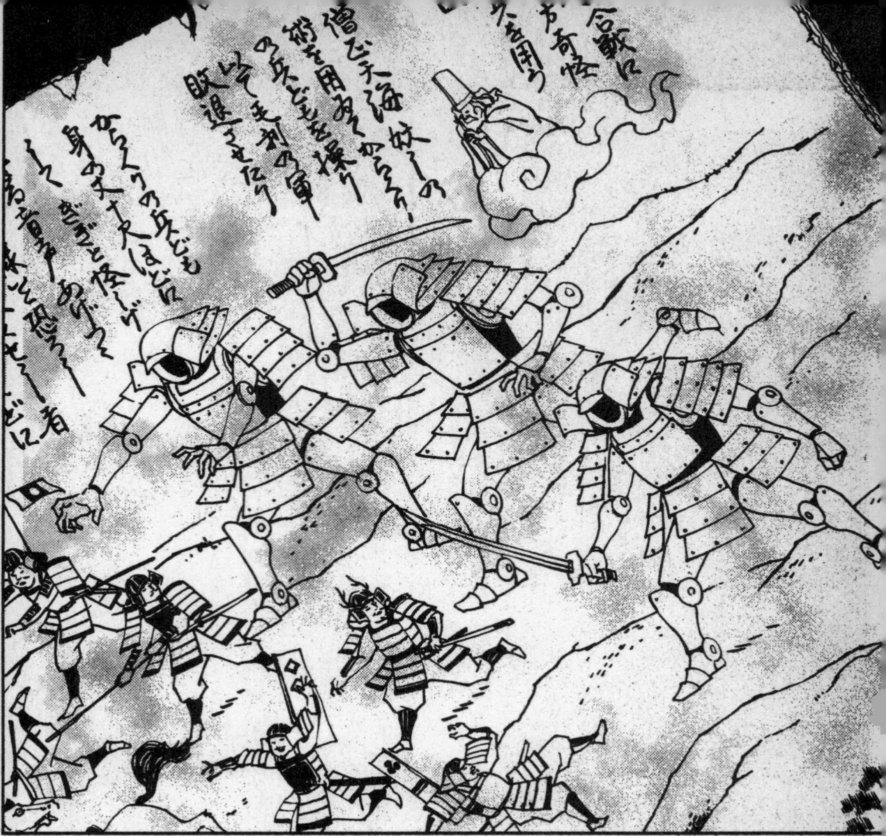

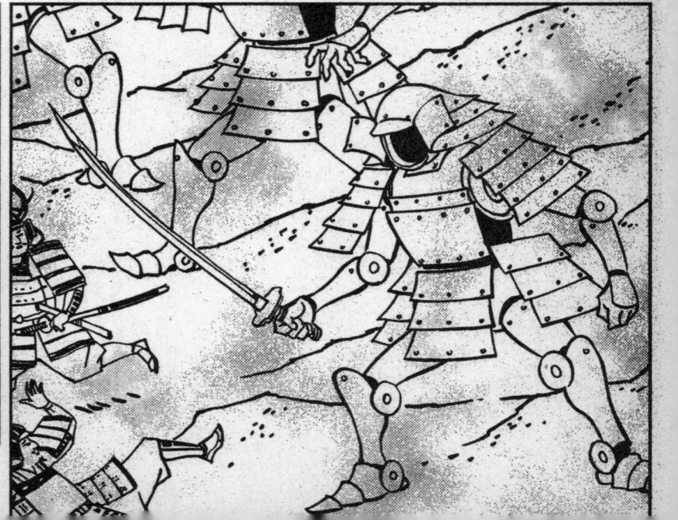

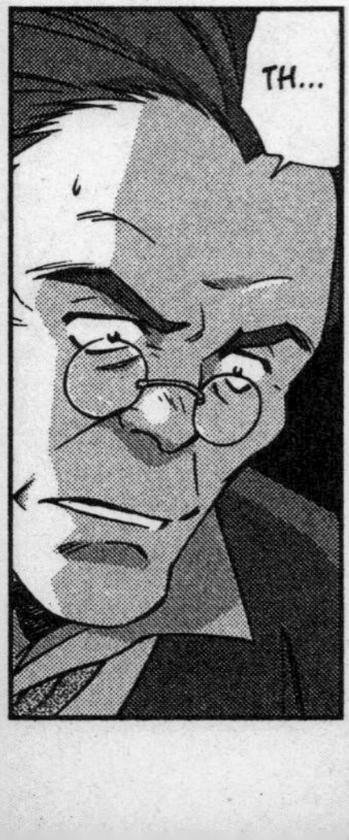
TH...

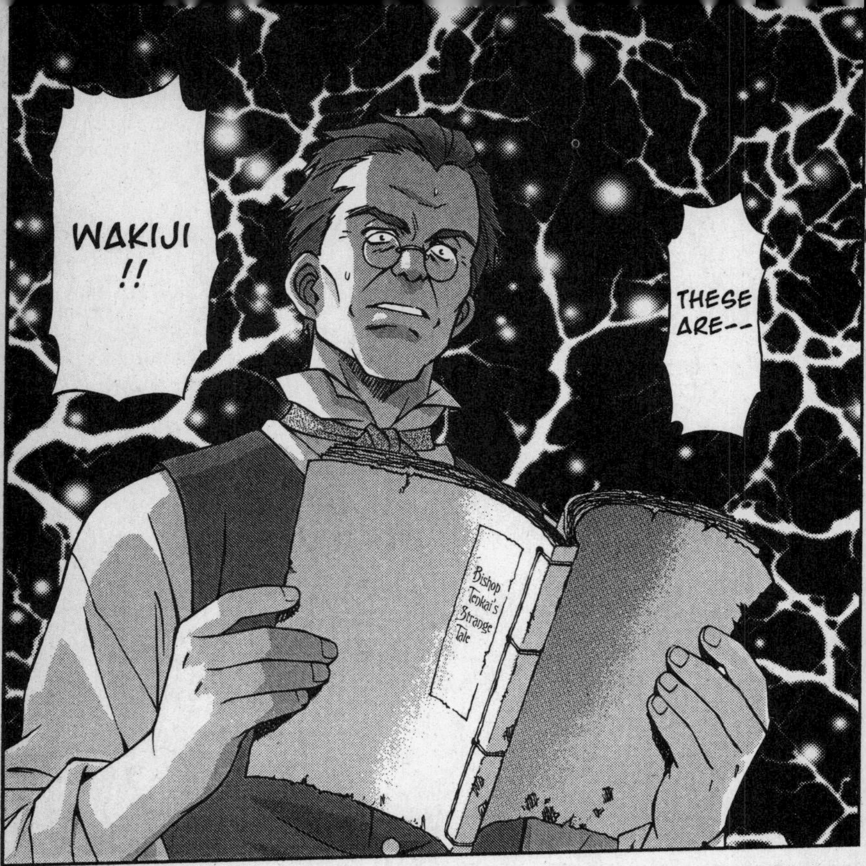
THESE ARE--
Bishop Tenkai's Strange Tale
WAKIJI !!
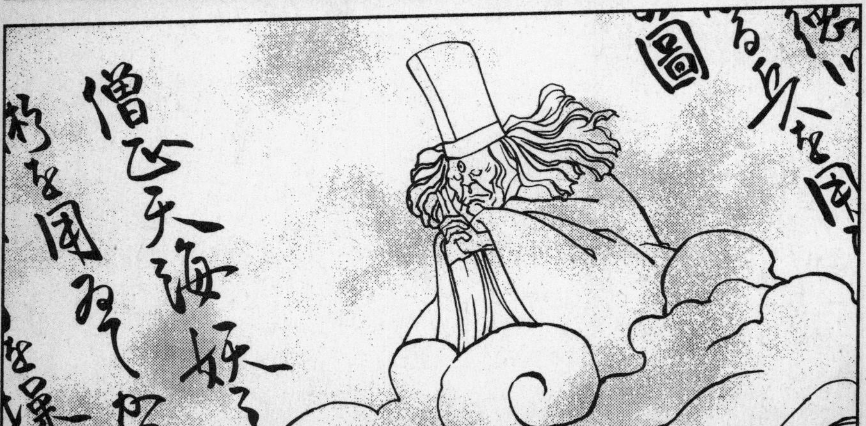

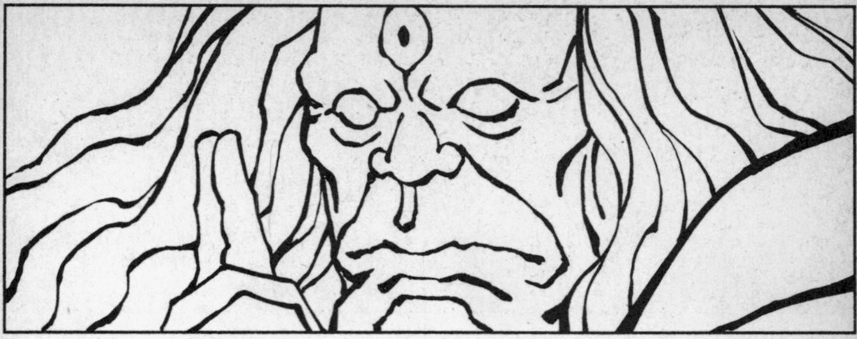

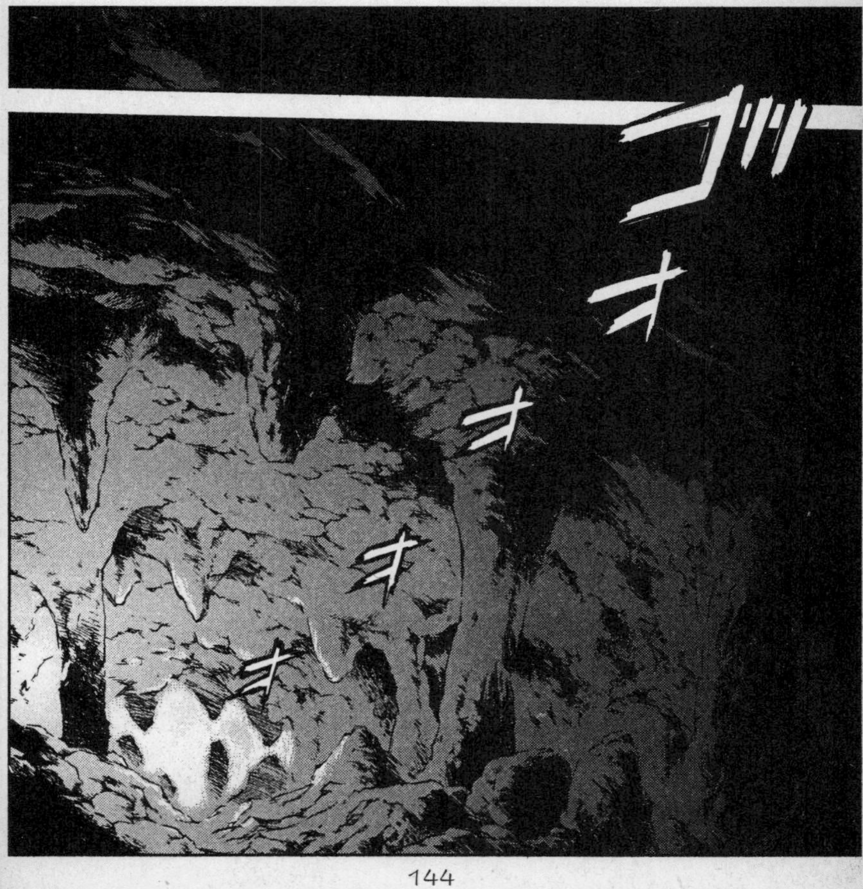
ゴォォォォ

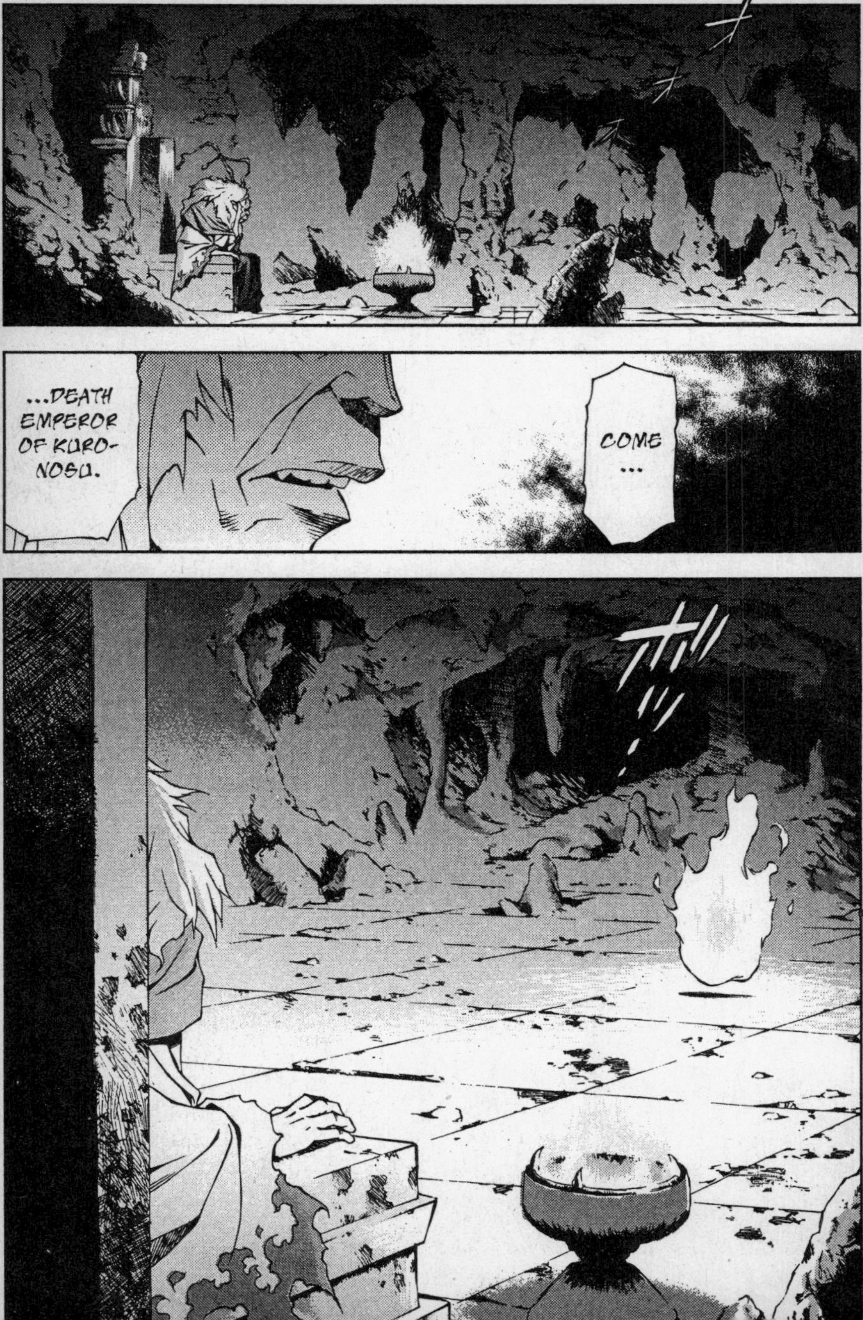
COME ...
...DEATH EMPEROR OF KURO-NOSU.

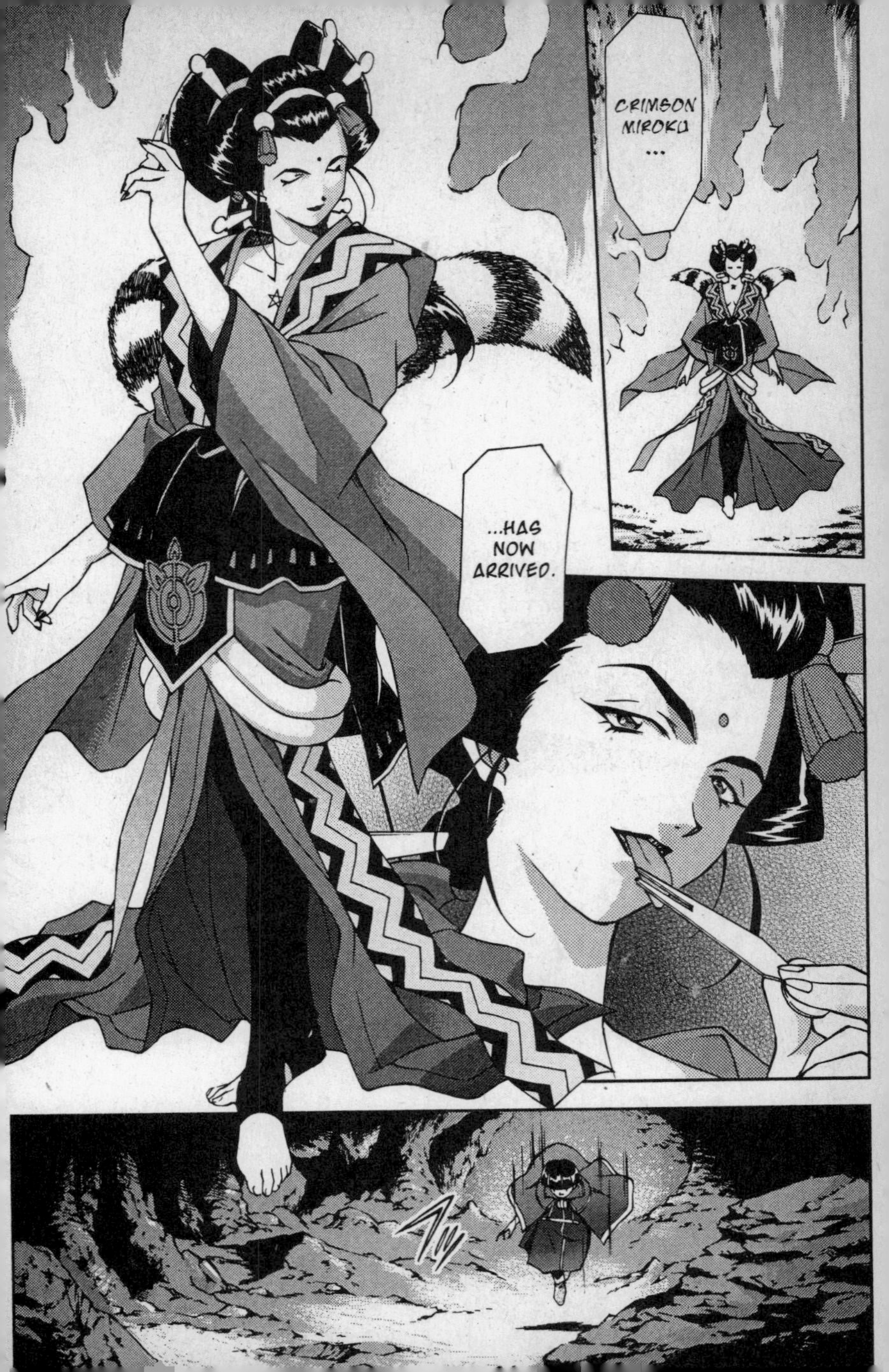
CRIMSON MIROKU ...
...HAS NOW ARRIVED.

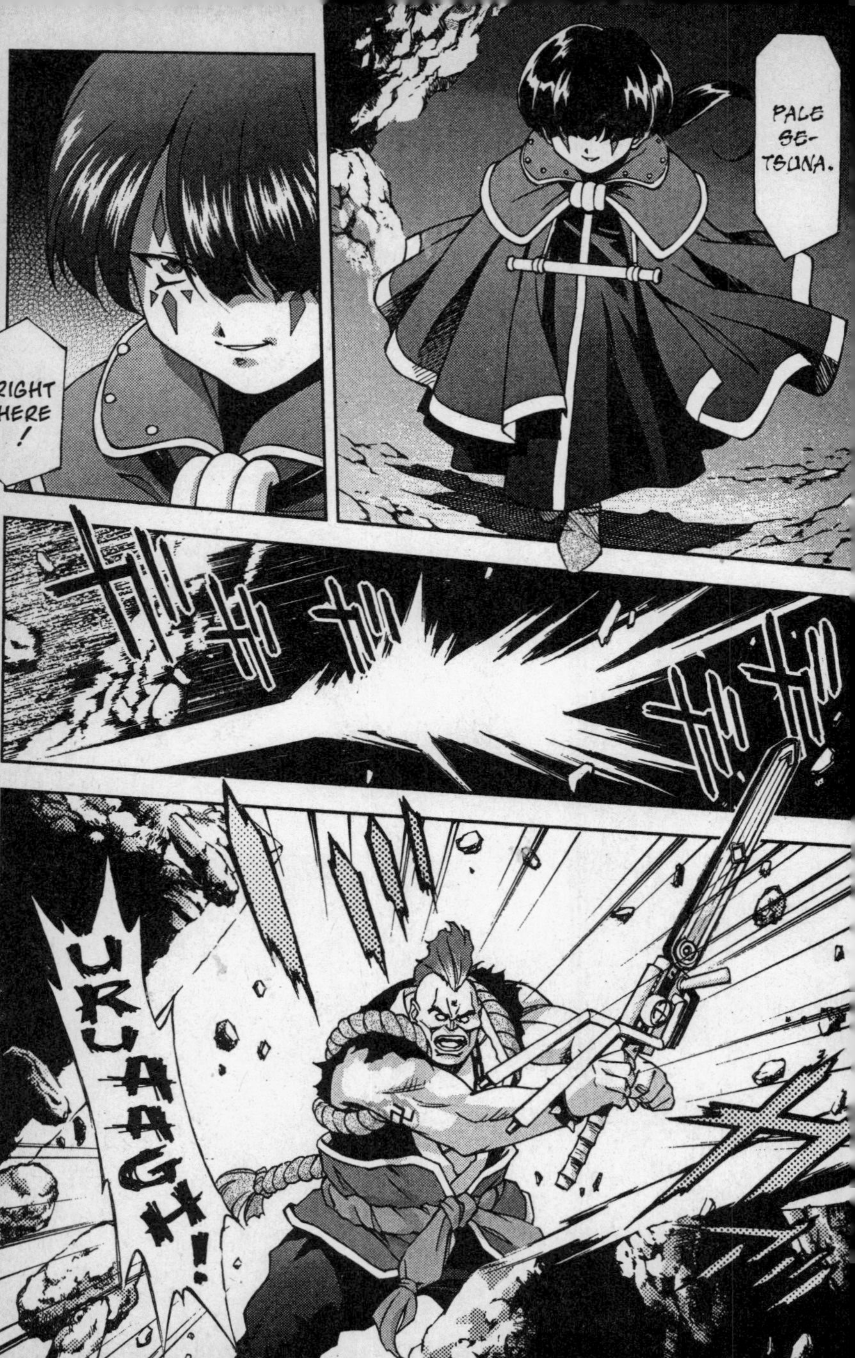

PALE SE-TSUNA.
RIGHT HERE!
URUAAGH!

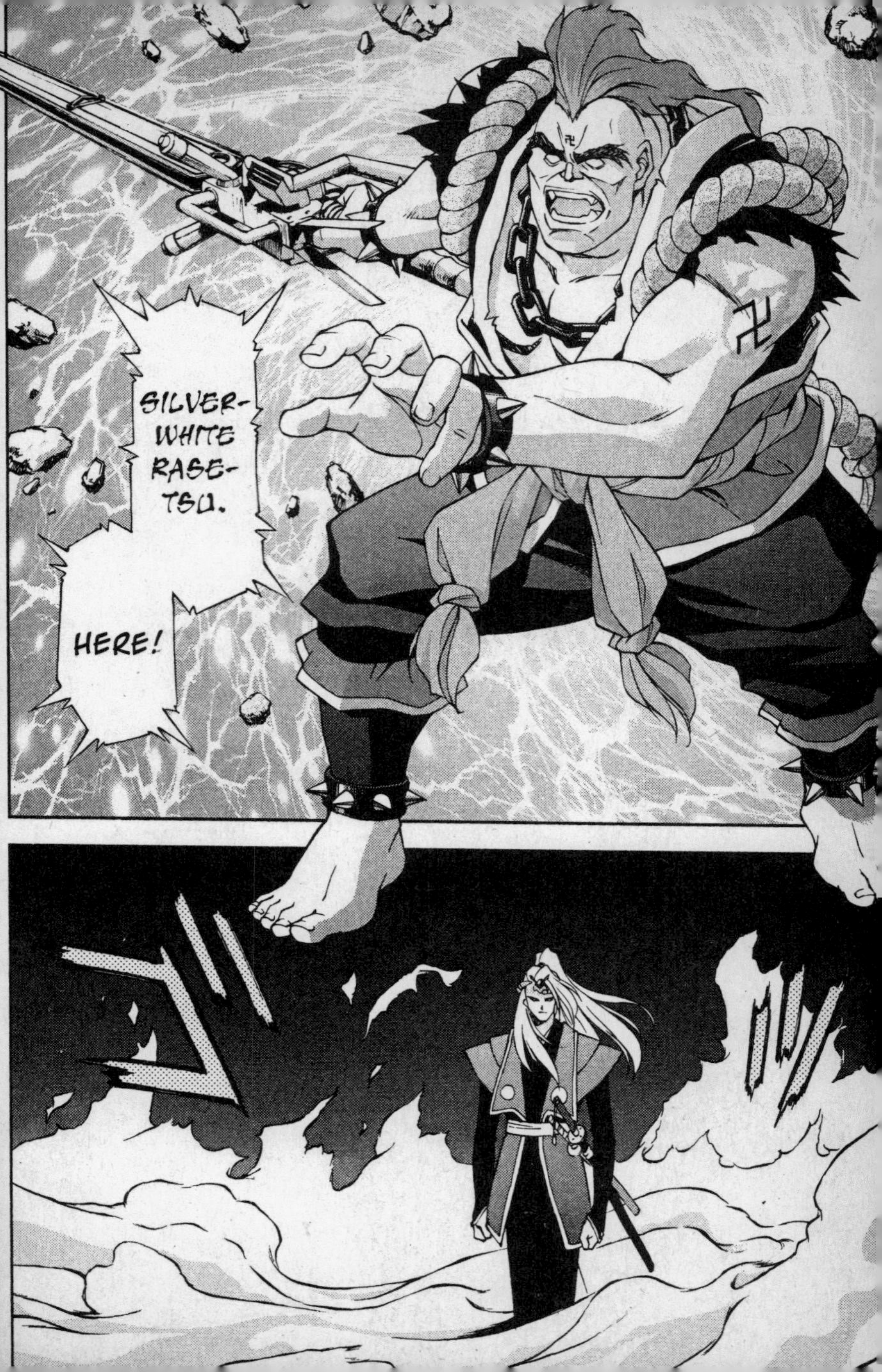
SILVER-WHITE RASE-TSU.
HERE!

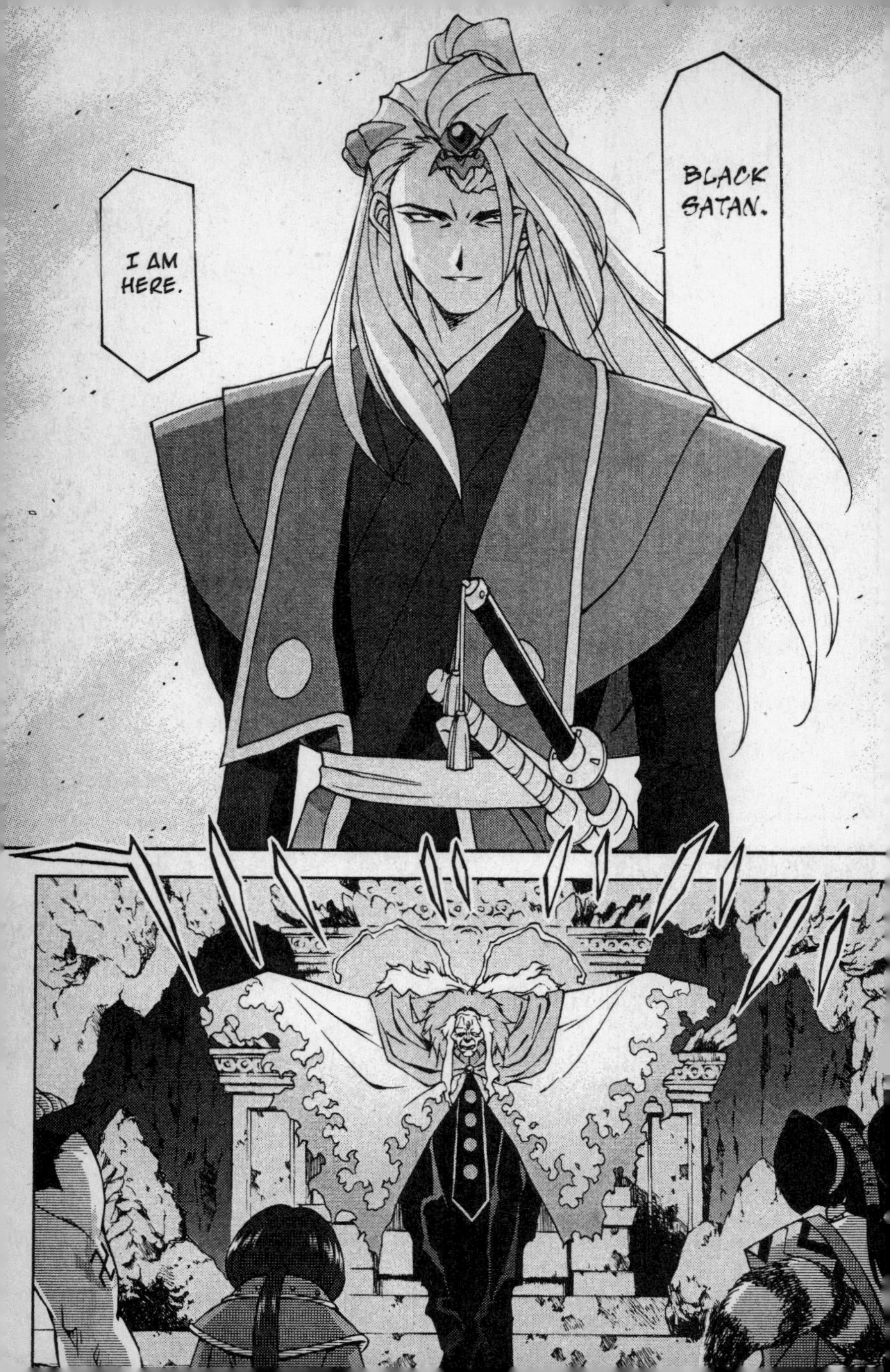
BLACK SATAN.
I AM HERE.

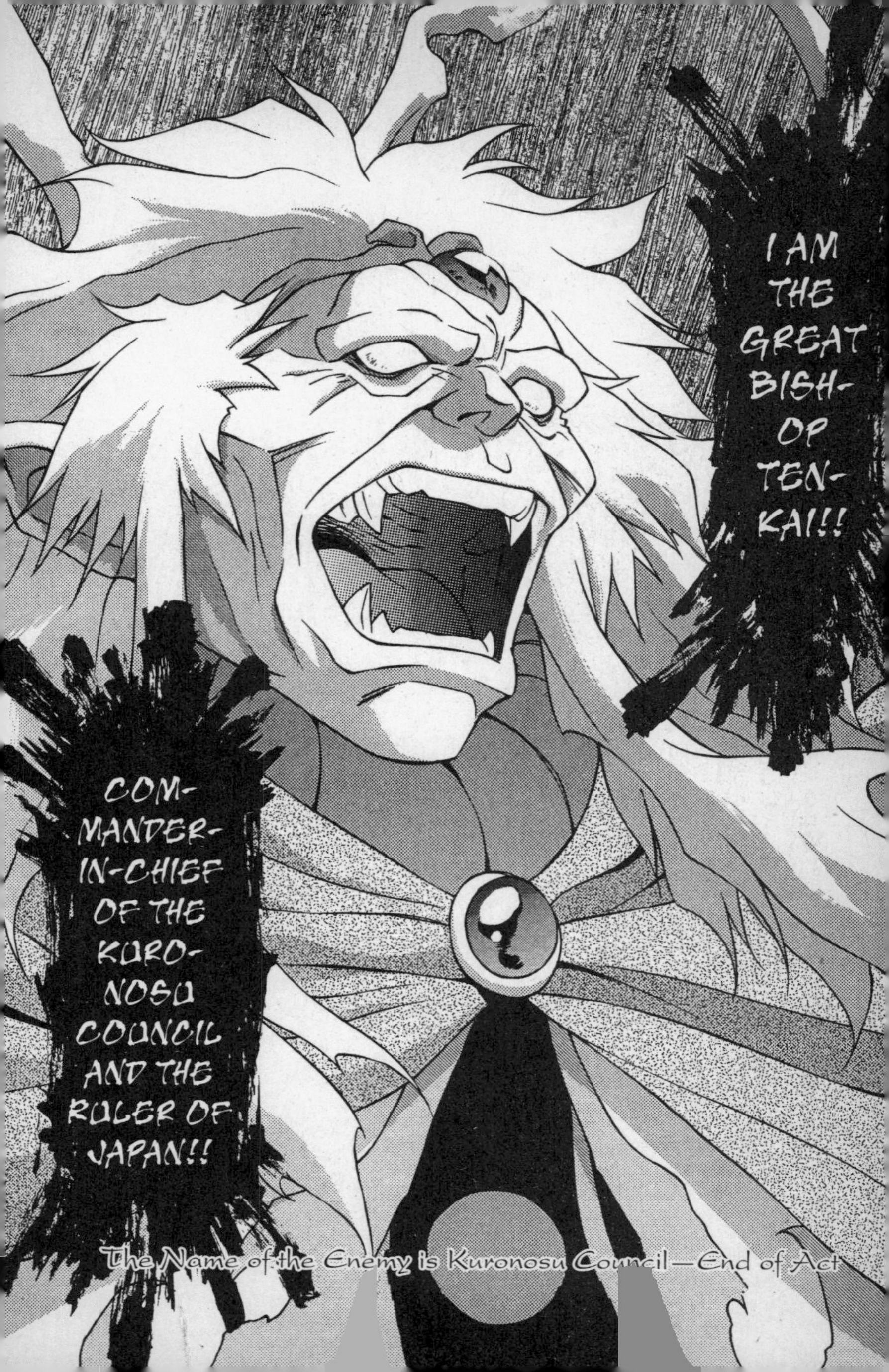
I AM THE GREAT BISH-OP TEN-KAI!!
COM-MANDER-IN-CHIEF OF THE KURO-NOSU COUNCIL AND THE RULER OF JAPAN!!
The Name of the Enemy is Kuronosu Council—End of Act

Chapter Eight
Commotion on the Stage

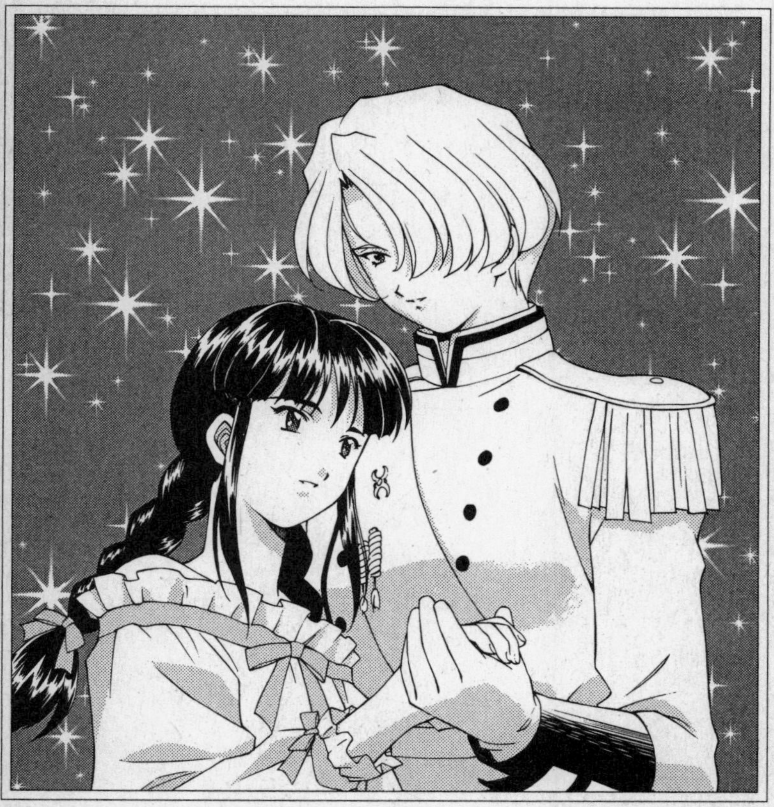

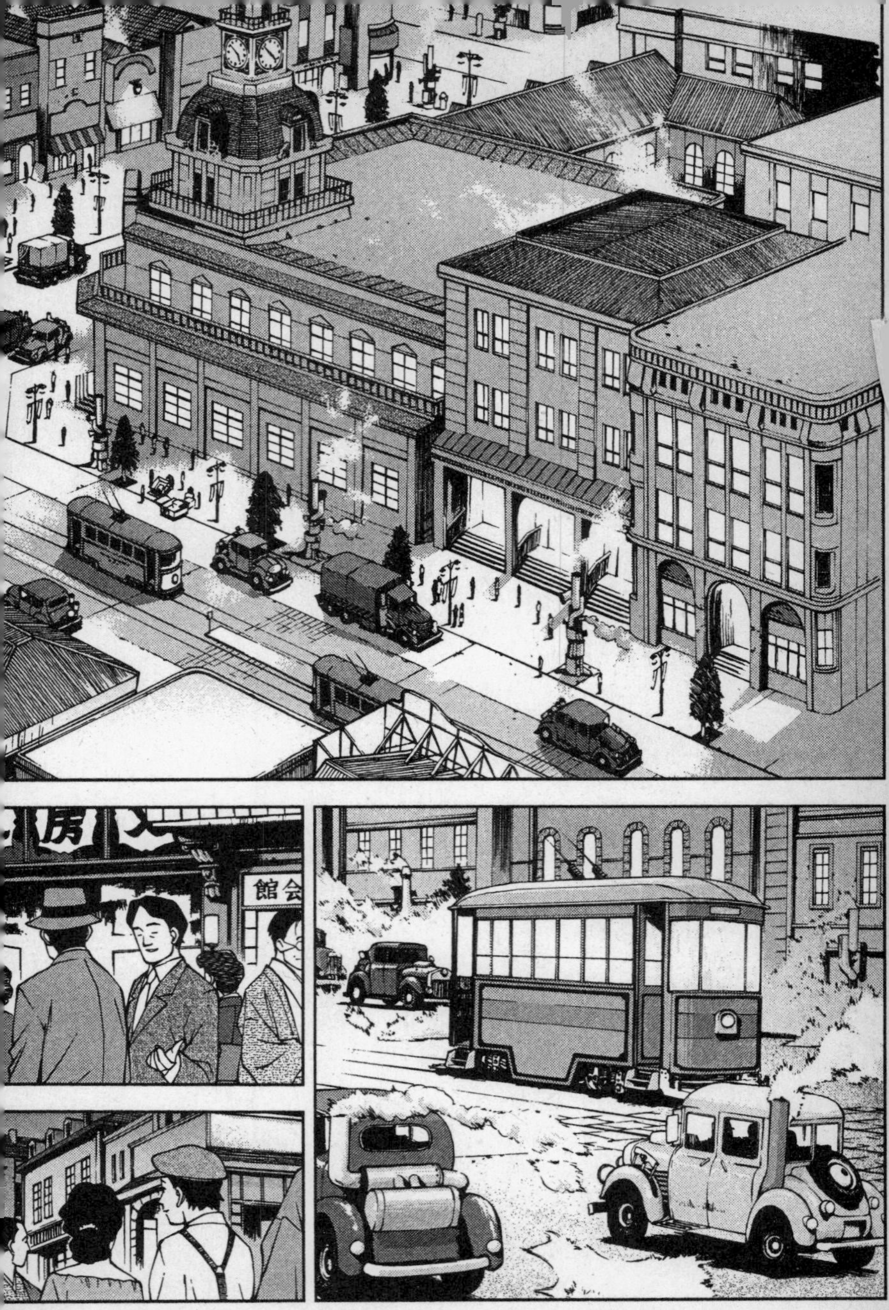
館会

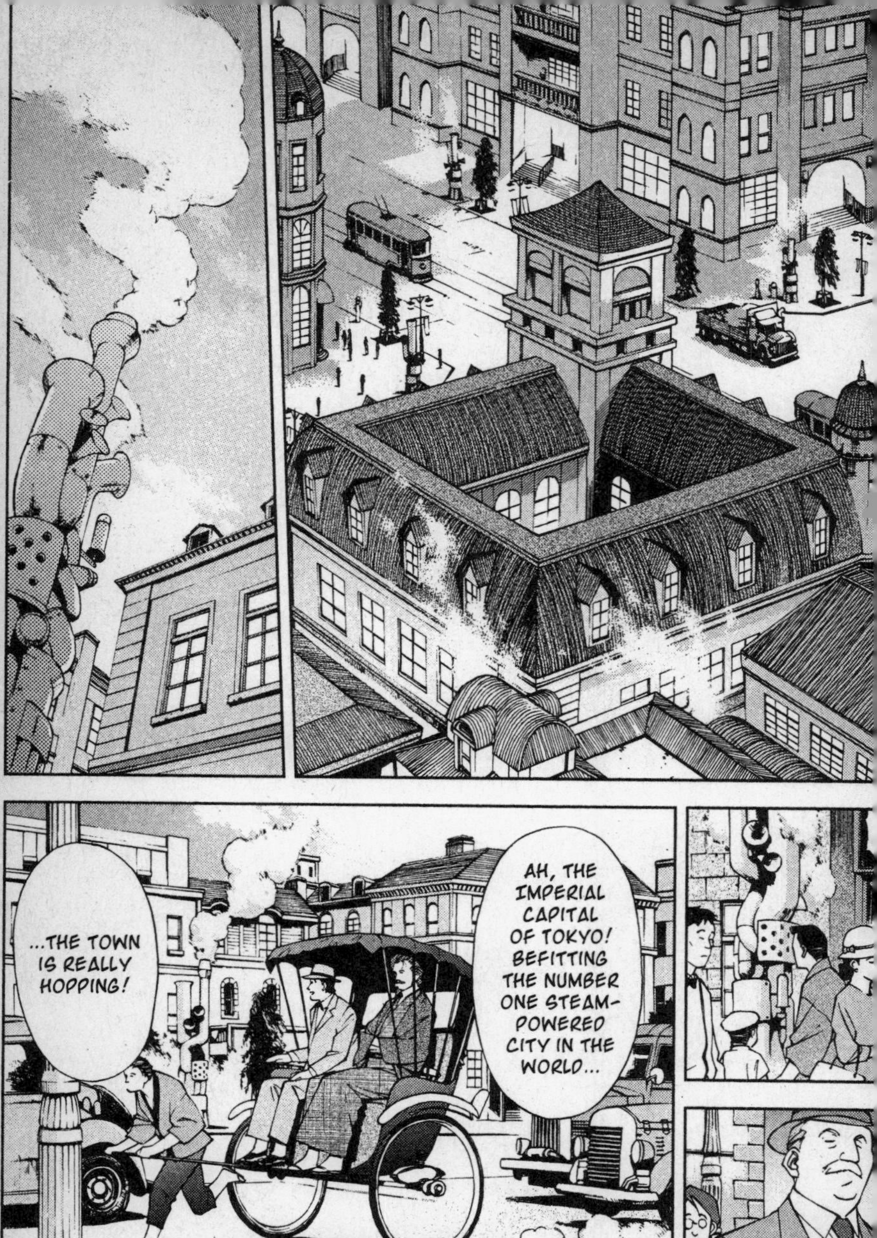
AH, THE IMPERIAL CAPITAL OF TOKYO! BEFITTING THE NUMBER ONE STEAM-POWERED CITY IN THE WORLD...
...THE TOWN IS REALLY HOPPING!

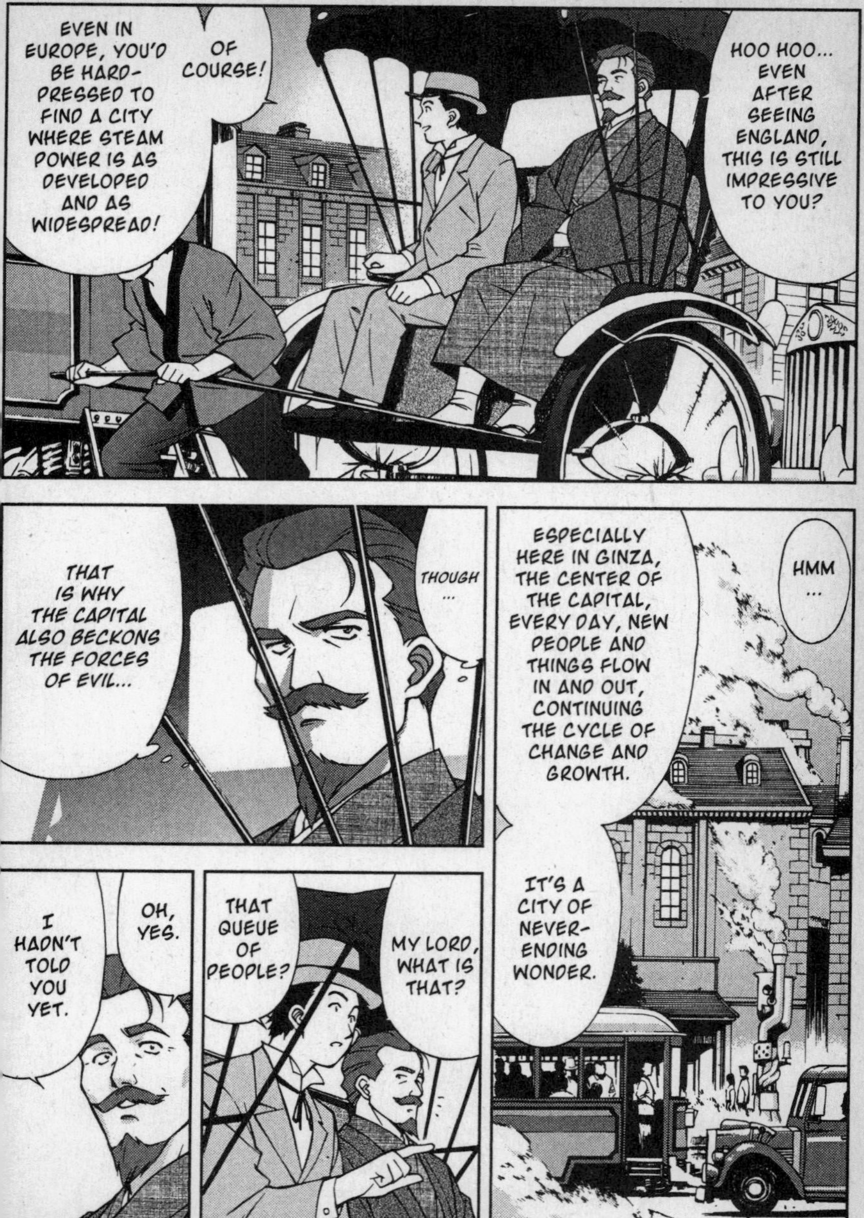
HOO HOO... EVEN AFTER SEEING ENGLAND, THIS IS STILL IMPRESSIVE TO YOU?
OF COURSE!
EVEN IN EUROPE, YOU'D BE HARD-PRESSED TO FIND A CITY WHERE STEAM POWER IS AS DEVELOPED AND AS WIDESPREAD!
HMM ...
ESPECIALLY HERE IN GINZA, THE CENTER OF THE CAPITAL, EVERY DAY, NEW PEOPLE AND THINGS FLOW IN AND OUT, CONTINUING THE CYCLE OF CHANGE AND GROWTH.
IT'S A CITY OF NEVER-ENDING WONDER.
THOUGH ...
THAT IS WHY THE CAPITAL ALSO BECKONS THE FORCES OF EVIL...
MY LORD, WHAT IS THAT?
THAT QUEUE OF PEOPLE?
OH, YES.
I HADN'T TOLD YOU YET.

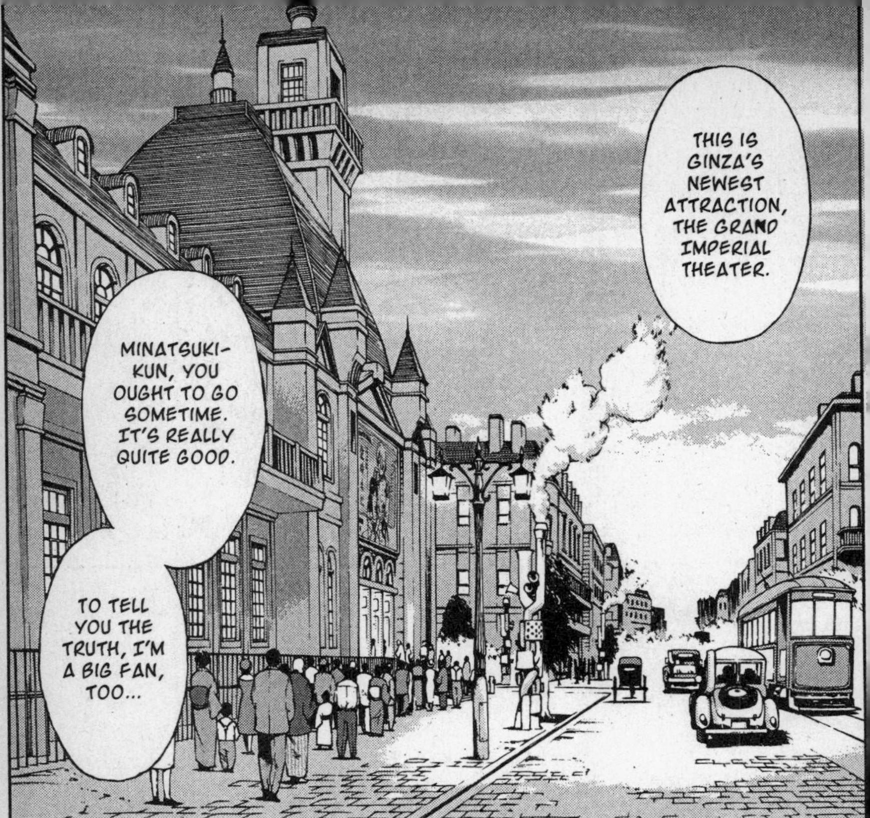
THIS IS GINZA'S NEWEST ATTRACTION, THE GRAND IMPERIAL THEATER.
MINATSUKI-KUN, YOU OUGHT TO GO SOMETIME. IT'S REALLY QUITE GOOD.
TO TELL YOU THE TRUTH, I'M A BIG FAN, TOO...

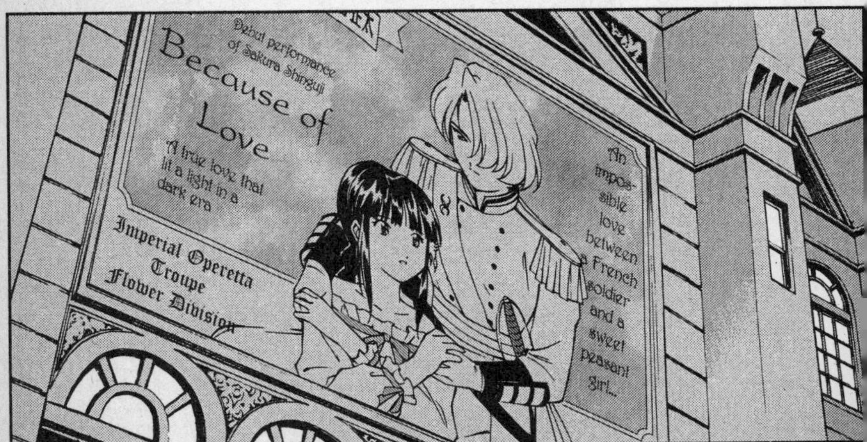
Debut performance of Sakura Shinguji
Because of Love
A true love that lit a light in a dark era
Imperial Operetta Troupe Flower Division
An impossible love between a French soldier and a sweet peasant girl...

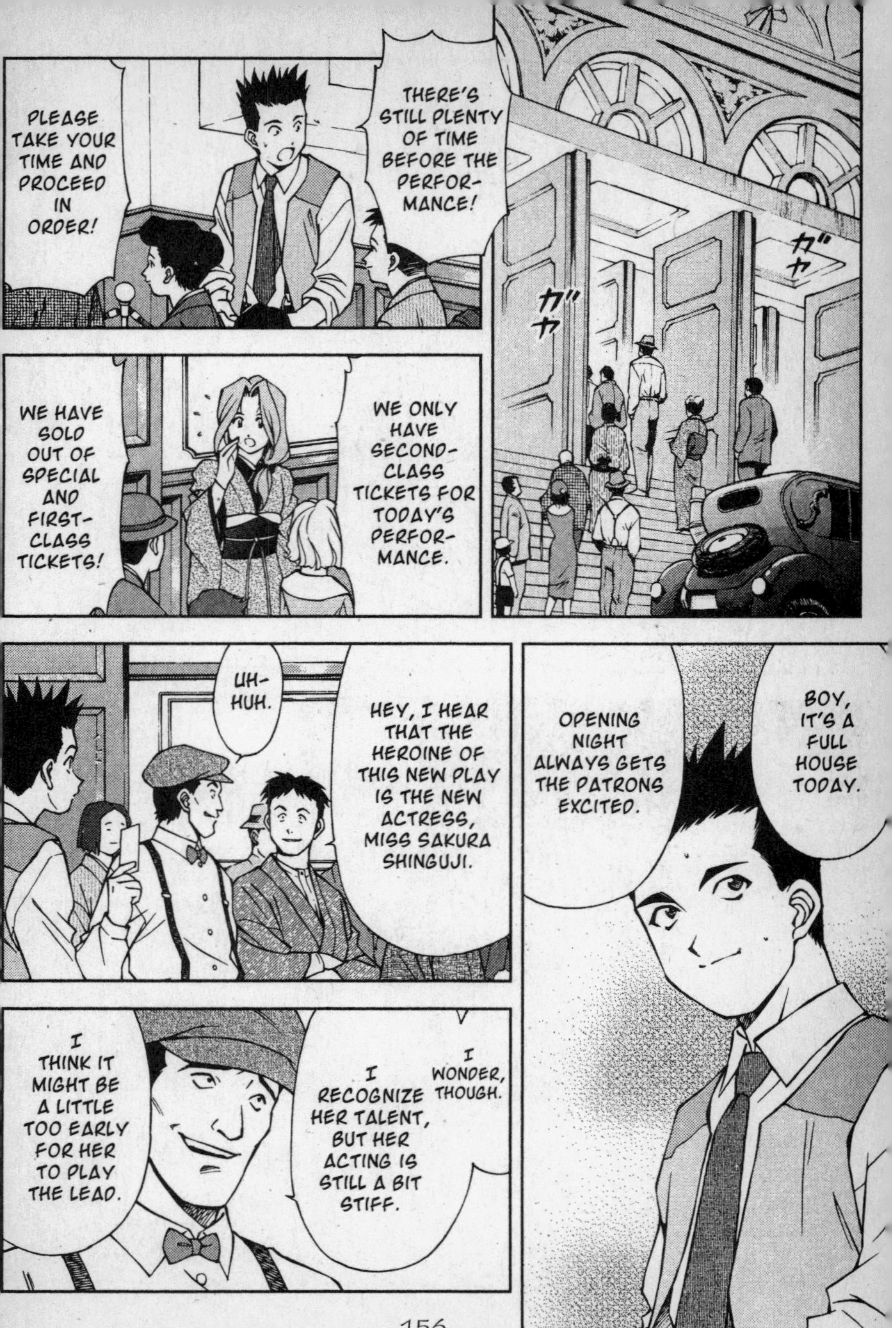
ガヤ
ガヤ
THERE'S STILL PLENTY OF TIME BEFORE THE PERFORMANCE!
PLEASE TAKE YOUR TIME AND PROCEED IN ORDER!
WE ONLY HAVE SECOND-CLASS TICKETS FOR TODAY'S PERFORMANCE.
WE HAVE SOLD OUT OF SPECIAL AND FIRST-CLASS TICKETS!
BOY, IT'S A FULL HOUSE TODAY.
OPENING NIGHT ALWAYS GETS THE PATRONS EXCITED.
HEY, I HEAR THAT THE HEROINE OF THIS NEW PLAY IS THE NEW ACTRESS, MISS SAKURA SHINGUJI.
UH-HUH.
I WONDER, THOUGH.
I RECOGNIZE HER TALENT, BUT HER ACTING IS STILL A BIT STIFF.
I THINK IT MIGHT BE A LITTLE TOO EARLY FOR HER TO PLAY THE LEAD.

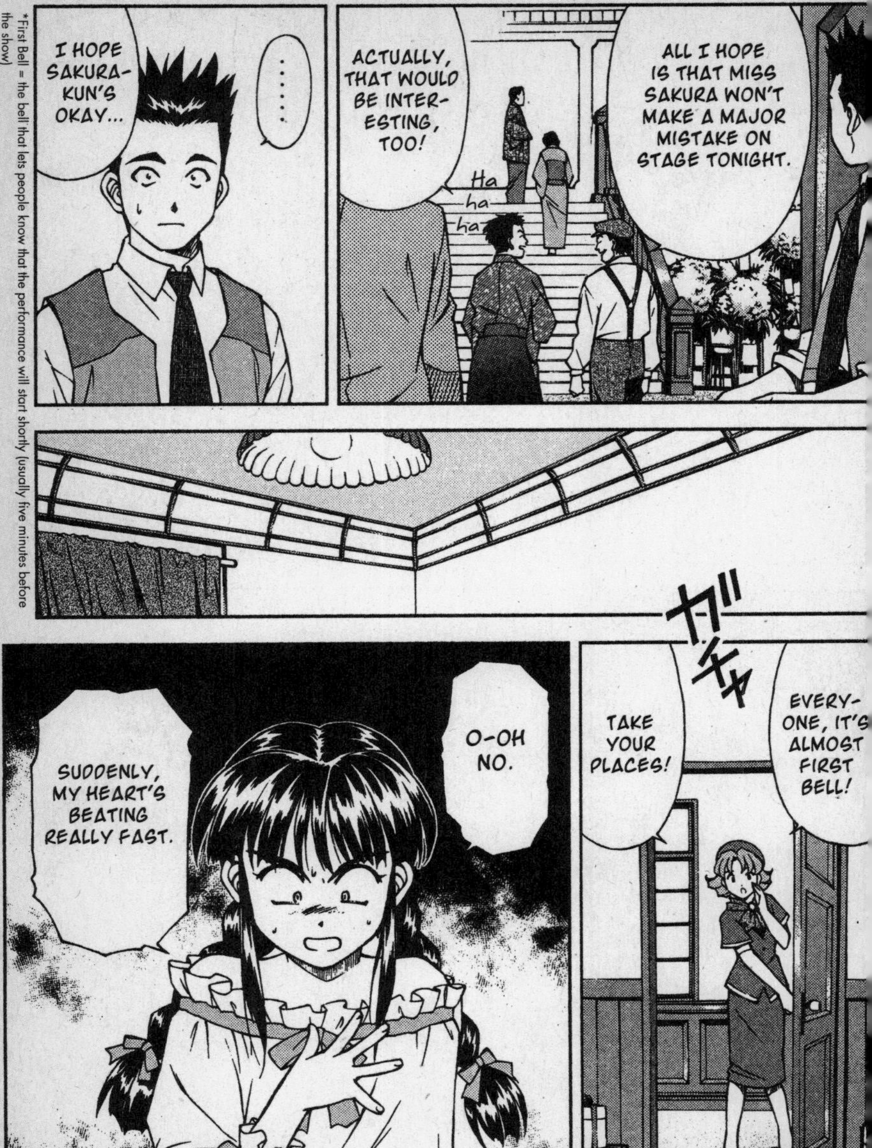
ALL I HOPE IS THAT MISS SAKURA WON'T MAKE A MAJOR MISTAKE ON STAGE TONIGHT.
ACTUALLY, THAT WOULD BE INTERESTING, TOO!
Ha ha ha
......
I HOPE SAKURA-KUN'S OKAY...
ガチャ
EVERYONE, IT'S ALMOST FIRST BELL!
TAKE YOUR PLACES!
O-OH NO.
SUDDENLY, MY HEART'S BEATING REALLY FAST.

*First Bell = the bell that lets people know that the performance will start shortly (usually five minutes before the show)

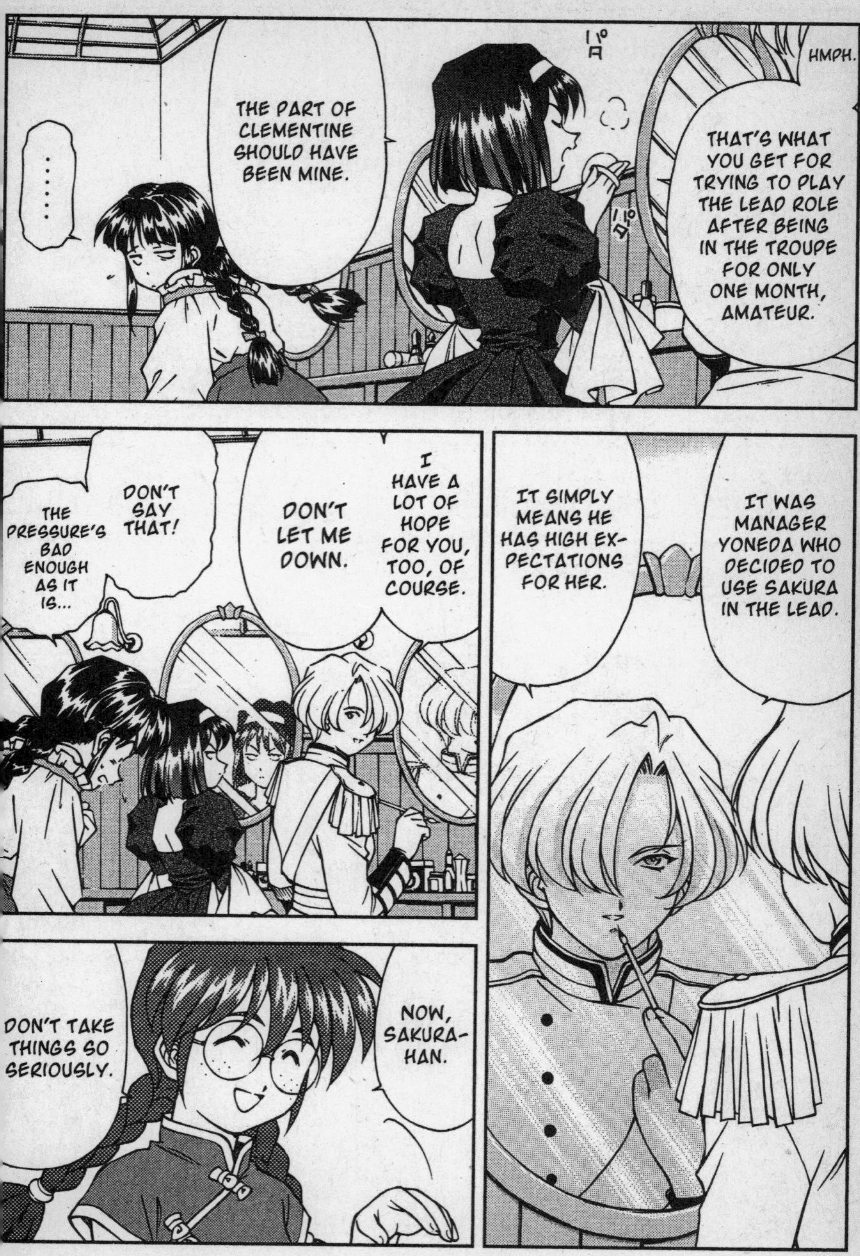
HMPH.
THAT'S WHAT YOU GET FOR TRYING TO PLAY THE LEAD ROLE AFTER BEING IN THE TROUPE FOR ONLY ONE MONTH, AMATEUR.
THE PART OF CLEMENTINE SHOULD HAVE BEEN MINE.
......
IT WAS MANAGER YONEDA WHO DECIDED TO USE SAKURA IN THE LEAD.
IT SIMPLY MEANS HE HAS HIGH EX-PECTATIONS FOR HER.
I HAVE A LOT OF HOPE FOR YOU, TOO, OF COURSE.
DON'T LET ME DOWN.
DON'T SAY THAT!
THE PRESSURE'S BAD ENOUGH AS IT IS...
NOW, SAKURA-HAN.
DON'T TAKE THINGS SO SERIOUSLY.

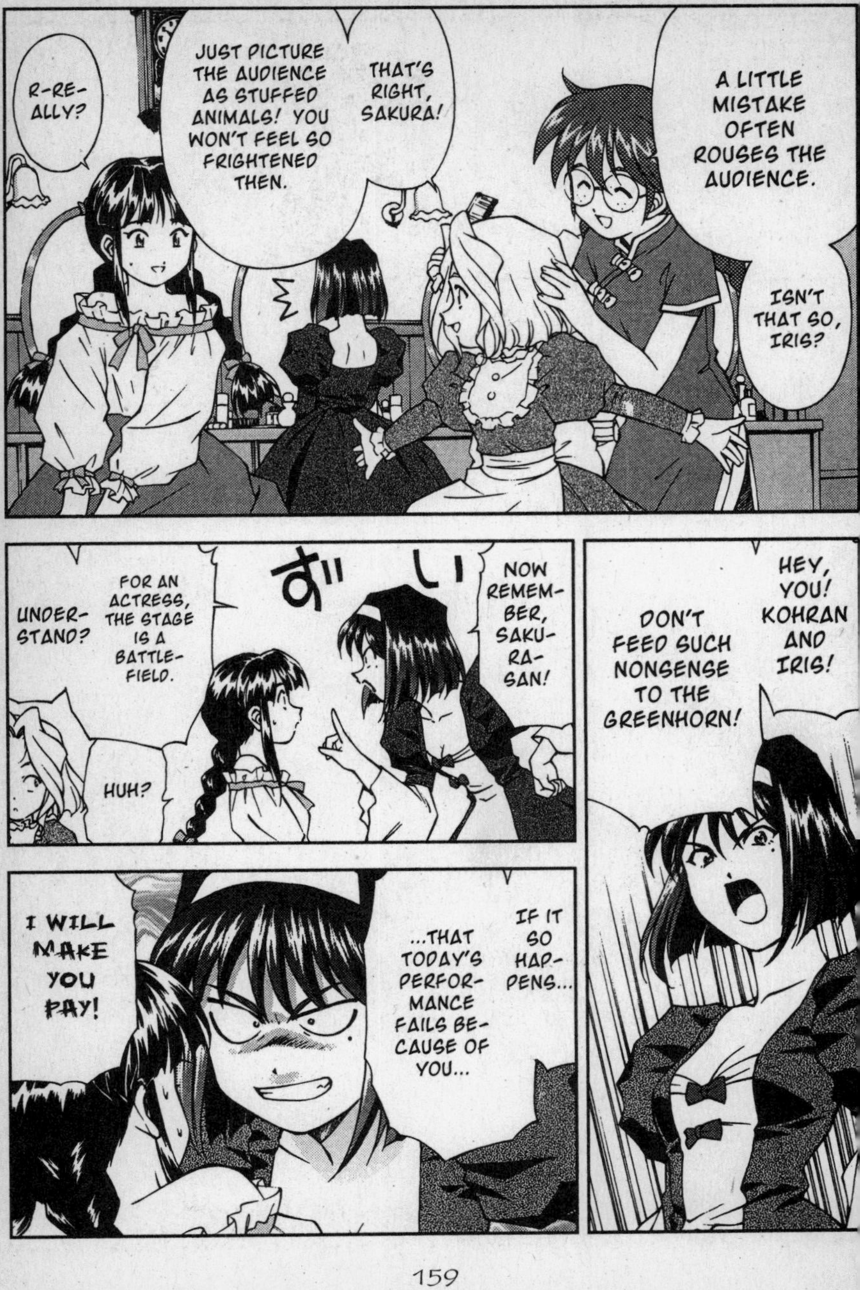
A LITTLE MISTAKE OFTEN ROUSES THE AUDIENCE.
ISN'T THAT SO, IRIS?
THAT'S RIGHT, SAKURA!
JUST PICTURE THE AUDIENCE AS STUFFED ANIMALS! YOU WON'T FEEL SO FRIGHTENED THEN.
R-RE-ALLY?
HEY, YOU! KOHRAN AND IRIS!
DON'T FEED SUCH NONSENSE TO THE GREENHORN!
ずい
NOW REMEM-BER, SAKU-RA-SAN!
FOR AN ACTRESS, THE STAGE IS A BATTLE-FIELD.
UNDER-STAND?
HUH?
IF IT SO HAP-PENS...
...THAT TODAY'S PERFOR-MANCE FAILS BE-CAUSE OF YOU...
I WILL MAKE YOU PAY!

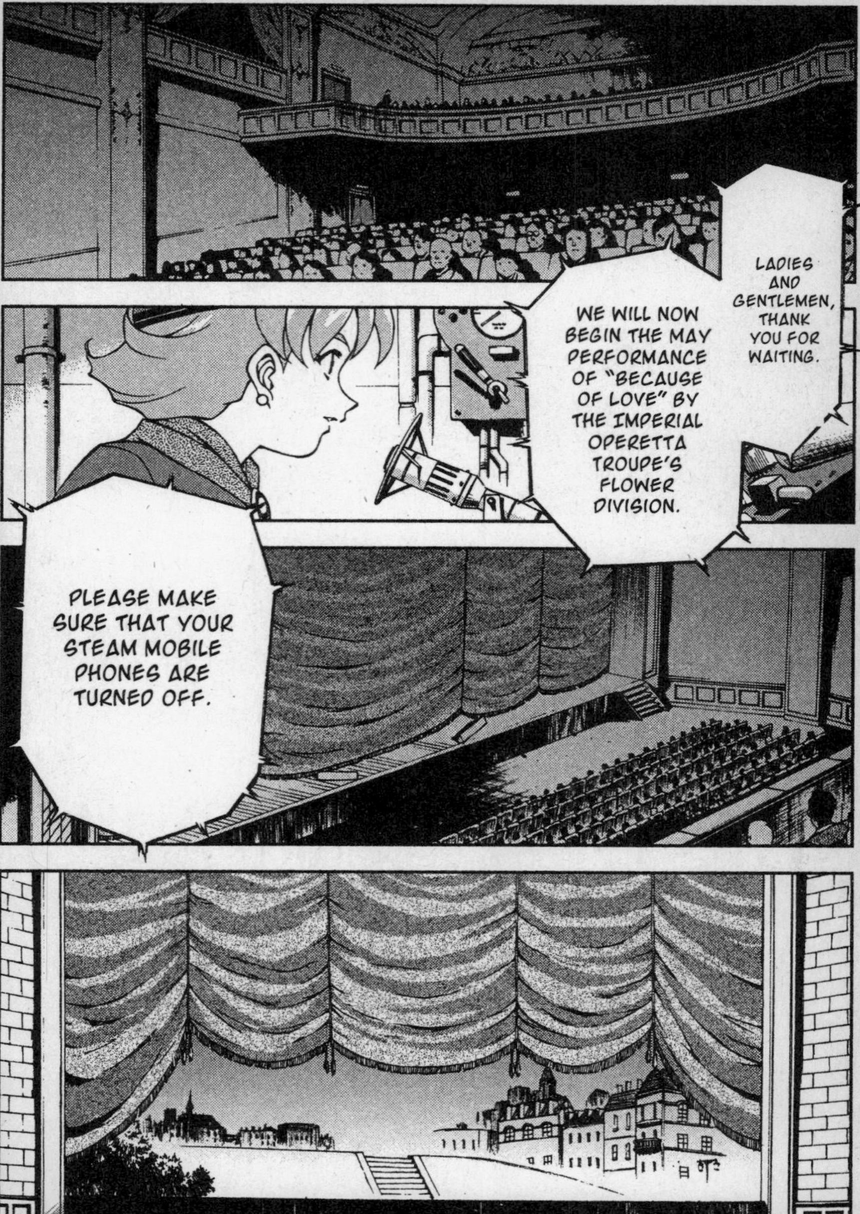
LADIES AND GENTLEMEN, THANK YOU FOR WAITING.
WE WILL NOW BEGIN THE MAY PERFORMANCE OF "BECAUSE OF LOVE" BY THE IMPERIAL OPERETTA TROUPE'S FLOWER DIVISION.
PLEASE MAKE SURE THAT YOUR STEAM MOBILE PHONES ARE TURNED OFF.

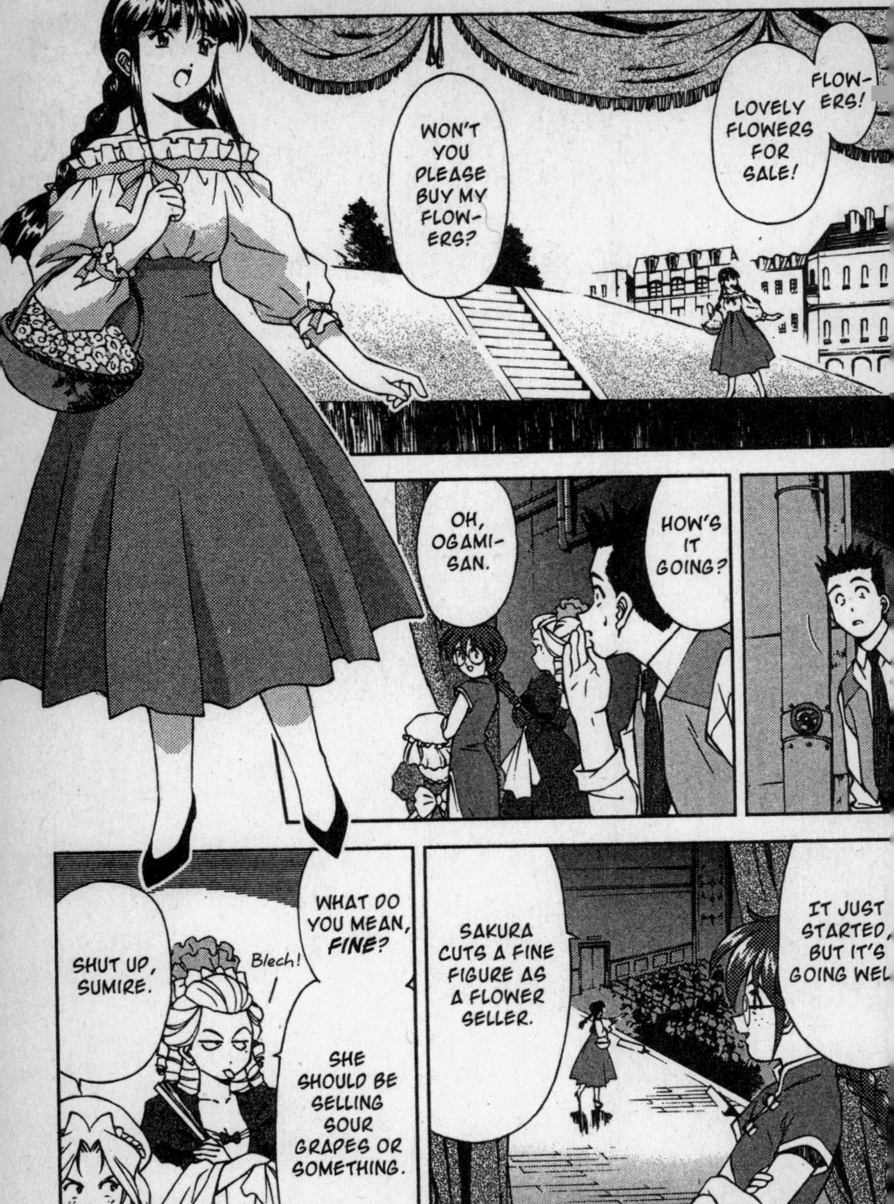
FLOW-ERS!
LOVELY FLOWERS FOR SALE!
WON'T YOU PLEASE BUY MY FLOW-ERS?
HOW'S IT GOING?
OH, OGAMI-SAN.
IT JUST STARTED, BUT IT'S GOING WEL
SAKURA CUTS A FINE FIGURE AS A FLOWER SELLER.
WHAT DO YOU MEAN, *FINE*?
SHE SHOULD BE SELLING SOUR GRAPES OR SOMETHING.
Blech!
SHUT UP, SUMIRE.

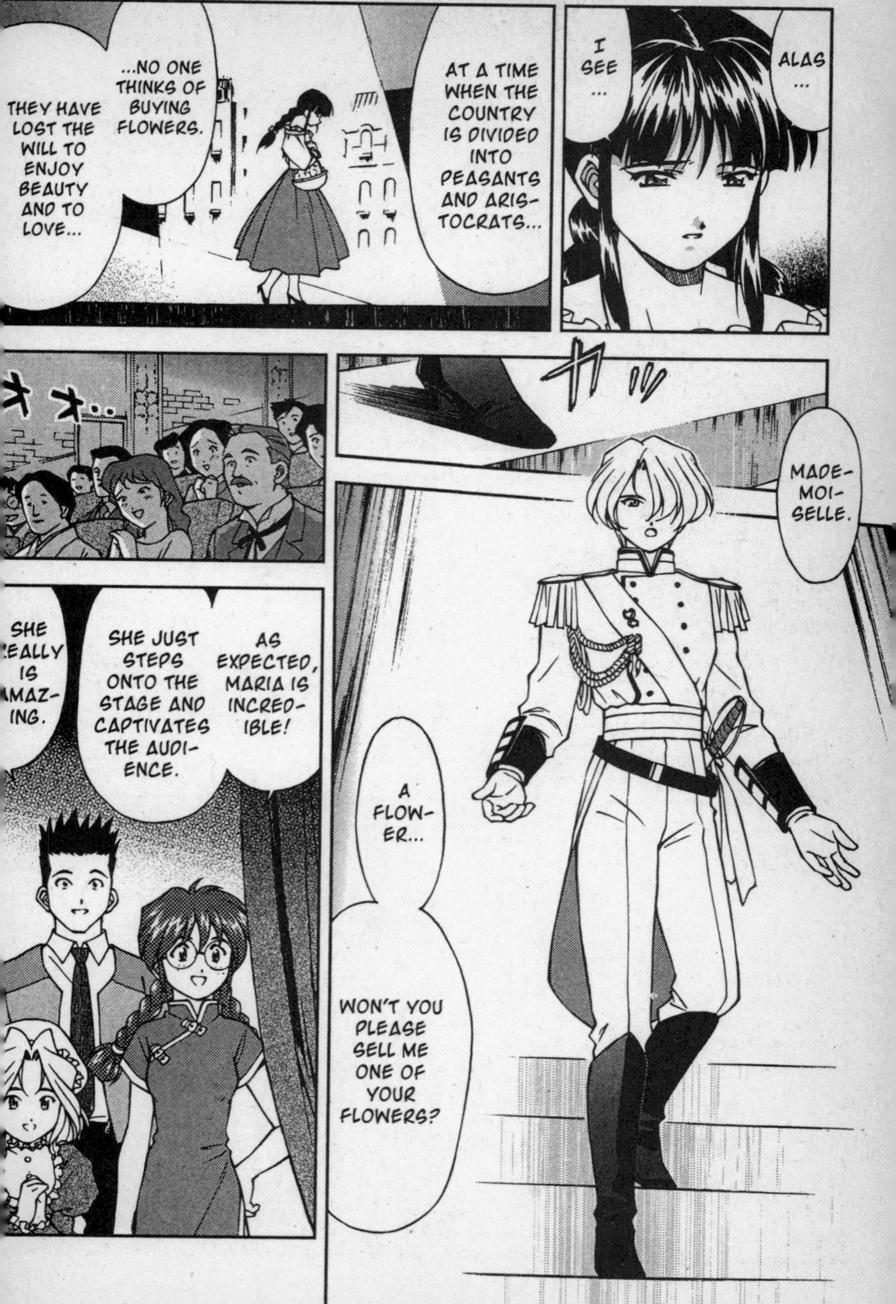
ALAS ...
I SEE ...
AT A TIME WHEN THE COUNTRY IS DIVIDED INTO PEASANTS AND ARIS-TOCRATS...
...NO ONE THINKS OF BUYING FLOWERS.
THEY HAVE LOST THE WILL TO ENJOY BEAUTY AND TO LOVE...
カッ
MADE-MOI-SELLE.
A FLOW-ER...
WON'T YOU PLEASE SELL ME ONE OF YOUR FLOWERS?
オオ...
AS EXPECTED, MARIA IS INCRED-IBLE!
SHE JUST STEPS ONTO THE STAGE AND CAPTIVATES THE AUDI-ENCE.
SHE EALLY IS MAZ-ING.

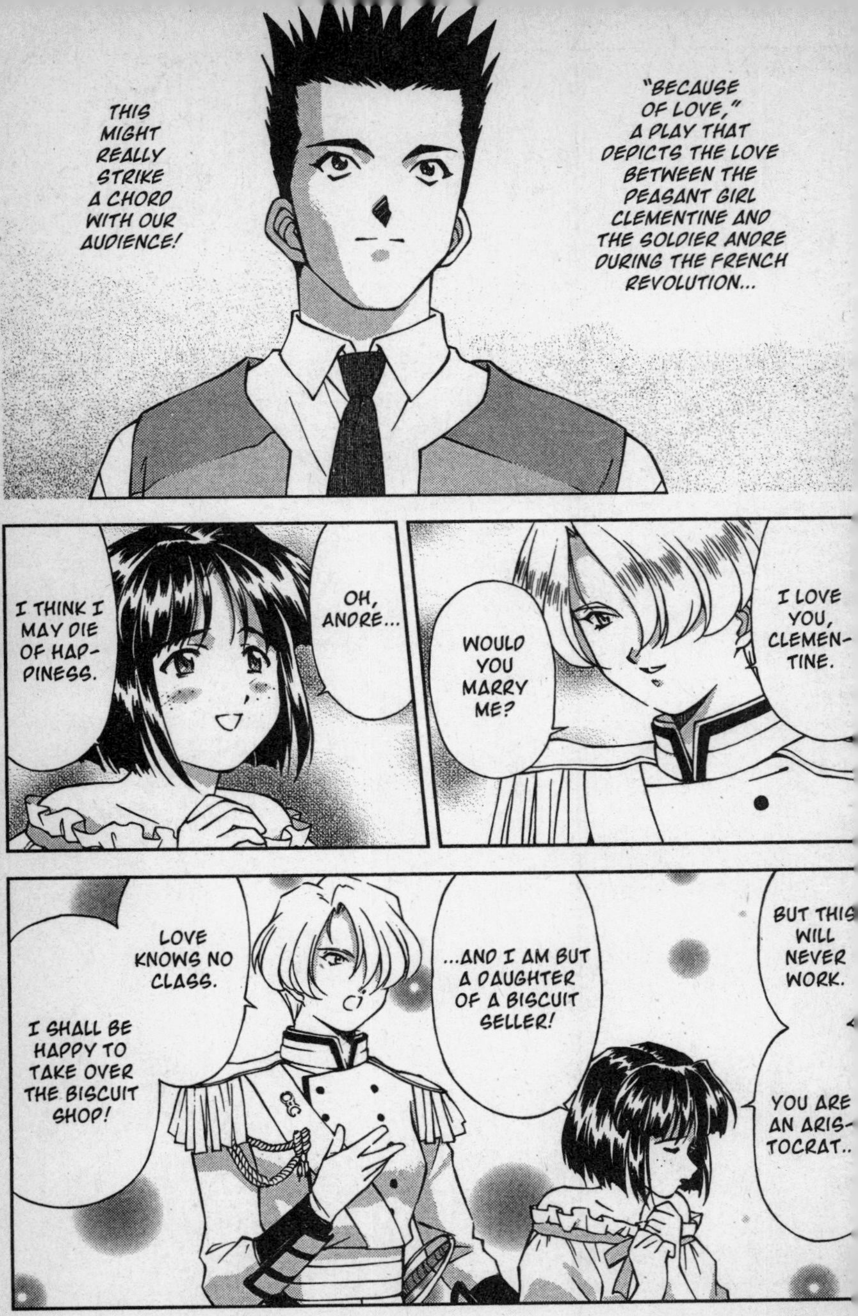
"BECAUSE OF LOVE," A PLAY THAT DEPICTS THE LOVE BETWEEN THE PEASANT GIRL CLEMENTINE AND THE SOLDIER ANDRE DURING THE FRENCH REVOLUTION...
THIS MIGHT REALLY STRIKE A CHORD WITH OUR AUDIENCE!
I LOVE YOU, CLEMENTINE.
WOULD YOU MARRY ME?
OH, ANDRE...
I THINK I MAY DIE OF HAPPINESS.
BUT THIS WILL NEVER WORK.
YOU ARE AN ARISTOCRAT..
...AND I AM BUT A DAUGHTER OF A BISCUIT SELLER!
LOVE KNOWS NO CLASS.
I SHALL BE HAPPY TO TAKE OVER THE BISCUIT SHOP!

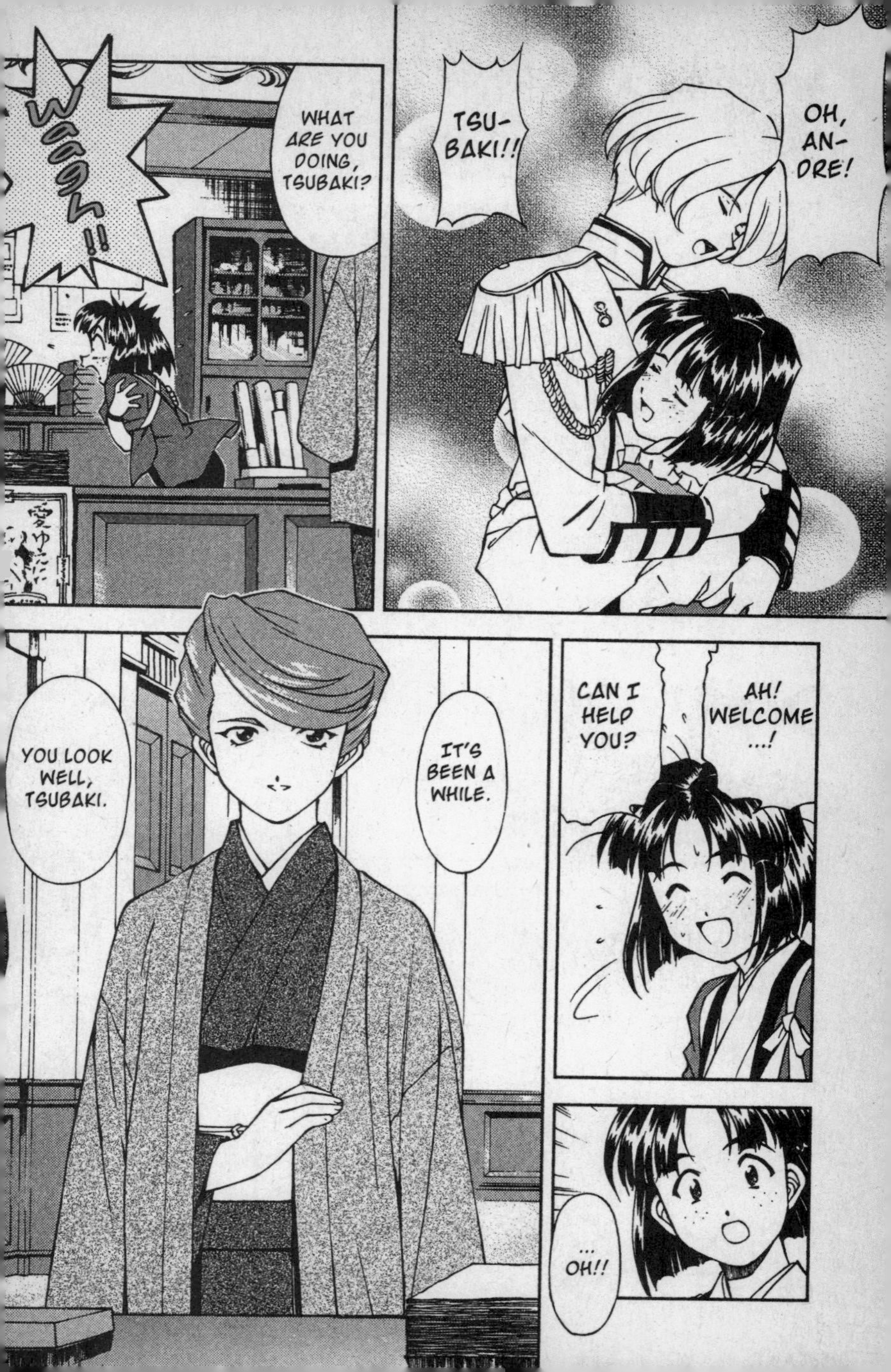
OH, AN-DRE!
TSU-BAKI!!
WHAT ARE YOU DOING, TSUBAKI?
Waagh!!
AH! WELCOME ...!
CAN I HELP YOU?
... OH!!
IT'S BEEN A WHILE.
YOU LOOK WELL, TSUBAKI.

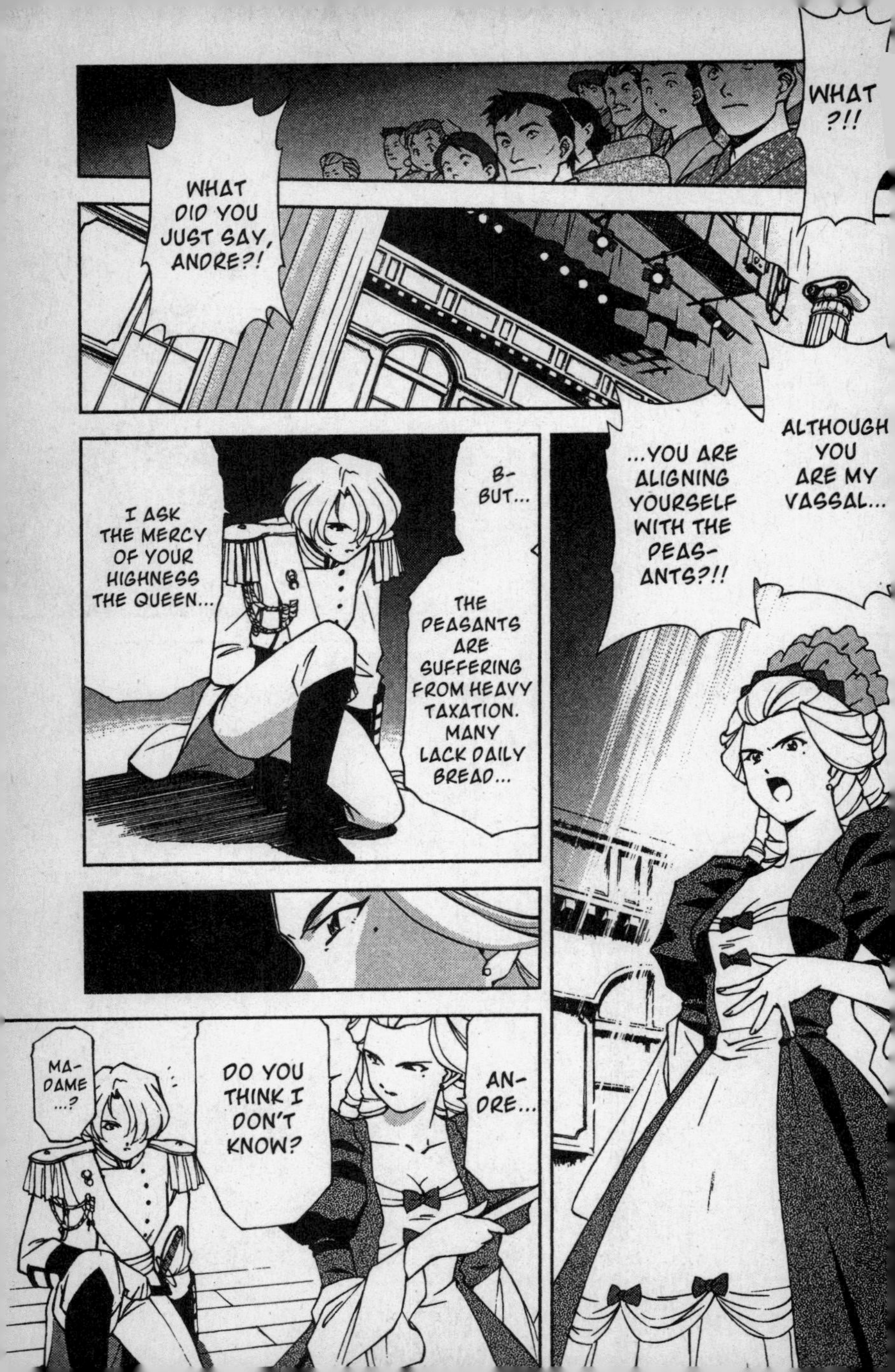
WHAT ?!!
WHAT DID YOU JUST SAY, ANDRE?!
ALTHOUGH YOU ARE MY VASSAL...
...YOU ARE ALIGNING YOURSELF WITH THE PEAS-ANTS?!!
B-BUT...
I ASK THE MERCY OF YOUR HIGHNESS THE QUEEN...
THE PEASANTS ARE SUFFERING FROM HEAVY TAXATION. MANY LACK DAILY BREAD...
AN-DRE...
DO YOU THINK I DON'T KNOW?
MA-DAME ...?

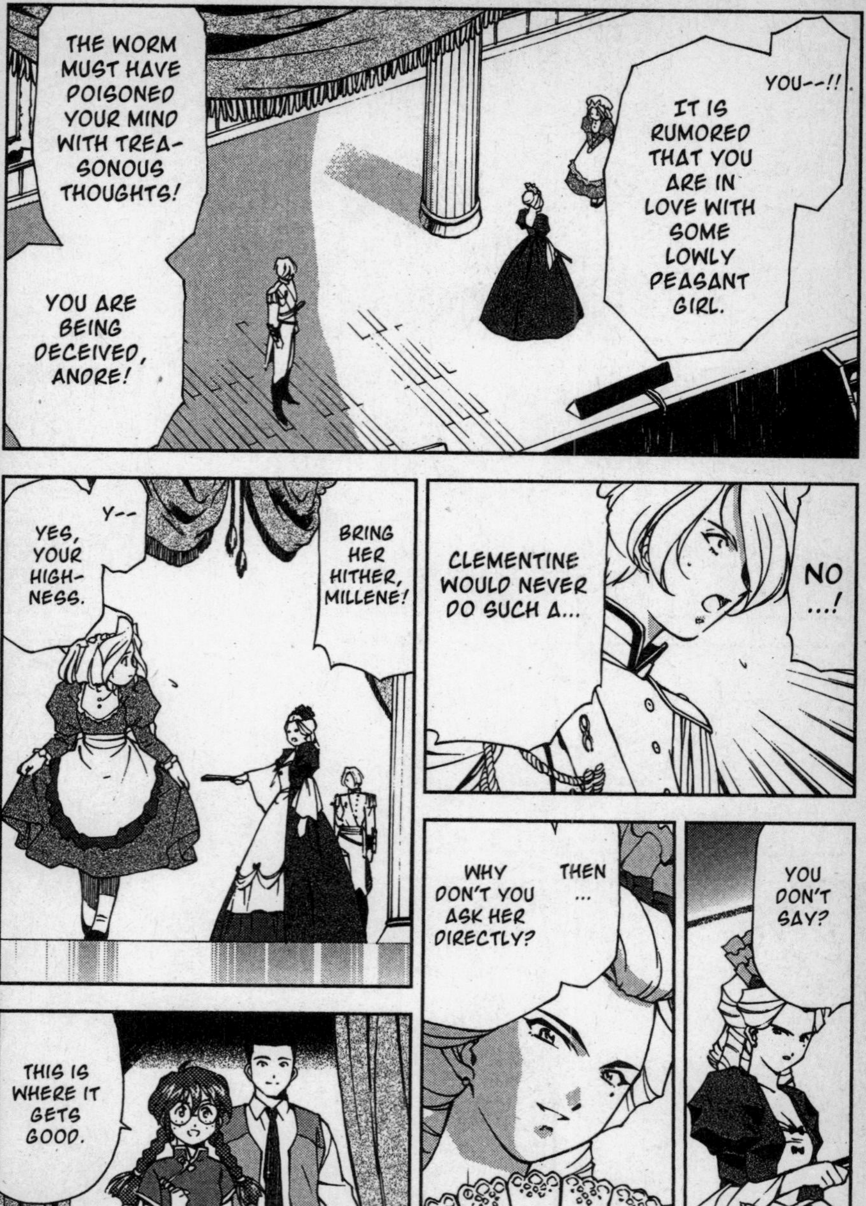

YOU--!!
IT IS RUMORED THAT YOU ARE IN LOVE WITH SOME LOWLY PEASANT GIRL.
THE WORM MUST HAVE POISONED YOUR MIND WITH TREA-SONOUS THOUGHTS!
YOU ARE BEING DECEIVED, ANDRE!
NO ...!
CLEMENTINE WOULD NEVER DO SUCH A...
BRING HER HITHER, MILLENE!
Y--
YES, YOUR HIGH-NESS.
YOU DON'T SAY?
THEN ...
WHY DON'T YOU ASK HER DIRECTLY?
THIS IS WHERE IT GETS GOOD.

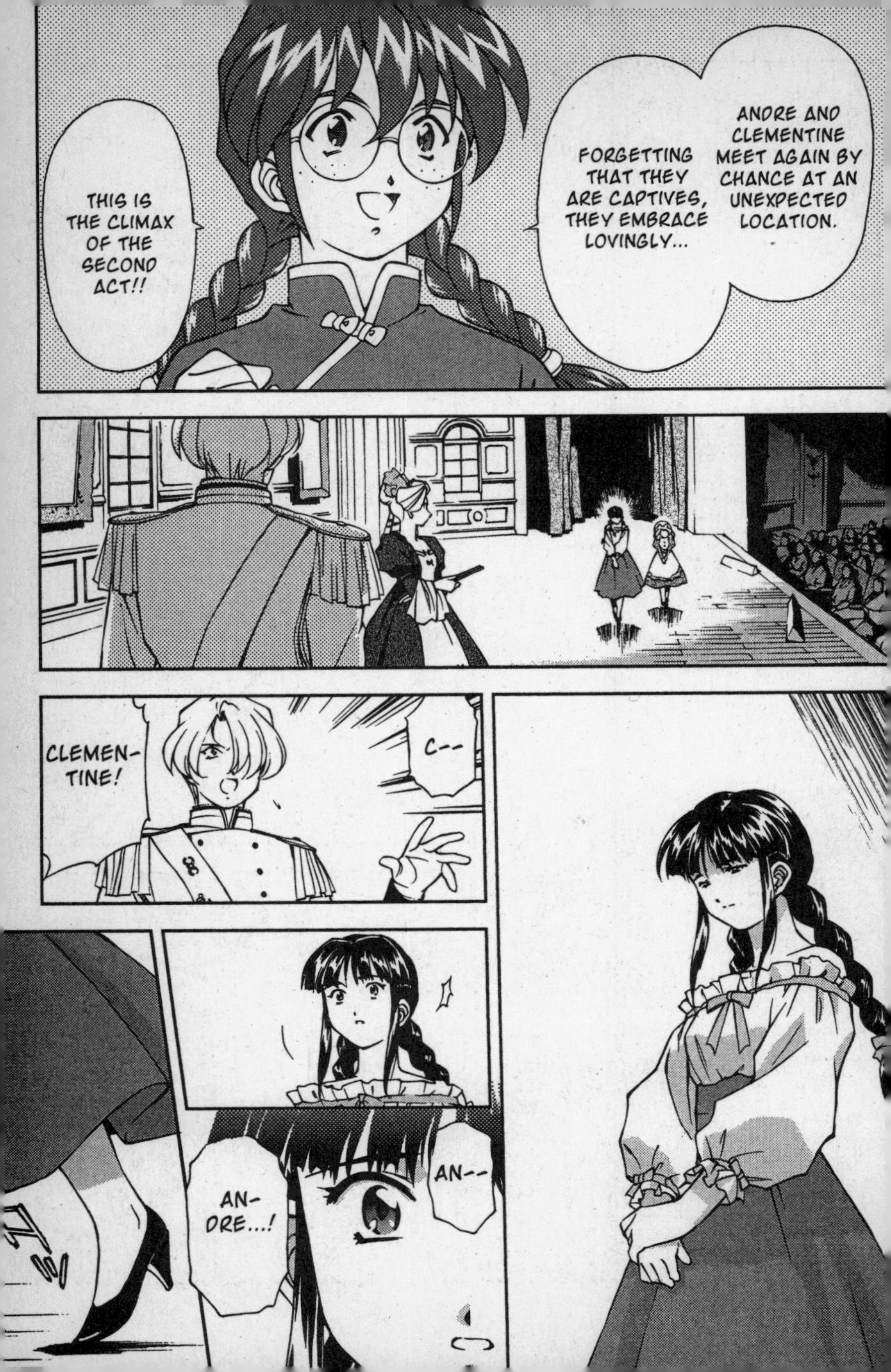
ANDRE AND CLEMENTINE MEET AGAIN BY CHANCE AT AN UNEXPECTED LOCATION.
FORGETTING THAT THEY ARE CAPTIVES, THEY EMBRACE LOVINGLY...
THIS IS THE CLIMAX OF THE SECOND ACT!!
C--
CLEMEN-TINE!
AN--
AN-DRE...!

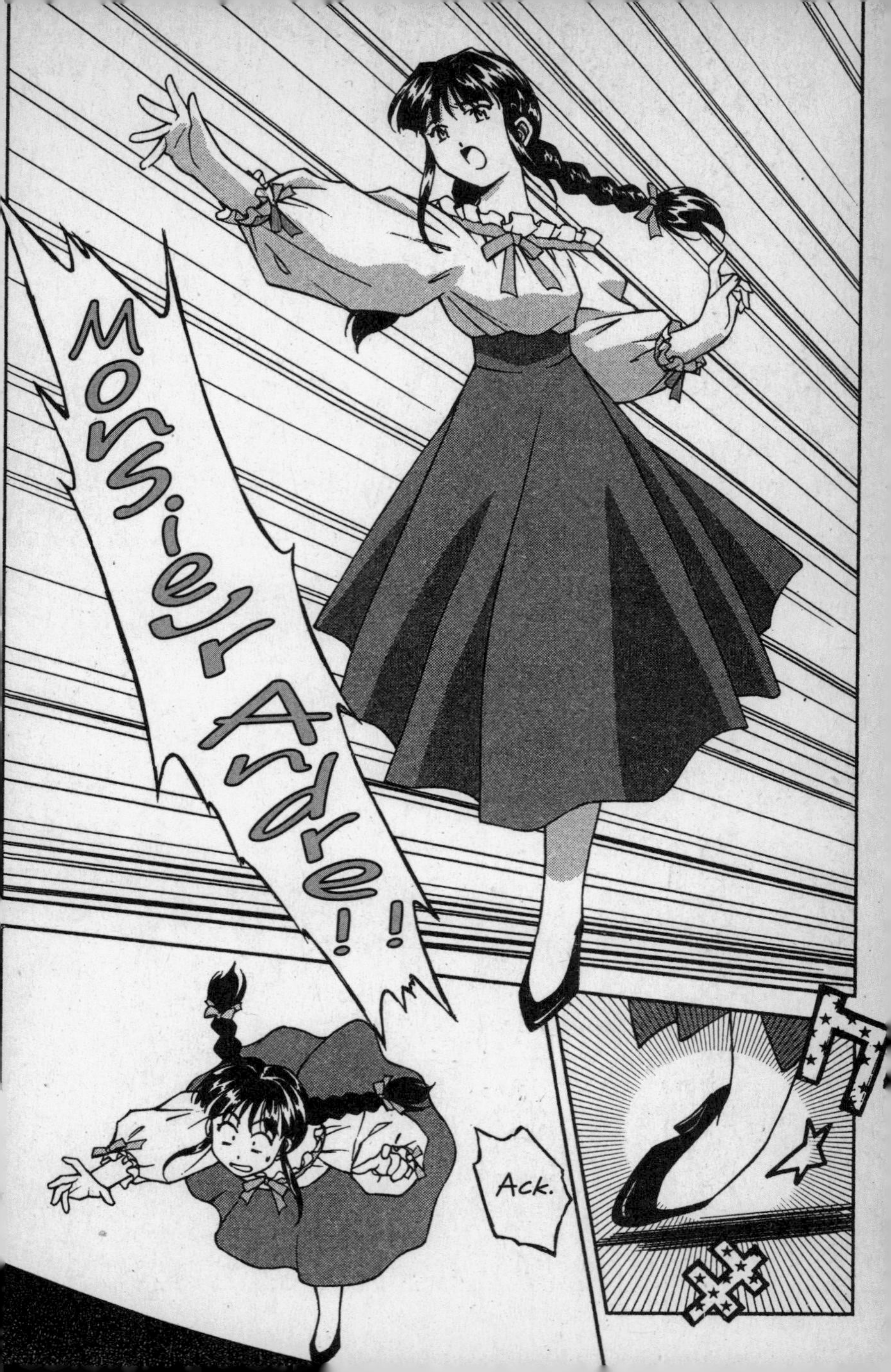
Monsieur Andre!!
Ack.

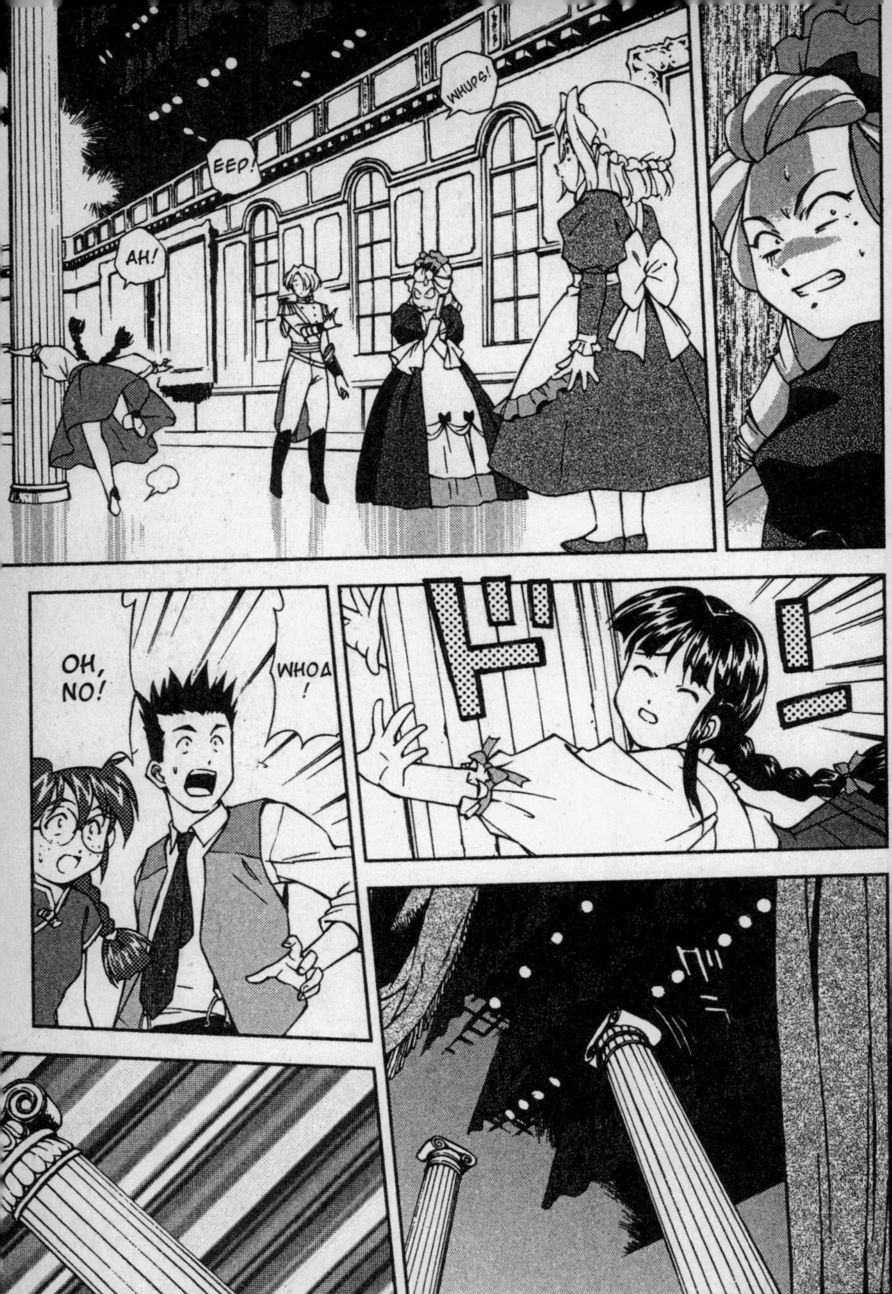
WHUPS!
EEP!
AH!
ド
WHOA!
OH, NO!

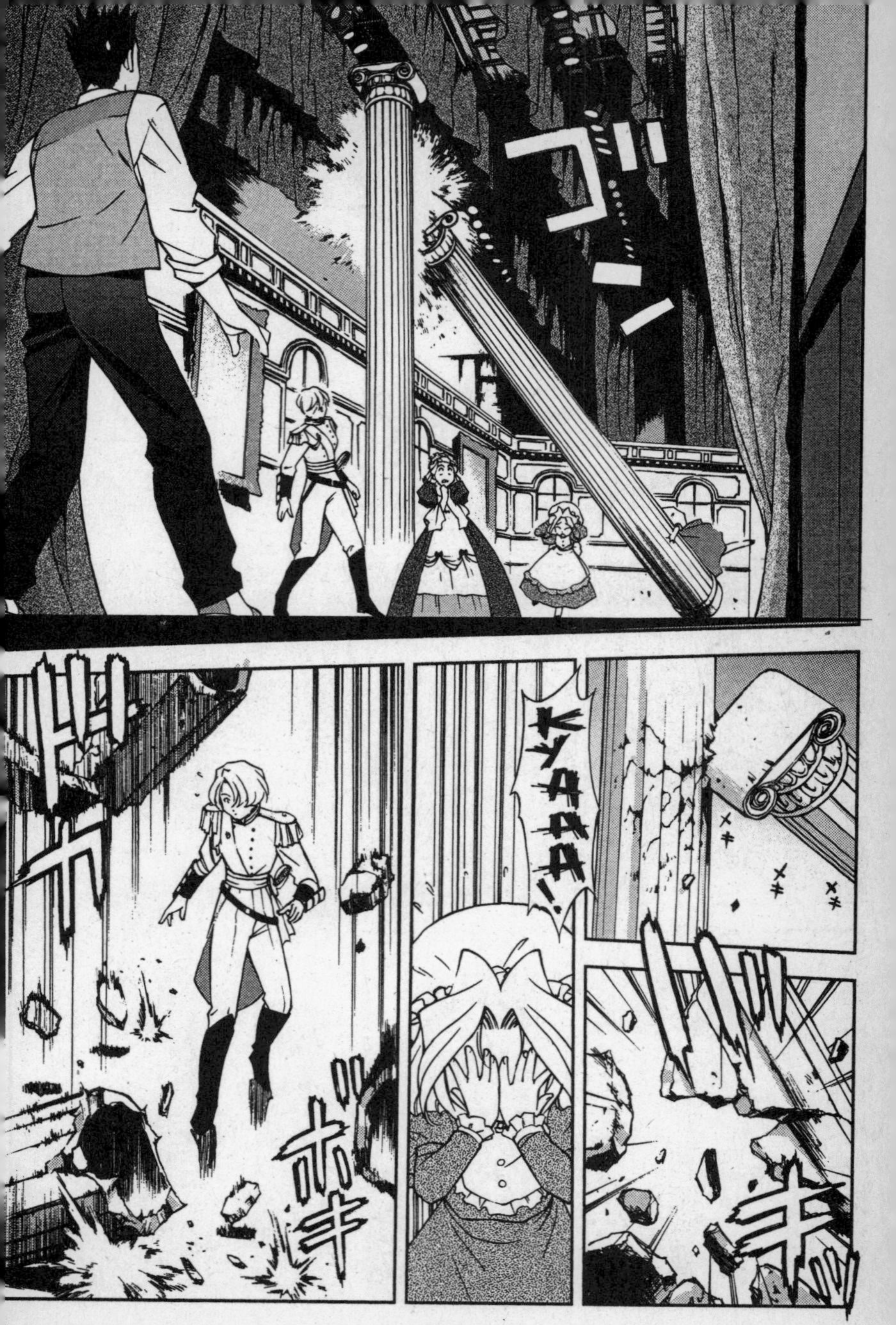
KYAAAA!

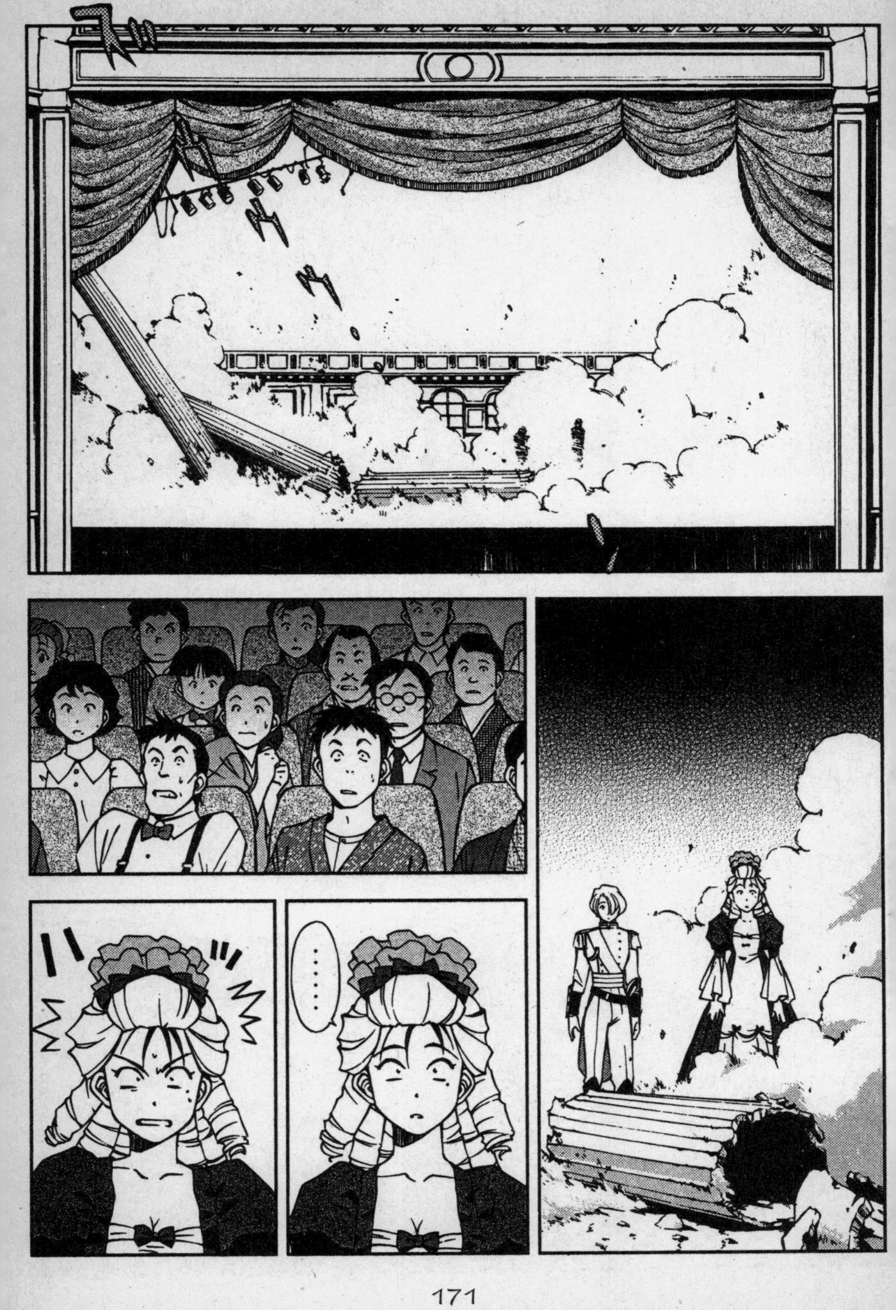
……

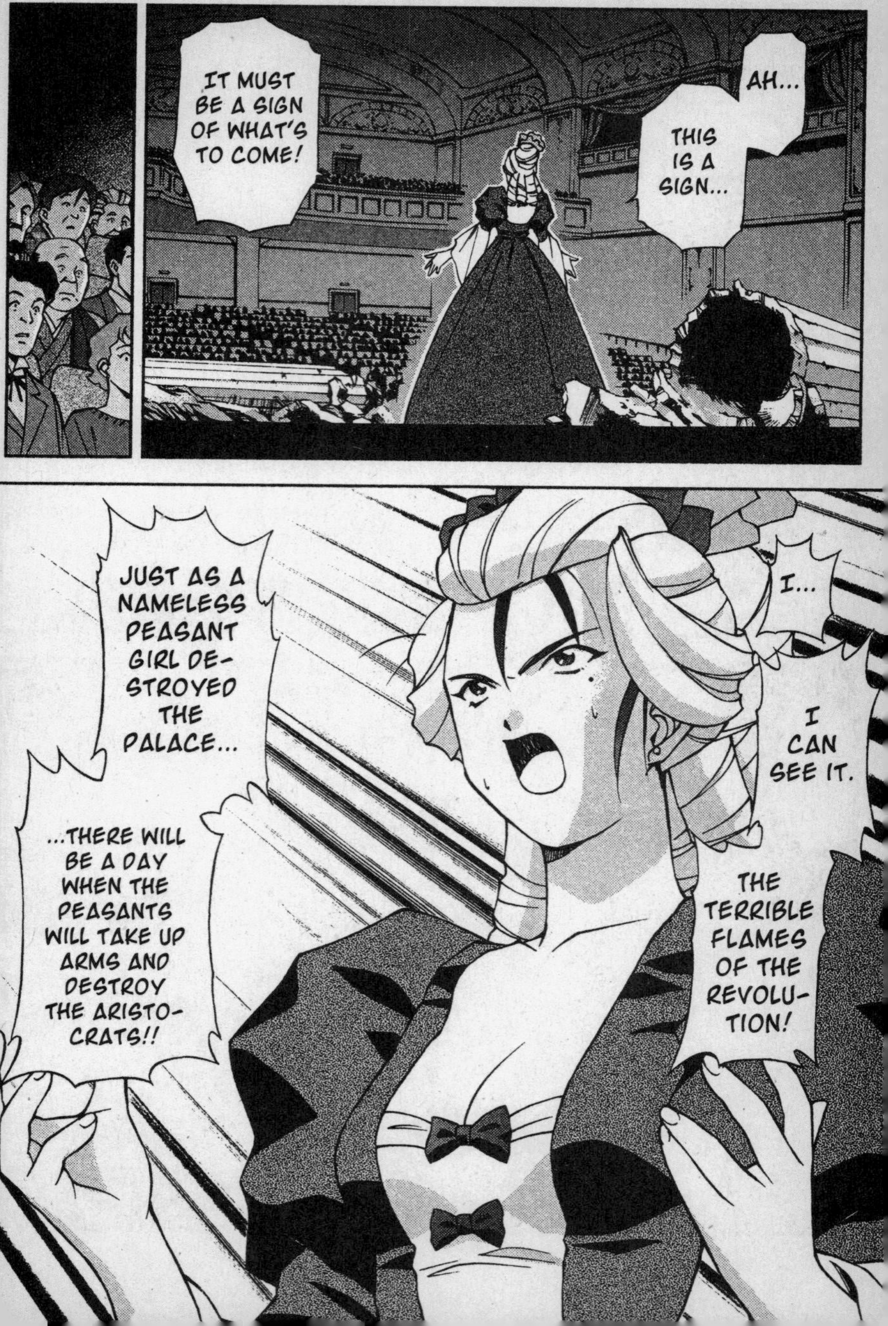
AH...
THIS IS A SIGN...
IT MUST BE A SIGN OF WHAT'S TO COME!
I...
I CAN SEE IT.
THE TERRIBLE FLAMES OF THE REVOLUTION!
JUST AS A NAMELESS PEASANT GIRL DESTROYED THE PALACE...
...THERE WILL BE A DAY WHEN THE PEASANTS WILL TAKE UP ARMS AND DESTROY THE ARISTOCRATS!!

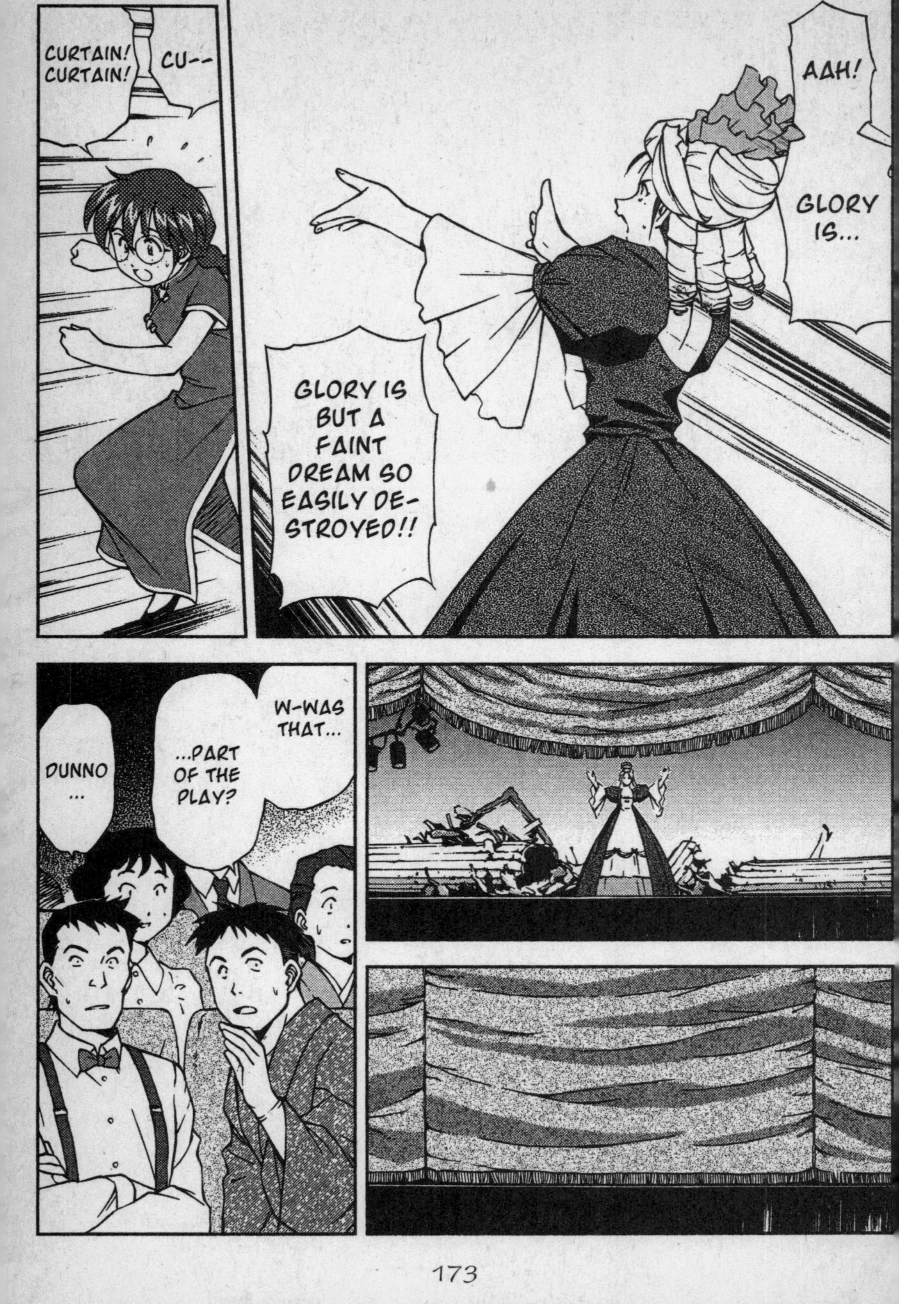
AAH!
GLORY IS...
GLORY IS BUT A FAINT DREAM SO EASILY DE-STROYED!!
CU--
CURTAIN! CURTAIN!
W-WAS THAT...
...PART OF THE PLAY?
DUNNO ...

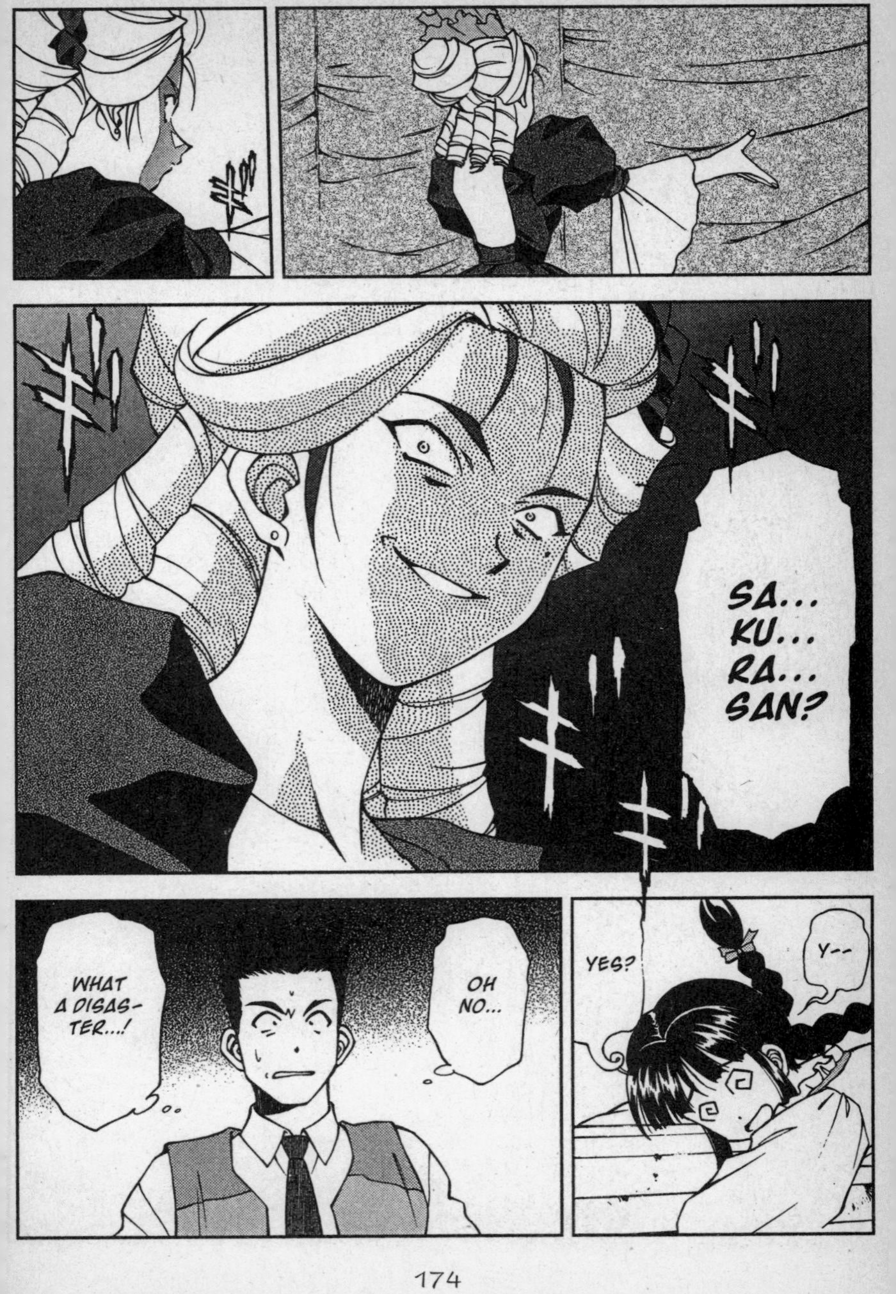
SA... KU... RA... SAN?
Y--
YES?
OH NO...
WHAT A DISASTER...!

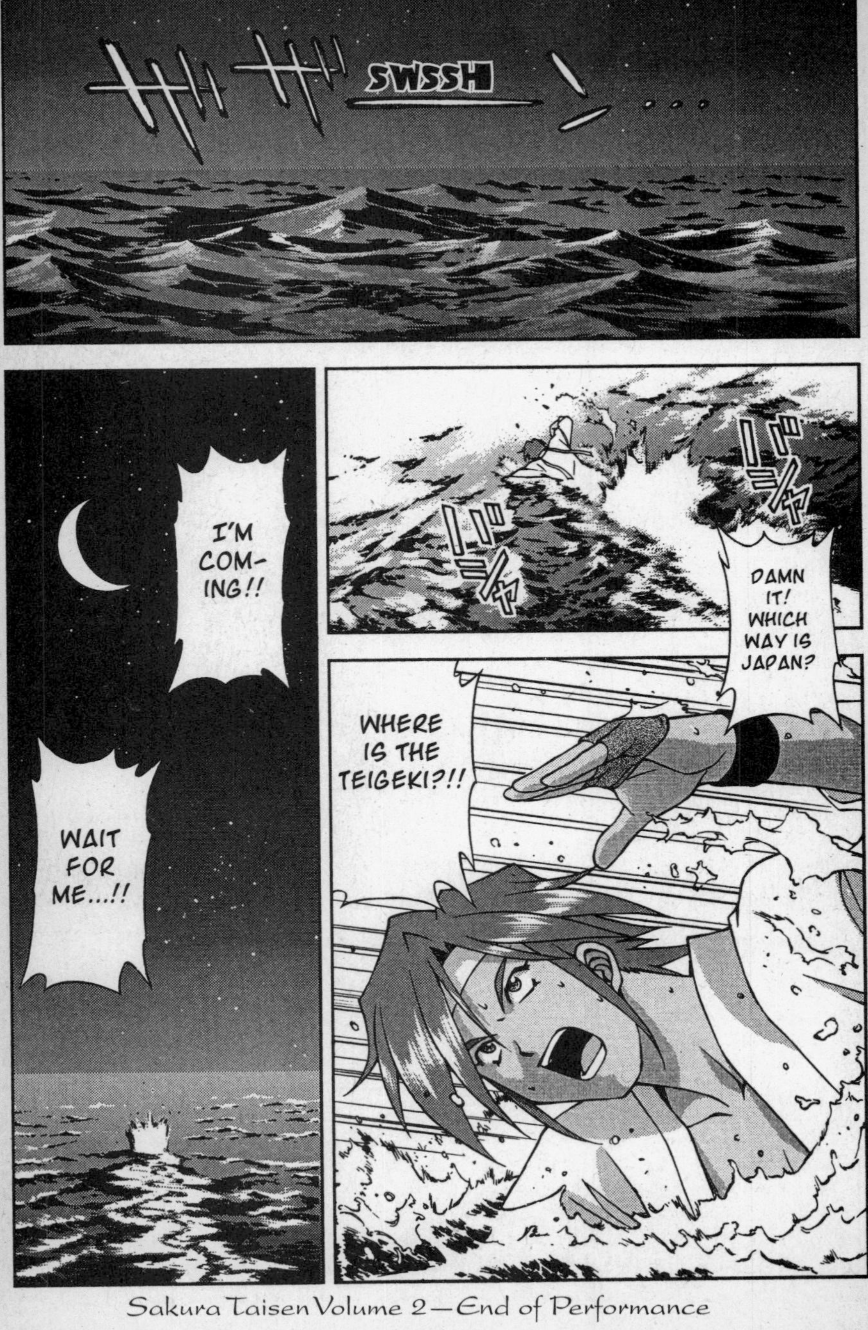
SWSSH
DAMN IT! WHICH WAY IS JAPAN?
WHERE IS THE TEIGEKI?!!
I'M COM-ING!!
WAIT FOR ME...!!

Sakura Taisen Volume 2—End of Performance

Spirit Armor

Human-shaped weapon that uses *reiryoku*-powered engines in place of steam-powered engines. One example is the Koubu used by the Imperial Fighting Troupe. The armor is constructed from a metal by the name of "Shirusu-usu", discovered during the American Civil War. Shirusu-usu metal is reported to have a strong resistance against curses and spells. The Spirit Armor's main engine can run on steam or *reiryoku*, making it a "dual steam-spirit-type engine." Only those who possess high levels of *reiryoku* can operate the armor's spirit engine.

Reiryoku

A spiritual energy generated by a person with supernatural powers. It is the power of the psyche that everyone possesses, although average people have so little that they are generally unaware of it. The power that is possessed by evil persons is called *demonic reiryoku*, but both kinds are fundamentally the same type of energy.

The Grand Imperial Theater

A theater located at 4-Chome, Ginza, Kyobashi-ku, Tokyo. Often referred to as "Teigeki" or "the Imperial." The construction on the building was begun in the fall of the 8th Year of the Taisho era (1919) and was finished in the spring of the 12th Year of the Taisho era (1923). It was the largest theater in Asia at the time.

The exterior of the building was designed in the Victorian style. The interior is a mix of Japanese and Western styles. Totally undetectable from the outside, it houses the headquarters of the Imperial Fighting Troupe in the basement and also stores secret weapons such as the Koubu and Gourai, or "Rolling Thunder," the bullet train. The second floor of the theater is used as a dormitory for the members of Flower Division.

The admission fees for the theater, as of 1923, are as follows: special seating (second floor) 15 yen, first class seating (first and second floors) 8 yen, second class seating 5 yen, third class seating 3 yen and standing room only 40 sen (that's 40/100 of one yen).

Imperial Fighting Troupe

The Imperial Capital Defense Force was incepted in 1922, the successor to the Army's Counter-Kouma Team. Also known as "Teigeki." The Commander of the force is Lieutenant General Ikki Yoneda, Second-in-Command is Ayame Fujie. There are five teams, "Hana" (Flower), "Kaze" (Wind), "Yume" (Dream), "Tsuki" (Moon), and "Yuki" (Snow). As the front assault team, the Flower Division is equipped with Koubu Spirit Armor. The Force belongs neither to the Army nor the Navy. It is a secret force whose existence is known only to a handful of people.

Imperial Operetta Troupe

Formed in the 11th Year of the Taisho era (1922), it is an all-girls opera troop that performs anything from palace plays to short comedy skits. They are based in the Grand Imperial Theater in Ginza.

Steam-Powered Robots

A manned weapon developed in the U.S. A generic term for all human-shaped weapons operated by steam engines. The weapon debuted in the Great European War. At that time, the weapon moved not on two legs as they do now, but on wheels and caterpillar tracks.

Koubu

Its formal name is "Tiger-Type Spirit Armor Koubu." The first generation Spirit Armor of the world's first counter-evil human-shaped steam weapon to be loaded with a dual *reiryoku* and steam-powered engine. Its schematic designs were done by Shinnosuke Yamazaki, though the final design and development was done by Kanzaki Heavy Industries. The Koubu is the main force of the Imperial Fighting Troupe's 1923 fighting power. What makes a Koubu special in terms of innovation is the use of the new dual-powered engine and the degree of freedom it allows the operator during battle by not having a fixed weapon.

Total height: 2428 mm
Dry weight: 647 kg
Operation time limit: 2 hours

Demon-Driven Reiryoku-Operated Robots

Human-shaped steam robots used by the Kuronosu Council. Currently, a manned version called "Kamui" and an unmanned version called "Wakiji" have been confirmed.

Wakiji

The main fighting force of the Kuronosu Council. They are unmanned and move as directed. Powered by evil *reiryoku* from items like the Kusabi, they are relics of the Tokugawa Era unearthed by Bishop Tenkai.

The Kuronosu Council

A mysterious secret society that appeared in the Imperial Capital in 1923. With Tenkai at its helm, it is composed of four officers who call themselves "Death Emperors," and their countless Wakiji.

Kusabi

An old ceremonial vessel that was stored at Ueno Kaneiji temple. It is shaped like a dokkosho (a type of pestle) used in esoteric Buddhism. It was recreated from a relic of the Tokugawa Shogunate by Satan Aoi.

Gourai, "Rolling Thunder"

Underground bullet train. The entirety of the train is composed of the Special D 505, the steam engine car and the cargo car (C-shaped to accommodate the aura armor machines).

Total length: 25.563 m
Total height, including projected area: 9.083 m
Designed by Shinnosuke Yamazaki in 6th Year of the Taisho era (1917) and constructed by Kanzaki Heavy Industries in 1922.
It departs from the basement of Ginza Headquarters and goes to the Flower Mansion Branch. With a maximum speed of 200 km/hour, it can move between Ginza and Asakusa in three minutes.

Flower Mansion Branch

Its formal name is "Imperial Attack Force Flower Mansion Branch and Underground Weapons Workshop." Branch Chief is Ayame Fujie. With most of the facility hidden underground, it is the Force's armory as well as the place where the Transport Specialty Division, the Wind Division, is based. The aboveground building is an amusement park called Flower Mansion. It is open to the public.

Taisho Era

In Sakura Taisen, the era name Taisho (using the characters for "Broad Truth") is used to differentiate from a similar Taisho era ("Great Truth") that occurred in the real world. The change from the Meiji era to the Taisho occurred in the same year as the actual Taisho era, and the 45th Year of Meiji is the first year of Taisho in 1912.

Kouma War

On April 4th, 1915, a number of small Kouma and one gigantic Kouma appeared from under the Nihonbashi area. The Kouma War refers to the events that followed. These Kouma brought great destruction to the central area of the Imperial Capital, but were finally crushed by the Army Counter-Kouma Unit in 1918.

Army Counter-Kouma Unit

An organization formed in 1912 by Ikki Yoneda and others, who foresaw the coming of evil monsters in the future and understood the necessity of defending the Imperial Capital with force and spell. Since they did not have Koubu, their only weapons were the body and the sword. The small but effective organization was dismantled in 1918.

Mie [Pose]

An acting method where the actor poses momentarily to emphasize an emotion in a scene. It was invented in Kabuki theater, and was later employed in close-ups in movies. When you use it to make yourself look good, it is still called mie, but is spelled differently.

Tate [Battle Scene]

The choreographed fight scene, from fistfights to battles or any other violent scene. Also called Tachimawari. A tateshi shows the actors how to move about in a fight scene. Various props may be used and new ideas are always welcomed.

Anten [Dark Change]

The lights are turned off when changing the scenery on the stage between scenes. Costumes and props are changed in the dark. The stage may be rotated. Anten can also indicate change of time or location. If the Anten is too long, it slows the pace of the show.

Kamite/Shimote [Stage left/Stage right]

The Japanese characters used for "stage left" and "stage right" can also be read as "skilled" and "inferior," though they should never be read this way. If you read a script that is written "Maria kamite, Sumire shimote" as "Maria is good, Sumire is bad," the rehearsal will become a hellish scene! In Japan, kamite is the right side of the stage as seen from the audience and shimote is the left side as seen from the audience.

Gene [Dress Rehearsal]

Also called "gene pro," it is shortened from the German term General Probe. The gene pro is the run-through rehearsal involving acting, music and everything, with all the costumes and props as it would be seen in a performance. Often in Europe and the U.S., VIPs are invited to the dress rehearsal on the day before or the day of the first performance.

Prompter

A person who gives the actors parts of lines or songs behind stage. Also called "Koh-Ken." In kabuki, they used to have a system called "mikkagojoho" (three days' leniency) where the actors openly received lines for up to three days after the show opened since the performance could not be expected to be perfected before three days' time.

Mogiri [ticket taker]

A person who tears the ticket in half at the entrance to a theater. Also the theater entrance itself. When a performance was good, the patron was to say, "Thank you, mogiri, for a great show" at the entrance to the theater.

Shonichi, Nakabi, Senshu-raku [First day of performance, middle day, end day of performance]

Shonichi is the first day of performance. Everyone celebrates the first day of performance, the fruit of many days and nights of labor, by wishing everybody "Happy First Day." Naturally, the lead actors and actresses must give "shugi" (money presents) to the cast. Patrons also come by with shugi and good luck wishes.

Nakabi is the middle day of the performance. Everybody wishes each other "Happy Middle Day" for having reached the midpoint safely, and also wish for a good rest of the run. The lead actors and actresses give shugi to the cast.

Senshu-raku is the last day of the performance. Everybody says, "Happy Last Day." No shugi is needed on the last day. The organizers usually put on a party to celebrate the end of the performance. In Japanese, senshu-raku is spelled with the same character as in the word "turtle" rather than the alternative, the character for "autumn." As the turtle is generally more auspicious than autumn, the latter variation is rarely included. When there are performances in remote areas, each performance is called "raku" and the last location is called "Dai-raku."

Ohiri [Full House]

When the audience reaches house capacity or more, it is a full house. It is customary for the organizers to give out ohiri bukuro ("full house bags," bags containing gift money). The general public also receives a gift equaling the cost of a snack or light meal. Sometimes, for good luck, these are given out even when the house is not full.

Maku [Curtain]

A piece of cloth that separates the stage and the audience. A boundary, a theatrical concept in a drama. A magic cloth that is used to signal reflection, transportation, beginning and end, tension and relaxation, change, etc.

Sajiki Seki [Box Seats]

Special seats at the same height as the stage. In kabuki, it is located in the front of the stage. In the West, these are the box seats to the left and right of the stage located on the first and second floors. The highest seats are called tenjo sajiki (close to the ceiling) and are commoners' seats.

Makumae [Space in Front of the Curtain]

A small space in front of the curtain. A makumae shibai (curtain play) is a small scene put on to buy time for changing props or costumes. They are often performed by lesser characters, as star performers do not like to appear in front of the curtain. However, many productions use this space nowadays to avoid long anten.

Hako [Box]

Theater. The building in which the performance takes place.

Seri [Sinking Stage]

A stage set where a part of the stage is made to go up and down. When an actor is brought up from under the stage, it is called "seri-a-ge," and, when taken down, it is called "seri-sa-ge." In kabuki, a small sinking stage in the hanamichi has a special name: suppon (snapping turtle). In traditional kabuki, actors that appear from this area are ghosts or monster characters, never live human beings, though they may appear to be one. This is a rule.

Hanamichi [Elevated Runway]

A dramatic space stretching from the back of the audience to the stage. It is used to change the concept of time, space, or to bring the actors closer to the audience. It is a uniquely Japanese stage device that expands the space of the stage infinitely.

Isho-awase [Costume Fitting]

The costumes procured or sewn by the people in charge of costumes are put on by the actors and shown to the staff, including the writer and director, for approval. Also called Costume Parade.

Tooshi geiko [Run-through Rehearsal]

A rehearsal that is done from the beginning of the play to the end without a break, using props and costumes. The tempo of the play and continuity is decided and adjusted in time for the performance.

Yomiawase [Read-through]

Done at the beginning stages of the rehearsal, the actors read their lines from the script in order to get a grasp of their characters. The whole image of the play is displayed for the first time. However, when the playwright gathers the actors and reads the script himself, it is called "honyomi" or "kao-awase" (first meeting). Sometimes, yomiawase follows such a reading.

Kao-awase [First Meeting]

Coming together of people of different upbringings and ways of thinking and living to create a single production before the start of rehearsals. They talk about how things will be done. Acting together for the first time is called "hatsu kao-awase."

Bonus Section

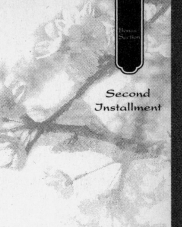

Second Installment

Cherry Blossoms Flourish in Otowa

By Ohji Hiroi

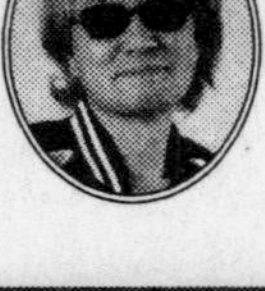

Shikishima no yamato gokorowo hitotohaba
Asahi ni nihohu yamazakurabana
[waka poem]

I think this was a poem by Nobunaga Motoi, a Japanese studies scholar from the Edo period. I remember learning it, but have forgotten the details. "Shikishima no" is a set phrase to go with "yamato." Perhaps "Dr. Shikishima" of Tetsujin 28 is a set epithet replacing "yamato" with "tetsujin?" As my thoughts turned, I had to yawn.
It was raining outside. It was depressing. It was already past spring and into the rainy season. I had been threatened and pleaded with by country samurai type Yamamoto and geeky Nomura to write this manga version of *Sakura Taisen,* but two months had already passed, and not a single line had I written. It was not as if I'd not done anything during those two months. I'd completed, though late, the setting script and casting for the game, the script for song shows and lyrics. I had decided that I would write the script for the manga for two hours after three a.m., but it'd already been two months since I'd decided this, and nothing. To begin with, I couldn't decide how the story should start, the reason being my feeling that following the game would be rather boring. A writer is a selfish animal. No matter how popular, it's painful to trace what one wrote before (and seven years ago at that!).

I lit another cigarette from habit. The phone rang. It was past four a.m.
"Yes."
"Oh, Hiroi-sensei."
"Y-yes?"
"It's Nomura from Kodansha. How is it going? The first episode?"
They called to see how things were going.

"I haven't written a thing," I said arrogantly.

"Hey, that's not right. You said you would write it!"

"I will. But I can't."

"You have to write if you said you would!" He started to sound like a little kid. Nomura is a weirdo. Talking straight to weirdos never gets anywhere.

"Well, when I try to write, some supernatural phenomenon occurs. I think this house must be cursed..."

"That's a lie!"

"No, really..."

"It's not nice to break your promise!" Nomura was becoming more and more like a little kid. "Breaking a promise is a bad thing, you know..."

Everybody knows that. But even though you know, sometimes you just end up breaking promises. Even countries make promises and then break them.

"I'm gonna tell. I'm gonna tell on you!" Nomura yelled at the end of the phone.

"W-wait! Who are you telling?"

"Igarashi-san!"

"Nomura-kun, let's talk calmly about this. I am, after all, the original scriptwriter for Sakura Taisen. I'm also the general producer..." I threatened in a soft tone of voice.

"If you won't write, I'm gonna tell!"

He wouldn't let up.

"I didn't say I won't write!"

"Then when are you going to write?"

"I just can't write!"

"Well, put your back into it, then!"

Is he ordering me?

"I am!"

"You're lying!"

"I'm not lying!"

"Fine. I will send Kodansha's Siberian special agent over right away!"

"Huh? Siberia? Special agent? What's that?"

"You'll know when you see him."

"Come on. I just don't have time to be involved in such a prank..."

He hung up the phone.

What an idiot. I mumbled as I hung up the phone. I took a shower to change my mood. When I put on my pajamas after brushing my teeth, I was overcome by sleepiness. I had a nightmare. I think I was moaning in my sleep.

"Hiroi-san...Hiroi-san, get up."

Someone was shaking me.

"Aaan?"

I finally managed to open my eyes.

An otherworldly beauty was staring at me.

"Whoa, wh–what? Who? Where?"

"Good morning."

A nice voice.

"M–morning. Who are you?"

"I'm Reiko Isomura, the Siberian Special Agent from Kodansha."

"Huh?"

"I received mobilization orders from Igarashi, so I came."

"Ah… How did you get in?!"

"Locks have no meaning to us. We have been trained to get in anywhere."

"Why such training?"

"For the safety of the writers. To safeguard against headhunting. To keep the deadline!"

"These three are the duty of Siberian Agents."

"You're joking, right?" My jaw dropped.

"All the major publishing houses have this kind of organization. Let's get working, okay?"

Reiko kissed me.

I was overtaken with this totally unexpected attack. My head was swimming in Reiko's sweet scent.

"Yes, ma'am!"

I stood up and noticed something else was, too.

"Okay, take him!"

Huh? Take me? What?

At that very moment, three men in black came from nowhere and grabbed me by my two arms.

"W–what do you think you're doing?!"

"You'll be locked up," Reiko said coldly.

"You idiot! I have other jobs, too!"

"What you need to do right now is the Kodansha job."

"You can't do that. That's simply not done."

"But Kodansha has always done it," she said categorically. There was not a speck of hesitation.

"Even if you lock me up, what can't be written can't be written!"

"Don't worry. I assure you. We, the Siberian Special Agents, will assist you."

"Huh? How are you going to assist me?"

"In every way. Selflessly. Now take him!"

With Reiko's last words, the black suits covered my nose and mouth with a piece of gauze. It smelled sweet.

"W–what…ngh…mogamoga…" I muttered as my mind faded quickly away. Far away, cherry blossoms flourished in the morning light.

(to be continued)

Sumire and I

On December 25, 1994, I was right in the middle of my Christmas concert. I was demanding that the audience chant "beautiful, svelte, elegant big sister," while my laughter ("Oh ho ho ho") echoed through the concert hall on the howling microphones. I was told it was that laughter that made Mr. Hiroi decide I was the perfect match for Sumire. I had thought that it was because of my beauty and body, but…well…

When *Sakura Taisen* began, I worked hard every day and night to act the part of a character very different from my own. But my colleagues always said, "You're just fine as you are." I guess there are many things in life that one is not aware of. So, Ma_mi-san, you're not that big after all.

Oh ho ho ho ho!

Michie Tomizawa
playing Sumire Kanzaki

The action heats up both onstage and on the streets of Tokyo. Sakura's first starring role in the theater is a complete disaster, but fortunately, Sakura can still hold more than her own on the battlefield! Demon invaders and sinister forces provide quite a challenge for our talented troupe, but it's nothing that a little teamwork and fighting spirit can't handle...and there's always time for a little romantic intermission! Love may be blossoming on the battlefield, in spite of all odds!

Find out in Sakura Taisen, Vol. 3!

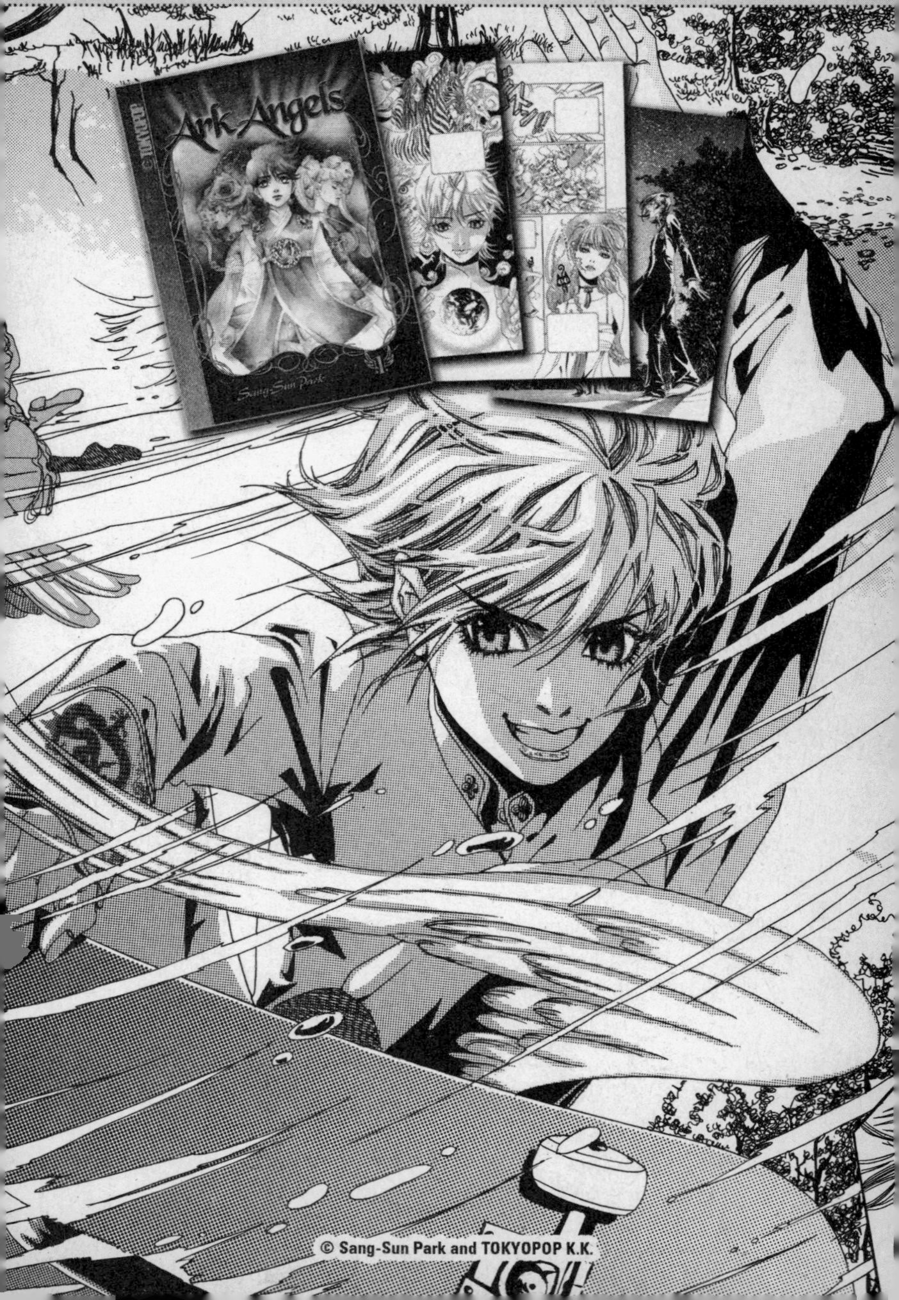
Ark Angels
Sang-Sun Park

Ark Angels

Girls just wanna have fun— while saving the world.

From a small lake nestled in a secluded forest far from the edge of town, something strange has emerged: Three young girls— Shem, Hamu and Japheth—who are sisters from another world. Equipped with magical powers, they are charged with saving all the creatures of Earth from extinction. However, there is someone or something sinister trying to stop them. And on top of trying to save our world, these sisters have to live like normal human girls: They go to school, work at a flower shop, hang out with friends and even fall in love!

FROM THE CREATOR OF THE TAROT CAFÉ!

T TEEN AGE 13+

STOP!

This is the back of the book.
You wouldn't want to spoil a great ending!

This book is printed "manga-style," in the authentic Japanese right-to-left format. Since none of the artwork has been flipped or altered, readers get to experience the story just as the creator intended. You've been asking for it, so TOKYOPOP® delivered: authentic, hot-off-the-press, and far more fun!

DIRECTIONS

If this is your first time reading manga-style, here's a quick guide to help you understand how it works.

It's easy... just start in the top right panel and follow the numbers. Have fun, and look for more 100% authentic manga from TOKYOPOP®!